P.

LIBRARY
Tel: 01244 375444   Ext: 3301

CHESTER COLLEGE

This book is to be returned on or before the
last date stamped below. Overdue charges
will be incurred by the late return of books.

IT

D1348639

New Perspectives in
Primate Evolution & Behaviour

Daubentoni madagascariensis: aye-aye   *Photo*. David Haring: *Duke Primate Center*

New Perspectives in
Primate Evolution & Behaviour

Edited by

Caroline S. Harcourt & Bryan R. Sherwood

WESTBURY

First published in 2002 by

Westbury Academic & Scientific Publishing
An imprint of Smith Settle Ltd
Ilkley Road, Otley
West Yorkshire LS21 3JP
Great Britain

ISBN 1 84103 008 2

British Library Cataloguing-in-Publishing Data
A catalogue record for this book is available from the British Library.

Printed by
Smith Settle Limited, Otley, West Yorkshire LS21 3JP

Contents

SECTION ONE: New Perspectives in Human Evolution & Systematics

SECTION TWO: New Perspectives in Mind & Cognition.

SECTION THREE: New Perspectives in Behaviour & Ecology

Contributing authors

Dr James R Anderson
Department of Psychology
University of Stirling
Stirling, Scotland FK9 4LA, UK

Dr Allison Bean
Survival Anglia Ltd.
Anglia House, Norwich NR2 3BY, UK

Dr Josep Call
Max Planck Institute for Evolutionary Anthropology
Inselstraße 22, D-04103 Leipzig,
GERMANY

Dr Andrew Chamberlain
Department of Archaeology
The University of Sheffield
Sheffield, UK

Professor Steven E Churchill
Department of Biological Anthropology & Anatomy
Duke University
Box 90383.
North Carolina 27708, USA

Dr Robin H Crompton
Faculty of Medicine
Department of Human Anatomy & Cell Biology
University of Liverpool
PO Box 147, Liverpool L69 3GE, UK

Dr Robert Foley
Human Evolutionary Biology Research Group
Department of Biological Anthropology
University of Cambridge
Downing Street, Cambridge CB2 3DZ, UK

Dr Piers J Gollop
Human Evolutionary Biology Research Group
Department of Biological Anthropology
University of Cambridge
Downing Street, Cambridge CB2 3DZ, UK

Professor Morris Goodman
Professor of Anatomy & Cell Biology
Department of Anatomy & Cell Biology
Wayne State University
School of Medicine
Gordon H Scott Hall, 540 E Canfield Avenue,
Detroit, Michigan 48201, USA

Professor John J A Gowlett
Department of Archaeology
University of Liverpool
School of Archaeology, Classics
and Oriental Studies
William Hartley Building
Liverpool, L69 3GS, UK

Dr Alexander H Harcourt
Department of Anthropology
University of California - Davis
Davis, California 95616, USA

Professor Philip Lieberman
Department of Cognitive & Linguistic Sciences
Department of Anthropology
Brown University
Providence, Rhode Island 02912-19, USA

Professor Edwin H McConkey
Professor Emeritus
Department of MCD Biology
University of Colorado
Boulder, Colorado 80309, USA

Dr Lindsay E Murray
Department of Psychology
University College Chester
Parkgate Road, Chester, CH1 4BJ, UK

Dr Nicholas E Newton-Fisher
Department of Anthropology
Washington State University
Pullman, Washington 99164, USA

Professor Scott I Page
Department of Biology
Norwich University
Northfield, Vermont 05663, USA

Professor Gordon McG Reid
Visiting Professor University of Liverpool & Director
North of England Zoological Society
Chester Zoo, Chester CH2 1LH, UK

Dr Daniel Schmitt
Department of Biological Anthropology & Anatomy
Duke University Medical Center
Box 3170
Durham, North Carolina 27710, USA

Professor Elwyn L Simons
James B. Duke Professor & Scientific Director
Duke University Primate Center
Duke University
3705 Erwin Road, Durham,
North Carolina 27705-5000, USA

Dr Ian Tattersall
Department of Anthropology
American Museum of Natural History
Central Park West at 79th Street
New York 10024, USA

Dr Susannah K S Thorpe
Department of Human Anatomy and Cell Biology
The University of Liverpool
PO Box 147, Liverpool L69 3GE, UK

Acknowledgements

The chapters presented here are original and exciting new perspectives on the evolution, behaviour and ecology of monkeys, apes and humans. It developed from the second international meeting on primatology, hosted by the North of England Zoological Society, with support from the University of Liverpool; Bernard Wood (Department of Human Anatomy), Robin Dunbar (Department of Psychology), and their staff.

Caroline Harcourt was persuaded to exercise her formidable scientific and editorial skills in preparing the draft manuscripts for publication and, for this, the publishers and the North of England Zoological Society are very grateful. Bryan Sherwood FLS must be thanked for skillfully managing the editing process and maintaining liaison between the authors and Westbury Publishing. Dick Byrne, Guy Cowlishaw, Kevin Hunt, Bill Jungers, Bill McGrew, Richard Wrangham, Elisabeth Visalbergi, and others, who are anonymous, should also be warmly acknowledged for their thorough and constructive comments on the individual chapters. Brian Gardiner, Kings' College London and Council Member of the North of England Zoological Society along with Phyllis Lee, Department of Biological Anthropology, University of Cambridge, gave invaluable advice on the final, overall form and content of the publication and have been most supportive of the whole endeavour.

Gordon McGregor Reid
North of England Zoological Society
November 2000

Preface

G. McG. REID

A comparison between the wealth of literature and the papers in the present volume provides a fascinating and valuable insight into the changing scientific pre-occupations of successive, overlapping generations of scholars. At any one time, the questions asked and the interpretation of the material or behavioural evidence depend on the analytical tools available and the philosophies employed. Nevertheless, the most fundamental questions persist, even if the answers sometimes differ and the level of resolution in enquiry is greatly increased. We still want to know how humans originated, evolved and functioned. In particular, we seek to understand better our systematic, social and psychological inter-relationships and our corresponding relationships with other primates. Now, however, there is far more evidence to be debated (*Section One*). The classical systematic discipline of comparative anatomy has, for example, increasingly been both complimented and challenged by molecular biology. This is particularly true in the case of arguments developed on the evidence of DNA and protein sequences. Some of these critical new data have been derived from investigations conducted for the groundbreaking Human Genome Project.

Accepting a fresh cladistic approach, we can surely welcome the proposition (Goodman *et al.*, This volume) that the traditional monotypic human family Hominidae is defunct. Further, we can reasonably agree that all living apes and humans are included in the subfamily Homininae; and that the chimpanzee and bonobo actually belong with man in the genus *Homo*.

There have also been remarkable new discoveries of fossil and recent primates and much more is known or surmised about their habitats, ecology, ethology, sociobiology and general biology. From this, important new questions in mind, cognition, language and social interactions have been formulated (*Section Two*) and in behaviour and ecology (*Section Three*). I am pleased to note that the naturalistic, socially well-integrated colony of chimpanzees at Chester Zoo has been able to support such studies, including those on the ontogeny and evolution of bipedalism, and on individual differences in personality and the evolution of mind. Romantically viewed as the 'seat of the soul', this particular mental property may have a physical locus as large 'self-awareness neurons' in the frontal lobe of the brain, near the *corpus callosum* – at least according to John Allman of the California Institute of Technology. Accepting self-consciousness in great apes or other taxa raises moral, ethical and spiritual issues. Ultimately, if admitted to be in the same broad 'mental taxon', one might consider extending basic human rights to these animals, as advocated by Peter Singer of Monash University, Australia.

Among those that teach and investigate evolution, we are having to address emerging controversies. For instance, the extent to which the processes of natural selection operate on humans and how these may be changing, or ceasing altogether – a debate being fanned by Stephen Jones of University College London, Christopher Wills of the University of California and Richard Dawkins, formerly of the University of Sussex. Some contemporary biologists have even begun to challenge the utility and scientific testability of the concept of natural selection in explaining evolution and biodiversity.

Beyond this, we may begin to wonder whether the existing Linnean system of classification and nomenclature can long survive in the new Millennium, given the impending theoretical, practical and strategic demands of systematic, evolutionary and conservation biology.

Finally, we must consider (A Harcourt, This volume) the crucial issue of primate extinctions as another means of understanding evolution and the survival of particular species and higher taxa. Sadly, twelve primate species managed in collaborative conservation breeding programmes by Chester Zoo are now on the *IUCN Red List of Threatened Taxa,* including mandrill, chimpanzee, Bornean and Sumatran orang-utan. Globally, this situation arises from the deleterious impact of familiar factors such as habitat loss and fragmentation, rainforest fires, poaching and the bushmeat trade. As a part of the vital worldwide process of conservation and restoration we will need – in addition to the present outstanding practitioners – even more biologists dedicated to understanding past and current situations, and concerned to apply this knowledge to conserving the future.

New Perspectives in
Human Evolution & Systematics

Adaptation, systematics and human evolution

I. TATTERSALL

Introduction

Palaeoanthropology is the only subdiscipline of vertebrate palaeontology that seeks to discover the origins and antecedents of a single living species. This unusual perspective has deeply affected the practice of palaeoanthropology from the very beginning, and has assured the development of this field in a distinctive direction. Palaeontologists of other stripes are concerned with diverse groups, and seek, at least initially, to discover the origins of this diversity, and to elucidate the relationships among the taxa comprising the groups they study. Palaeoanthropologists, in contrast, have been overwhelmingly preoccupied with projecting the single species *Homo sapiens* as far back in time as possible. There is thus a linearity to their thinking that is largely absent among their colleagues, and that imparts a very individual flavour to their science. Yet there is little reason to believe that, at least for the vast majority of their time on Earth, hominids have interacted with each other and with the external environment in a materially unusual way. And there is hence no case for arguing that fossil hominids should be analysed and understood in ways any different from those we use to analyse and understand any other components of the vertebrate fossil record.

It is certainly true that a convincing case can be made that modern *Homo sapiens* is a totally unprecedented presence on the landscape, and one that does indeed demand understanding in its own individual terms (Tattersall, 1998). But the arrival of behaviourally modern *Homo sapiens* was clearly a recent event, having taken place well under 100 kyr ago. It is thus best regarded as an epiphenomenon as far as the analysis of the antecedent human fossil record is concerned. The problems this recency of origin poses lie much more in the realm of predicting future outcomes of human interaction with the environment than in the exegesis of how, and out of what sort of background, *Homo sapiens* emerged. For, if our species is a special kind of entity that cannot be regarded simply as an extrapolation of the trends that had gone before it, modern *Homo sapiens* clearly cannot embody any appropriate yardsticks by which to evaluate the evolutionary history that preceded it.

Yet the palaeoanthropological mindset remains resolutely linear, denying diversity whenever possible. The hominid fossil record, which is much better than is commonly supposed, contains as rich a morphological variety as can be found in the archive of any mammalian family. But in the interests of linearity this variety is compressed in some quarters into a mere two successive species in the entire 2 Myr-plus history of the genus *Homo* (e.g. Wolpoff *et al.*, 1993).

Ironically, given the fact that much of the variety we perceive must be adaptive at some level, palaeoanthropologists have been abetted in their denial of taxic diversity by their adherence to a particularly fundamentalist form of the adaptationist paradigm, and I would like to draw particular attention to this here. For among palaeoanthropologists, it seems, adaptation is almost invariably seen as something that applies to individual characters rather than to organisms or to species. Limiting the notion of adaptation in this way powerfully reinforces the 'transformationist' (as opposed to 'taxic') mindset (Eldredge, 1979) that prevails in palaeoanthropology: the view that minimises the importance of taxa in evolution in favour of a concern with changes in genes and their products. Indeed, much of what passes for evolutionary analysis in palaeoanthropology consists of drawing lines between fossils on stratigraphic charts and then concocting scenarios of 'adaptation' to 'explain' differences between earlier and later forms in whatever characters have caught the investigator's eye. Of course, adaptation is a necessary corollary of natural selection, and it would be unwise indeed to deny that either of these processes plays a central role in evolution. But it is important to examine the *levels* at which they act in order to understand what those roles actually are.

Adaptation and natural selection

More than half a century ago, Theodosius Dobzhansky (1937:13) characterised the evolutionary process as one encompassing three levels of action. The first level involves the origin of genetic novelties; the second, the ordering of those novelties in moulding 'the genetic structures of populations into new shapes'; and the third, 'the fixation of the diversity already attained on the preceding two levels'. Incomplete though it is as a comprehensive account of the evolutionary process, Dobzhansky's tripartite scheme remains as valid today as when he proposed it. Level one is accounted for by mutations and recombinations, and is accomplished by a variety of processes that, it is crucial to realise, have nothing to do with either adaptation or natural selection. Genetic novelties simply arise, and can acquire functions and selective value only once they have arisen. Clearly, innovations never appear *for* anything.

Most species with reasonably wide distributions are divided into a number of local populations; and through the action of level two processes, which include but are not limited to natural selection, such local populations routinely differentiate from each other. It is at this second level of action that adaptation will occur, normally to local rather than to species-wide environmental circumstances. It is important to remember that while adaptations, in the sense of phenotypic characters, are obviously the property of individuals, adaptation *per se* is a population characteristic.

Finally, level-three fixation is achieved by speciation, the establishment of genetic isolation in one or more local populations of the differentiating species. It is this irreversible process that awards discrete historical identity to such populations. Speciation may involve one (or possibly more) of a variety of processes, none of which has any necessary relation to natural selection or adaptive change (Tattersall, 1994); and it will rarely if ever occur simply as a passive result of adaptive change in the local population (Tattersall, 1993). Speciation and morphological differentiation are thus fundamentally – and, for palaeontologists, inconveniently – disconnected.

This three-level process as articulated by Dobzhansky accounts nicely for microevolutionary innovation, but far less satisfactorily for macroevolutionary change. Of course, speciation is an obvious prerequisite for macroevolution, but the simple appearance of new species is inadequate to account for larger-scale patterns in the history of life. These patterns result instead from competition among species, whether each other's close relatives or not: a process that involves a winnowing among taxa that is broadly analogous to the winnowing of individuals achieved by natural selection. As Gould & Eldredge (1993: 224) recently remarked, *"Most macroevolution must be rendered by asking what kinds of species within a clade did better than others ... or what biases in direction of speciation prevailed within a clade."* Of course, sorting of this kind need not necessarily be strictly adaptationist either: environments fluctuate constantly, and species may become extinct, or may have the good fortune to lose competitors, for reasons that have nothing to do with how well they are adapted for survival in a specific habitat. Environmental changes are, after all, random with regard to adaptation, and although certain traits may well, on average, predispose to survivability in a wider rather than narrower range of environments, this is not something that can simply be assumed.

The evolutionary process and human evolution

Where does all this leave us in regard to the analysis of the human fossil record? Most importantly, it strongly suggests that we should stop thinking of human evolution principally in terms of the evolution of traits: 'human brain evolution', the 'evolution of bipedality', the 'evolution of language', and so forth. We need to shed our comfortable 'transformationist' tendencies that allow us to dissect the human physical and behavioural records into individual characteristics that can be dealt with independently of each other. We need to bear in mind that the 'trends' we think we observe are not only entirely retrospective, but may very well be products of our own perceptions, or worse, preconceptions. For example, it is a truism that human brain sizes have increased over time. Yet, after years of research, can we yet say anything useful about the nature of this 'trend'? Indeed, can we even say whether we are, perhaps, actually looking not at a single trend, but at an aggregate of two or more possibly dissimilar subtrends, or at no gradual trend at all? The answer appears to be that we are far indeed from being able to say anything useful. Thus, for instance, when I recently tried to plot human fossil brain sizes against time I was forced to abandon the attempt when I realised two things. First, for many of the relevant fossils, ages are not known with adequate precision, or even with any precision at all. For the moment this is not simply a procedural difficulty and its resolution will have to await technological progress.

But more revealing of the underlying problems of palaeo-anthropology was the second, and larger, problem. I was unable to assign many of the available specimens to species units I could consider biologically meaningful; and without the ability to do this I was unable to make sense of the information on brain size they contained. Individual fossil specimens are unhelpful in phylogenetic analysis (unless a particular specimen is the only one of its species you have), for individuals are simply components of species, and it is species that are the essential units of ecological competition and the source of macroevolutionary pattern. The minimalist tradition of palaeoanthropological systematics has assured that fewer accepted species are available than are necessary to cover the morphological variety that the human fossil record offers; and although the few names generally accepted do provide umbrellas under which to group all of the fossils available, any attempt to detect evolutionary pattern among them, whether in terms of systematic relationship or of the evolution of individual characters, is doomed to meaninglessness. It might be argued that wastebasket taxa have a value if by accepting them you are enabled to put aside currently insoluble problems and thereby to proceed to questions that *can* be productively broached; but it is evident that any phylogeny consisting exclusively of wastebasket taxa is viciously misleading.

The palaeoanthropological rejection of the taxic paradigm in favour of the transformationist one has thus cut two ways. In downplaying the importance of species recognition in the human fossil record, and in demonstrating their antitypologist sophistication by minimising the number of species recognised in that record, palaeoanthropologists have inflicted on their profession a totally unrealistic schema of human phylogeny, and have condemned themselves to an eternity of mindless and perfunctory arguments over whether such-and-such a fossil is an 'advanced *Homo erectus*' or a 'primitive archaic *Homo sapiens*'. What's more, in concentrating on the 'evolution' of specific functional systems and on their 'selective significance', they have lost sight of the fact that every organism – and for that matter, every species – is an integrated whole, which succeeds or fails as a whole.

As we have seen, natural selection plays a crucial role in shaping the population diversification that is central to the evolutionary process. But it remains true that natural selection is a 'one individual, one vote' function. Natural selection can only vote up or down on the success of an organism as a whole, not on its individual components.

An individual – or a species, for that matter – succeeds or fails as a total entity, not simply as the bearer of this trait or that. Let's briefly look at the implications of this for one functional system.

The origin of bipedalism

Few if any palaeoanthropologists would now disagree that it was the adoption of bipedalism that initially set the ancestral hominids on their unique evolutionary trajectory. Leaving aside the dubious *Ardipithecus ramidus*, whose hominid status must remain uncertain for the moment, it is clear that the earliest recognisable representatives of our family Hominidae (*Australopithecus anamensis*: Leakey *et al.*, 1995) possessed the ability to walk upright with relative ease, 'bipedal apes' though they may have been in other ways. This recent discovery has served only to sharpen the debate on the 'why' of hominid bipedalism. Every possible notion as to why early hominids stood and moved upright has been explored at one time or another – even including a 'wading ape' ancestry (Morgan, 1997).

More mainstream suggestions include improved efficiency of locomotion in open environments (e.g. Rodman & McHenry, 1980); freeing the hands to carry objects (e.g. Lovejoy, 1981) or food (Hewes, 1961), or to make tools (Washburn, 1960) or brandish weapons (Kortlandt, 1980); seeing over tall grasses and more effectively scanning the horizon (Day, 1986); discouraging the attentions of carnivores, which are more quickly triggered by horizontal silhouettes (NB Todd, *pers. comm.*); and keeping cool away from the shade of the forest by minimising the surface area of the body available to receive the direct rays of the sun while maximising its cooling surface (Wheeler, 1984). The recent realisation that bipedalism was probably not adopted in an open savannah context has redirected attention to ape postures in woodland environments, and to the possibility that an habitual upright posture somehow resulted from an exaptation that was present in a woodland-living ancestor (Hunt, 1994).

Regardless of the mechanism favoured, however, such proposals have usually been made under the assumption that there was a single underlying cause that promoted bipedalism. From this it is but a short step to assume that bipedalism 'evolved' as a result of the posited advantage(s). This, of course, is to misunderstand totally the nature of the evolutionary process. Habitual bipedalism is a behaviour that is accompanied by at least a minimal degree of skeletal modification from the principally quadrupedal state. As we learn more about *Hox* genes and other aspects of developmental genetics, we will doubtless come to understand how a relatively minor genetic change can give rise to such modification in an individual, and in time become entrenched in the gene pool of its deme. For the time being, though, it is sufficient to know that such effects do routinely occur, as demonstrated by the well-documented tendency of demes to differentiate from each other. It is also evident that, once an advantageous modification has been acquired, its possessors will enjoy *all* of the advantages – and disadvantages, for it is rare that advantage comes without cost of some kind – that it offers. Quite simply, it is not necessary, or even always possible, to debate which asset is the crucial one. Bipedalism offers different suites of advantages under different circumstances, and, once again, the individual or population prospers or perishes as a whole, rather than as the bearer of a particular 'adaptation'. This realisation refocuses attention on the importance of Dobzhansky's level one of the evolutionary process: a salutary thing, for the origin of novelty is nowadays all too often simply taken for granted, while level two – adaptation – receives all the attention.

Taxic and transformationist palaeoanthropologies

What would a taxic palaeoanthropology look like, in contrast to the linear and minimally branching scheme encouraged by the transformationist mindset? To answer this, we first have to look at the hierarchy of hypothesis formation in systematic palaeontology (Tattersall & Eldredge, 1977). The most fundamental task is to sort the fossils that comprise the evolutionary record into the basic biological unit, species. As what I've said above about the disconnection of speciation from morphological shifts implies, this is in practice no easy matter; but as I have argued elsewhere (Tattersall, 1986), fully recognisable morphs do represent a basis for species recognition, even if to proceed on the basis of such morphs carries a risk of underestimating actual species diversity.

Once the basic units of analysis have been established, relationships among them can be expressed in the form of a *clad-ogram*, a branching diagram in which all known taxa are terminal, and are grouped together into nested sets on the basis of the common possession of derived character states. Such sharing of derived states is taken as evidence of an evolutionary relationship, whose exact nature – ancestor/descendant, descendants of the same common ancestor – remains unspecified. The cladogram is the only potentially testable type of statement in systematic palaeontology, although, again, formulation in practice is complicated by such factors as homoplasy, which is particularly rampant in evolutionary close-knit groups such as the genus *Homo* (Tattersall, 1993).

Once formulated, the cladogram can then serve as the basis for a *phylogenetic tree*, in which the nature of the relationships involved is specified, and time is also factored in. The tree is thus an inherently more complex and interesting statement than the cladogram, but is essentially untestable since it is impossible to demonstrate con-clusively that two forms lie in an ancestor — descendant relationship (for, logically, any ancestor must be primitive in all characters relative to its putative descendant).

A single cladogram can, indeed, yield a number of different trees; and a single tree can produce several different *scenarios*, the most complex and interesting formulation of all, a narrative in which

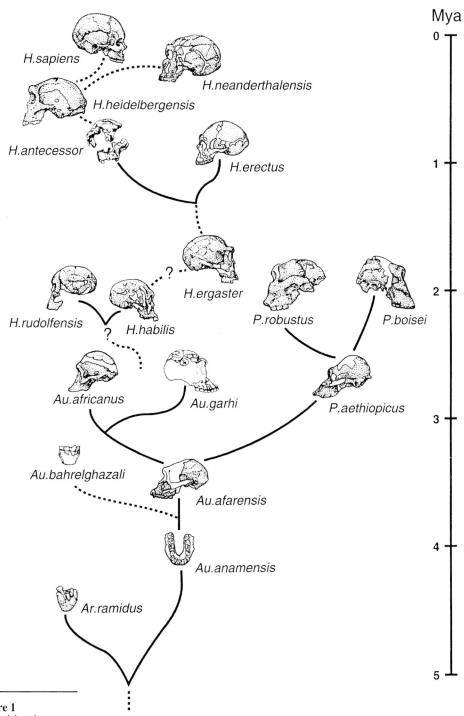

Figure 1
A provisional
phylogenetic tree
of Hominidae.
© Ian Tattersall.

All species named on this chart have received at least a reasonable degree of acceptance among palaeoanthropologists, but the number shown probably under-estimates the
taxic variety actually present. (Adapted from Tattersall & Schwartz, 2000.)

considerations of adaptation, function, ecology, and so forth are added to the information present in the chosen tree. It is not too much to claim that at present all higher levels of analysis of the human fossil record are vitiated by the fact that we do not have a robust and generally agreed alpha taxonomy. If we do not know within reasonable limits how many species we are dealing with in the known human fossil record, there is no way in which we can proceed to a reliable cladogram, let alone tree or scenario. Yet the general feeling among palaeoanthropologists, fuelled by transformationist bias, seems to be that species are no more than names, arbitrary sections of lineages, and are therefore simply insignificant. Or worse, that it is important to show sophistication and population awareness by striving to reduce the names accepted to the minimum number possible. Clearly, for as long as such attitudes persist, there is little hope for progress or even for a modicum of agreement in this famously contentious field. In any study the basic units of analysis are critical. To proceed as if this were otherwise in palaeoanthropology is like trying to study cartography without general agreement on the length of the metre.

One of the consequences of the general neglect of the importance of taxa in palaeoanthropology, has been a concomitant neglect of morphology (Tattersall & Schwartz, 1998). Quite simply, detailed morphology has been regarded as secondary to time in determining the affinities of far too many fossil hominids. As a result, it is impossible at this point to know reliably how many hominid species are represented in the known fossil record. Figure 1 provides what will doubtless ultimately prove to be a fairly minimalist rendering of the record as it is known today; but even so, it dramatically shows that from the beginning hominid phylogeny has been a story of incessant experimentation: of the continuous birth and extinction of species. The topography produced by this process is that of a bush, rather than a ladder; and it emphasises the fact that *Homo sapiens* is simply the single surviving twig on a large ramifying natural edifice rather than the occupant of a summit gained through a long, single-minded slog. This has profound implications for humanity's view of its own place in nature.

If the taxic approach ultimately achieves nothing more than to erode the seductive but profoundly flawed transformationist notion that human evolution has consisted of a drawn-out and largely undeviating progress from primitiveness to perfection, it will have had a salutary effect.

References

Day MH. 1986. Bipedalism: Pressures, origins and modes. In: Wood B, Martin L, Andrews P. eds. *Major Topics in Primate and Human Evolution*. Cambridge: Cambridge University Press. 188-202.

Eldredge N. 1979. Alternative approaches to evolutionary theory. *Bulletin of the Carnegie Museum of Natural History.* **13:** 7-19.

Gould SJ, Eldredge N. 1993. Punctuated equilibria comes of age. *Nature.* **366:** 223-227.

Hunt K. 1994. The evolution of human bipedality: Ecology and functional morphology. *Journal of Human Evolution.* **26:** 183-203.

Kortlandt A. 1980. How might hominids have defended themselves against large predators and food competitors? *Journal of Human Evolution.* **9:** 79-112.

Leakey MG, Feibel C, MacDougall I, Walker AC. 1995. New four million year-old hominid from Kanapoi and Allia Bay, Kenya. *Nature.* **376:** 565-571.

Lovejoy O. 1981. The origin of man. *Science.* **211:** 341-350.

Morgan E. 1997. *The Aquatic Ape Hypothesis.* London: Souvenir Press.

Rodman PS, McHenry H. 1980. Bioenergetics and the origin of hominid bipedalism. *American Journal of Physical Anthropology.* **52:** 103-106.

Tattersall I. 1986. Species recognition in human paleontology. *Journal of Human Evolution.* **22:** 341-349.

Tattersall I. 1993. Speciation and morphological differentiation in the genus *Lemur.* In: Kimbel WH, Martin LB. eds. *Species, Species Concepts and Primate Evolution.* New York: Plenum Press. 163-176.

Tattersall I. 1994. How does evolution work? *Evolutionary Anthropology.* **3 (1):** 2-3.

Tattersall I. 1998. *Becoming Human: Evolution and Human Uniqueness.* New York: Harcourt Brace.

Tattersall I, Eldredge N. 1977. Fact, theory and fantasy in human paleontology. *American Scientist.* **65 (2):** 204-211.

Tattersall I, Schwartz JH. 1998. Morphology, paleoanthropology and Neanderthals. *The Anatomical Record (New Anatomist).* **253 (3):** 113-117.

Tattersall I, Schwartz JH. 2000. *Extinct Humans.* Colorado: Westview Press.

Washburn SL. 1960. Tools and human evolution. *Scientific American.* **303 (3):** 3-15.

Wheeler PE. 1984. The evolution of bipedality and loss of functional body hair in hominids. *Journal of Human Evolution.* **13:** 91-98.

Wolpoff MH, Thorne AG, Jelinek J, Zhang Y. 1993. The case for sinking *Homo erectus*: 100 years of *Pithecanthropus* is enough! *Courier Forschungsinstitut Senckenberg.* **171:** 341-361.

The fossil record of human origins among the Anthropoidea

E. L. SIMONS

Introduction

This subject has several layers of meaning, depending on which stages of transition from the most primitive primates to anatomically modern *Homo sapiens* are being dealt with. Humans today exhibit a mosaic of structural and behavioural features that were acquired at different times in our ancestry and the more primitive characteristics that still survive link us to our origins among apes and earlier anthropoid primates. In general, our inferences about the past have to be drawn from the interpretation of fossilised bones and teeth, and in some cases these indicate elements of behaviour or ancient lifestyles as well. Since characteristics that we now know to be essential features of human anatomy have appeared in quite different times and places, it is the history of these successive modifications that reveals the story of our past.

We do not know, in most cases, the exact line of descent that has led to *Homo sapiens,* but the fossil record of ancient higher primates is now sufficient to enable scientists to outline several broad stages through which our ancestry appears to have passed. This history took place in the Old World and almost entirely in Africa. For purposes of discussion one simplification is to consider the evidence in four main stages: 1) The origin of anthropoids or anthropoideans in the African Eocene epoch; 2) the appearance of more advanced catarrhines during Oligocene times; 3) the nature of the first hominoids (the Miocene ape radiation); and 4) the differentiation of the first hominids in the Plio-Pleistocene. When one thinks of the origins of the various characteristics that link us to our primate ancestry the primary questions are: 'what? when? how? and where?' Just as the skeletal elements which detail stages in our ancestry arose at various widely separated times, the acquisition and loss of anatomical features involved in the transformation from primitive primate to human are similarly spread out.

Beginning early in this century, scientists have told a story of a sequence of events through time that led to modern humans. For some of the first writers an unacceptable orthogenetic or directed slant was given to the account – note Elliot Smith having written in 1924 of *"Man's ceaseless struggle to achieve his destiny."* Apart from this, the story of the successive stages of development in our ancestry was at various times reported somewhat fancifully or even incorrectly and this storytelling element led Landau (1984, 1991) to conclude that accounts of the evolutionary events in the past history of humans resemble folk tales or 'hero-myth' accounts, rather than a scientific narration. Nevertheless, in the past decade or so, we have learned so much more about *all* stages in our derivation from the basal prosimian ancestor up to modern humans that, today, a much more coherent account can be produced. Scientists may differ about details of this narrative but no one should suppose any longer that the basic sequence of events is mythical.

Eocene epoch

When considering the first stages of anthropoid evolution in the late Eocene, we know that the earliest anthropoids or anthropoideans (members of suborder Anthropoidea) are typified by a complex of distinctions that separate them as a group from earlier ancestors among the prosimians. These distinctions evolved for a reason, or set of reasons, and what were originally behavioural changes eventually became fixed in the skeletal and dental anatomy so that they can now be observed and characterised from fossils.

There are three major problems in discerning these beginnings. First not all changes – reflected in fossil bone and teeth – that are used to define early Anthropoidea would have appeared at the same time. Second, there are major gaps in the temporal sequences of the relevant fossils and, third, there is only a spotty spatial distribution of the evidence. Were we to have fossils representing all sequential stages they would imperceptibly intergrade and it would become much more difficult to draw defining lines between them.

As to where the anthropoids originated there are two continents that might have mattered. Europe, North America, and South America can be eliminated since their early Tertiary mammalian faunas are well documented from numerous faunal samples without any putative stem anthropoids having been found in these continents. In fact, primates that are, or may be, the earliest anthropoideans have only been found beginning in the middle Eocene in northern Africa and in southern Asia. Of all these earliest sites the most complete fossil materials come from Africa in late Eocene and early Oligocene sites located in the badlands north of the great lake, Birket Qarun, in the Fayum Province of Egypt. Discoveries there, made first by Richard Markgraf and later through expeditions under my direction, have been in two phases. Initially, from about 1906 until 1987 only Oligocene primates (including extensive parts of their skeleton and skulls) were found. Hence during that period of research the definition of what typifies early anthropoids was based in large part on these finds.

Beginning in the late 1980s, fossil primates from a distinctly older horizon in the Egyptian late Eocene began to turn up and by now these have become even better documented than the Oligocene Fayum primates. These older anthropoids are, in general, smaller and more primitive than the Oligocene forms and, being earlier, show more clearly what the ancestral anthropoideans were like.

Figure 1
Field crew
excavating the unique
late Eocene Site, L –
41. Lower Sequence,
Fayum Province,
Egypt. Age about 36
million years.
This site has yielded
a greater variety of
the earliest
Anthropoidea than
any other in the
world.
*Photo. Richard
Lovesy*

The effect of this two-stage discovery of early higher primates in Egypt has shifted considerably the suite of features that we use when we identify extinct species as early anthropoids.

For instance, it was once believed that the first anthropoideans had unusually deep jaws and very flattened molars (above and below) whose cusps were inflated (not crescentic) and all lower molars were believed to lack the paraconid cusp. Now we know that this is not true of Eocene anthropoideans from the Fayum such as *Catopithecus, Serapia, Arsinoea* and *Proteopithecus.* Any effort to understand the anatomical nature and even the identification of purported early species as belonging to the first higher primates must start with the species of these four genera. Two genera, *Algeripithecus* and *Tabelia* from the middle Eocene of Algeria resemble the Fayum forms but, so far, have been documented only by isolated teeth. They are, however, contemporary with the earliest Asian forms so far proposed as anthropoids, so that one cannot say for sure which of the two continents produced the earliest higher primates.

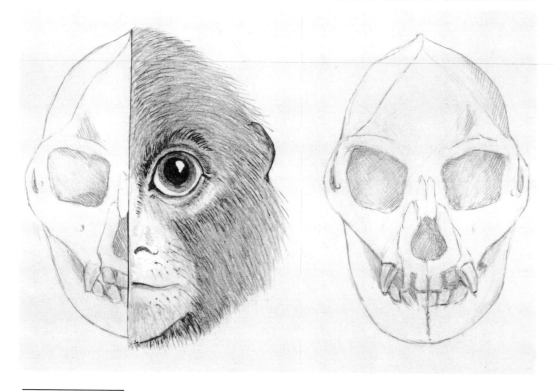

Figure 2
Reconstruction of the
face of *Catopithecus
browni,* a late Eocene
catarrhine monkey
from the Fayum
Depression, Egypt.
*Illustration by Elwyn
Simons*

Regrettably, these possible early higher primates from parts of
north Africa other than Egypt and those from southern Asia, as well,
are documented only by finds of scattered teeth or fragmentary upper
and lower jaws. Nevertheless, for certain identification of any fossil
as an undoubted member of Anthropoidea the cranium must be
preserved. It is only in such skulls that the essential anthropoid
characters of the facial and basicranial regions can be observed.
Long discussions can be, and have been, written about the taxonomic
status of possible early Asian anthropoids, the most completely
documented of which are now *Siamopithecus, Pondaungia* and
Amphipithecus. Unfortunately, until skulls are known for these
primates, a definite taxonomic assignment as to major group
affinities cannot be made. It is known from the ancient distribution
of other fossil mammals, and from plant fossils as well, that there
were weak ties between northern Africa and southern Asia in the
Eocene so that there could have been faunal migration between them
at approximately middle Eocene time, that is between about 42-36
Myr.

Recently the claim has been made that an Asian anthropoid
radiation, culminating in the gibbon and orang-utan, is documented

by *Siamopithecus* from Thailand and *Pondaungia* and *Amphipithecus* from Myanmar. But we now know, from what happened in primate evolution later than the Eocene, what and where the main stream of primate evolution to humans was. Until geologically recent times it has always been in Africa. In various ways the four Egyptian Eocene genera *Arsinoea, Proteopithecus, Catopithecus* and *Serapia* resemble each other and, in addition, the latter two particularly resemble and are taxonomically ranked with Egyptian Oligocene anthropoids, the first of the two, *Catopithecus,* with *Propliopithecus* and *Aegyptopithecus,* and the last, *Serapia,* with *Apidium* and *Parapithecus.* *Propliopithecus* and *Aegyptopithecus,* in turn, bear striking details in the dentition and skull that link them to Miocene east African *Proconsul, Afropithecus* and several other genera among their east African contemporaries.

Similarly, the recently described skull of the oldest undoubted catarrhine monkey, *Victoriapithecus,* from the middle Miocene of east Africa bears many striking similarities to skulls of *Aegyptopithecus.* These relationships document that catarrhine evolution began, and continued for a long time, solely on the isolated African continent. The three known Asian forms do not seem to have led anywhere as there are no demonstrable descendants in the Oligocene and earliest Miocene of Asia.

In addition, the southeast Asian Eocene primates show features which are unlike those seen in the earliest well-known Egyptian anthropoids. Such characteristics include very deep and massive mandibles, long third molars, hyperflattened molar crown surfaces, a 'twinned' metaconid, and typically, loss of M/1 paraconid and M/1-2 hypoconulids. In contrast, both *Catopithecus* and *Proteopithecus* have relatively gracile mandibles, short third molars, distinct and somewhat crescentic cusps that stand much higher when unworn, a twinned hypoconulid/entoconid on M/1-3, a M/1 paraconid cusp and never a twinned metaconid. Judging from photographs published by Takai *et al.,* (2000), a frontal fragment recently found associated with a maxilla of *Amphipithecus* appears to lack postorbital closure and shows, other, non-anthropoidean features.

Returning to the Eocene Fayum anthropoids, it is clear that a composite description of their nature can now be made. Firstly, their teeth and limb bones show that the best preserved of them were sexually dimorphic and distinctly adapted for arboreal living (Gebo *et al.,* 1994; Simons, Plavcan & Fleagle, 1999). The fauna and flora contemporary with these primates indicates a warm climate rain forest environment with seasonal monsoons (Bown & Kraus, 1988). These anthropoids were marmoset sized, and because of the dimorphism are thought to have associated in polygynous, fairly large sized social groups. Comparatively small orbits show that these primates were diurnal. Their tooth structure indicates insectivory and some folivory and/or fruit eating. Hence it would seem that we owe, today, our diurnality and residual dimorphism to these 36 Myr old ancestors. Basal anthropoidean social groups imply a dominant leader initiating group movements and choice and times of feeding. (This ancient inheritance may help to explain the seemingly ingrained tendency of modern humans to seek group leaders.) In sum, the beginning of the higher primates as we know it was in the tropical forest as arboreal, diurnal and group living creatures.

Oligocene epoch

The record of presumed stages in human ancestry during this epoch is also documented only in the African Fayum. The two most completely known Oligocene primates from Africa in terms of preservation of cranial, dental and postcranial remains are the parapithecid *Apidium phiomense* (Simons, 1995; Fleagle & Simons, 1995) and the propliopithecid *Aegyptopithecus zeuxis* (Kay, Fleagle & Simons, 1981; Fleagle & Simons, 1982; Fleagle *et al.,* 1996; Ankel-Simons, Fleagle & Chatrath 1998). These two different families, Parapithecidae and Propliopithecidae, have very different relevance for primate evolutionary history, since the parapithecids are a highly derived and distinct group without subsequent descendants while *Aegyptopithecus* and the other propliopithecids appear to stand at or near the base of the catarrhine radiation. Thus, the conditions found in the propliopithecids document the stage just before the appearance of true apes. At this stage, basal catarrhines are very generalised and hence there is not much to be seen in *Aegyptopithecus* that is still with us today. Just possibly the existence of Carabelli's cusp in some modern humans is a survival from the large lingual, beaded cingula that are present in *Aegyptopithecus.*

Relative size of the brain in *Aegyptopithecus* is still at the prosimian level but continued pronounced sexual dimorphism in these and other related but less well documented species strongly indicates multi–male/multi–female societies. Before sexual dimorphism became a characteristic of anthropoideans it may be presumed that primate social groups were smaller, monogamous family units similar to those among most extant prosimians. For such groups individual members would have had to be able to distinguish only four or five individuals from external non-group members. With the larger, polygynous groups characteristic of earliest known higher primates, selection would have put a premium on the ability to distinguish from non-group members the individual identities of a distinctly larger number of individuals, say fifteen or sixteen in the home social group. Clearly the development of complex social systems had begun in the Eocene, and it would have been one of the factors selecting for relatively larger and larger brain size. Nevertheless, brain volume/body size estimates put *Aegyptopithecus* on the low side compared to Miocene-Recent anthropoids. A brain to body size ratio of 1:22 was calculated by Simons (1993) from the most complete endocranial cast, but this proportion may well be affected by inaccuracies in estimating body size (thought to be approximately 6000g).

Figure 3
Collecting at Quarry M in the Upper Sequence (Oligocene deposits) of the Jebal Qatrani Formation, Fayum Province, Egypt. The author holding a face of *Aegyptopithecus* that has just been discovered. Age about 32-33 million years.
Photo. Herbert H. Covert.

A series of studies by Fleagle and Simons (e.g. Fleagle & Simons, 1982) and, more recently, by Ankel-Simons, Fleagle & Chatrath (1998) have shown that *Aegyptopithecus* is a generalised arboreal quadruped, broadly similar in its postcranial adaptation to present day howling monkeys. This Fayum genus differs, however, from any modern form in possessing robust, stocky limb bones and, for its size, massive mandibular and temporal muscles. The mandible and skull are equally robust and show a thick and deep horizontal ramus with buttressed symphysis coupled with a thick cranium showing well-developed sagittal and nuchal crests. Caudal vertebrae have been found and these document the retention of a long tail. Teaford, Maas & Simons (1996) studied the dental microwear on teeth of *Aegyptopithecus* and other Fayum primates. In the case of *Aegyptopithecus* they concluded that diet was frugivorous but tending toward hard object feeding – perhaps seasonally.

Benefit (1999) has reviewed known fossils of the Kenyan middle Miocene monkey, *Victoriapithecus*, and has demonstrated that in cranial anatomy it is quite like *Aegyptopithecus,* (see also Benefit & McCrossin (1997). Both of these primates share many details of a generalised cranio-facial morphotype, including a long, low neurocranium with temporal lines forming a frontal trigon and converging backward into a distinct saggital crest, flanked by strong nuchal crests. Orbital openings are taller than wide and with the low-set zygomatics are angled upward relative to the plane of the palate, above the eye-sockets are superorbital arches or costae. Benefit believes that these and other shared features place *Aegyptopithecus* closer than any other fossil primate to the common ancestor of catarrhine monkeys and apes. This conclusion, with which I agree, is important because it provides strong evidence that during the Oligocene Epoch, Africa was still the home of the primate lineage leading to the later apes and humans, and the likely place for catarrhine differentiation. We can see that the lifestyle of these basal catarrhines was not yet different from that which their ancestors had in the Eocene. They were tree dwelling, fruit and hard object feeding quadrupeds with long tails.

Miocene epoch

Fossils from this long lasting Tertiary Epoch document the separation of early hominoids and cercopithecoids in Africa and was also the period when catarrhines dispersed from Africa to Europe and Asia. Almost all Miocene African primates come from Uganda and Kenya. Sites from this area can be sorted temporally as being early, middle or late Miocene. The most completely documented primates are the early Miocene finds made on Rusinga Island in Lake Victoria, Kenya and at several mainland sites around the Kivarando Gulf of the lake (Songhor, Koru) and west of Lake Turkana (Kalodirr, Buluk, etc.). Genus *Proconsul,* established in 1934, is the best known of these primates and total assessment of the nearly complete skeleton (based on several individual finds) makes it possible to rank species of this genus as being among the earliest known hominoids (see Ward, Walker & Teaford, 1991). Contra Benefit (1999) and Harrison (1998) who believe that *Proconsul* had a tail, Ward, Walker & Teaford (1999) maintain that there is no evidence for an external tail in *Proconsul* and, hence, this derived character of hominoids, may remain valid for species of this genus.

Species of *Proconsul* are rather large, ranging from siamang to chimpanzee or even small gorilla size. Several, mainly smaller, primate genera are contemporary members of this African radiation. They belong to the genera *Micropithecus, Nyanzapithecus, Rangwapithecus, Simiolus, Dendropithecus, Turkanapithecus, Kalepithecus* and *Limnopithecus* (see Fleagle, 1999 for references). Several of the smaller of these primates appear to have been highly folivorous (Benefit, 1999; Kay & Ungar, 1997). Apart from *Dendropithecus,* which has a long straight humerus resembling those of suspensory primates, all species of the preceding genera, where known in the postcranium, are adaptively similar to *Proconsul*. Another genus, *Morotopithecus,* from the early Miocene of Uganda, has been described as having a postcranial skeleton resembling that of extant hominoids (Gebo *et al.,* 1997). If this is correct, then this might be the earliest documentation of the modern type of hominoids.

The relationship of *Proconsul* to the Oligocene primate *Aegyptopithecus* is significant as was initially indicated in the description of the latter genus (Simons, 1965); the two share enlarged beaded lingual cingula on the upper molars and a molar size sequence increasing posteriorly, as well as many other details of dental morphology. The relatively recent discovery of *Afropithecus* in the Kenyan Miocene has provided evidence that links the two genera further because they share numerous morphological similarities in the cranium (as discussed already in connection with *Victoriapithecus).* This extends to details not seen in other genera such as their sharing a broadened ascending wing of the premaxilla with a central foramen. The morphometric studies of Leakey *et al.* (1991) and Seiffert (1998) have also found striking similarities in the upper facial morphology of *Afropithecus* and *Aegyptopithecus* that are unique among living and extinct catarrhines. It therefore may be concluded with reasonable certainty that *Proconsul* and allied Miocene forms are derived from the larger group represented by the propliopithecids.

Proconsul has a type of locomotion unlike that of any living anthropoid, but may be close to that posited for primitive catarrhines generally. General similarities to living apes include: 1) similar morphology of the elbow region 2) the robusticity of the fibula 3) the shape of the tarsal bones and 4) loss of the tail. Some of the differences from living hominoids that have been noted are: 1) comparatively elongated olecranon process 2) a lengthened styloid process of the ulna and 3) only slight curvature of the phalanges. Taken together, the combination of these and other features of the teeth and skeleton of *Proconsul* suggest a generalised arboreal quadrupedal mode of locomotion, devoid of habitual suspensory behaviours. Kay & Ungar (1997) have suggested that *Proconsul* was predominantly frugivorous. At the end of the early Miocene, advanced anthropoids were still only found in Africa and were still arboreal frugivores. Since subgroups of higher Hominoidea had not yet differentiated, there can have been no independent derivation of the hylobatids and *Pongo* in Asia, directly from the amphipithecids, as recently suggested by Jaeger, Chaimanee & Ducrocq (1998). There is no evidence that propliopithecids or proconsulids occurred in Asia in the Eocene, Oligocene or early Miocene.

Middle Miocene sites in east Africa provide further evidence about higher primate evolution. From Maboko Island in Lake Victoria, Kenya, fossils of the first cercopithecoid, *Victoriapithecus,* and of an ape, *Kenyapithecus,* have been found and dated at about 15 Myr. *Kenyapithecus* also occurs at the 14 Myr Fort Ternan site.

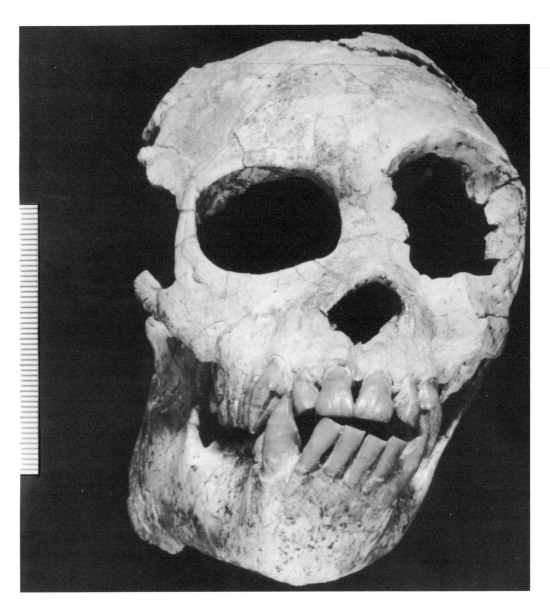

Figure 4
Skull of *Proconsul eseloni* recovered by Mary Leakey on Rusinga Island in 1948.
Courtesy Nairobi Museum of Natural History – Photo. Natural History Museum, London.

Benefit (1999) has reviewed the cranial, dental and postcranial anatomy of *Victoriapithecus* and has presented a case that this earliest cercopithecoid monkey was probably semi-terrestrial, constituted the family ancestral to modern catarrhine monkeys, and may have been locally outcompeted by *Kenyapithecus*.

Benefit explains the absence of any monkeys from the early Miocene east African sites (where early Miocene hominoids are so common) on environmental grounds, suggesting that the hominoids were wet forest primates which were mainly folivorous and soft fruit eating while the victoriapithecids seem to have inhabited more xeric riverine forest bush and savannah country. *Afropithecus* and *Kenyapithecus* appear to have shared with *Victoriapithecus* a diet of hard fruits and seeds (Benefit, 1999 and references therein). *Kenyapithecus* is of great interest in terms of the story of human descent because it also seems to have been a semi-terrestrial chimpanzee-sized ape existing from 15 to 12.5 Myr – too early to belong to the hominine clade, but without crossing specialisations that would eliminate it from the ancestry of the African ape – hominine clade. Publications on newly found skeletons of *Kenya- pithecus* are forthcoming but information about the skeleton available to date does not present nearly as complete a picture of its adaptation as do several finds of the *Proconsul* group. Nevertheless, progress is being made in interpreting its lifestyle. McCrossin (1997) and McCrossin, Benefit & Gitau (1998) have suggested that *Kenyapithecus* had a terrestrial form of locomotion resembling that of African apes and that these anatomical features indicate that it was an early member of the African great ape/human clade.

Other scholars, such as Alan Walker and Steven Ward (*pers. com.*), doubt that its adaptations were very different from those of *Proconsul*. Late Miocene sites in Africa have provided little information about hominoid evolution. As I have been pointing out for many years, further evidence about the ancestry of hominines after about 12.5 Myr and all the way up to about 4.4 Myr is severely restricted by what is called 'the gap'. In this period there are no significant fossil specimens that can be referred to species of the chimpanzee – human clade. From East Africa there are hominine teeth from sites such as Ngorora (10 Myr), Leukeino (7 Myr) as well as isolated teeth and a mandible with one tooth from Lothagam (7 Myr).

Another problem for reconstructing the evolution of the higher Hominoidea is that some molecular anthropologists would put all the split point times for all branches of living members of the group within this time period (Pilbeam, 1996), and hence all connections remain hypothetical in the absence of fossils.

Plio-Pleistocene epochs

From 4.4 Myr sites in the Awash river valley in Ethiopia come fossils that have been named *Ardipithecus ramidus* (White, Suwa & Asfaw, 1994; 1995). Although several partial skeletons of this species have been found they have not yet been described and it is still unclear if this species had any bipedal adaptations. What little is known about this species indicates that, unlike later hominins, *Ardipithecus* had relatively large canines, comparatively smaller cheek teeth and thin tooth enamel. Its relationship to the oldest bipedal hominin, *Australopithecus anamensis* (represented by carpal bones, distal humerus, radius and tibia) from 3.9-4.2 Myr sites at Kanapoi, on the southwestern side of Lake Turkana, and Allia Bay, on the eastern shore, has yet to be established. It seems likely that *Australopithecus anamensis* is more closely related to still younger species of the genus *Australopithecus* than is *Ardipithecus.*

The genus *Australopithecus,* which was first described by Dart in 1925, has now come to be recognised as the connecting link between apes and members of the genus *Homo.* Reviewing the very extensive literature concerning the considerable number of species of *Australopithecus* that have been described is beyond the scope of this chapter. Nevertheless, it is appropriate here to itemise some of the many ways in which *Australopithecus* serves as a connecting link. Perhaps the most advanced feature is its possession of a fully bipedal adaptation, although details of the anatomy differ in many ways from the exact bipedal characters of modern humans. Hence, when the curtain goes up at about 4.4 Myr, after the late Miocene early Pliocene gap, the hominins have become mainly terrestrial. This adaptation of *Australopithecus* is apparent throughout the skeleton so that there are changes away from the ape condition in the base of the skull, the vertebral column, the pelvis, femur, knee and ankle joint, and foot. All but the earliest species of the genus show striking reduction of the canines when contrasted to those of chimpanzees and gorillas. On the other hand, the cranium of *Australopithecus africanus* has a rather chimpanzee-like outline as seen in STS 5 from Sterkfontein, South Africa. In addition, the average brain volume of *Australopithecus* is much more comparable in size to that of a chimpanzee than to that of later hominins of the genus *Homo.*

Many authors, e.g. Susman, Stern & Jungers (1984), have pointed out that phalanges of both hand and foot of *Australopithecus* indicate that this creature must have continued to be adept at tree climbing and probably slept in trees as a means of evading the whole range of contemporary (mainly terrestrial) carnivores. Asfaw *et al.* (1999) described a new species of *Australopithecus*, *A. garhi*, thought to be more primitive than *A. africanus* with an unusual combination of comparatively large anterior teeth coupled with large post-canine teeth lacking the exaggerated enamel thickness of these same teeth in robust *Australopithecus (Paranthropus).*

Unfortunately the first stage of the 'Hero Myth' remains shrouded in mystery due to the lack of transitional fossils from the late Miocene. However, the traditional perspective of early twentieth century researchers that there was an adaptive shift from exclusive arboreality directly to habitual bipedalism has recently been challenged by re-evaluations of the anatomical evidence linking hominins to the African apes. Richmond & Strait (1999) have recently proposed that *Australopithecus* retained morphological features of the wrist from a knuckle-walking ancestor.

This view echoes the recent work of Gebo (1996), who has demonstrated that members of the African ape/human clade have a stabilised wrist together with a foot morphology associated with heel-strike, plantigrade footfalls. These features together suggest a common ancestor that was a terrestrial quadruped, and possibly a

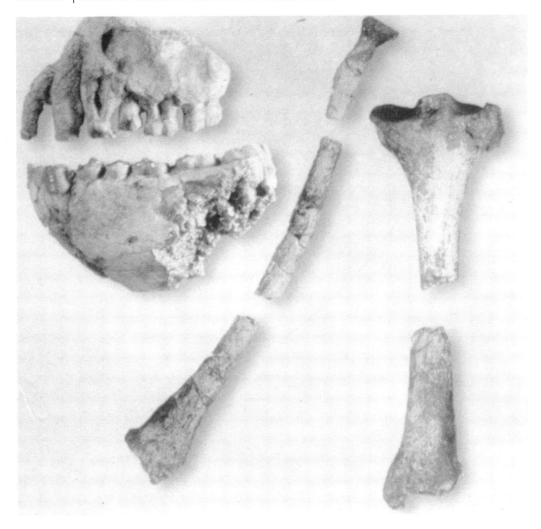

Figure 5
Maxilla, mandible, radius, and tibia of the 3.9-4.2 Myr hominid *Australopithecus anamensis* from Kanapoi and Allia Bay, northern Kenya. Note the distinct flaring of the proximal and distal ends of the tibia – these are features functionally associated with shock absorption during bipedal walking. *Courtesy National Museums of Kenya.*

knuckle-walker. Since none of these features are seen in fossils earlier than *Australopithecus,* such hypotheses will require new fossil discoveries for confirmation. Moving to a consideration of the nature of Pleistocene hominins the oldest well-preserved skeleton that can be placed in the genus *Homo* is the Nariokotome skeleton found in 1.5 Myr deposits west of Lake Turkana, Kenya. Some students place it as an early member of the species *Homo erectus* and others consider it a distinct species referable to *Homo ergaster.* As far as the postcranial skeleton of this individual, a sub-adult male, is concerned, hominin evolution had progressed to the point that there is little difference from modern humans, although the brain is only about two thirds as large as the modern average.

The summated anatomical changes that have come about in the course of human evolution since our ancestry split, approximately five million years ago, from the branch leading to the African apes, make us seem very different from the apes. Nevertheless, these changes are in many ways little more than 'skin deep' for it remains almost commonplace knowledge that we share with the chimpanzee 98% of the genome, and numerous other features such as mutually understandable cries of pain and terror, chuckling when tickled, and the ability to culturally transmit knowledge and tool-making skills.

Acknowledgements

I thank Erik Seiffert, Cornelia Simons and Friderun Ankel-Simons for criticism and comments on the manuscript. Part of the research reported was funded by the US National Science Foundation Grant No. 9729422. This is Duke Primate Center Publication No. 691.

References

Ankel-Simons FA, Fleagle JG, Chatrath PS. 1998. Femoral anatomy of *Aegyptopithecus zeuxis,* an early Oligocene anthropoid. *American Journal of Physical Anthropology.* **106:** 413-434.

Asfaw B, White T, Lovejoy O, Latimer T, Simpson S, Suwa G. 1999. *Australopithecus garhi:* A new species of early hominid from Ethiopia. *Science.* **284:** 629-635.

Benefit BR. 1999. *Victoriapithecus:* The key to Old World monkey and catarrhine origins. *Evolutionary Anthropology.* **7(5):** 155-174.

Benefit BR, McCrossin ML. 1997. Earliest known Old World monkey skull. *Nature.* **388:** 368-371.

Bown TM, Kraus MJ. 1988. *Geology and Paleontology of the Oligocene Jebel Qatrani Formation and Adjacent Rocks, Fayum Depression, Egypt.* U.S. Geological Survey Professional Paper 1452. Washington, D.C.: U.S. Government Printing Office.

Dart RA. 1925. *Australopithecus africanus:* the man-ape of South Africa. *Nature.* **115:** 195-199.

Elliot Smith G. 1924. *Essays on the Evolution of Man.* Oxford: Oxford University Press.

Fleagle JG, Simons EL. 1982. The humerus of *Aegyptopithecus zeuxis,* a primitive ape. *American Journal of Physical Anthropology.* **59:** 175-193.

Fleagle JG, Simons EL. 1995. Limb skeleton and locomotor adaptation of *Apidium phiomense,* an Oligocene anthropoid from Egypt. *American Journal of Physical Anthropology.* **97:** 235-289.

Fleagle JG, Richmond HF, Ankel-Simons FA, Chatrath PS, Simons EL. 1996. *Aegyptopithecus zeuxis* and the evolution of Old World higher primates. *Proceedings of the Geological Survey. Egypt Centenary Conference.* 277-287.

Fleagle JG. 1999. *Primate Adaptation and Evoution.* (Second Edition). San Diego: Academic Press.

Gebo DL, Simons EL, Rasmussen DT, Dagosto M. 1994. Eocene anthropoid postcrania form the Fayum, Egypt. In: Fleagle JG, Kay RF. eds. *Anthropoid Origins.* New York : Plenum Press. 203-233.

Gebo DL, MacClatchy L, Kiflo R, Demo A, Kingston J, Pilbeam D.1997. A new hominoid genus from the Uganda early Miocene. *Science.* **276:** 401-404.

Harrison T. 1998. Evidence for a tail in *Proconsul heseloni. American Journal of Physical Anthropology.* (supplement.) **26:** 96.

Jaeger JJ, Chaimanee Y, Ducrocq S. 1998. Origin and evolution of Asian hominoid primates. Paleontological data versus molecular data. *C. R. Academy of Science IIA.* **321:** 73-78.

Kay RF, Fleagle JG, Simons EL. 1981. A revision of the Oligocene apes of the Fayum Province, Egypt. *American Journal of Physical Anthropology.* **55:** 293-322.

Kay RF, Ungar P. 1997. Dental evidence for diet in some Miocene catarrhines with comments on the effects of phylogeny on the interpretation of adaptation. In: Begun DR, Ward CV, Rose MD. eds. *Function, Phylogeny and Fossils: Miocene Hominoid Evolution and Adaptations.* New York: Plenum Press. 131-150.

Landau M. 1984. Human evolution as narrative. *American Science.* **72:** 262-268.

Landau M. 1991. *Narratives of Human Evolution.* New Haven: Yale Univ. Press.

Leakey MG, Leakey RE, Richtsmeier JT, Simons EL, Walker AC. 1991. Similarities in *Aegyptopithecus* and *Afropithecus* facial morphology. *Folia Primatologica.* **56:** 65-85.

McCrossin ML. 1997. New postcranial remains of *Kenyapithecus* and their implications for understanding the origins of hominoid terrestriality. *American Journal of Physical Anthropology.* (supplement) **24:** 164.

McCrossin ML, Benefit BR, Gitau SN. 1998. Functional and phylogenetic analysis of the distal radius of *Kenyapithecus,* with comments on the origin of the African great ape and human clade. *American Journal of Physical Anthropology.* (supplement) **26:** 158.

Pilbeam DR. 1996. Genetic and morphological records of the Hominoidea and hominid origins: a synthesis. *Molecular Phylogenetics and Evolution.* **5:** 155-168.

Richmond BG, Strait DS. 2000. Evidence that humans evolved from a knuckle-walking ancestor. *Nature.* **404:** 382-385.

Seiffert ER. 1998. A comparative morphometric analysis of the catarrhine orbital aperture. [Unpublished M.A. thesis], University of Texas at Austin.

Simons EL. 1965. New fossil apes from Egypt and the initial differentiation of Hominoidea. *Nature.* **205:** 135-139.

Simons EL. 1993. New endocasts of *Aegyptopithecus:* Oldest well-preserved record of the brain in Anthropoidea. *American Journal of Science.* **293:** 383-390.

Simons EL. 1995. *Crania of Apidium:* Primitive Anthropoidean (Primates: Parapithecidae) from the Egyptian Oligocene. *American Museum Novitates.* **3124:** 1-10.

Simons EL. 1995. Skulls and anterior teeth of *Catopithecus* (Primates: Anthropoidea) from the Eocene and anthropoid origins. *Science.* **268:** 1885-1888.

Simons EL, Plavcan JM, Fleagle JG. 1999. Canine sexual dimorphism in Egyptian Eocene anthropoid primates *Catopithecus* and *Proteopithecus. Proceedings of the National Acadamy of Science. U.S.A.* **96:** 2559-2562.

Susman RL, Stern JT Jr, Jungers WL. 1984. Arboreality and bipedality in the Hadar hominids. *Folia Primatologica.* **43:** 113-156.

Takai M, Shingehara N, Tsubamoto T, Egi N, Aung AK, Thein T, Soe AN, Tun ST. 2000. The latest middle Eocene Primate Fauna in Pondaung area, Myanmar, *Asian Paleoprimatology.* **1:** 7-28.

Teaford MF, Maas MC, Simons EL. 1996. Dental microwear and microstructure in early Oligocene primates from the Fayum, Egypt: Implications for diet. *American Journal of Physical Anthropology.* **101:** 527-543.

Ward CV, Walker A, Teaford MF. 1991. *Proconsul* did not have a tail. *Journal of Human Evolution.* **21:** 215-220.

Ward CV, Walker A, Teaford MF. 1999. Still no evidence for a tail in *Proconsul heseloni. American Journal of Physical Anthropology.* (supplement) **28:** 273.

White TD, Suwa G, Asfaw B. 1994. *Australopithecus ramidus,* a new species of early hominid from Aramis, Ethiopia. *Nature.* **371:** 306-333.

White TD, Suwa G, Asfaw B. 1995. Corrigendum*: Australopithecus ramidus, a* new species of early hominid from Aramis, Ethiopia. *Nature.* **375:** 88.

CHAPTER THREE

Evolutionary geography, habitat availability and species distributions among early African hominids

P. J. GOLLOP & R. A. FOLEY

Introduction

The recognition of the relatively high levels of taxonomic diversity among the Pliocene African hominids has led to a greater interest in the relationship between patterns of hominid evolution and evolutionary mechanisms. This has taken the form of questions about the number of species (Kimbel & Martin, 1993; Foley, 1991; Reed & Fleagle, 1995) and their relationship to climatic and environmental change (Vrba, 1993, 1995; Foley 1993, 1994; deMenocal, 1995; Potts 1998). Vrba has argued that speciation patterns are confined to major periods of climatic change (the pulse-turnover hypothesis), although the analytical support for this has been questioned (Foley, 1994). Potts (1998) has also suggested that long term adaptive trends in hominid evolution have been shaped by the increasing level of environmental and climatic variability that developed during the Pliocene and Pleistocene.

All these models ultimately depend upon the relationship between the formation of new taxa and the distribution of habitats. Most theories of speciation are dependent upon some level of allopatry and isolation as a prerequisite for the formation of reproductive barriers. Reduction of preferred habitats leads to loss of gene flow, increased competition and selection, and reduced population sizes and higher probabilities of extinction. Expansion of suitable habitats results in population expansions and dispersals across larger areas. This perspective implies that geography rather than time should be the starting point for understanding evolutionary patterns.

Three reasons can immediately be cited for paying close attention to the spatial patterns in evolution. The first is that the two major events in evolution – speciation and extinction – occur geographically. It is widely accepted that speciation is predominantly, if not exclusively, allopatric – that is, it depends upon some form of physical separation of populations. Equally, species undergoing a process of extinction will go through a succession of smaller and smaller geographical ranges, until they survive not at all, or perhaps as geographical isolates in refugia. Second, evolutionary biologists have long recognised that the current geographical distributions of taxa reflect their historical past, and so an understanding of evolutionary relationships must take into account biogeographical patterns. Third, as ecological approaches to evolution have become more central to the subject, it is clear that there is a strong relationship between habitat distributions and evolutionary patterns.

The purpose of this chapter is to explore certain aspects of evolutionary geography among the Pliocene and early Pleistocene African hominids.

Evolutionary geography is defined as that branch of evolutionary biology that examines spatial factors in evolution (Lahr & Foley, 1998; Foley, 1999). It is concerned with such aspects as the biotic and abiotic conditions that shape evolutionary patterns, and is explicitly demographic in its approach. In previous papers this approach has been used to consider the origins of modern humans (Lahr & Foley, 1998), and evolutionary patterns among Pliocene African hominids (Foley, 1999). The focus of this chapter is somewhat different. There has been considerable debate about the habitat preferences of the early hominids – for example, whether they are confined to savannah regions, or whether they occupied more forested regions. Reconstruction of hominid habitat is critical in building adaptive models to explain such characteristics as bipedalism or more carnivorous behaviour. Another dimension, however, is how the availability of certain habitats will affect the extent of isolation and the potential for dispersal and expansion among hominids. Here we use palaeoclimatic modelling to estimate the availability of distinct biomes in Africa, and provide some estimates for species range areas for hominids with specific habitat preferences. These will be used to discuss the role of climate and environmental change on early hominid evolutionary patterns.

Methods

There are two components to the methods used here. The first is to use false colour satellite maps, linked to marine oxygen isotope data to calculate the distribution of specific habitats under various climatic conditions. The second is to build model species with varying habitat preferences. The analysis then focuses on the relationship between these, and in particular, generates model species range areas and distributions.

Modelling palaeoenvironments

In order to examine the geographical distribution of hominids with different habitat preferences it is necessary to map the distribution of habitat types at various times in the past. Present-day Africa contains a huge diversity of environments. In East Africa alone the vegetation ranges from sparse semi-desert vegetation to dense rain forest including various bushland and grassland types, as well as mangroves, other swamps and the afro-alpine vegetation found on the highest mountains (Pratt & Gwynne, 1977). The distribution of different vegetation types is largely controlled by moisture availability and altitude (Justice *et al.,* 1986). Foley (1987) has described how increasing rainfall leads to an increase in plant cover, biomass and plant production, thereby affecting the structure and pattern of habitats. The variation in the vegetation of savannah environments, for example, depends on rainfall. However, while primary production in savannahs is generally low in comparison with rain forest environments, African savannahs are characterised by the abundance and diversity of their large mammal fauna, so though plant foods are of low quality there is a rich supply of animal resources. Nevertheless, both these resources vary dramatically in abundance, distribution and availability throughout the year because of the seasonal nature of rainfall.

The traditional source for information on the distribution of vegetation on the Earth's surface has been mapping by ground survey. Land cover maps have been assembled from a variety of ground-based sources such as atlases, local maps and country reports for specific purposes such as input into climate models (DeFries & Townshend, 1994). One problem with using such approaches on a large scale is that the observations of many different observers must be synthesised and disparate observations must be reconciled (Tucker *et al.*, 1985). The size of the task is apparent in the maps of, and ancillary texts on, the vegetation of Africa (White, 1983). Equally, the eclectic way in which these data sets have been compiled makes them difficult to reproduce and to repeat over time to obtain information on changes in land cover. The variation in estimates of the area occupied by major cover types is so great that a comparison of three ground-based global data sets shows that they agree that a common land cover type is present on only 26% of the land surface (DeFries & Townshend, 1993).

Mapping present vegetation distributions is problematic but reconstructing those of the past is an even more complex task. Probably the best empirically-derived palaeovegetation maps available at the moment are those produced by the Quaternary Environments Network (Adams, 1995). These maps are a laudable attempt to review and unite evidence and opinion on palaeoenvironments and are reinforced by a comprehensive synopsis of available data. However, despite this, the resolution of the maps is poor for the simple reason that palaeodata are sparse (Adams, 1995). Resolution varies greatly from region to region depending on the density of sites from which useful data have been obtained.

While low-resolution maps such as that shown in Figure 1a are valuable, they do not fully represent the heterogeneous nature of African environments. Therefore they are of little use in exploring the relationships between ecological fragmentation and the distribution of species at a population scale. For the purposes of this chapter, which deals with exactly this sort of question, high resolution maps of Africa's palaeovegetation are required.

Figure 1b shows a land cover image derived from satellite remote-sensing data. Such data have been used to distinguish between land cover types at a continental scale primarily using seasonal changes in vegetative cover as displayed in temporal variation of the spectral vegetation index known as the normalised difference vegetation index or NDVI (DeFries & Townshend, 1994), a measure of the amount and vigour of vegetation. High values of the index are obtained for areas covered by green vegetation and low values for unvegetated areas and those that are cloud-covered (Townshend & Justice, 1986).

a)

Water
Tropical rainforest
Tropical woodland
Tropical thorn scrub/woodland
Tropical semi-desert
Tropical grassland
Tropical extreme desert
Savannah
Mediterranean sclerophyll scrub
Temperate scrub
Temperate desert
Temperate semi-desert
Sparser, short grass steppe

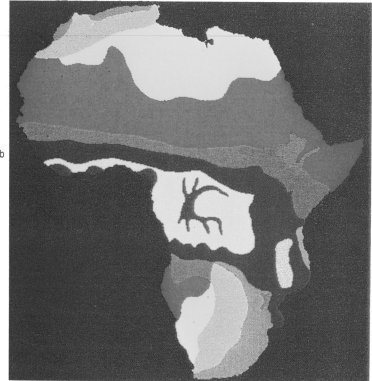

b)

Waterbodies
Barren/sparse
Open shrubland
Closed shrubland
Grassland
Savannah
Woody savannah
Forest

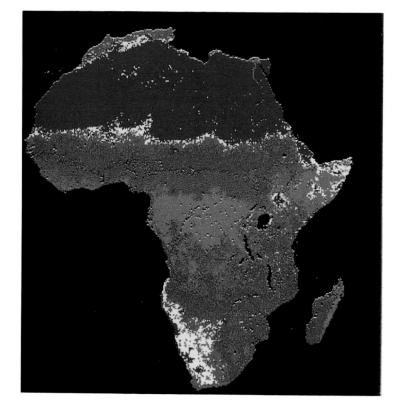

Figure 1a
Africa at 18 kya
(based on Adams,
1995).

Figure 1b
A remotely-sensed
land cover image
(USGS, 1998).

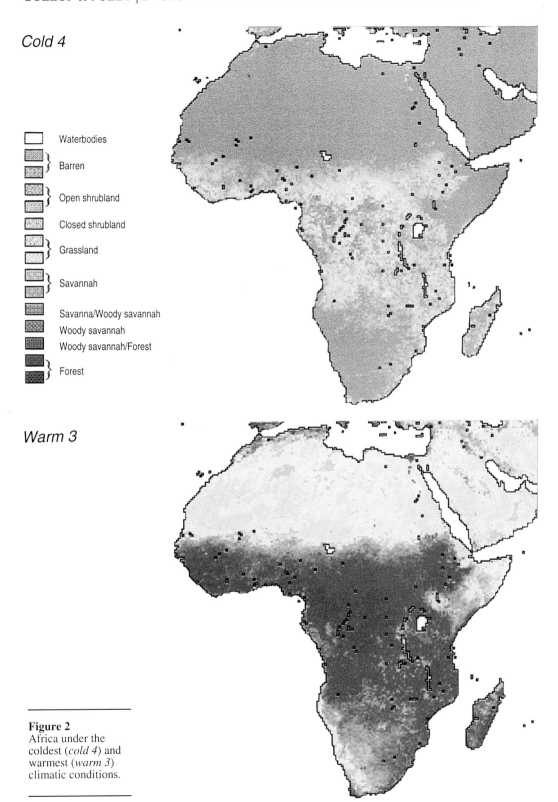

Figure 2
Africa under the coldest (*cold 4*) and warmest (*warm 3*) climatic conditions.

Multitemporal data sets of the NDVI have been used to classify land cover types for Africa (Tucker *et al.,* 1985) (see Figure 1b) and South America (Townshend *et al.,* 1987). There is a high correlation between temporally integrated NDVI images and the major land cover types found in Africa as defined by White (1983) for example.

Thus the highest NDVI values correspond to the forest and wetter savannah areas and the lowest values to desert and semidesert areas (Tucker *et al.,* 1985). One of the most striking features of such land cover maps is that they are available at extremely fine resolutions (~ 1 km) therefore they provide a clear picture of the degree to which habitats are fragmented.

Gollop (in prep.) has developed a method for using satellite remote-sensing data to produce models of palaeoenvironments. The method relies on two factors. First, the relationship between particular NDVI values and different land cover types; for example, that between high values and forest/woodland habitats. Second, the fact that broadly speaking, Africa is wetter when global climate is warmer and drier when climate is colder. Hence, under full glacial conditions forest areas all but disappear and are replaced by woodland while during interglacial periods, savannah areas are replaced by more closed, wooded environments.

Bearing this in mind, NDVI images can be manipulated to reflect changing climatic conditions. For example, to simulate a full glaciation an NDVI image might be altered such that its values are reduced by the difference between values associated with forest and those associated with savannah. When the image is reclassed so that NDVI values are associated with their particular land cover types, the effect of the alteration will be that forest areas have been replaced by savannahs. At the other end of the spectrum, areas with low NDVI values such as shrubland will have had their values further reduced such that they now represent desert. This process can of course be reversed to model wetter conditions.

In this chapter the difference between forest and savannah NDVI values has been partitioned into equal parts and a present day mean NDVI image (a composite of monthly images) has been manipulated in stages to reflect the gradual increase or decrease in moisture resulting from climatic warming or cooling. Both the NDVI data and the land cover map shown in Figure 1b were obtained from the United States Geological Survey website (see USGS, 1998). The two most extreme palaeoenvironmental maps, those reflecting Africa under the driest (*cold 4*) and wettest (*warm 3*) conditions are shown in Figure 2.

Under the full transition from forest to savannah or *vice versa*, there is a major expansion of desert and open habitat when Africa is dry and a broad west to east spread of closed habitat (and 'greening' of the Sahara) when Africa is at its wettest. In addition, the resolution of the original image is maintained so that changes in environmental heterogeneity associated with the changes in habitat distribution are apparent. While it should be remembered that this method only provides a way of modelling palaeoenvironments, it does provide a means of examining the effect of climate change on habitat at a very fine scale. In this sense it has major advantages over empirically-derived but low-resolution maps.

Fitting the palaeovegetation maps to the palaeoclimatic record

The method described above produces maps of African vegetation under different climatic conditions. To link these with particular times in the past the maps must be related to climatic history. Figure 3 shows an oxygen isotope curve for the past 6 million years (Shackleton, 1995). From the curve it is clear that global climate has been extremely variable over this period and also that there has been an overall decrease in temperature. To relate the palaeovegetation maps to this climatic history, the variation between the highest and lowest values on the curve was partitioned into 8 bands and each of these temperature bands was equated with a habitat map. The relationship between the temperature variation described by the oxygen isotope curve and the palaeoenvironment maps is shown in Figure 4. Table 1 shows the earliest and latest appearance of each of the habitat maps, and indicates the periods when particular habitats' distributions were likely to have been relatively common.

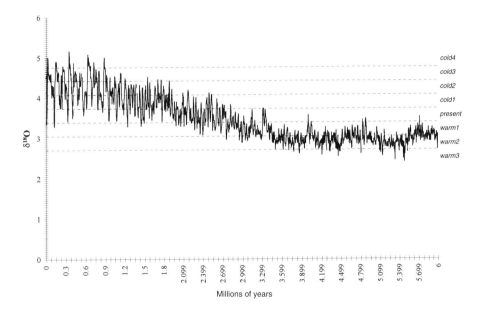

Figure 3
Oxygen isotope curve for the past 6 million years and temperature bands with their associated habitat maps.

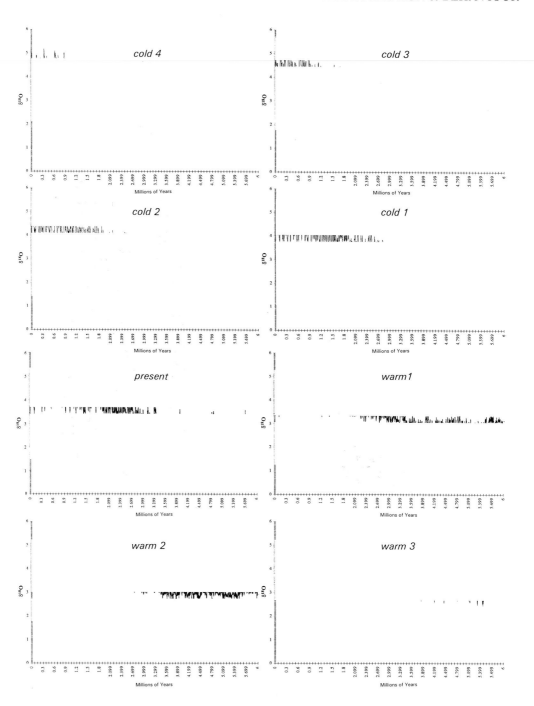

Figure 4
Distribution of the palaeoenvironment maps across the past 6 million years.

Table 1 The earliest and latest appearance (in millions of years) of each habitat map based on the oxygen isotope core and the bands used to define palaeo-environments (see Figure 3).

Habitat map		Earliest occurrence	Latest occurrence
cold 4	Short and rare periods in later Pleistocene	0.088	0.015
cold 3	Relatively common in last 1 Myr	1.875	0.027
cold 2	Relatively common in last 1.8 Myr	2.528	0.012
cold 1	Relatively common between 1.8 and 0.9 Myr	3.344	0.009
present	Predominant climate between 2.7 and 1.9 Myr, then rare short periods	5.711	0
warm 1	Very rare since 2.7 Myr	5.996	0.003
warm 2	Predominant climate between 6 and 3.3 Myr	6	2.75
warm 3	Rare occurrences between 5 and 3.8 Myr	5.525	3.779

For example, the harshest conditions (*cold 3* and *cold 4*) are not found before ~1.9 Myr. Likewise, the wettest conditions (*warm 3*) are not found after ~3.8 Myr.

Modelling hominid species' habitat associations

There have been many attempts to reconstruct habitat preferences of hominid species using palaeoenvironmental and chemical evidence. Broadly speaking these have shown that hominids occupied a wide range of habitats within the drier parts of Africa. The primary areas of debate have concerned whether the early hominids occupied forests and woodlands as well as savannahs, whether there is a trend towards more open habitats over time, and whether there are any measurable differences in habitat association between taxa. Reed (1997) has provided the most comprehensive recent analysis, and has broadly shown that early hominids tend to be associated with more closed habitats, that the megadontic or robust australopithecines are associated with more open environments, and that early *Homo* is found in a range of relatively open environments (see Table 2).

The approach adopted here is somewhat different. Instead of pre-defining the habitats of particular hominid taxa we have chosen to define a number of 'model species' with particular habitat preferences and constraints. For example, Model 1 is a forest-specific species, and thus in the analyses run here can only exist in those areas where forest cover occurs. Model species 2, on the other hand is more tolerant, and can exist in environments ranging from forest to woody savannah. A total of six such model taxa are defined, providing a range of alternative habitat preferences and specificities (see Table 3). These taxa can be said to broadly conform to the range of associations proposed by Reed (1997), without at this stage specifying which actual hominid species may correspond to each model taxon.

Table 2 Reconstructions of the environments of early hominid taxa in Africa. Reconstructions based primarily on (Reed 1997).

Taxon	Habitats
A. ramidus	Woodland
A. anamensis	?
A. afarensis	Closed to open woodland, with edaphic grassland / shrubland / deltaic floodplain / water and trees present
A. africanus	Woodland and bushland with riverine forest
A. aethiopicus	Bushland to open woodland / edaphic grassland
A. robustus	Open or wooded/bushed grassland / edaphic grassland
A. boisei	Woodland to shrubland / edaphic grassland
H. habilis + H. rudolfensis	Open grasslands / dry shrublands / edaphic grasslands
H. ergaster	Shrubland / riparian woodland / arid open landscapes

Table 3 Definition of early hominid model species used here. The range of habitats that each one is able to occupy is used to explore maximum distributions under different palaeoenvironmental conditions.

Model Species	Habitat Tolerance
Model 1	Forest-specific
Model 2	Forest to woody savannah
Model 3	Woody savannah to savannah
Model 4	Woody savannah to grassland
Model 5	Woody savannah to shrubland
Model 6	Savannah to shrubland

Table 4 Estimates of the area of different habitat types under different climatic conditions, based on the link between the NDVI categories and the palaeo-environmental reconstructions from the oxygen isotope core.

NDVI category	Habitat	Habitat area (km² x 10⁶)							
		cold4	*cold3*	*cold2*	*cold1*	*present*	*warm1*	*warm2*	*warm3*
1	Barren	16931	14821	12747	10786	2405	69	0	0
2	Barren	2166	1650	1382	1571	7018	1133	5	0
3	Open shrub	1934	1472	1078	1134	1822	5334	142	0
4	Open shrub	1819	1776	1262	974	1112	3696	1054	27
5	Closed shrub	1661	1974	1472	1134	1134	1389	5334	264
6	Grassland	1829	2315	2445	1832	1330	1506	4250	4078
7	Grassland	1291	1912	2464	2286	1650	1339	1571	5862
8	Savannah	834	1395	2126	2557	2005	1565	1458	1797
9	Savannah	616	979	1741	2237	2557	1912	1394	1462
10	Savannah	318	787	1389	2206	2976	3090	2224	1717
11	Woody savannah	43	318	858	1389	2333	2976	2955	2224
12	Woody savannah	0	43	435	974	1766	2710	3621	3600
13	Forest	0	0	43	362	1336	2707	5074	7262
14	Forest	0	0	0	0	0	18	362	1149

Results and discussion

Habitat areas under different climatic conditions

Table 4 shows the geographical area of Africa covered by different habitats under the various climatic conditions considered here. As can be seen, and has been well established in the palaeoenvironmental literature, during colder periods the area of forest and woodland decreases and the more open environments expand. For example, under *present* conditions there are 1.336 million square kilometres of forest; under increasingly closed conditions this area decreases very markedly – by 73% under the '*cold 1*' conditions, and by 99% under '*cold 2*'.

Beyond these conditions, forest would have been virtually absent in Africa. Conversely, forest distribution would double under 'warm 1' conditions, and increase more than fivefold under conditions of extreme warmth such as those that occurred relatively frequently prior to 3.8 Myr.

At the other end of the habitat spectrum, grassland and savannah conditions increase in distribution as the climate becomes increasingly colder, as occurred progressively during the Pleistocene. What can broadly be described as 'open' environments currently occupy 81% of the continent. Under '*cold 1*' conditions this increases to 90%, and then successively through to almost 100% under the extreme conditions of '*cold 4*'. Under the warmer, wetter conditions open environments decrease successively until they cover only 52% of the continent.

These results indicate the extent of variation in the areas covered by different habitats as climate changes. They also show that the general vectors of change observed using the NDVI models of habitat conform to those expected using palaeobiological evidence. The main difference between the habitat distribution maps here is that they show a much greater loss of forest than is consistent with current African biogeographical patterns, and thus there is likely to be an underestimate of forest conditions during cold stages, and an overestimate of more open environments.

Range areas of model hominid species

Table 5 shows the estimated maximum range areas of the model hominid species under different climatic regimes. These show the obvious corollary of the habitat areas, that as conditions become colder, the ranges of those species preferring closed habitats decline very markedly, and those of the open-dwelling species increase accordingly. The more interesting question is the extent of range contraction and expansion. For example, from the warmer conditions typical of the late Miocene and the early Pliocene to periods as cold or colder than the present day, forest dwelling species would lose over 80% of their range. Even under conditions warmer than those of today, but colder than the warmer Pliocene, the loss may have been as much as 60% (Figure 5). This change is likely to have led to very considerable local extinction, isolation of populations, and a general reduction in population sizes, and a relatively extreme change in evolutionary patterns.

Conversely, increasingly cold and dry conditions would favour those species able to survive in more open habitats. Again, it is the scale of the change rather than its general direction that is important. A hominid capable of living in all savannah environments would see an expansion of available habitats from the warm Miocene to the conditions prevalent in the Pliocene of nearly 10%. However, what is striking is that the availability of such habitats does not vary anything like the changes in forest habitats. Furthermore, as the conditions become increasingly cold and dry during the course of the Pleistocene there is a loss of habitat as more areas come under desertic conditions.

Table 5   Potential range sizes of the model hominid species based on the palaeo-environmental maps. All figures in thousands of square kilometres.

Habitat range	cold 4	cold 3	cold 2	cold 1	present	warm 1	warm 2	warm 3
Model 1 Forest and closed habitats	0	0	43	362	1336	2707	5074	7262
Model 2 Forest, woody savannah	43	361	1336	2725	5435	8411	12012	14235
Model 3 All savannahs	1811	3522	6549	9363	11637	12253	11652	10800
Model 4 All savannahs and open grassland	4931	7749	11458	13481	14617	15098	17473	20740
Model 5 All savannahs, grassland and shrubland	10345	12971	15270	16723	18685	25517	24003	21031
Model 6 Open savannah, grassland and shrubland	9984	11823	12588	12154	11610	16741	15203	13490

Under the extreme glacial conditions of the late Pleistocene such a species would be reduced to less than 15% of its total range. This would imply as extreme an evolutionary effect on savannah species as would occur for hominids or hominoids confined to closed habitats.

Those creatures able to survive in the more extreme open habitats would fare better. Their maximum range would still occur under conditions warmer than today, but their loss of habitat under extreme cold and dry climatic regimes would be less than 40% in the case of the model 6 species (open savannah, grassland and shrubland).

What these results show is the vector of habitat change as climate changes, but this has already been well established. More importantly, they indicate the scale of habitat change, and thus provide more insight into the evolutionary consequences of climatic changes. They indicate that the climatic changes that occurred throughout the Pleistocene would have had major effects on species' distributions and the probability of isolation and extinction, and that these would affect both open-dwelling and closed-habitat taxa, although to different extents.

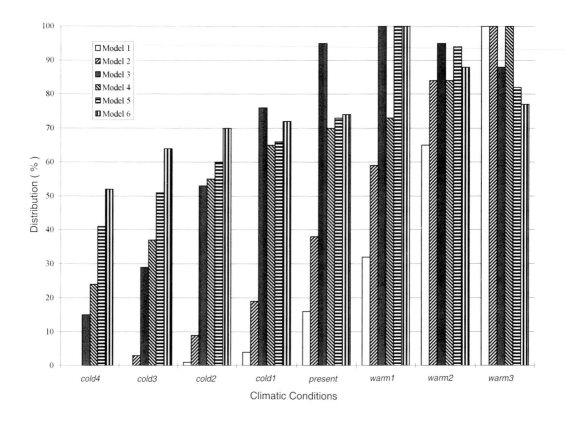

Figure 5
Species distributions
under different
climatic conditions.
Shown as percent-
ages of each species'
maximum.

Chronological patterns

Figure 3 and Table 1 show how the various climatic regimes
were distributed over time during the last six million years. This
information can be used to indicate the periods under which different
taxa may have been most widely dispersed or most fragmented.
Overall, all the model taxa would have larger potential ranges during
periods warmer than today, and in effect the Pleistocene cooling has
reduced habitat availability across the whole range of probable
preferences and tolerances. For the two model species preferring
closed environments, the period of maximum extension would have
been the later Miocene, since when there has been a continuous loss
of environment, with only occasional reversals. For the more open
living species conditions *'warm 1'* and *'warm 2'* would have been
the periods of greatest expansion, and were in the Pliocene,
occurring only sporadically during the Pleistocene. Effectively, after
around 2.7 Myr all hominids would have been likely to have suffered
range contractions, not specifically at this time, but repeatedly over
the later Pliocene and during the Pleistocene.

One further point should be added to this observation. The environmental reconstructions shown here employ a number of static categories, and we have discussed how these show broad temporal trends. However, this implies much greater stability than actually occurred. During any one of the major periods the climate would have fluctuated considerably. For example, between 1.8 and 2.4 million years ago, a critical period in hominid evolution, conditions ranging from 'cold 2' to 'warm 1' would have occurred, and more importantly the environment would have fluctuated across these conditions many times. It is this repeated expansion and fragmentation of habitats that is likely to have been significant in evolutionary terms, and also make it less likely that there will be a simple relationship between climate and evolutionary change. There is simply too much ecologically relevant climate change.

Linking real hominid taxa to the patterns of habitat change

Table 2 shows some estimates of the habitat associations of the known hominid taxa. In attempting to address the issue of the extent to which the model taxa conform to the specific model taxa, it should be noted that many of the associations between real hominid fossils and their environments relate to specific local environments, particularly lake, river and deltaic margins. The models discussed here do not have the resolution to take these micro-habitats into account. However, it is likely that the early hominids would have ranged more broadly, and the question of gross habitat types remains important.

The earliest known hominid, *Ardipithecus ramidus* is associated with relatively wooded environments, although not closed forest. It probably lies closest to the Model 2 taxon, which would have been most widespread under conditions of 'warm 3', which was relatively rare for most of the period, and 'warm 2', conditions that had virtually disappeared by 3 Myr. For its known stratigraphic range, it would have seen only relatively small contractions in its range area.

The australopithecines are found in a range of relatively open environments, with some evidence for virtually all taxa of at least a degree of occupation of woodland savannahs. They thus lie in the range of Models 3 to 5. There is some reason to think that the later and more robust australopithecines are more associated with the drier and more open range of savannah and grassland habitats. The earlier taxa – *A. afarensis* and *A. africanus* would have seen an expansion of available habitats across their stratigraphic range. However, for the later australopithecines, from 2.9 Myr there would have been a gradual decrease in range area, probably amounting to between 10 and 25% of their maximum range. Perhaps of greatest significance is that from around 1.5 Myr, with a great prevalence of 'cold 2' conditions, their habitat would have been reduced by nearly 50%, and this may have been a significant factor in both the occurrence of different lineages at this time and the disappearance of the robust australopithecines prior to 1.0 Myr.

Homo may have been less of a woodland genus, except along rivers, and more adapted to open environments (Reed 1997). If so, then this would make at least *Homo ergaster* closer to Model 6. Its peak range would have been during '*warm 1*' climates, but these were largely, if not completely, absent by the time they appear in the fossil record. However, across the range of climates that characterise the period 2.3 to 1.0 Myr, their tolerable habitats would have fluctuated only by less than 10%, suggesting that *Homo* may have been more buffered than other hominids from the effects of climatic change. The characteristics that may have enabled it to survive in these more open environments – changes in stature and shape for thermo-regulatory reasons, greater use of technology, greater levels of meat eating – should perhaps be seen in this environmental context, as should the persistence of *Homo* after the extinction of the australopithecines.

Habitat fragmentation

The results and discussion presented here have focused on the overall scale of habitat change, and range expansion and contraction has been measured at a continental scale. While this provides a useful measure of the likely effects of climatic change on hominid distributions, it is unlikely that such effects would occur across the whole area. At one level the figures deployed here – for example, the idea of a 10% fluctuation in habitat availability for early *Homo*, and of a 50% loss of habitat for the australopithecines – can be simply extrapolated to the local level; in other words, for any hominid population there is a probability of these levels of habitat change. However, the biogeography of Africa is such that it is unlikely that there would have been such an even pattern of change. Habitats may have been completely lost in some areas, and unaffected in others. The key point is that these changes occur locally and at a small scale. The overall impact would have been changes in the probability of extinction or dispersals and range expansions, but there would have been significant variation. In particular, as climate changed, pockets of habitat would have become isolated, and under these conditions both drift and selection could operate to lead to evolutionary change.

Conclusions

This chapter has addressed the problem of the effect of habitat change on early African hominids. Using a modeling approach to both palaeoenvironmental reconstruction and the distributions of species, we have attempted to quantify the amount and pattern of potential range expansion and contraction for the early hominids. We have argued that the patterns of climatic change would have led to habitat shifts on closed-environment dwelling species that would reduce ranges by more than 50%; that all hominids are likely to have seen significant loss of habitat during the Pliocene and Pleistocene; and that perhaps early *Homo* may have been more buffered from these changes, with habitat availability fluctuating by closer to 10%. Beyond these observations and inferences, however, we have argued that an understanding of evolutionary patterns among the hominids requires a detailed consideration of spatial patterns, and that evolutionary geography has the potential to throw new light on the patterns and processes of evolution more generally.

References

Adams J. 1995. Quaternary Environments Network (QEN) website: http://www.soton.ac.uk/~tjms/adams1.html

DeFries R, Townshend J. 1993. Global land cover: comparison of ground-based data sets to classifications with AVHRR data. In: Foody G, Curran P. eds. *Environmental Remote Sensing from Regional to Global Scales.* Chichester: John Wiley and Sons. 84-110

DeFries R, Townshend J. 1994. NDVI-derived land cover classifications at a global scale. *International Journal of Remote Sensing.* **15:** 567-3586.

de Monacal P. 1995. Plio-Pleistocene African climate. *Science.* **270:** 53-59.

Foley RA. 1987. *Another Unique Species: patterns in human evolutionary ecology.* UK: Longman Scientific and Technical.

Foley RA. 1991. How many hominid species should there be? *Journal of Human Evolution.* **20:** 413-428.

Foley RA. 1993. African terrestrial primates: comparative evolutionary biology of the Hominidae and *Theropithecus*. In: Jablonski N. ed. *Theropithecus as a Case Study in Primate Evolutionary Biology.* Cambridge: Cambridge University Press. 245-270.

Foley RA. 1994. Speciation, extinction and climatic change in hominid evolution. *Journal of Human Evolution.* **26:** 275-289.

Foley RA. 1999. The evolutionary geography of Pliocene hominids. In: Broamge T, Schrenk F. eds. *African Biogeography, Climatic Change, and Hominid Evolution.* Oxford: Oxford University Press. 328-348.

Lahr MM, Foley RA. 1998. Towards a theory of modern human origins: geography, demography and diversity in recent human evolution. *Yearbook of Physical Anthropology.* **41:** 137-176.

Gollop PJ. in preparation. Using remotely-sensed data to model the effect of past climate change on habitat distribution in Africa.

Justice C, Holben B, Gwynne M. 1986. Monitoring East African vegetation using AVHRR data. *International Journal of Remote Sensing.* **7:** 1453-1474.

Kimbel WH, Martin LB. eds. 1993. *Species, Species Concepts, and Primate Evolution.* New York and London: Plenum Press.

Potts R. 1998. Variability selection in hominid evolution. *Evolutionary Anthropology.* **7:** 81-96.

Pratt D, Gwynne M. 1977. *Rangeland management and ecology in East Africa.* London: Hodder and Stoughton.

Reed K. 1997. Early hominid evolution and ecological change through the African Plio-Pleistocene. *Journal of Human Evolution.* **32:** 289-322.

Reed KE, Fleagle JG. 1995. Geographic and Climatic Control of Primate Diversity. *Proceedings of the National Academy of Sciences of the United States of America.* **92:** 7874-7876.

Shackleton NJ. 1995. New data on the Evolution of Pliocene Climatic Variability. In: Vrba E, Denton G, Partridge T, Burckle L. eds. *Paleoclimate and Evolution.* New Haven and London: Yale University Press. 242-248.

Townshend J, Justice C. 1986. Analysis of the dynamics of African vegetation using the normalized difference vegetation index. *International Journal of Remote Sensing.* **7:** 1435-1445.

Townshend J, Justice C, Kalb V. 1987. Characterization and classification of South American land cover types using satellite data. *International Journal of Remote Sensing.* **8:** 1189-1207.

Tucker C, Townshend J, Goff T. 1985. African land-cover classification using satellite data. *Science.* **227:** 369-375.

USGS. 1998. Global Land 1-KM AVHRR Project: http://edcwww.cr.usgs.gov/landdaac/1KM/1kmhomepage.html

Vrba ES. 1993. Turnover-pulses, the Red Queen, and related topics. *American Journal of Science.* **293a:** 418-452.

Vrba ES. 1995. On the Connections between Paleoclimate and Evolution. In: Vrba E, Denton G, Partridge T, Burckle L. eds. *Paleoclimate and Evolution.* New Haven and London: Yale University Press. 24-45.

White F. 1983. *The Vegetation of Africa.* UNESCO, Paris: Natural Resource Research. **20:** 356.

Reconstructing human evolution in the age of genomic exploration

M. GOODMAN, E. H. McCONKEY & S. L. PAGE

Introduction

The Human Genome Project aims to produce a complete nucleotide sequence map of the 3,000 million nucleotides contained within the 24 different types of human chromosomes, along with identifying the approximately 100,000 different genes and their functions. Technical advances in automating the sequencing of megabase portions of genomes now give assurance that a complete reference DNA sequence for the human genome will soon be finalised. Concurrently, efforts to determine the detailed nucleotide sequence map of mouse chromosomes are accelerating. However, knowing all the genetic similarities and differences between humans and mice will not reveal the genetic basis for the unique features of our anatomy (e.g. bipedal locomotion, greatly enlarged brain), physiology (e.g. susceptibility to AIDS and hepatitis B) and behaviour (e.g. speech, higher order cognitive functions). A Human Genome Evolution Project is needed to organise and focus research on the goal of deciphering the genetic basis of being human (McConkey & Goodman, 1997).

To achieve this overall goal requires sequencing the genomes of a chimpanzee and a pygmy chimpanzee or bonobo (our nearest relatives) and a gorilla (our next nearest relative). Then phylogenetic comparisons, utilising these genome sequences, can identify all the genic mutations (DNA sequence changes) that became fixed in the lineage to modern humans since our lineage last shared a common ancestor with chimpanzees and bonobos.

Ultimately, to define the genetic roots of being human, the comparative genomic data should include extensive DNA sequence data on a broad range of primates. The reason is that some of our most striking human features, such as greatly enlarged brains and prolonged childhoods in nurturing societies, have deep roots in our evolutionary history. Brain capacity is significantly larger in the Miocene fossil primates of suborder Anthropoidea than in the earlier Eocene fossil primates (Fleagle, 1988; Martin, 1990). Also, among living primates, the neocortical portions of the brain are much larger in simian primates (the living platyrrhines and catarrhines of Anthropoidea) than in non-simian primates (the tarsiers and the lemuriform and loriform strepsirhines). Similarly, fetal life and the infant and childhood stages of postnatal development are more prolonged in the simian primates, especially in apes and humans, than in the non-simian primates. We may surmise that the genetic blueprints for the inherited aspects of our morphology, metabolism, and mental functions have both anciently conserved features common to all living primates and phylogenetically more restricted features that arose later in evolution, ranging from the simian-specific ones that arose within the early Anthropoidea in the lineage to the last common ancestor of platyrrhines and catarrhines to the human-specific ones that arose in the last few million years in the lineage to modern humans.

The functionally important DNA sequences, such as the coding sequences of genes and the *cis* regulatory elements that are proximal to genes, constitute less than 5% of the total nuclear DNA in a human or other mammalian genome, as may be inferred from the comparative genomic data that have already been gathered. The remaining (more than 95% of such total genomic DNA) consists of noncoding sequences that are not scrutinised by natural selection nearly as much as are the functionally important DNA sequences, i.e. most mutations in these noncoding sequences are likely to be selectively neutral mutations. Thus, the vast majority of sequence changes that have occurred during evolution have not had direct effects on phenotypes. Clearly, on looking to the future in this age of genomic exploration, the major effort in reconstructing human evolution at the DNA level will be to separate out from the mass of randomly fixed neutral mutations the positively selected mutations that shaped the genes and gene expression patterns that define the genetic basis of being human.

During evolution two kinds of nucleotide substitutions, synonymous and non-synonymous, occur in the genic coding sequences (exons) that specify the primary structures (amino acid sequences) of proteins. Although a gene's synonymous substitutions are likely to be selectively neutral because they cause no change in the amino acid sequence of the protein chain encoded by that gene, the non-synonymous (i.e. amino acid changing) substitutions are not nearly as likely to be selectively neutral. In particular, on recon-structing the course of non-synonymous substitutions in an evolving lineage, if we observe that the non-synonymous rate speeded-up at an earlier period and then markedly slowed-down, we can attribute the speed-up to positive selection spreading non-synonymous substitutions through the lineage, and the subsequent slow-down to purifying selection preserving the substitutions that had previously spread through the lineage. Moreover, if during the speed-up the percentage of non-synonymous (N) change at nucleotide positions where such change is possible is greater than the percentage of synonymous (S) change at the nucleotide positions where synonymous change is possible, this finding (N/S >1) is a strong indicator that positive selection drove the course of genic change.

The speed-up/slow-down pattern of non-synonymous change is especially useful for spotting the positively selected substitutions that occurred earlier in our evolutionary history (e.g. the stem of the Anthropoidea) and were then conserved (i.e. unchanged) in later lineages. During the last stage of our evolutionary history, i.e. in the lineage to modern humans after this lineage separated from the lineage to chimpanzees and bonobos, the speed-up/slow-down analysis cannot be applied, but we can look for non-synonymous amino acid substitutions that occurred in the human lineage. In order to do this, we must have comparative data on amino acid sequences from at least chimpanzees, bonobos and gorillas, so that a hypothetical ancestral sequence for the human-chimpanzee-bonobo clade can be calculated. This information could be obtained for every human protein-coding sequence, by using information from the human genome to make PCR primers to amplify the corresponding exons from the apes. Because of the very close overall similarity of DNA sequences among those species, at least 90% of human primers should suffice to amplify ape exons.

However, a logical first step in searching for human-specific amino acid changes would be to identify candidate genes for comparative genomic analysis. Among the candidates would be genes known to be involved with development of the hind limbs or the cranium, genes involved in any aspect of human cognition, transcription factors, and genes coding for proteins that modify other proteins (e.g. kinases and phosphatases). Because of the short evolutionary time since the human lineage separated from the chimp/bonobo lineage, there will in general be few nucleotide changes that are specific to humans, even for the synonymous category. Therefore, any non-synonymous amino acid change that is specific to humans should be viewed as being of potential evolutionary interest. The first step would be to document that a given amino acid change is present in all humans (i.e. fixed in our species) and that the putative ancestral sequence is not an artefact of polymorphism within ape genomes.

Cis-regulatory elements and other functional noncoding elements, such as those involved in maintaining chromatin structure, not only occur in the immediate proximity of the coding sequences of genes but also occur distally scattered among non-functional noncoding sequences. Thus to detect all the functional *cis* elements will require the determination of complete genome sequences not just genic coding sequences. Considerable experimental work has already identified over 4000 different regulatory elements, these being relatively short sequence motifs (5-25 bp in length) that are detected by their binding of regulatory proteins (Duret & Bucher, 1997). Phylogenetic analysis of aligned homologous sequences have showed that such *cis* regulatory elements are evolutionarily conserved (Tagle *et al.*, 1988; Gumucio *et al.,* 1996; Duret & Bucher, 1997; Hardison *et al.*, 1997). Indeed the phylogenetic approach offers promise of detecting many as yet unknown regulatory and other functional sequence motifs.

To conduct an effective search in the human genome for all functional noncoding elements, each genomic region under study needs to be represented by extensive comparative sequence data on primates. Then by reconstructing the evolutionary history of these likely functional noncoding elements, just as with the genic coding sequences, it will be possible to identify not only those elements that are anciently conserved, being unchanged in all or almost all primate lineages, but also those that arose at successively later stages in our evolutionary history from the simian-specific to the human-specific elements. A functionally important *cis* element that was simian-specific as a result of previous nucleotide substitutions, fixed in a common ancestor of platyrrhines and catarrhines, would be spotted by showing no, or almost no, further nucleotide substitutions in the descending simian lineages. This rate slow-down would be due to purifying selection preserving the nucleotide substitutions that earlier had been spread by positive selection. In contrast, the non-functional noncoding sequences that flank the functional element would continue to accumulate selectively neutral nucleotide substitutions at a relatively rapid rate.

A functionally important human-specific *cis* element could arise from a modification of a pre-existing functional *cis* element. If so, it could be spotted by its conservation (slow rate of change) in most non-human simian lineages. Moreover, if a large enough population of healthy adult humans (say several thousand individuals) were to be analysed for DNA polymorphisms, a lower incidence of polymorphic variants would be expected for a functionally important human-specific *cis* element than for typical noncoding, selectively neutral DNA. The reason for expecting this is that the positive selection that spread the adaptive *cis* changes would be followed by purifying selection to preserve these changes.

Evidence has already been gathered that DNA sites in human genes under purifying selection show a much lower incidence of polymorphic variants in human populations than selectively neutral DNA sites (Cargill *et al.*, 1999; Halushka *et al.*, 1999).

In addition to nucleotide substitutions, among other genomic changes that occur in evolution are insertions and deletions, gene duplications, retrotranspositions of retrotransposons (mobile DNA elements), and chromosomal rearrangements. Like nucleotide substitutions, the vast majority of these other genomic changes are selectively neutral. Often after a gene duplication, one or the other nonallelic duplicate accumulates mutations that change the functional gene into a pseudogene, which then is part of the non-functional noncoding DNA. However, sometimes there is a physiological advantage to have increased synthesis of a gene product and thus have more than one nonallelic copy of the functional gene, each copy coding for the same or nearly the same gene product. In that event, gene conversions, which maintain identity between the coding sequences of the duplicate genes, are favoured by natural selection. Also, on rarer occasions, natural selection might favour mutations that reshape a duplicate gene so that it codes for a modified gene product that offers a new or improved physiological advantage to the carriers of the reshaped gene.

Table 1 DNA studies that elucidate primate phylogeny.

Major Clades	Cercopithecid Clades
Bailey *et al.* (1991)	Benveniste (1985)
Bailey *et al.* (1992)	Disotell *et al.* (1992)
Goodman *et al.* (1998)	Goodman *et al.* (1998)
Koop *et al.* (1989)	Harris & Disotell (1998)
Porter *et al.* (1995)	Messier & Stewart (1997)
Porter *et al.* (1997a)	Page *et al.* (1999)
Zietkiewicz *et al.* (1999)	Van der Kuyl *et al.* (1995)

Strepsirhine Clades

Hominid Clades

Strepsirhine Clades	Hominid Clades
Bailey *et al.* (1991)	Arnason *et al.* (1998)
Bailey *et al.* (1992)	Bailey *et al.* (1991)
Bonner *et al.* (1980)	Bailey *et al.* (1992)
Bonner *et al.* (1981)	Benveniste (1985)
Goodman *et al.* (1998)	Caccone & Powell (1989)
Porter *et al* (1995)	Goodman *et al.* (1998)
Porter *et al.* (1997a)	Horai *et al.* (1995)
Yoder *et al.* (1996)	Perrin-Pecontal *et al.* (1992)
Yoder (1997)	Porter *et al.* (1997a)
	Ruvolo (1997)

Platyrrhine Clades

Platyrrhine Clades	
Barroso *et al.* (1997)	Satta *et al.* (2000)
Benveniste (1985)	Sibley & Ahlquist (1987)
Canavez *et al.* (1999)	Takahata & Satta (1997)
Chaves *et al.* (1999)	
Chiu (1997)	
Goodman *et al.* (1998)	
Harada *et al.* (1995)	
Meireles *et al.* (1999)	
Porter *et al.* (1995)	
Porter *et al.* (1997a)	
Porter *et al.* (1997b)	
Porter *et al.* (1999)	
Schneider *et al.* (1993)	
Schneider *et al.* (1996)	
Tagliaro *et al.* (1997)	
Von Dornum (1997)	
Von Dornum & Ruvulo (1999)	

The retrotransposition of retrotransposons that are situated within or by genes provides a mechanism for copying, along with the retrotransposons, non-retrotransposon sequences (such as exons and promotors) into new genomic locations (Moran *et al.*, 1999). It has been suggested that this may be another general mechanism for the evolution of new genes and new arrangements of *cis* regulatory elements (Moran *et al.*, 1999; Eickbush, 1999; Boeke & Pickeral, 1999). Once extensive genomic sequence data are obtained for a range of primates, a search of the human genome could be conducted for any such new genes and new regulatory arrangements.

Research directed at deciphering the genetic basis of being human will be facilitated by having an objective, non-biased view of humankind's place in primate phylogeny. Considerable evidence on primate phylogeny already exists, the most objective being the DNA evidence. The main studies that have gathered this DNA evidence are listed in Table 1. The phylogenetic analyses carried out in these studies have utilised DNA hybridisation data and both mitochondria and nuclear DNA sequence data, the latter from a growing number of unlinked nuclear genomic loci. The non-functional noncoding sequences of the nuclear loci due to their relatively fast nucleotide substitution rates have provided some of the best evidence on the phylogenetic relationships of humans and other living primates (Goodman *et al.*, 1998). Moreover the rates at which selectively neutral mutations accumulate are less variable than the rates at which positively selected mutations accumulate. Thus the evolution rates of non-functional noncoding sequences, in conjunction with fossil evidence on the time course of primate phylogeny, can provide relatively reliable molecular clock estimates of the ages of branch points in descent from the strepsirhine-haplorhine branch-point (the last common ancestor of all living primates) to the present-day primate species.

The phylogenetic relationships that exist among primate clades and the estimated ages of these clades from the more anciently separated to the more recently can be depicted by a phylogenetic classification in which each taxon represents a monophyletic group (a clade) and the estimated ages of the clades determine the ranks of the taxa, i.e. higher ranking taxa (e.g. semiorders, suborders, infraorders) represent clades that are older in age than lower ranking taxa (e.g. subfamilies, tribes, subtribes), and taxa at the same rank (hierarchical level) are of roughly equivalent age (Goodman *et al.*, 1998; 1999). Such a classification allows us to define, free of anthropocentric bias, the taxonomic place of humankind in primate phylogeny (Table 2). The DNA evidence for the phylogenetic information in the classification is complemented by morphological evidence including that from fossils on key branch-points in primate phylogeny. With this objective phylogenetic framework for assessing the genetic processes that have operated in the evolution of primate genomes, we present some examples of how molecular evolution shaped functionally important genic coding sequences and *cis-*

regulatory elements in the human genome. We then renew our call for a Human Genome Evolution Project directed at discovering the crucial genetic correlates of being human.

Table 2 DNA Based Phylogenetic Classification of Primates.

An age placed in parenthesis after the name of a higher taxon in this hierarchical classification represents the estimated age of that higher taxon, treated as a *crown goup*, but also of the next lower ranking taxa, treated as *total groups*. Common names for extant species are from Rowe (1996). Estimated ages are either the same or very close to previous estimates (Goodman *et al.*, 1998, 1999). Additional information from the molecular phylogenetic trees produced in recent studies were used in recalculating the estimated ages for taxa within Platyrrhini (Meireles *et al.*, 1999; Chaves *et al.*, 1999) and within Cercopithecidae (Page *et al.*, 1999).

Subgeneric names are used here for any collection of species with an estimated LCA age of 6 Myr or less and with at least some species in the collection having different full generic names in Groves (1993), also in Rowe (1996) who follows Groves in his use of generic names. In fact to have a rough equivalance for taxa at the same rank, subgeneric names should also have been used for the subdivisions within *Tarsius, Cebus, Saguinus, Callicebus, Ateles,* and *Macaca* as the estimated crown group ages of these genera are 6, 5, 6, 7, 4, and 4 Myr, respectively.

Order Primates (63 Myr)

Semiorder Strepsirhini (50 Myr)
  Suborder Lemuriformes (45 Myr)
    Infraorder Chiromyiformes
      Family Daubentoniidae
        Daubentoni madagascariensis: aye-aye
    Infraorder Eulemurides
      Superfamily Lemuroidea (28 Myr)
      Family Cheirogaleidae (22 Myr)
        Subfamily Microcebinae
          Microcebus murinus: grey mouse lemur
        Subfamily Cheirogaleinae
          Cheirogaleus medius: fat-tailed dwarf lemur
      Family Indridae
        Propithecus verreauxi: Verreaux's sifaka
      Family Lemuridae
        Eulemur fulvus: brown lemur
  Suborder Loriformes
    Family Loridae (23 Myr)
      Subfamily Galagoninae
        Otolemur crassicaudatus: thick-tailed greater bush baby
      Subfamily Perodicticinae
        Perodicticus potto: potto
      Subfamily Lorinae
        Nycticebus coucang: slow loris
Semiorder Haplorhini (58 Myr)

Suborder Tarsiiformes
 Family Tarsiidae
  Tarsius (6 Myr)
   T. syrichta: Philippine tarsier
   T. bancanus: western tarsier
Suborder Anthropoidea (40 Myr)
 Infraorder Platyrrhini
  Superfamily Ceboidea (26 Myr)
  Family Cebidae (22 Myr)
   Subfamily Cebinae (20 Myr)
   Tribe Cebini
    Cebus (5 Myr)
     C. albifrons: white-fronted capuchin
     C. olivaceus: weeper capuchin
     C. kaapori: capuchin
   Tribe Saimiriini
    Saimiri (2 Myr)
     S. sciureus: common squirrel monkey
     S. boliviensis: Bolivian squirrel monkey
   Subfamily Aotinae
    Aotus (3 Myr)
     A. azarae: red-necked night monkey
     A. nancymai: red-necked night monkey
   Subfamily Callitrichinae
   Tribe Callitrichini (14 Myr)
    Subtribe Saguinina
    Saguinus (6 Myr)
     S. fusicollis: saddleback tamarin
     S. bicolor: bare-faced tamarin
     S. midas: golden-handed tamarin
    Subtribe Leontopithecina
     Leontopithecus rosalia: golden lion tamarin
    Subtribe Callimiconina
     Callimico goeldii: Goeldi's monkey
    Subtribe Callitrichina
    Callithrix (5 Myr)
     C. (Callithrix) (<1 Myr)
      C. (C.) jacchus: common marmoset
      C. (C.) geoffroyi: Geoffroy's tufted-eared marmoset
     C. (Cebuella) pygmaea: pygmy marmoset
     C. (Mico) (3 Myr)
      C. (M.) argentata: bare-ear marmoset
      C. (M.) humeralifer: tassel-eared marmoset
      C. (M.) mauesi: Maves marmoset
  Family Pitheciidae
  Subfamily Pitheciinae (19 Myr)
   Tribe Callicebini
    Callicebus (7 Myr)
     C. moloch: dusky titi monkey
     C. torquatus: collared titi monkey
   Tribe Pitheciini

Subtribe Pitheciina (11 Myr)
  Pithecia irrorata: bald-faced saki
  Chiropotes (6 Myr)
    C. (*Cacajao*) *calvus*: bald uacari
    C. (*Chiropotes*) *satanas*: bearded saki
Family Atelidae
  Subfamily Atelinae (17 Myr)
  Tribe Alouattini
    Alouatta (3 Myr)
      A. caraya: black-and-gold howler
      A. belzebul: red-handed howler
      A. seniculus: red howler
  Tribe Atelini (12 Myr)
    Subtribe Atelina
    Ateles (4 Myr)
      A. paniscus: black spider monkey
      A. geoffroyi: black-handed spider monkey
    Subtribe Brachytelina (10 Myr)
      Lagothrix lagotricha: woolly monkey
      Brachyteles arachnoides: woolly spider monkey
Infraorder Catarrhini
  Superfamily Cercopithecoidea (25 Myr)
  Family Cercopithecidae
    Subfamily Cercopithecinae (15 Myr)
    Tribe Colobini (10 Myr)
      Subtribe Colobina
      Colobus guereza: Abyssinian colobus
      Subtribe Presbytina (7 Myr)
        Trachypithecus obscuris: spectacled leaf monkey/langur
        Nasalis larvatus: proboscis monkey
    Tribe Cercopithecini (10 Myr)
      Subtribe Cercopithecina (9 Myr)
      Cercopithecus
        C. cephus: mustached guenon
      Erythrocebus
        E. patas: patas monkey
      Chlorocebus
        C. aethiops: green monkey
      Subtribe Papionina (9 Myr)
      Macaca (4 Myr)
        M. mulatta: rhesus macaque
        M. nigra: Celebes macaque
      Cercocebus (5 Myr)
        C. (*Mandrillus*) (4 Myr)
          C. (*M.*) *sphinx*: mandrill
          C. (*M.*) *leucophaeus*: drill
        C. (*Cercocebus*) *galeritus*: Tana river mangabey
      Papio (4 Myr)
        P. (*Papio*) *hamadryas cynocephalus*: yellow baboon
        P. (*Theropithecus*) *gelada*: gelada baboon
        P. (*Lophocebus*) *aterrimus*: black mangabey

Family Hominidae
  Subfamily Homininae (18 Myr)
   Tribe Hylobatini
    Subtribe Hylobatina (8 Myr)
     Symphalangus syndactylus: siamang
     Hylobates lar: white-handed gibbon
   Tribe Hominini (14 Myr)
    Subtribe Pongina
     Pongo pygmaeus: Borneo orang-utan
    Subtribe Hominina (7 Myr)
     Gorilla gorilla: gorilla
    Homo (6 Myr)
     H. (*Pan*) (3 Myr)
      H. (*P.*) *troglodytes*: chimpanzee
      H. (*P.*) *paniscus*: pygmy chimpanzee or bonobo
     H. (*Homo*) *sapiens*: humankind

Our place in primate phylogeny

Traditional primate classifications, such as advocated by Fleagle (1988) and Martin (1990), use the pre-Darwinian idea of a *scala naturae*, or grades of advancement, to divide the order Primates into Prosimii and Anthropoidea. Prosimii is the suborder for small-brained primates, i.e. the tarsiers and lemuriform and loriform strepsirhines. Anthropoidea is the suborder for larger-brained primates, i.e. the New World monkeys, Old World monkeys, so-called lesser apes, greater apes, and humans.

Also by using the idea of grades of advancement for some of the groupings within Anthropoidea, the traditional primate classifications place the African great apes (chimpanzees, bonobos, and gorillas) with the Asian great apes (orang-utans) in subfamily Ponginae of family Pongidae. In turn, humans on being treated as the most advanced primates are the sole living members of family Hominidae. This traditional anthropocentric view of the primates is not a reliable guide to their phylogeny, i.e. to the primate clades produced by evolution. There is mounting DNA evidence that tarsiers and the simians are more closely related to each other than either is to the strepsirhines (see Figure 1 and studies listed under Major Clades in Table 1). If we accept this evidence, the traditional Prosimii is not a monophyletic taxon, i.e. does not represent a clade, because by definition a clade contains only species that are more closely related to each other than to any outside species. Similarly, the traditional Pongidae and Ponginae do not represent clades. The DNA evidence not only strongly groups the African great apes with humans rather than with orang-utans but has the clade of chimpanzees and bonobos as the sister-group of humans rather than of gorillas (see Figure 2 and studies listed under Hominid Clades in

Figure 1
Sister-grouping of tarsiers with simians in the maximum parsimony tree constructed for γ-globin DNA sequences. The sequences employed are from Bailey *et al.* (1992), Meireles *et al.* (1999), and Page *et al.* (1999). Numbers by stems of clades are bootstrap proportions (% of 1000 replications). Values above 95% provide very strong parsimony support for the clades with such values.

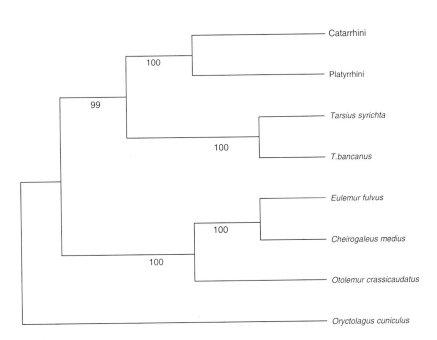

Figure 2
The sister-grouping of *Homo* (*Pan*) (the subgenus for chimpanzees and bonobos) with *Homo* (*Homo*) (the subgenus for humans) in the maximum parsimony tree constructed for γ-globin DNA sequences (see legend to Figure 1). Numbers by stems of clades are bootstrap proportions (% of 1000 replications).

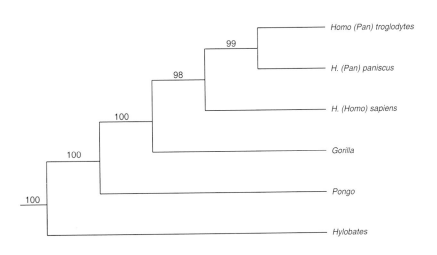

Table 1). Recent cladistic analyses of morphological characters also depict the tarsiers as most closely related to simians, the clade of chimpanzees and bonobos as the sister-group of humans, and gorillas as their sister-group (Shoshani *et al.*, 1996; Goodman *et al.*, 1998). In contrast to traditional taxonomy with its use of the idea of grades of advancement, a strictly phylogenetic taxonomy (one free of arbitrary anthropocentric biases) can provide an objective framework for viewing humankind's evolutionary place in nature. By this objective view humans are genealogically very close to apes, grouping with chimpanzees and bonobos in the genus *Homo* and with all living apes in the subfamily Homininae.

The phylogenetic classification for primate clades that presents this radically different view of our place among the primates (Table 2) was constructed by synthesising the DNA evidence on phylogenetic relationships with the fossil and molecular evidence on branch times in primate phylogeny. In constructing the classification, three principles proposed by Hennig (1966) were followed. The first principle is that each taxon should represent a monophyletic group or clade – that is, it should represent all species descended from a common ancestor. The second principle is that the hierarchical groupings of lower-ranked taxa into higher-ranked taxa should describe the phylogenetic relationships of the clades. The third principle is that, ideally, taxa at the same hierarchical level or rank should represent clades that are equally old – that is, at an equivalent evolutionary age. The fossil record by itself allowed estimates of the ages of only a scattering of branch-points in primate phylogeny. However the model of local molecular clocks applied to the branch lengths of phylogenetic trees constructed from the DNA data allowed estimates of the ages of all branch-points in these trees. The model of local molecular clocks differs from that of a global molecular clock by not assuming that all lineages accumulate nucleotide substitutions at the same rate; local molecular clock calculations are much more constrained by fossil evidence on branch-times than are global molecular clock calculations (Goodman, 1986; Bailey *et al.*, 1991, 1992; Porter *et al.*, 1997a,b, 1999; Barroso *et al.*, 1997; Meireles *et al.*, 1999; Chaves *et al.*, 1999). Even though nucleotide substitutions in the non-functional noncoding DNA tend to accumulate at a less variable rate than do the positively selected nucleotide substitutions, selectively neutral substitution rates can still show considerable variation between lineages. For example the non-functional noncoding DNA evolution rate is almost twice as fast in loriform strepsirhines than in lemuriform strepsirhines (Bonner *et al.*, 1980, 1981; Koop *et al.*, 1989; Porter *et al.*, 1997a). As another example, leaf-eating Old World monkeys show a faster rate than cheek-pouched Old World monkeys (Page *et al.*, 1999). Local molecular clock estimates of branch-times adjust for such lineage variation in rates by having each base substitution occur over a longer period of time in a more slowly evolving lineage than in a more rapidly evolving lineage.

To use the model of local molecular clocks for estimating lineage divergence dates from the percentages of sequence change on the branches of the molecular phylogenetic trees, reference dates based on fossil evidence (reviewed in Goodman *et al.*, 1998) were used to calibrate the local clocks. This fossil evidence placed the lineage divergence date or last common ancestor (LCA) of Old World monkeys (family Cercopithecidae) and humans and apes (family Hominidae) at 25 Myr, the LCA of platyrrhines and catarrhines at 40 Myr, and the LCA of strepsirhines and haplorhines (i.e., of all living primates) at 63 Myr. The palaeontologically based age of 25 Myr for the LCA of cercopithecids and hominids served as the starting reference date for estimating the divergence dates for lineages within the hominid clade and separately within the cercopithecid clade. The age of 40 Myr for the LCA of platyrrhines and catarrhines served as the starting date for estimating the divergence dates for lineages within the platyrrhine clade. The age of 63 Myr for the LCA of strepsirhines and haplorhines served as the starting date for estimating the divergence dates for lineages within the strepsirhine clade and also for the haplorhine lineage to tarsiers.

The phylogenetic classification for primate clades (Table 2) records the results that were obtained from the molecular phylogenetic trees on the phylogenetic relationships and ages of the clades. This classification portrays a series of phylogenetic branchings during the course of primate evolution from the Palaeocene epoch to the present day. The division of a higher-ranked taxon into subordinate lower-ranked taxa denotes a phylogenetic branching. The age (in Myr) placed after the name of a taxon is the estimated age of that taxon treated as a *crown group* but also of that taxon's closest (at a step below in rank) subordinate taxa treated as *total groups*. A crown group includes both the LCA of the extant species in a clade and all descendant species (extinct and extant) of the LCA but does not include the stem of the LCA (Jeffries, 1979).

The total group includes, in addition to all members of the crown group, the stem of the LCA and all extinct offshoots of the stem. Thus the age of 63 Myr for the LCA of all living primates - that is, the age for Primates as a crown group - is the age for both Strepsirhini and Haplorhini as total groups. In turn, the ages of 50 Myr and 58 Myr listed alongside Strepsirhini and Haplorhini, respectively, are the ages for these two taxa treated as crown groups.

After this first major branching, in the early Palaeocene epoch, into semiordinal clades, subordinal clades emerged. The late Palaeocene haplorhines divided into Tarsiiformes and Anthropoidea. The anthropoideans of the middle Eocene epoch (at ~40 Myr) divided into the infraorders Platyrrhini and Catarrhini. As total groups, families originated from superfamilial clades within infraorders in the middle to late Oligocene epoch (~28-25 Myr), subfamilies in the early Miocene epoch (~23-22 Myr), tribes in the early to middle Miocene (~20-15 Mry), subtribes in the middle to late Miocene (~14-10 Myr), genera in the late Miocene (~10-7 Myr), and subgenera in the late Miocene to early Pliocene epoch (~7-4 Myr). Estimated branch times at the infrageneric level for the species examined at the DNA level in this study ranged from 7 to <1 Myr.

In this primate classification, in which taxa represent clades and the ages of the clades determine the ranks of the taxa, many of the names for taxa are the same as those commonly used in other primate classifications. This is possible because in traditional primate classifications, despite the use of the grade concept to name some of the taxa, most taxa do represent monophyletic groups. For example, in the traditional primate classification used by Martin (1990), there are extant members in 5 infraorders, 6 superfamilies, 12 families, and 13 subfamilies. The molecular evidence shows that: all these extant infraorders and superfamilies, 9 of the 12 extant families and 10 or, possibly, 11 of the 13 extant subfamilies are monophyletic taxa. However, sister-group relationships are not well depicted, nor are taxa at the same rank necessarily at an equivalent age in traditional primate classifications. However, a crude correlation does exist between age of origin of a taxon and its rank.

As Romer (1962, p. 32) observed, the rise of modern orders and suborders of mammals occurred in the Eocene epoch, the rise of modern families in the Oligocene epoch, and the rise of modern subfamilies in the Miocene epoch. In correlation, the strictly phylogenetic classification of primate taxa, with its age equivalence among taxa at the same rank, places suborders, families, and sub-families, when treated as total groups, in the Eocene, Oligocene, and Miocene geologic epochs, respectively. The names for genera used in tabulations of the living primates (e.g., see Groves 1993) are also used in the phylogenetic classification (Table 2), in most cases as full generic names but in a few cases as subgeneric names. An exception is that Groves (1993) treats gibbons and siamangs as members of the same genus, *Hylobates*. However, the estimated LCA age for gibbons and siamangs is 8 Myr. Thus in this case, the phylogenetic classification places these two apes in separate genera but groups them together in the same subtribe.

In contrast with the traditional family Hominidae, which has *Homo sapiens* as its only living species, the age-equals-rank system places all living apes and humans in subfamily Homininae. A phylogenetic branching (at ~18 Myr) divided this subfamily into tribes Hylobatini and Hominini. Within Hylobatini, the phylogenetic branching (at ~8 Myr) in the subtribe Hylobatina separated *Symphalangus* (siamangs) from *Hylobates* (gibbons). Within Hominini, a phylogenetic branching (at ~14 Myr) separated the monogeneric subtribe Pongina for *Pongo* (orang-utans) from Hominina. Within Hominina, a phylogenetic branching (at ~7 Myr) separated *Gorilla* from *Homo*.

Within *Homo*, a phylogenetic branching (at ~6 Myr) separated the subgenus for common chimpanzees and bonobos - that is, *H.* (*Pan*) - from the subgenus for humans - that is, *H.* (*Homo*). Thus, the principle of rank equivalence with other primate clades of the same age requires grouping the chimpanzee clade with the human clade within the same genus.

Humans and chimpanzees are more than 98.3% identical in their typical nuclear noncoding DNA and more than 99.5% identical in the active coding nucleotide sequences of their functional nuclear genes (Goodman *et al.*, 1989, 1990). In mammals such high genetic correspondence is commonly found between sibling species below the generic level but not between species in different genera. The genetic and phylogenetic evidence that groups humans and chimpanzees together as sister subgenera of the same genus justifies the belief that the two chimpanzee species can provide insights into distinctive features of humankind's own evolutionary origins. Indeed chimpanzees use tools, have material cultures, are ecological generalists, and are highly social (McGrew, 1992; DeWaal, 1995; Goldberg, 1998). Their anatomical inability to produce most of the sounds of human speech long obscured the fact that they are also capable of understanding and using rudimentary forms of language, as shown by recent studies on communication via sign language and lexigrams (Fouts & Mills, 1997; Savage-Rumbaugh, Shanker & Taylor, 1998).

Selected genic changes in our evolutionary history

Positively selected genic changes, coding and regulatory, occurred in the evolutionary history of our two fetally expressed γ-globin genes. The reconstruction of this history from comparative data (reviewed in Goodman, 1999) reveals that the early primates had a single γ-globin gene, and this early γ gene was expressed solely in embryonic life as is the γ gene of living strepsirhines. In the simian stem-lineage to the LCA of platyrrhines and catarrhines, the γ-globin gene tandemly duplicated, an upsurge of nucleotide substitutions in the γ promoter and coding sequences occurred, and the transition to fetal γ expression began.

The first steps in the transition from embryonic to fetal γ expression may be inferred from the platyrrhine (e.g. capuchin monkey) γ expression pattern, which is intermediate to the strepsirhine (e.g. galago) embryonic pattern and the catarrhine (e.g. human) fetal pattern. The switch from γ to β-globin gene expression occurs at the start of fetal life in strepsirhines, in mid-fetal life in platyrrhines, and at birth in catarrhines.

Moreover, of the two γ genes produced by the tandem duplication ($5'$-γ^1-γ^2-$3'$), platyrrhines tend to have only one (most often γ^2) fetally expressed, whereas catarrhines have both γ genes fetally expressed. Right after the tandem duplication, the nascent γ^1 gene continued to be embryonically expressed and fetally repressed, whereas the nascent γ^2 gene was largely silent throughout ontogeny and thus was free to accumulate nucleotide substitutions. Some of the substitutions permitted fetal expression by reducing the promoter's ability to bind fetal repressors. Other substitutions - *non-*

synonymous ones - shaped a distinct fetal hemoglobin with advantageous properties, subsequently, gene conversions spread such promoter and coding sequence changes to both γ genes.

The upsurge of promoter and *non-synonymous* base substitutions in the stem-simians, during the first steps of the transition from embryonic to fetal γ expression, was followed by conservation of most of these simian specific nucleotides in the functional γ genes of platyrrhines and catarrhines (Fitch *et al.*, 1991; Hayasaka *et al.*, 1992, 1993; Goodman *et al.*, 1996). This rate speed-up slow-down pattern is evidence that selection favoured the emergence of a distinct fetal hemoglobin. Among the amino-acid changing substitutions that were fixed in the γ genes of the common ancestor of present-day simian primates, three occurred in codons specifying DPG-binding sites: valine at the first amino acid position of the γ chain mutated to glycine, and histidine at the 143rd position mutated through two amino acid replacements to serine. In addition in the early platyrrhines, glycine at the first amino acid position mutated to serine and histidine at the second amino acid position mutated to asparagine. By drastically reducing the DPG-binding capacity of fetal hemoglobin, these amino acid changes ensured a favourable balance in the transport of oxygen from mother to foetus, and thereby helped make possible the prolonged intrauterine fetal life and extensive prenatal brain development of simian primates.

Functional studies have provided evidence that the substitutions in *cis*-regulatory elements caused or permitted the simian γ genes to be fetal genes rather than exclusively embryonic. An analysis of galago and human γ genes in transgenic mice has demonstrated that the *cis* differences between galago and human sequences in a 4.0 kb region surrounding the γ gene resulted in distinctly different expression patterns: the galago γ transgene expression was embryonic and was silenced in the mouse fetal liver, whereas the activity of the human γ transgene peaked in fetal life (TomHon *et al.*, 1997).

Using a strategy called differential phylogenetic footprinting, Gumucio *et al.* (1994) identified some *cis* changes that are good candidates for further investigation in transgenic studies; in particular, they found evidence of a two-step change in the nucleotide sequences of the γ promoter-proximal CCAAT box region. In the first step, simian-specific base substitutions occurred in the stem of the simians. In the second step, catarrhine-specific base substitutions occurred in the stem of the catarrhines. Each step resulted in an alteration in the binding affinity of a set of putative fetal repressor proteins: these proteins bind galago and lemur sequences with high affinity, platyrrhine sequences with moderate affinity, and human sequences with very low affinity (Gumucio *et al.*, 1994). Simian-specific base substitutions also occurred in the γ promoter -50 region; these substitutions permitted the binding of a fetal activator that favours the competitive expression of γ over β during fetal life (Jane *et al.*, 1992). These γ promoter *cis*-regulatory changes permitted the γ genes to be fetally expressed, while the coding sequence changes favoured the transport of oxygen from maternal hemoglobin to the new fetal hemoglobin.

As suggested above, a likely evolutionary pressure for these selected changes in γ genes was the emergence in the simian primates of a larger neocortex, one of the most aerobic and most energy consuming tissues. This same evolutionary pressure may have been in part responsible for positively selected changes in the evolution of cytochrome *c* oxidase subunit IV in simian primates (Wu *et al.*, 1997). Cytochrome *c* oxidase (COX) is the multisubunit enzyme complex that catalyses the final step of electron transfer through the respiratory chain. Thus COX plays a vital role in aerobic tissues. Phylogenetic analysis of rodent, cow, and primate gene sequences that encode COX IV, i.e. *COX 4* nucleotide sequences, revealed an accelerated *non-synonymous* rate in the earlier evolution of catarrhines followed later by a decelerated rate. Pronounced positive selection for adaptive amino acid replacements was evident by higher N than S rates in the lineage encompassing catarrhine and hominid stems. A marked deceleration of N rates with much lower N than S rates in the terminal lineages to gorilla, human, and chimpanzee *COX 4* genes indicated that the positively selected changes were then preserved by purifying selection. Phylogenetic analyses of gene sequence data for other COX subunits as well as other proteins active in the respiratory chain has also provided evidence for positively selected changes in our earlier simian ancestors (Adkins *et al.*, 1996; Schmidt *et al.*, 1999; Wu *et al.*, 2000).

Future direction of genomic exploration

We have argued above that major progress toward identifying the genetic basis for unique features of human anatomy, physiology and behaviour can be achieved by comparative genomic analysis of DNA sequence data from other primates. Without that information, the overall goals of the Human Genome Project will not be completely achieved. This establishes an inescapable need for virtually complete genomic sequences from our nearest relatives among the apes (chimpanzees, bonobos, and gorillas), supplemented by sequence information from a wide range of primates for regions of special interest. The technology and resources developed for the Human Genome Project will be invaluable as the era of comparative genomics develops, but the research will be complex and costly. Some form of administrative organisation to focus and co-ordinate the efforts that will arise internationally is needed. With that in mind, we and others (McConkey *et al.*, 2000) have proposed that the Human Genome Organisation (HUGO) formally establish a Human Genome Evolution Project (HGEP). The proposal is currently under study by HUGO.

Comparative genomic analysis will identify many human-specific nucleotide substitutions and other genomic changes from the presumed human-chimpanzee-bonobo ancestral genome, but the phenotypic consequences (if any) of those genomic changes will at best be hypothetical and often will be unpredictable. When feasible and ethically permissible the functional effects of human-specific genomic features should be documented experimentally. In many cases, the necessary experimental proof can be obtained with cultured cells and even more information will become available by construction of transgenic mice. However, there will surely be human-specific genetic functions that cannot be analysed in those systems. When we have candidate genes for bipedal locomotion, for cranium development, or for any complex aspect of cognition, how will we demonstrate their function in shaping our unique human anatomy and behaviour?

To answer such questions, proposals to perform genetic experiments on apes are likely to be offered. This would raise enormously complex and intense ethical issues. Chimpanzees and bonobos are so close to humans at the genetic level that we argue for including them in the genus *Homo*. Transfer of human genes to chimpanzees or bonobos would raise questions about the concept of humanness. Genetic experiments on any of the great apes, if they are done at all, will have to be scrutinised in as much detail as genetic experiments on humans, with extensive input from ethicists, philosophers, animal rights activists, and other interest groups, as well as by the appropriate scientific authorities and administrators. Only those experiments that did not compromise bodily integrity and bodily liberties and that would be permissible to be performed on humans should warrant consideration. Ethical considerations may require that some putative human-specific genetic functions remain nothing more than educated guesses, at least for the foreseeable future.

Nevertheless the age of genomic exploration will ultimately produce encyclopaedic information on the expression of human genes in health and disease and on the sites (base positions) in human genomes where mutations harmful to health have occurred. We propose that such encyclopaedic information should also include, for each base position, its pattern of rates of base substitution during the course of primate phylogeny and whether its present allelic (mutant non 'wild-type') variants are at frequencies high enough as to indicate absence of purifying selection or, conversely, so low as to be due to the scrutiny of purifying selection. Correlative studies performed on these different types of information in this massive human genomic data bank should then be able to reveal the positively selected mutations that shaped the genetic basis of being human.

Acknowledgement

This work has been supported by grants from the National Science Foundation and National Institutes of Health.

References

Adkins RM, Honeycutt RL, Disotell TR. 1996. Evolution of eutherian cytochrome *c* oxidase subunit II: heterogeneous rates of protein evolution and altered interaction with cytochrome *c*. *Molecular Biology and Evolution.* **13:** 1393-1404.

Arnason U, Gullberg A, Janke A. 1998. Molecular timing of primate divergences as estimated by two nonprimate calibration points. *Journal of Molecular Evolution.* **47:** 718-727.

Bailey WJ, Fitch DHA, Tagle DA, Czelusniak J, Slightom JL, Goodman M. 1991. Molecular evolution of the ψη-globin gene locus: gibbon phylogeny and the hominoid slowdown. *Molecular Biology and Evolution.* **8:** 155-184.

Bailey WJ, Hayasaka k, Skinner CG, Kehoe S, Sieu LC, Slightom JL, Goodman. 1992. Reexamination of the African hominoid trichotomy with additional sequences from the primate β-globin gene cluster. *Molecular Phylogenetics and Evolution.* **1:** 97-135.

Barroso CML, Schneider H, Schneider MPC, Sampaio I, Harada ML, Czelusniak J, Goodman M. 1997. Update on the phylogenetic systematics of New World monkeys: further DNA evidence for placing the pygmy marmoset (*Cebuella*) within the marmoset genus *Callithrix. International Journal of Primatology.* **18:** 651-674.

Benveniste RE. 1985. The contributions of retroviruses to the study of mammalian evolution. In: MacIntyre RJ, ed. *Molecular Evolutionary Genetics.* New York: Plenum. 359-417.

Boeke JD, Pickeral OK. 1999. Retroshuffling the genomic deck. *Nature.* **398:** 108-111.

Bonner TI, Heinemann R, Todaro GJ. 1980. Evolution of DNA sequence has been retarded in Malagasy primates. *Nature.* **286:** 420-423.

Bonner TI, Heinemann R, Todaro GJ. 1981. A geographical factor involved in the evolution of the single copy DNA sequence of primates. In: Scudder GGE, Reveal JL. eds. *Evolution Today.* Pittsburgh: Hunt Institute for Botanical Documentation. 293-300.

Caccone A, Powell JR. 1989. DNA divergence among hominoids. *Evolution.* **43:** 925-942.

Canavez FC, Mireira MAM, Ladasky JJ, Pissinatti A, Parham P, Seuanez HN. 1999. Molecular phylogeny of New World primates (Platyrrhini) based on β$_2$-microglobulin DNA sequences. *Molecular Phylogenetics and Evolution.* **12:** 74-82.

Cargill M, Altshuler D, Ireland J, Sklar P, Ardlie K, Patil N, Lane CR, Lim EP, Kalyanaraman N, Nemesh J, Ziaugra L, Friedland L, Rolfe A, Warrington J, Lipshutz R, Daley GQ, Lander ES. 1999. Characterization of single-nucleotide polymorphisms in coding regions of human genes. *Nature Genetics.* **22:** 231-238.

Chaves R, Sampaio I, Schneider MP, Schneider H, Page SL, Goodman M. 1999. The place of *Callimico goeldii* in the callitrichine phylogenetic tree: evidence from von Willebrand factor gene (vWF) intron II sequences. *Molecular Phylogenetics and Evolution.* **13:** 392-404.

Chiu C-H. 1997. Evolution and Expression of the γ-Globin Genes in New World Monkeys (Infraorder *Platyrrhini*). [Ph. D. Thesis], Wayne State University at Detroit.

DeWaal FBM. 1995. Bonobo sex and society. *Scientific American.* **272:** 82-88.

Disotell TR, Honeycutt RL, Ruvolo M. 1992. Mitochondrial DNA phylogeny of the Old World monkey tribe Papionini. *Molecular Biology and Evolution.* **9:** 1-13.

Duret L, Bucher P, 1997. Searching for regulatory elements in human noncoding sequences. *Current Opinion in Structural Biology.* **7:** 399-406.

Eickbush T. 1999. Exon shuffling in retrospect. *Science.* **283:** 1465.

Fitch DHA, Bailey WJ, Tagle DA, Goodman M, Sieu L, Slightom JL. 1991. Duplication of the γ-globin gene mediated by L1 long interspersed repetitive elements in an early ancestor of simian primates. *Proceedings of National Academy of Sciences USA,* **88:** 7396-7400.

Fleagle JG, 1988. *Primate Adaptation and Evolution.* New York: Academic Press.

Fouts R, Mills ST. 1997. *Next of Kin: What Chimpanzees Have Taught Me About Who We Are.* New York: William Morrow and Company.

Goldberg TL. 1998. Biogeographic predictors of genetic diversity in populations of eastern African chimpanzees (*Pan troglodytes schweinfurthi*). *International Journal of Primatology.* **19:** 237-254.

Goodman M, 1986. Molecular evidence on the ape subfamily Homininae. In: Gershowitz H, Rugknagel DR, Tashian RE. eds. *Evolutionary Perspectives and the New Genetics.* New York: AR Liss. 121-132.

Goodman M, Koop BF, Czelusniak J, Fitch DHA, Tagle DA, Slightom JL. 1989. Molecular phylogeny of the family of apes and humans. *Genome.* **31:** 316-335.

Goodman M, Tagle DA, Fitch DHA, Bailey WJ, Czelusniak J, Koop BF, Benson P, Slightom JL. 1990. Primate evolution at the DNA level and a classification of hominoids. *Journal of Molecular Evolution.* **30:** 260-266.

Goodman M, Slightom JL, Gumucio DL. 1996. Molecular evolution in the β-globin gene family of mammals, emergence of redundant genes, important new genes, and new expression patterns. In: Holmes RS, Lim HA. eds. *Gene Families: Structure, Function, Genetics, and Evolution.* Singapore: World Scientific. 43-52.

Goodman M, Porter CA, Czelusniak J, Page SL, Schneider H, Shoshani J, Gunnell G, Groves CP. 1998. Toward a phylogenetic classification of primates based on DNA evidence complemented by fossil evidence. *Molecular Phylogenetics and Evolution.* **9:** 585-598.

Goodman M, Page SL, Meireles CM, Czelusniak J. 1999. Primate phylogeny and classification elucidated at the molecular level. In: Wasser SP. ed. *Evolutionary Theory and Processes: Modern Perspectives.* The Netherlands: Kluwer Academic Publishers. 193-212.

Goodman M, 1999. The genomic record of humankind's evolutionary roots. *American Journal of Human Genetics.* **64**: 31-39.

Groves CP. 1993. Order primates. In: Wilson DE, Reader DM. eds. *Mammalian Species of the World: A Taxonomic and Geographic Reference*, 2nd ed. Washington, DC:Smithsonian Institution Press. 243-277.

Gumucio DL, Shelton DA, Blanchard-McQuate K, Gray T, Tarle S, Heilstedt-Williamson H, Slightom JL, Collins F, Goodman M. 1994. Differential phylogenetic footprinting as a means to identify base changes responsible for recruitment of the anthropoid γ gene to a fetal expression pattern. *Journal of Biological Chemistry.* **269**: 15371-15380.

Gumucio DL, Shelton DA, Zhu W, Millinoff D, Gray T, Bock JH, Slightom JL, Goodman M. 1996. Evolutionary strategies for the elucidation of *cis* and *trans* factors that regulate the developmental switching programs of the β-like globin genes. *Molecular Phylogenetic and Evolution.* **5**: 18-32.

Halushka MK, Fan J-B, Bentley K, Hsie L, Shen N, Weder A, Cooper R, Lipshutz R, Chakravarti A. 1999. Patterns of single-nucleotide polymorphisms in candidate genes for blood-pressure homeostasis. *Nature Genetics.* **22**: 239-247.

Harada ML, Schneider H, Schneider MP, Sampaio I, Czelusniak J, Goodman M. 1995. DNA evidence on the phylogenetic systematics of New World monkeys: support for the sister grouping of *Cebus* and *Saimiri* from two unlinked nuclear genes. *Molecular Phylogenetics and Evolution.* **4**: 331-349.

Hardison R, Slightom JL, Gumucio DL, Goodman M, Stojanovic N, Miller W. 1997. Locus control regions of mammalian β-globin gene clusters: combining phylogenetic analyses and experimental results to gain functional insights. *Gene.* **205**: 73-94.

Harris EE, Disotell TR. 1998. Nuclear gene trees and the phylogenetic relationships of the mangabeys (Primates: Papionini*). Molecular Biology and Evolution.* **15**: 892-900.

Hayasaka K, Fitch DHA, Slightom JL, Goodman M, 1992. Fetal recruitment of anthropoid γ-globin genes: findings from phylogenetic analyses involving the 5'- flanking sequences of the ψγ[1] globin gene of spider monkey *Ateles geoffroyi. Journal of Molecular Biology.* **224**: 875-881.

Hayasaka K, Skinner CG, Goodman M, Slightom JL. 1993. The γ-globin genes and their flanking sequences in primates: findings with nucleotide sequences of capuchin monkey and tarsier. *Genomics.* **18**: 20-28.

Hennig W. 1966. *Phylogenetic Systematics.* Urbana, Illinois: University of Illinois Press. (Reissued 1979).

Horai S, Hayasaka K, Kondo R, Tsugane K, Takahata N. 1995. Recent African origin of modern humans revealed by complete sequences of hominoid mitochondrial DNAs. *Proceedings of National Academy of Sciences USA.* **92**: 532-535.

Jane SM, Ney PA, Vanin EF, Gumucio DL, Nienhuis AW. 1992. Identification of a stage selector element in the human γ-globin promoter that fosters preferrential interaction with the 5' HS2 enhancer when in competition with the β-promoter. *The EMBO Journal.* **11:** 2961-2969.

Jeffries RSP. 1979. The origin of the chordates - a methodological essay. In: House MR. ed. *The Origin of Major Invertebrate Groups,* London: Academic Press. 443-477.

Koop BF, Tagle DA, Goodman M, Slightom JL. 1989. A molecular view of primate phylogeny and important systematic and evolutionary questions. *Molecular Biology and Evolution.* **6:** 580-612.

Martin RD. 1990. *Primate Origins and Evolution: a phylogenetic reconstruction.* London: Chapman and Hall.

McConkey EH, Goodman M. 1997. A human genome evolution project is needed. *Trends in Genetics.* **13:** 350-351.

McConkey EH. Fouts R, Goodman M, Nelson D, Penny D, Ruvolo M, Sikela J, Stewart C-B, Varki A, Wise S. 2000. Human genome evolution project proposal. *Molecular Phylogenetics and Evolution.* **15:** 1-4.

McGrew WC. 1992. *Chimpanzee Material Culture - Implications for Human Evolution.* Cambridge: Cambridge University Press.

Meireles CM, Czelusniak J, Schneider MPC, Muniz JAPC, Brigido MC, Fereira HS, Goodman M. 1999. Molecular phylogeny of ateline New World monkeys (Platyrrhini: Atelinae) based on γ-globin gene sequences: evidence that *Brachyteles* is the sister group of *Lagothrix. Molecular Phylogenetics and Evolution.* **12:** 10-30.

Messier W, Stewart C-B. 1997. Episodic adaptive evolution of primate lysozymes. *Nature.* **385:** 151-154.

Moran JV, DeBerardinis RJ, Kazazian, Jr. HH. 1999. Exon shuffling by L1 retrotransposition. *Science.* **283:** 1530-1534.

Page SL, Chiu C-H, Goodman M. 1999. Molecular phylogeny of Old World monkeys (Cercopithecidae) as inferred from γ-globin DNA sequences. *Molecular Phylogenetics and Evolution.* **13:** 348-359.

Perrin-Pecontal P, Gouy M, Nigon V-M, Trabuchet G. 1992. Evolution of the primate β-globin region: nucleotide sequence of the δ-β globin intergenic region of gorilla and phylogenetic relationships between African apes and man. *Journal of Molecular Evolution.* **34:** 17-30.

Porter CA, Sampaio I, Schneider H, Schneider MPC, Czelusniak J, Goodman M. 1995. Evidence on primate phylogeny from ε-globin gene sequences and flanking regions. *Journal of Molecular Evolution.* **40:** 30-55.

Porter CA, Page SL, Czelusniak J, Schneider H, Schneider MPC, Sampaio I, Goodman M. 1997a. Phylogeny and evolution of selected primates as determined by sequences of the ε-globin locus and 5' flanking regions. *International Journal of Primatology.* **18:** 261-295.

Porter CA, Czelusniak J, Schneider H, Schneider MPC, Sampaio I, Goodman M. 1997b. Sequences of the primate ε-globin gene:

implications for systematics of the marmosets and other New World primates. *Gene.* **205:** 59-71.

Porter CA, Czelusniak J, Schneider H, Schneider MPC, Sampaio I, Goodman M. 1999. Sequences from the 5' flanking region of the ε-globin gene support the relationship of *Callicebus* with the pitheciins. *American Journal of Primatology.* **48:** 69-75.

Romer AS. 1962. *The Vertebrate Body.* Philadelphia: WB Saunders.

Rowe N. 1996. *The Pictorial Guide to the Living Primates.* East Hampton, New York: Pogonias Press.

Ruvolo M. 1997. Molecular phylogeny of the hominoids: inferences from multiple independent DNA sequence data sets. *Molecular Biology and Evolution.* **14:** 248-265.

Satta Y, KLein J, Takahata N. 2000. DNA archives and our nearest relative, the trichotomy problem revisited. *Molecular Phylogenetics and Evolution.* **14:** 259-275.

Savage-Rumbaugh S, Shanker SG, Taylor TJ. 1998. *Apes, Language, and the Human Mind.* Oxford: Oxford University Press.

Schmidt TR, Goodman M, Grossman LI. 1999. Molecular evolution of the COX7A gene family in primates. *Molecular Biology and Evolution.* **16:** 619-626.

Schneider H, Schnider MPC, Sampaio MIC, Harada ML, Stanhope M, Czelusniak J, Goodman M. 1993. Molecular phylogeny of the New World monkeys (Platyrrhini: Primates). *Molecular Phylogenetics and Evolution.* **2:** 225-242.

Schneider H, Sampaio I, Harada ML, Barroso CML, Schneider MPC, Czelusniak J, Goodman M. 1996. Molecular phylogeny of the New World monkeys (Platyrrhini: Primates) based on two unlinked nuclear genes: IRBP intron 1 and ε-globin sequences. *American Journal of Anthropology.* **100:** 153-179.

Shoshani J, Groves CP, Simons EL, Gunnell GF. 1996. Primates phylogeny: morphological vs molecular results. *Molecular Phylogenetics and Evolution.* **5:** 102-154.

Sibley CG, Ahlquist JE. 1987. DNA hybridization evidence of hominoid phylogeny: results from an expanded data set. *Journal of Molecular Evolution.* **26:** 99-121.

Tagle DA, Koop BF, Goodman M, Slightom JL, Hess D, Jones RT. 1988. Embryonic and γ globin genes of a prosimian primate (*Galago crassicaudatus*): nucleotide and amino acid sequences, developmental regulation, and phylogenetic footprints. *Journal of Molecular Biology.* **203:** 439-455.

Tagliaro CH, Schneider MPC, Schneider H, Sampaio IC, Stanhope MJ. 1997. Marmoset phylogenetics, conservation perspectives, and evolution of the mtDNA control region. *Molecular Biology and Evolution.* **14:** 674-684.

Takahata N, Satta Y. 1997. Evolution of the primate lineage leading to modern humans: phylogenetic and demographic inferences from DNA sequences. *Proceedings of National Academy of Sciences USA.* **94:** 4811-4815.

TomHon C, Zhu W, Millinoff D, Hayasaka K, Slightom JL, Goodman M, Gumucio DL. 1997. Evolution of a fetal expression pattern via *cis* changes near the γ globin gene. *Journal of Biological Chemistry.* **272:** 14062-14066.

Van der Kuyl AC, Kuiken CL, Dekker JT, Goudsmit J. 1995. Phylogeny of African monkeys based upon mitochondrial 12S rRNA sequences. *Journal of Molecular Evolution.* **40:** 173-180.

Von Dornum MJ. 1997. DNA Sequence Data from Mitochondrial COII and Nuclear G6PD Loci and a Molecular Phylogeny of the New World Monkeys (Primates: Platyrrhini). [Ph.D. Thesis], Harvard University at Cambridge.

Von Dornum M, Ruvolo M, 1999. Phylogenetic relationships of the New World monkeys (Primates, Platyrrhini) based on nuclear G6PD sequences. *Molecular Phylogenetics and Evolution.* **11:** 459-476.

Wu W, Goodman M, Lomax MI, Grossman LI. 1997. Molecular evolution of cytochrome *c* oxidase subunit IV: evidence for positive selection in simian primates. *Journal of Molecular Evolution.* **44:** 477-491.

Wu W, Schmidt TR, Goodman M, Grossman LI. 1999. Molecular evolution of cytochrome *c* oxidase subunit I in primates: is there co-evolution between mitochondrial and nuclear genomes? *Molecular Phylogenetics and Evolution.* (In press).

Yoder AD, Cartmill M, Ruvolo M, Smith K, Vilgalys R. 1996. Ancient single origin for Malagasy primates. *Proceeding of National Academy of Sciences USA.* **93:** 5122-5126.

Yoder AD. 1997. Back to the future: a synthesis of strepsirrhine systematics. *Evolutionary Anthropology Issues, News, and Reviews.* **6:** 11-22.

Zietkiewicz E, Richer C, Labuda D, 1999. Phylogenetic affinities of Tarsier in the context of primate Alu repeats. *Molecular Phylogenetics and Evolution.* **11:** 77-83.

CHAPTER FIVE

Biomechanics in palaeoanthropology: engineering and experimental approaches to the study of behavioural evolution in the genus *Homo*

S. E. CHURCHILL & D. SCHMITT

Introduction

Biomechanics – the study of the action of forces on biological structures, is playing an increasingly important role in the investigation of behavioural and adaptive evolution in the Hominidae. Biomechanical approaches have proven useful in all aspects of palaeoanthropology – from generating inferences about the behavioural ecology of Miocene hominoids (e.g. Rose, 1988; Ruff, 1989) to understanding subsistence and economic shifts in Holocene human groups (e.g. Ruff & Hayes, 1983; Bridges, 1989, 1991; Fresia, Ruff & Larsen, 1990). A biomechanical perspective is often embedded in broader, comparative functional-morphological analyses, and thus its utility in understanding the biobehavioural characteristics of extinct taxa has been largely under-appreciated. As the application of mechanics – kinetics, statics and kinematics – to biological materials, biomechanics often serves as the inferential basis for going from analysis of form to deduction of function. In the broader field of biology, biomechanical investigations are usually employed to elucidate the mechanical solutions that natural selection has fostered in response to adaptive challenges (see Lauder, 1995, 1996 for a review and critique of this approach), and thus biomechanics serves to teach us about adaptation and the constraints that limit adaptive responses to the action of selection. In palaeoanthropology, the focus is more on reconstructing major behavioural/adaptive shifts in human evolutionary history than on understanding selection and adaptation as processes. Biomechanics, as a commonly used inferential framework for deducing behaviour from morphology – function from form – thus plays a key but often less conspicuous role in biological anthropology. So, while explicitly biomechanical studies are relatively rare in palaeoanthropology, the use of biomechanical principles is widespread.

Rather than review the broad application of biomechanics to human evolutionary studies, we choose instead to review the use of one biomechanical approach – the structural analysis of long bones – to one on-going issue in palaeoanthropology – the behavioural characteristics of Neanderthals – in order to illustrate the potential and limitations of biomechanics in palaeoanthropology. In so doing, we hope to both highlight the power and utility of biomechanical analyses for studying past human behaviour, and underscore the inferential limits of such an approach. Comparative structural analysis functions as a powerful tool for generating behavioural hypotheses, but without further testing with additional comparative data or experimental investigation, these inferences remain nothing more than untested hypotheses. While those researchers that use biomechanical approaches appreciate this limitation, there is a widespread tendency for consumers of this work – archaeologists and primatologists – to take biomechanically-generated behavioural hypotheses at face value as complete explanations. It is our goal to show this practice to be unsound.

Current debate about Neanderthal behaviour

One contentious, on-going issue in palaeoanthropology concerns the behavioural attributes of archaic members of the genus *Homo*, and especially late Pleistocene forms such as the Neanderthals. While debate abounds about every aspect of Neanderthal behaviour, from cannibalism (e.g. Tomic-Karovic, 1970; Ullrich, 1978; Trinkaus, 1985; Stiner, 1991a; Defleur *et al.*, 1993) to their capacity for speech, symbolic communication, ritual and culture (e.g. Lieberman & Crelin, 1971; Gargett, 1989 and comments; Arensburg *et al.*, 1990; Laitman *et al.*, 1990, 1991, 1993; Lieberman, 1992; Hayden, 1993; Schepartz, 1993), the issue of hunting and subsistence organisation has probably received the most attention. One point of general agreement is that Neanderthal diet included a high percentage of meat, and that the Neanderthals exploited a diverse spectrum of prey species (Laquay, 1981; Chase, 1986; Fizet, Mariotti & Bellon, 1995; Mellars, 1996). It is also generally accepted that Neanderthals were capable of directed hunting of small-to-moderate sized herbivores, such as reindeer (Chase, 1986, 1988; Binford, 1984, 1985, 1991), wild goats and sheep (Marean, 1998). But here agreement ends, and how the Neanderthals obtained larger prey – whether by hunting or scavenging – remains an issue of considerable discussion. Animal part representation in Mousterian faunal assemblages from the French sites of Combe Grenal and Grotte Vaufrey, and patterns of carnivore damage on human modified (cut-marked) bones in these assemblages led Binford to argue that scavenging of large animals was an important component of archaic human meat procurement (Binford, 1982, 1985, 1987, 1989; see also Binford, 1984 for a comparable argument concerning MSA hominids from Klasies River Mouth, South Africa). Binford suggested that Neanderthals may have lacked the behavioural or technological sophistication sufficient to hunt the full range of available prey species regularly, and that Neanderthal subsistence may have been dependent upon scavenging for success (Binford, 1984, 1985). Stiner (1990, 1991a,b,c, 1993, 1994; Stiner & Kuhn, 1992) presents zooarchaeological evidence from the Italian Mousterian sites of Grotta Guattari and Grotta dei Moscerini that reflects a reduction in the frequency of scavenging and an increase in hunting during the Mousterian rather than at the Middle to Upper Palaeolithic transition (as usually assumed), which she feels reflects adaptive responses to changing ecological conditions. Thus, by Stiner's view, Neanderthals shared with modern humans a well-developed degree of adaptive flexibility, and may better be characterised as 'opportunistic', rather than 'obligate', scavengers. Nonetheless, Binford's claims of obligate scavenging, coupled with an inferred single-animal hunting focus (based on lack of evidence for co-operative game drives and mass kills) suggestive of opportunistic hunting practices in the Mousterian of some regions (Freeman, 1973; Binford, 1982; Straus, 1983; Straus & Clark, 1986), have developed into a general view of Neanderthal subsistence behaviour as lacking planning depth, tactical behaviour and long-term curation of subsistence technology (Binford, 1982, 1989: see also Simek, 1987 for corroborating evidence from spatial patterning of bones and artifacts at two Mousterian sites). By this view, true logistical foraging behaviour is a fully modern human trait that arose at the time of, or after, the appearance of modern humans (Binford, 1985).

A less logistically organised foraging system has also been argued to characterise Levantine Neanderthal subsistence behaviour (Lieberman, 1993; Lieberman & Shea, 1994). Based on season-of-death indicators in gazelle teeth from presumably Neanderthal-generated deposits at Kebara (units VII-X), Tabun (level B) and Qafzeh (levels VII-XV) Caves, Lieberman has argued that Neanderthals may have occupied single sites on a year-round basis. Levantine Mousterian modern humans, on the other hand, are argued to have followed a circulating mobility pattern of seasonal residential moves between sites, as evidenced by seasonality indicators in fauna from the presumably modern human-generated levels at Hayonim (level E), Tabun (levels C and D) and Qafzeh (levels XVI-XXIII). The year-round occupation of sites by Neanderthals must have aggravated the problem of local biodepletion faced by all foragers, necessitating increased foraging mobility and increased hunting intensity. This intensification of hunting and foraging is reflected in the proportions of lithic points – many with impact damage referable to spear use – relative to other tool types in Levantine Neanderthal sites (Shea, 1998; Lieberman & Shea, 1994), and also in elevated muscularity and skeletal robusticity in these hominids relative to Levantine Middle Palaeolithic early modern humans (see Trinkaus, 1992, 1995) (Figure 1). Lieberman & Shea's model of Near Eastern Mousterian subsistence does not address issues of Neanderthal hunting capabilities or reliance on scavenging, but does argue that Levantine Neanderthals were more predatory than their modern human counterparts in order to compensate for resource depletion problems inherent to their mobility strategies (Shea, 1998).

That Neanderthal behaviour differed from that of early modern humans is by no means the consensus view, and numerous arguments have been made that subsistence organisation and hunting behaviour differed little between the Middle and Upper Palaeolithic (e.g. Chase, 1986, 1988, 1989; Farizy & David, 1989; Patou, 1989; Patou-Mathis, 1996; see also Jelinek, Debénath & Dibble, 1989 for purported evidence of mass hunting in the French Mousterian). Most recently, Marean (1998; Marean & Kim, 1998) has argued that the original pattern of faunal part representation upon which Binford based his arguments owes to taphonomic processes and collector bias, not to hominid behaviour. By refitting long bone diaphyseal shaft fragments from small faunal assemblages from Kobeh (Iran) and Die Kelders (South Africa) Caves, Marean has shown the assemblages to be dominated by limb elements (characteristic of hominid access to meaty portions of a carcass and, by inference, hunting) and not foot and axial skeletal parts (characteristic of hominid access to carcasses after they have been ravished by carnivores) as claimed by Binford and others. Marean's conclusions are not universally accepted (see Klein & Cruz-Uribe, 1998; Stiner, 1998), and the debate about Neanderthal subsistence remains open.

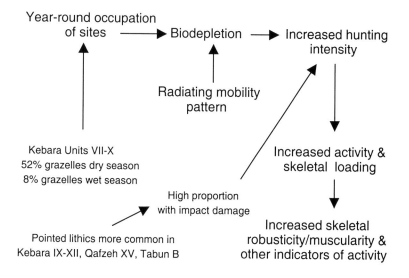

Figure 1
In a model of Levantine Neanderthal subsistence organisation proposed by Dan Lieberman and John Shea (Lieberman, 1993; Lieberman & Shea, 1994), faunal and lithic evidence is argued to reflect a subsistence system based on limited residential mobility that relied on increased foraging intensity to offset local biodepletion. Greater hunting and foraging intensity is reflected in the greater skeletal robusticity of Near Eastern Neanderthals relative to neighbouring Middle Palaeolithic modern humans (see text for details).

Neanderthals contrast with early modern humans, and modern humans generally, in a large number of skeletal features (Trinkaus, 1983, 1986; Churchill, 1996, 1998). These contrasts have proven to be fertile ground for biomechanical and comparative functional-morphological approaches to inferring their behavioural characteristics. One of the most fruitful approaches in the past decade has been the application of geometric analysis of long bone diaphyseal cross-sections, using principles of beam theory, to elucidate the relative magnitude and orientations of habitual loads incurred by the postcranial skeletons of these hominids. Armed with inferred knowledge of these loading regimes in fossil humans, it is possible to postulate the behavioural repertoires that may have produced those loads.

Before reviewing the inferences that have been drawn from this work, it may be helpful to review the biological basis for structural analysis.

Structural analysis of long bones

While working from morphological analysis to behavioural inference is not always straight forward, we do expect skeletal morphology to reflect behaviour, for two reasons.

First, we assume that natural selection has operated to optimise morphology for important behaviours performed by a species (Smith & Savage, 1956), given limitations imposed by genetic, developmental and functional constraints. We can thus think of morphology as having been 'designed' (see Sommerhoff, 1950; Rudwick, 1964; Williams, 1966) to function effectively in the repertoire of behaviours that were critical to the survival and reproduction of our ancestors (notably, food acquisition and predator avoidance) (but see below, and Lauder, 1995, for cautions against uncritically adopting this thinking).

Second, we know from a wealth of experimental and comparative studies that living bone tissue actively adapts to its bio-mechanical environment (e.g. Goodship, Lanyon & McFie, 1979; Lanyon, Magee & Baggott, 1979; Woo *et al.*, 1981; Lanyon & Rubin, 1984). Beginning with early work by Culmann (1866), von Meyer (1867), Roux (1883), Wolff (1892) and Koch (1917), there has been a growing appreciation of the remarkable capacity of the mammalian skeleton to alter its material properties and the shapes of bones in response to changes in mechanical loads (although not all aspects of the skeleton are equally plastic to activity, see below). Cortical tissue in the shafts of long bones is especially responsive to the amount and patterns of stress that habitually pass through them. By examining the amount of cortex in long bone diaphyses, we can say something about the load levels to which the bone was adapted, and make inferences about the activity levels of their owners (see Ruff, 1992 for a review and justifications for this type of research).

Bone modelling (addition or subtraction of bone resulting in changes of gross size and shape) and remodelling (strengthening of bone tissue at the histological level, without change in gross morphology)[1] occurs in the order of a few months (Goodship *et al.*, 1979), thus the amount and distribution of cortical bone tissue likely reflects the average loading history of a particular bone over the last year or so of the life of the individual. Perhaps nowhere is the idea that the geometric structure of bones closely reflects the bone's habitual loading environment, and that bone modelling and remodelling processes result in a certain mechanical economy of bone tissue, more strongly developed than in the early work of Pauwells (1948, 1950, 1954). It was Pauwell's assertions of this relationship that led to the first attempts by Endo & Kimura (1970) to apply long bone cross-sectional analysis to Neanderthals remains.

[1]
See Martin & Burr (1989: 143) for a more complete definition of these terms.

Since skeletal elements add bone tissue in places where stresses and resultant strains are high (and resorbs bone where strain is low), we should, in theory, be able to use the distribution of bone tissue to determine how the average forces to which the bone was subjected were distributed. Armed with the knowledge of loading patterns to which the bone was subjected, we may generate insights into prehistoric behaviour patterns.

In actuality, the relationship between bone shape and loading patterns is not always straightforward. In some cases, there seems to be a direct and predictable relationship between increased loads and bone apposition. In a classic study by Goodship, Lanyon & McFie (1979), a small section of the ulnar shaft was removed from a number of young pigs, resulting in a doubling of the strain produced during locomotion in the associated radius. Within three months, adaptive modelling had added cortical tissue to the radius such that its new cortical area equalled that of the radius plus ulna prior to surgery, with the result that strains in the radius during locomotion had reduced to normal levels. The greatest amount of bone apposition occurred on the surface adjacent to the ulna, resulting in a widening of the bone in the plane of the radius and ulna. This suggests that bone adaptively responds to increased strains by altering both the amount of tissue and the placement of tissue to keep strain levels within a certain range, and supports the idea that there is a direct correspondence between loading regimes and skeletal morphology. However, a number of recent analyses of strain distribution in the craniofacial and postcranial skeletons of a variety of animals indicate that structural reinforcement of skeletal elements is not always in line with usual strains engendered during mastication or locomotion (Lanyon & Rubin, 1985; Rubin, McLeod & Bain, 1990; Hylander & Johnson, 1992; Daegling, 1993; Demes *et al.*, 1998). These results prompted Demes and colleagues (1998: 96) to remark that "*… bone cross-sectional geometry may not be a simple mirror reflection of functional loads*", calling into question the sagacity of uncritically reading prehistoric behaviour from analysis of bone geometry.

It should also be noted that different aspects of the skeletal system vary in their ability to adaptively remodel under changing stress levels and patterns. The lengths of long bones and the size and morphology of their articular surfaces show limited adaptability, generally only prior to skeletal maturity (Ruff, Scott & Liu, 1991; Ruff & Runestad, 1992; Trinkaus, Churchill & Ruff, 1994). Thus, between-group differences in mean measures of joint size or shape are more likely to reflect the evolutionary-selective history of the group (and, to some degree, juvenile behaviour of the individuals), while studies of long bone shaft morphology provide more fine-grained information about individual behaviour.

The vast majority of structural studies have relied on geometric analysis of long bone diaphyseal cross-sections. In this method, bones are modelled as hollow, cylindrical beams and the contribution of bone geometry to the resistance of biomechanical loads is calculated using

2)
The term 'robusticity' was originally employed in physical anthropology to refer to ratios of external bone dimensions (usually long bone diaphyseal diameters) to bone length, and hence as a measure of the relative stoutness of the bones. Traditional robusticity ratios have been shown to be unreliable measures of the mechanical strength (or more accurately, the contribution of bone geometry to mechanical strength) of long bones (Ruff *et al.*, 1993; Jungers, Burr & Cole, 1999). Ruff and colleagues (1993) have argued that cross-sectional geometric properties, standardised to the appropriate power of bone length, are better indicators of relative bone strength. These ratios serve as static measures of relative strength, and are directly analogous to the indices of athletic ability (or manoeuverability) championed by Alexander (1989). Despite the historical context of the term, it is this later meaning that is invoked in most recent discussions of robusticity. We are also quick to point out that robusticity ratios, while producing relative measures of bone strength, are not free of size effects (see Jungers & Burr, 1994; Jungers *et al.*, 1999), and thus robusticity comparisons across groups of different mean body sizes should be done with caution.

principles of engineering beam theory (see Ruff & Hayes, 1983; Ruff, 1992; Lieberman, 1997 for details of the conceptual basis, analytical methods and potential pitfalls of this type of research). When considered relative to mechanically relevant measures of body size, these measures provide an indication of the relative strength, or robusticity (*sensu* Ruff *et al.*, 1993)[2] of the skeleton and thus the magnitude of the loads to which it was subjected. Strength measures determined from cross-sections serve as more sensitive indicators of robusticity than do measures of external dimensions of long bone shafts, since they also take into consideration the internal geometry of the compact bone (Ruff *et al.*, 1993; Jungers, Burr & Cole, 1999). Since direct sectioning of fossil human long bones is unthinkable, cross-sections are generally determined non-invasively by radiographic means. Measures of cross-sectional cortical area provide an indication of the strength of the diaphysis in compression and tension, while second and polar moments of area (determined from both the amount and distribution of cortical tissue in the section) reflect the resistance of the shaft to bending and torsional moments at that diaphyseal level. Measures of cross-sectional shape, such as the ratio of two orthogonal second moments of area, provide an indication of the orientation of predominant bending moments in the diaphysis. The relationship of these variables to diaphyseal biomechanical strength is discussed in more detail in Jungers & Minns (1979), Ruff & Hayes (1983), and Ruff (1992).

Structural analysis applied to Neanderthals

Biomechanical approaches to Neanderthal behaviour have involved three very different comparative frameworks.

The first of these concerns comparisons between Eurasian Middle Palaeolithic-associated Neanderthals and Upper Palaeolithic-associated early anatomically modern humans (and sometimes also including more recent Holocene foraging groups). This comparison is done in the context of an archaeological artefactual record that indicates substantial behavioural differences between the groups.

The cultural transition from Middle-to-Upper Palaeolithic, at least as reflected in the archaeological record, was one of technological refinement of lithic core reduction techniques and an emerging emphasis on blade production, a shift in emphasis on certain tool types (notably an increased abundance of well-defined end scrapers and burins) and introduction of 'new' types (e.g. crescents and obliquely retouched blades), increased standardisation of lithic blanks and finished pieces, and refinement of bone and antler working techniques (reviewed in Mellars, 1989). The extent to which these technological changes reflect changes in the adaptive realm (especially with respect to subsistence behaviour) remains an open question, and it is with regard to this issue that structural analyses have been most profitably applied.

The second comparative framework concerns the elucidation of behavioural similarities and differences between Near Eastern Neanderthals and early modern humans, both associated with Levantine Middle Palaeolithic technology. The association of two morphologically distinct hominid groups with typologically similar – if not identical – Mousterian industries (Binford, 1968; Jelinek, 1982; Trinkaus, 1984; Clark & Lindly, 1989) and very similar faunal assemblages has raised a host of questions about the adaptive strategies of these two groups, as well as about the relationships between the typological characteristics of lithic assemblages, hominid behaviour, and morphology (see Smith, Falsetti & Donnelly, 1989; Trinkaus, 1992, 1995; Harrold, 1992; Churchill, 1997). Studies of the lithic record of the Levantine Mousterian that go beyond traditional typological comparisons have suggested that important behavioural differences existed between Neanderthals and early modern humans in this region (Shea, 1989, 1998; Lieberman & Shea, 1994), and as discussed above, this conclusion has been supported by interpretations of seasonality indicators in the fauna from Neanderthal and early modern human sites in the Levant (Lieberman, 1993; Lieberman & Shea, 1994).

Functional morphological studies of the two groups have long suggested important behavioural-adaptive contrasts, as reflected in differences in postcranial robusticity and muscularity, anterior dental wear, ulnar trochlear notch orientation, femoral neck-shaft angles and femoral shaft dimensions (Trinkaus, 1992). Structural analysis of long bones has recently been used to refine our understanding of the behavioural contrasts between these groups, and to develop a greater appreciation of why two independent records of behaviour – one archaeological and one morphological – provide such contrasting pictures.

Finally, structural analyses have been applied to the question of behavioural contrasts between early Upper Palaeolithic-associated Neanderthals and early modern humans in Europe. The recovery of Neanderthals from the typologically Upper Palaeolithic (but with technological ties to the earlier Mousterian) Châtelperronian industry at La Roche à Pierrot (St. Césaire: Lévêque & Vandermeersch, 1980) and Arcy-sur-Cure (Grotte du Renne: Hublin *et al.*, 1996) has raised new questions about behavioural shifts that occurred at the time the Upper Palaeolithic was becoming established in Europe, and how those shifts might relate to morphological differences between Neanderthals and early modern humans.

Three general scenarios have been put forth to account for the Châtelperronian phenomenon, including the idea that the Châtelperronian represents an intermediate, transitional stage in the unilineal evolution of European Middle into Upper Palaeolithic culture; the idea that the Châtelperronian is the result of acculturation of Neanderthal populations through contact with Aurignacian-bearing peoples (presumably modern humans); and the idea that the Châtelperronian was the result of ecological competition with invading

Aurignacian peoples, which forced the Neanderthals to invent new technological means of exploiting resources (see D'Errico *et al.*, 1998 for a review). By better defining the habitual behaviour patterns of Châtelperronian Neanderthals, structural analysis may be able to contribute some resolution to this issue. Of the three sets of comparisons, this last is the most hampered by sample size constraints, since only one Châtelperronian Neanderthal – the adult male from St. Césaire – preserves long bones (and very fragmentary ones at that). Structural analyses of Neanderthal long bones have generally been applied to questions concerning two behavioural realms: mobility patterning and manipulative differences. We will address each of these in turn, within the context of the comparative frameworks outlined above.

Mobility patterning

Geometric analyses of lower limb long bone (femoral and tibial) cross-sections have been used to compare European Mousterian Neanderthals with Upper Palaeolithic modern humans (Lovejoy & Trinkaus, 1980; Trinkaus & Ruff, 1989a,b; Ruff *et al.*, 1993), Levantine Mousterian Neanderthals with Levantine Mousterian modern humans (Endo & Kimura, 1970; Trinkaus, Ruff & Churchill, 1998), and the St. Césaire Châtelperronian Neanderthal with early Upper Palaeolithic modern humans (Trinkaus *et al.*, 1998, 1999). All of these studies have produced consistent results. Relative to early modern humans (regardless of archaeological context), Neanderthals tend to have lower limb bones that are robust (having elevated measures of resistance to compressive, tensile, bending and torsional loads) when long bone length (as a measure of stature) is used to standardise the strength measures. However, relative to measures of body mass (such as femoral head diameter, or mass estimated from long bone length and bi-iliac breadth) there is no significant difference between groups. Body mass is arguably the most mechanically relevant measure of body size when considering lower limb remains, since it is body mass under the acceleration of gravity and the acceleration and deceleration of body mass during locomotion, that produces the predominant forces on the lower limb. Thus, when the greater breadth of the trunk (and hence greater mass for a given stature) of Neanderthals is taken into consideration, the apparent differences in lower limb robusticity disappear. This suggests (but see below) that mobility levels overall were similar between Neanderthals and early modern humans, across each of the comparative contexts. This result holds for comparison of lower limb bone strength between Levantine Neanderthals and early modern humans as well (Trinkaus *et al.*, 1998), which does not support the idea of significant differences in mobility levels between these groups (*contra* Lieberman & Shea, 1994). Similar adult mobility levels (but not necessarily subadult levels, see below) in Levantine Mousterian groups is further indicated by similarities in femoral histology (Abbott, Trinkaus & Burr, 1996), talar proportions and pedal phalangeal dimensions (Trinkaus & Hilton, 1996).

However, differences in cross-sectional shape of the lower limb bones suggest that important differences existed in the patterns of locomotion between these groups. Early modern human femora have mid-shaft cross-sections that are teardrop shaped with large pilasters on the dorsal surface. This results in bones with large second moments of inertia in the anteroposterior plane, and thus resistant to the kinds of bending stresses incurred by the femur during bipedal locomotion. Neanderthal femoral shafts tend to be sub-circular in section (i.e., having nearly equal second moments of inertia in both the anteroposterior and mediolateral planes), reflecting greater mediolateral expansion of the shaft (Trinkaus & Ruff, 1989a,b; Trinkaus *et al.*, 1998, 1999). In all of the comparisons, Neanderthal femora are generally more resistant to mediolaterally directed bending stresses, thus showing a greater resistance to bending moments in all directions, relative to the anteroposteriorly reinforced femora of early modern humans. This pattern is reflected as well, albeit not as markedly, in the tibia.

A number of behavioural explanations have been posited to account for these morphological differences, including the possibility that Neanderthal movement on the landscape was more irregular and less directed than those of modern humans, or that Neanderthals experienced high levels of lateral upper body movement (as in forcefully thrusting a spear) that required greater effort with the legs to stabilise the body, or that the more lateral body build (i.e., wider trunks) of Neanderthals created greater mediolateral bending moments in their lower limbs, or some combination of two or more of these explanations (Trinkaus & Ruff, 1989a).

Differences in the relative strength of the lower limbs of recent (Holocene) peoples have typically been argued to reflect differences in mobility levels between groups (Ruff, Larsen & Hayes, 1984; Bridges, 1985, 1989; Holt, 1997; Stock & Pfeiffer, 1998), and these inferences have generally accorded very well with ethnohistoric or archaeological evidence of mobility in these groups. While the similarity in lower limb bone strength in Neanderthals and early modern humans would suggest similarities in locomotor levels, it is not entirely certain that differences between individuals or groups in mobility levels *should* be reflected in the robusticity of the lower limb.

There is a growing consensus among bone biologists that the critical stimulus triggering adaptive remodelling is the magnitude of the strain engendered in the bone during loading, not the number of loading cycles. For instance, Rubin & Lanyon (1984) found that a small number of loading cycles (36) that produce strain levels above a certain threshold were sufficient to stimulate adaptive modelling and remodelling, while an increase beyond 36 (up to 1800 cycles) had no appreciable effect on further osteogenic activity. Numerical models (Whalen, Carter & Steele, 1988; Beaupré, Orr & Carter, 1990a,b) and numerous clinical/experimental studies (reviewed in Skerry & Lanyon, 1995) support the claim that only a small number of cycles is needed to reach a saturated osteogenic response if the load is of sufficient magnitude. This has important implications for analyses of between group variation in lower limb robusticity.

If lower limb loads produced during walking are of sufficient magnitude to either prevent bone loss or stimulate bone formation, a saturated osteogenic response would be achieved within the first hundred metres of locomotion (within 36 loading cycles, or strides), and thus one would not predict a difference in bone mass or distribution in the lower limbs of human groups differing in mobility – humans that walk one kilometre a day should have the same relative bone strength (robusticity) as people who walk 40 kilometres a day.

Bone biologists disagree about the primary 'mechanical stimulus' in osteoregulation, and all of the following have been proposed: fatigue damage, strain energy density, strain rate, strain gradients, and abnormal strain distributions (see Martin & Burr, 1989 for a review). Of these, the only mechanism that would be consistent with the observed patterning in human skeletal material would be fatigue damage. Microfractures may develop from a few cycles of high magnitude loading or, more importantly, from many cycles of a lower magnitude load. Thus mobility differences between groups may result in different amounts of fatigue damage and hence different modelling and remodelling responses. However, at physiological loading levels during walking, roughly 10^8 loading cycles would be required to bring a femur to failure through fatigue (King & Evans, 1967), and as noted by Currey (1984:82): "*A person walking at a brisk 100 steps a minute, 10 hours a day, would take 9 years to reach this number of cycles on one leg bone.*" If the risk of fatigue damage from walking is so low, we might reasonably wonder if even the highest foraging or residential mobility levels among humans would ever be sufficient to stimulate appositional modelling and increased lower limb diaphyseal robusticity.

Additionally, if a mechanism other than fatigue damage provides the primary osteogenic signal, the conventional interpretation of variation in human lower limb skeletal robusticity would still require re-evaluation. While this remains an open issue, it is important to bear in mind that the lack of difference in lower limb robusticity, and by inference mobility levels, between Neanderthals and early modern humans may have more to do with the inadequacy of structural analysis for detecting mobility differences than in actual similarity between groups.

The Levantine Neanderthals do contrast with their modern human sympatriots in femoral neck-shaft angle, which may suggest that differences in mobility levels did exist between these groups (Trinkaus, 1993). The orientation of the femoral neck is very responsive to loading during childhood (Tardieu & Trinkaus, 1994), and the lower neck-shaft angle seen in Neanderthals has been taken to imply differing levels of childhood mobility in the Levantine Mousterian groups (Trinkaus, 1993). This difference has been suggested to reflect differences in social organisation in Levantine Neanderthals and early modern humans, with Neanderthal children having remained with foraging parties (thus engaging in long distance mobility from an early age) while modern human children stayed at the residential site without accompanying foraging parties.

Manipulative behaviour

As with studies of the lower limb, structural analyses of upper limb remains have been conducted within the context of European Mousterian Neanderthals – Upper Palaeolithic modern human comparisons (Ben-Itzhak, Smith & Bloom, 1988; Churchill, 1993, 1994; Ruff *et al.*, 1993; Churchill, Weaver & Niewoehner, 1996), Levantine Mousterian Neanderthal – Levantine Mousterian modern human comparisons (Smith, Bloom & Berkowitz, 1983; Trinkaus *et al.*, 1998; Trinkaus & Churchill, 1999), and a comparison of the St. Césaire Neanderthal with early Upper Palaeolithic modern humans (Trinkaus *et al.*, 1999).

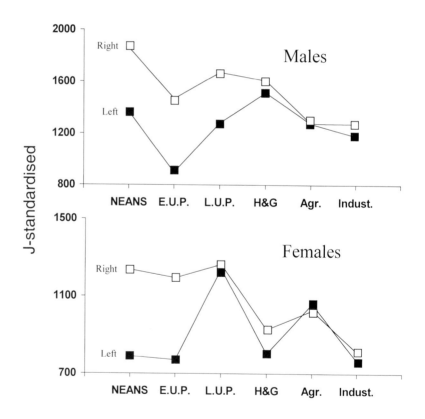

Figure 2
Average polar moment of inertia (J) standardised to body size in Neanderthal (NEANS), Early Upper Palaeolithic (E.U.P.), Late Upper Palaeolithic (L.U.P.) and recent modern human male and female samples. Recent modern human samples include hunter-gatherers (H&G) and pre-European contact agriculturalists from the Georgia Coast, and autopsy samples of recent European-Americans (data from Churchill *et al.*, 1996). Body size standardisation was done using humeral length raised to the forth power (J-standardised = $[J/HL^4] * 10^9$).

Where lower limb robusticity seemed to reflect similarity between groups in load levels, upper limb robusticity consistently reflects differences between Neanderthals and early modern humans in loads produced by manipulation, at least in members of one sex. Among males, there is a statistically significant difference in mean measures of body-size standardised humeral strength between the more robust Neanderthals and the more gracile early Upper Palaeolithic-associated modern humans (Churchill *et al.*, 1996) (Figure 2). This temporal decline is followed by an increase in humeral strength in the later Upper Palaeolithic (Figure 2).

Some of this temporal change in robusticity is attributable to temporal variation in mean body size, but body size change alone cannot account for the whole pattern (Churchill, Wall & Schmitt, unpublished data). Sample sizes are smaller for the comparisons concerning females, and in some instances comparisons are based on single specimens representing a fossil group. Based on these meagre samples, Neanderthals and early modern European females do not appear to differ substantially in size-corrected measures of humeral strength (Figure 2). With respect to humeral robusticity, it appears that there was a trend in males for a significant reduction from Neanderthals to early Upper Palaeolithic humans indicating a reduction in upper limb activity levels between these groups. This trend is also evident in measures of articular robusticity and muscularity (Churchill, 1994).

However, overall diaphyseal cross-sectional shape and patterns of right-left asymmetry are similar in these two groups (Churchill, 1994; Churchill *et al.*, 1996), suggesting similarity in manipulative patterns. A similar pattern is seen when Levantine Neanderthals and early modern humans are compared (Trinkaus & Churchill, 1999). Again, the early modern humans are, as a group, significantly weaker in measures of humeral strength (especially in the right limb), but tend to have similar diaphyseal shapes and similar levels of right-left asymmetry (Trinkaus & Churchill, 1999). In this regard not much can be said about Châtelperronian-associated Neanderthals, since the single specimen with adequate postcranial remains (St. Césaire 1) preserves only fragmentary remains of the left humerus, radius and ulna. In measures of diaphyseal robusticity of these bones, St. Césaire falls with other Neanderthal left-side upper limb remains, or in-between Neanderthal and early Upper Palaeolithic males. Neanderthal upper limbs, then, show a pattern opposite that seen in the lower limbs – with diaphyseal shapes similar to those of early modern humans, but with robusticity differences suggesting higher levels of habitual manipulative loads having been resisted by the arms of Neanderthals. This pattern has been used to argue that Neanderthals and early modern humans may have engaged in similar foraging practices, perhaps reflecting an emphasis among males on close-range hunting with thrusting spears (Churchill *et al.*, 1996), albeit in the context of differences in subsistence organisation that may have reduced the total need for labour input by early modern humans. The results of the analysis of Near Eastern hominid upper limbs support the model proposed by Lieberman & Shea (1994; Lieberman, 1993; Shea, 1998) suggesting greater predatory frequency among Levantine Neanderthals.

Previous functional analyses of the morphology of the scapular glenoid fossa led to the suggestion that the Neanderthal shoulder joint – which tends to be relatively dorsoventrally narrow – was not well adapted to the high dorsoventral joint reaction forces generated at this joint during throwing (Churchill & Trinkaus, 1990). Both Neanderthals and early Upper Palaeolithic males tend to have anteroposteriorly reinforced right-side humeral shafts – that is, to have diaphyses with greater second moments of inertia in the anteroposterior plane, and are hence more resistant to bending in that plane. Churchill *et al.*, (1996) have argued that this kind of reinforcement would be consistent with habitual thrusting spear use, since substantial bending moments would be expected to occur in the dominant limb as the humeral flexors (e.g. *M. pectoralis major*) work against resistance. Late Upper Palaeolithic males tend to have right-side humeral shafts that are more rounded in section – a configuration more conducive to resisting bending in multiple planes as well as torsional moments. Forceful throwing produces high torsional loads in the humerus (references in Churchill *et al.*, 1996), and the appearance of this morphology in male arms is coincident with archaeological evidence (namely spear throwers) of increased emphasis on throwing-based, long range hunting technology in the late Upper Palaeolithic. An unexpected finding concerns the similar, high amounts of humeral bilateral asymmetry in all three groups (Figure 2). Churchill *et al.*, (1996) argue that use of thrusting spears is an *apparently* bimanual behaviour but is mechanically better seen as a unimanual activity – that is, the real force of the thrust and withdrawal (and hence bending moments in the humerus) comes from the dominant limb. Thus asymmetry signatures may be the same for habitual hand-held, thrusting spears use and for habitual throwing (but humeral diaphyseal shape would still be expected to differ).

Thus recent structural analyses suggest important differences between Neanderthals and early modern humans in patterns of lower limb loading and in levels of upper limb loading. Null hypotheses of similarity in levels of lower limb loading and patterns of upper limb loading cannot currently be rejected. At face value, these results support claims of important adaptive/behavioural contrasts between these late archaic and modern humans, although the exact nature of these differences remains uncertain. Having arrived at this position, it would be tempting to treat these findings as conclusive and to use them to winnow archaeologically derived inferences. We hope that we have drawn attention to the challenges inherent in reconstructing behaviour from long bone structure – the main difficulties being uncertainty about the precise mechanical stimulus to which bone adaptively responds and the empirical finding that maximum *in vivo* bone strains do not always fall along the planes of maximum bone strength – and because of these complications we concur with Daegling (1993: 247) that "… *the inference of … stress patterns from purely morphological criteria in the absence of experimental corroboration is problematic*."

Experimental testing of biomechanical inferences

Engineering models, such as structural analysis based on beam theory, are a critical first step in determining structure-function relationships for fossil hominids and inferring behaviour from these relationships. Engineering models represent an important part of an 'argument from design' approach to functional morphology, as reviewed and critiqued by Lauder (1995, 1996). They must not, however, be viewed as conclusive explanations, but rather as hypotheses to be tested.

This is not a new caveat for functional morphologists in either basic biology (as reviewed by Homberger, 1988) or biological anthropology (as reviewed by Fleagle, 1979, and Jouffroy, 1989). There is a long history in both fields of experimental studies being used effectively to test functional/engineering models, and recently, the field of ecomorphology, with its emphasis on 'performance studies', has further developed the use of experimental protocols to test engineering-based hypotheses (e.g. Losos, 1990). Nonetheless, the majority of functional morphologists concerned with primate evolution do not test their functional models with independent experimental data, a problem that extends to researchers interested in reconstructing behaviour in extinct members of the genus *Homo* as well (a situation that has forced us to rely heavily on examples from primate functional morphology in illustrating the experimental approaches discussed below).

In the absence of experimental data, researchers tend to rely on comparative anatomy for confirmation of their models (as an example from primate functional morphology, the prediction that long legs are mechanically critical for leaping primates is seen to be confirmed by the observation that other leaping animals have long legs). This mode of checking functional models generally leads to correct conclusions, but as Bock (1977), Homberger (1988) and others have noted, this is not always the case. Most recently, both Michael Rose and George Lauder (Lauder, 1996; Rose, Nusbaum & Chippendale, 1996) have reviewed and described in detail the limitations of a simple modelling approach in the absence of experiment. In an extensive analysis of the problem, Lauder (1996) rejects the widely-held notion that engineering models can somehow be used to discern the function (mechanical role) of a structure and, by extension, its biological role (the mechanical role for a given organism in a given ecological context). He points out two critical weaknesses in drawing conclusions from engineering models, models that he deems fundamentally 'assumptive in character': (1) structure and mechanical function are not necessarily closely related, and (2) relevant design criteria cannot be easily identified *a priori*. He concludes by calling for rigorous experimental analysis of structure-function relationships: "... *in our desire to draw conclusions about biological design and to support theoretical views of how organism are built, we have been too willing to make assumptions about the relationship between structure and mechanical function ... and ... we have not often conducted the mechanical and performance tests needed to assess the average quality of organismal design.*" (Lauder, 1996:56) Rose *et al.* (1996: 221) add that evolutionary theories are like "... *Victorian schoolgirls, dressed up entirely in white and severely scrubbed*', cautioning that "... *while theories may be pretty to look at, they may not be that robust after all when confronted with the dangers of the real, empirical world."*

This view is not new to biological anthropology. In 1950, Sherwood Washburn called for "... *a modern, experimental comparative anatomy to take its place among the tools of the students of human evolution*" (Washburn, 1950:68). When Washburn called for this approach, experimental analysis in biological anthropology was in its infancy, with the work of Hildebrand (1931), and Elftman and Manter (1935) representing the bulk of experimental work on primate functional morphology. Since 1950 a great deal of progress has been made with the advent of detailed kinematic (e.g. Hildebrand, 1967, 1977; Alexander & Maloiy, 1984), cineradiographic (e.g. Jenkins, 1972; Whitehead & Larson, 1994; Wall, 1995), electromyographic (e.g. Tuttle & Basmajian, 1974; Stern *et al.*, 1977, 1980; Hylander & Johnson, 1985), force plate (e.g. Kimura, Okada & Ishida, 1979; Reynolds, 1985; Demes *et al.*, 1994; Schmitt, 1999), and strain gauge studies (e.g. Hylander, 1979; Demes *et al.*, 1998) [a thorough review of all of these techniques is beyond the scope of this chapter, but a detailed discussion of the appropriate use and technical requirements of all these methods can be found in Biewener (1992)]. In a hallmark article published in 1979, Fleagle reviewed the progress made since 1950 and renewed the call for experimentation, saying "*Regardless of how mechanically plausible and convincing [functional] explanations may be, they can be rigorously tested only by in-vivo studies.*" (Fleagle, 1979: 316).

To anyone familiar with the experimental studies cited above, it is clear that Fleagle's call has been heeded for studies of living primates, and that a marriage of mechanical arguments from design with experimental analyses has brought us to a new understanding of structure-function relationships in primates and furthered our understanding of primate evolution. This increased appreciation of form-function relationships has also lent itself readily to the business of inferring behaviour in early hominids. This dual approach has not, however, extended into studies of the biobehavioural characteristics of pre-modern members of the genus *Homo*. This phenomenon is both emblematic of the immaturity of experimental approaches in hominid palaeoanthropology and illustrative of how the limits of the conceptual design of experimental studies restrict their application to palaeo-anthropology.

Experimental analysis in primate palaeoanthropology follows a 'bracketing' approach (see Lauder, 1995; Witmer, 1995 for reviews) in which experimental data are collected from closely related extant forms that appear to lie to either side of the fossil in question in terms of relevant morphological or behavioural condition (for example, African apes and living humans are generally seen as bracketing the locomotor repertoire of *Australopithecus afarensis*), an approach that has been argued to serve "... *as the rationale for experimental studies of early hominid behaviour*" (Susman, 1998: 27). What are the possible outcomes of using a bracketing approach to determine structure-function relationships, and how might this method be applied to Neanderthal morphology? Certainly one possibility is that a given biomechanical model will be supported, a common but not universal outcome. An example of this kind of outcome is the finding, from airflow studies in modern humans (Churchill *et al.*, 1999), that downwardly directed nostrils, as found in modern Europeans and as inferred for Neanderthals based on the morphology of the skeletal nasal aperture, function (as has long been thought – based on arguments from design) to increase airflow turbulence and facilitate heat and moisture exchange across the nasal mucosa.

Alternatively, the mechanical model relating structure to function may be found to be in error but the underlying correlation between structure and behaviour will remain. In this case experimental studies lead researchers to a new understanding of the mechanical relationship between a trait and its function, and may lead to novel areas for investigation that were previously obscured by the spurious functional relationship espoused in the model. As an example from primate functional morphology, it is well known that terrestrial primates can be separated effectively from arboreal primates by the presence on the proximal humerus of a large protruding tuberosity for attachment of *M. supraspinatus*. Based on an argument from design, this feature was initially believed to be related to rapid protraction of the forelimb during the swing phase in terrestrial locomotion. Larson & Stern (1989) analysed the EMG activity patterns of *M. supraspinatus* in baboons, vervets and macaques, and found that, contrary to the intuitively appealing and sensible conclusions of previous functional models, *M. supraspinatus* is not active during the swing phase of locomotion. Rather, the muscle shows strong bursts during support phase (when the limb is being retracted). Larson & Stern (1989) suggested that in both arboreal and terrestrial species *M. supraspinatus* prevents excessively rapid flexion at the glenohumeral joint, thus the difference in joint morphology between arboreal and terrestrial primates appears to be related to a need for mobility in arboreal primates, rather than being related to muscle function.

A final possibility is that experimental studies will change our perception of mechanical relationships and also change our inferences about behaviour. An example of this type of outcome, again from the primate functional morphology literature, is the conclusion of Stern & Susman (1983) that the orientation of the iliac blade in apes, when combined with a flexed hindlimb posture, employs the lesser gluteal muscles as pelvic stabilisers. This result provided an entirely new (albeit controversial) interpretation of the functional significance of the pelvis in *Australopithecus*. A more startling example, and one integral to structural analysis of Neanderthal postcrania, concerns strain gauge research discussed above (e.g. Lanyon & Rubin,1985; Demes *et al.*, 1998) that suggests that the direction and magnitude of principal strain is not only difficult to predict from skeletal morphology, but often the opposite of what is expected. This raises questions about the functional interpretation of Neanderthal limb morphology reviewed above, and

Stiner MC. 1991a. The faunal remains from Grotta Guattari: A taphonomic perspective. *Current Anthropology.* **32:** 103-117.

Stiner MC. 1991b. Food procurement and transport by human and non-human predators. *Journal of Archaeological Science.* **18:** 455-482.

Stiner MC. 1991c. An interspecific perspective on the emergence of the modern human predatory niche. In: Stiner MC. ed. *Human Predators and Prey Mortality.* Boulder, Colorado: Westview Press.

Stiner MC. 1993. Small animal exploitation and its relation to hunting, scavenging, and gathering in the Italian Mousterian. In: Peterkin GL, Bricker HM, Mellars PA. eds. *Hunting and Animal Exploitation in the Later Paleolithic and Mesolithic of Eurasia.* Archeological Papers of the American Anthropological Association Number **4:** 107-125.

Stiner MC. 1994. *Honor Among Thieves: A Zooarchaeological Study of Neandertal Ecology.* Princeton: Princeton University Press.

Stiner MC. 1998. Comment on 'Mousterian large-mammal remains from Kobeh Cave: Behavioral implications for Neanderthals and early modern humans' by Marean CW, & Kim SY. *Current Anthropology.* **39:** S98-S103.

Stiner MC, Kuhn SL. 1992. Subsistence, technology, and adaptive variation in Middle Paleolithic Italy. *American Anthropologist.* **94:** 306-339.

Stock J, Pfeiffer S. 1998. Structural variability in the long bone diaphyses of small-bodied hunter-gatherers. Paper presented at the Dual Congress of the International Association for the Study of Human Palaeontology and the International Association of Human Biologists, Johannesburg RSA, July 1998.

Straus LG. 1983. From Mousterian to Magdalenian: Cultural evolution viewed from Vasco-Cantabrian Spain & Pyrenean France. In: Trinkaus E. ed. *The Mousterian Legacy: Human Biocultural Change in the Upper Pleistocene.* Oxford: British Archaeological Reports International Series.

Straus LG, Clark G. 1986. *La Riera Cave.* Tempe, AZ: Arizona State University Anthropological Research Papers Number 36.

Susman RL. 1994. Fossil evidence for early hominid tool use. *Science.* **265:** 1570-1573.

Susman RL. 1998. Hand function and tool behavior in early hominids. *Journal of Human Evolution.* **35:** 23-46.

Tardieu C, Trinkaus E. 1994. Early ontogeny of the human femoral bicondylar angle. *American Journal of Physical Anthropology.* **95:** 183-195.

Tomic-Karovic K. 1970. Krapinski Neandertalac i Kanibalizam. In: Malez M, ed. *Krapina 1899-1969.* Zagreb: Jugoslavenska Akademija Znanosti i Umjetnosti.

Trinkaus E. 1983. Neandertal postcrania and the adaptive shift to modern humans. In: Trinkaus E. ed. *The Mousterian Legacy: Human Biocultural Changes in the Upper Pleistocene.* Oxford: British Archaeological Reports International Series.

Trinkaus E. 1984. Western Asia. In: Smith FH, Spencer F. eds. *The Origins of Modern Humans: A World Survey of the Fossil Evidence.* New York: Alan R. Liss, Inc.

Trinkaus E. 1985. Cannibalism and burial at Krapina. *Journal of Human Evolution.* **14:** 203-216.

Trinkaus E. 1986. The Neandertals and modern human origins. *Annual Review of Anthropology.* **15:** 193-218.

Trinkaus E. 1992. Morphological contrasts between the Near Eastern Qafzeh-Skhul and late archaic human samples: Grounds for a behavioral difference? In: Akazawa T, Aoki K, Kimura T. eds. *The Evolution and Dispersal of Modern Humans in Asia.* Tokyo: Hokusen-sha Publishing.

Trinkaus E. 1993. Femoral neck-shaft angles of the Qafzeh-Skhul early modern humans, and activity levels among immature Near Eastern Paleolithic hominids. *Journal of Human Evolution.* **25:** 393-416.

Trinkaus E. 1995. Near Eastern late archaic humans. *Paléorient.* **21:** 9-23.

Trinkaus E, Churchill SE. 1999. Diaphyseal cross-sectional geometry of Near Eastern Middle Paleolithic humans: The humer. *Journal of Archeological Science.* in press.

Trinkaus E, Hilton CE. 1996. Neandertal pedal proximal phalanges: Diaphyseal loading patterns. *Journal of Human Evolution.* **30:** 399-425.

Trinkaus E, Ruff CB. 1989a. Cross-sectional geometry of Neandertal femoral and tibial diaphyses: Implications for locomotion. *American Journal of Physical Anthropology.* **78:** 315-316 (abstract).

Trinkaus E, Ruff CB. 1989b. Diaphyseal cross-sectional morphology and biomechanics of the Fond-de-Foret and the Spy 2 femur and tibia. *Anthropologie et Prehistoire.* **100:** 33-42.

Trinkaus E, Churchill SE, Ruff CB. 1994. Postcranial robusticity in *Homo.* II: Humeral bilateral asymmetry and bone plasticity. *American Journal of Physical Anthropology.* **93:** 1-34.

Trinkaus E, Churchill SE, Ruff CB, Vandermeersch B. 1999. Long bone shaft robusticity and body proportions of the Saint-Césaire 1 Châtelperronian Neandertal. *Journal of Archeological Science.* **26:** 753-773.

Trinkaus E, Ruff CB, Churchill SE. 1998. Upper limb versus lower limb loading patterns among Near Eastern Middle Paleolithic hominids. In: Akazawa T, Aoki K, Bar Yosef O. eds. *Neanderthals and Modern Humans in Western Asia.* New York: Plenum Press.

Trinkaus E, Ruff CB, Churchill SE, Vandermeersch B. 1998. Locomotion and body proportions of the Saint-Césaire 1 Châtelperronian Neandertal. *Proceedings of the National Academy of Sciences USA.* **95:** 5836-5840.

Tuttle R, Basmajian J. 1974. Electromyography of the brachial muscles in *Pan, Gorilla* and hominoid evolution. *American Journal of Physical Anthropology.* **41:** 71-90.

Ullrich H. 1978. Kannibalismus und Leichenzerstuckelung beim Neandertaler von Krapina. In: Malez M. ed. *Krapinski Pracovjek i Evolucija Hominida.* Zagreb: Jugoslavenska Akademija Znanosti i Umjetnosti.

Von Meyer H. 1867. Die architektur der spongiosa. *Archiv fur Anatomie, Physiologie und Wissenschaftliche Medicin.* **34:** 615-628.

Wall CE. 1995. Form and function of the temporomandibular joint in anthropoid primates. [Unpublished PhD thesis], State University of New York at Stony Brook.

Washburn SL. 1950. The analysis of primate evolution with particular reference to the origin of man. *Cold Spring Harbor Symposium on Quantitative Biology.* **15:** 67-78.

Whalen RT, Carter DR, Steel CR. 1988. Influence of physical activity on the regulation of bone density. *Journal of Biomechanics.* **21:** 825-837.

Whitehead PF, Larson SG. 1994. Shoulder motion during quadrupedal walking in *Cercopithecus aethiops:* Integration of cineradiographic and electromyographic data. *Journal of Human Evolution.* **26:** 525-544.

Williams GC. 1966. *Adaptation and Natural Selection.* Princeton: Princeton University Press.

Witmer LM. 1995. The extant phylogenetic bracket and the importance of reconstructing soft tissues in fossils. In: Thomasen JJ. ed. *Functional Morphology in Vertebrate Paleontology.* Cambridge: Cambridge University Press.

Wolff J. 1892. *Das Gesetz der Transformation der Knochen.* Berlin: A. Hirschwald.

Woo SL-Y, Kuei SC, Amiel D, Gomez MA, Hayes WC, White FC, Akeson WH. 1981. The effect of prolonged physical training on the properties of long bone: A study of Wolff's Law. *Journal of Bone and Joint Surgery.* **63A:** 780-787.

New Perspectives in
Mind & Cognition

The evolution of speech in relation to language and thought

P. LIEBERMAN

Introduction

In recent years, as linguists have begun to study the evolution of language they have followed the course set by Noam Chomsky, focussing on syntax which they often equate with 'true' language. This discussion differs. I shall argue that speech is the key element of human language, the derived property that sets it apart from the communications systems of other species. I shall also propose that subcortical basal ganglia structures are crucial components of the neural system that regulates human speech and language. Structures such as the basal ganglia, usually associated with motor control are key elements of the distributed neural system, the 'Functional Language System' (FLS), that regulates human language. The 'function' of this system is to transmit information rapidly and frame thoughts by means of speech; the FLS is adapted for the production and perception of vocal language. The subcortical structures of the FLS reflect its evolutionary history. Natural selection modified neural motor control systems that provide timely responses to environmental challenges and opportunities in other species. The structure of the FLS is neither 'modular' (Fodor, 1982) nor an amorphous distributed network. It is similar to functional neural systems that regulate other aspects of behaviour in human beings and other species. Through the FLS, speech, syntax and certain aspects of cognitive ability are functionally and morphologically related. Although the soft tissue of the brain is not preserved in the fossil record, I shall also discuss studies of the evolution of human speech producing anatomy which suggest that both the anatomy and neural substrate necessary for human language were present in anatomically modern human beings at least 100,000 years ago. These studies also suggest that some form of speech and language were present in other extinct hominid species.

The argument structure of this present discussion also differs from that of linguists who have followed the precepts of 'Evolutionary Psychology,' inventing untestable scenarios to account for the evolution of human syntactic ability. For example, Calvin & Bickerton (2000) claim that syntactic ability evolved through competition for sexual access to females. Bickerton replaces the familiar cartoon of a caveman dragging a female by her hair. According to Bickerton, early humans lived in groups in which all childbearing females were the sexual property of a hypothetical 'alpha' male. Other, lesser, males occasionally gained access to a female by means of co-operative subterfuge. According to Bickerton's script, some of the lesser males distracted the alpha male, while one would rush forth and couple with a willing female. The hypothetical 'cheater-detector' gene postulated by Evolutionary Psychologists yielded reciprocal altruism, furnishing the preadaptive basis for the basic noun-verb distinction of human language and subsequent complex syntax. While this tale of life in the Pleistocene perhaps might have some commercial value, the behaviour of humans in historical situations that bear passing similarity to Bickerton's scenario does not accord with the script. The keepers of harems often did not die in bed. Poison, a knife in the back, or a military coup, leading to the ascent of a new Sultan, would furnish more plausible endings to the script. With equal plausibility, we might propose a scenario in which the success of silver-tongued seducers resulted in selection for linguistic ability. In truth, a scenario can be devised that 'accounts' for the evolution of virtually any aspect of human behaviour.

Primitive and derived characteristics of human language

Crafting scenarios to account for the process of evolution is unnecessary. The comparative method, central to Charles Darwin's *On The Origin of Species* (1859), can provide insights into the evolution of human language. The comparative method can establish some of the primitive and derived aspects of human language. Living apes retain many of the primitive characteristics of our common ancestral species. Whatever features 'ape-language' and human language share must have existed in the extinct hominids who are in, or close to, our line of descent.

It is apparent that normal human children reared in any normal situation usually start to talk before the third year of life. Conversely, children raised without exposure to language never develop normal linguistic or normal cognitive ability. Children who have severe forms of mental retardation, such as Down's syndrome, never acquire normal language in any situation (Benda, 1969). Therefore, exposure to a normal human child-rearing environment is a necessary and sufficient condition for the acquisition of language, *if* the neural substrate necessary for language is present. This being the case, the linguistic potential of the chimpanzee brain can be assessed by rearing chimpanzees in an human environment.

Speech Production

Hayes & Hayes (1951) raised the infant chimpanzee Viki, together with their son, as though it were a human child. The human infant and chimpanzee were exposed to both normal human conversation and to the 'motherese' variety of speech commonly directed towards young children (Fernald *et al.,* 1989). The chimpanzee initially was 'completely unable to make any sound at all on purpose'. Despite intensive speech training, Viki could produce only four human words, that were barely intelligible, when the project ended because of Viki's death at age seven years. The absence of speech was consistent with Goodall's observations of chimpanzees in their natural habitat. Goodall notes that:

*"Chimpanzee vocalizations are closely bound to emotion. The production of a sound in the **absence** of the appropriate emotional state seems to be an almost impossible task for a chimpanzee...*

*Chimpanzees can learn to **suppress** calls in situations when the production of sounds might, by drawing attention to the signaler, place him in an unpleasant or dangerous situation, but even this is not easy"*. (Goodall, 1986, p. 125).

It is apparent that chimpanzees can not produce speech or, for that matter, vocalizations that are not 'bound' to specific emotional states (Lieberman, 1994c). Therefore, the speech is a probable derived feature of human language.

Lexical Ability

A different approach to the cross-fostering experiment was employed by Beatrix & Alan Gardner. The Gardners proposed to see what would happen if a chimpanzee was raised as though it were human in a linguistic environment using American sign language (ASL). The Gardners' project (Gardener & Gardener, 1969) commenced with the ten-month-old female chimpanzee Washoe who lived with the Gardners and their research team between 1966 and 1970. During that period she was treated as though she was a child, albeit one who was in contact with an adult during all of her waking hours. She was clothed, wore shoes, played with toys and learned to use cups, spoons and the toilet. She observed ASL conversations between adults and communications in ASL directed towards her, without the adults necessarily expecting her to understand what was being signed in the early stages of the project. Washoe acquired about fifty ASL words in the first year of cross-fostering.

In November 1972, four newborn chimpanzees, Moja, Pili, Tatu and Dar, were placed in four adoptive 'families' at the Gardner's laboratory. One or more of the human members of each family remained with each chimpanzee between 07.00 h and 20.00 h throughout the year. Each family had one or more people who were proficient in ASL. Records of the chimpanzees' ASL productions were kept; the chimpanzees' ASL vocabularies were also formally tested (Gardner & Gardner, 1971, 1984). In the first two years, the chimpanzees' ASL vocabularies reached 50 signs, a performance roughly equivalent to that of either hearing human children or deaf children raised from birth onwards in homes using ASL. However, the performance of the chimpanzees and human children diverges after age two. When the Gardners' project ended, the chimpanzees had a vocabulary of about 140 words after 60 months of cross-fostered life. The rate, about 3 signs per month, at which they had acquired words was about the same over the entire period. This stands in marked contrast to normal children raised under normal conditions. Near age three, it generally becomes very difficult to keep track of the number of words that a child knows. A 'naming explosion' occurs.

These findings have been replicated by Rumbaugh & Savage-Rumbaugh using a somewhat different cross-fostering techniques and a visual-manual communication's system at the Yerkes Language Research Center. The linguistic behaviour of Kanzi, a bonobo or pygmy chimpanzee *Pan paniscus*, has been noted in many publications and films. The published evidence (Rumbaugh & Savage-Rumbaugh, 1993) indicates that Kanzi's abilities, though superior to the other 'common' chimpanzees *Pan troglodytes* at the Yerkes Laboratories, are on a par with Tatu, the most proficient of the Project Washoe chimpanzees. Kanzi, like the Project Washoe chimpanzees, uses toys, goes on excursions with his human family members, is engaged in conversations directed to him and can hear people talking to each other. In contrast to Project Washoe, Kanzi's human companions talk to each other and to him in English. Kanzi's 'utterances' are formed as he points to 'lexigrams' on boards or computer terminals. Each lexigram represents an English word and can, when Kanzi is using a terminal connected to a speech synthesizer, trigger the English word that corresponds to the lexigram.

Using somewhat different methods, the Yerkes research group replicated the Project Washoe findings on the referential nature of Kanzi's vocabulary. The lexigrams represent concepts that correspond to the words that form the vocabularies of young human children. Kanzi at age six years seems to have about the same linguistic ability as the five-year old Project Washoe chimpanzees. A qualitative difference clearly exists that differentiates the lexical capacities of human beings and chimpanzees. However, it is clear that the lexical ability must be a primitive feature of human language. It undoubtedly existed in the species that was the common ancestor of human beings and non-human apes.

Syntax

Syntax is, to most linguists, the key feature of human language. Bickerton, for example, differentiates between 'proto-language', that makes use of words, but lacks syntax, and 'true' language, that makes use of syntax to communicate distinctions in meaning. However, it is apparent that cross-fostered chimpanzees have limited syntactic ability. Rumbaugh & Savage-Rumbaugh (1993) report that Kanzi's responses to sentences such as: *'Put the pine needles on the ball'* – *'Put the ball on the pine needles'*, indicates that he has mastered the canonical form of English in which subject proceeds the object. Kanzi responded correctly about 75 percent of the time when he heard these sentences, recovering the deleted subject 'you' which starts each command. This is significant since it meets the operational test proposed by Bickerton for productive syntax.

Bickerton's operational test for the presence of syntax is the ability to 'recover' deleted words from sentences.

According to Bickerton, the syntactic structure of a sentence is the factor that allows a human child to infer the deleted subject 'you' from a command such as: 'Put the plate on the table'. However, the data of Savage-Rumbaugh & Rumbaugh (1993) show that an ape can, as noted above, make use of the cannonical form of English to interpret correctly the meaning of a sentence; Kanzi followed the instructions in sentences that asked him to place the ball on the needles or the needles on the ball. Similar data reported by Gardner & Gardner (in press) show that chimpanzees can achieve this level of linguistic ability. Therefore, syntactic ability is a primitive feature that undoubtedly was present to a degree in early hominid language. The distinction again appears to be quantitative rather than qualitative; the limited syntactic ability of chimpanzees may derive from constraints on working memory that involve the neural bases of speech production as well as 'executive' capacity (Baddeley, 1986; Lieberman, 1998, 2000). Other data reported by the Yerkes group are consistent with Kanzi's having a limited verbal working memory span. Recent findings show that the brain mechanisms that regulate human speech also play a central role in the comprehension of syntax and other aspects of cognition. We will return to these issues below.

The neural bases of human language

Clearly, the human brain must have some derived characteristics that allow us to produce vocal speech or alternate symbols that signify words, such as manual sign language, or even tactile stimulation as in the case of Helen Keller. The traditional view of the neural bases of human language is a product of the nineteenth century. Phrenological theorists (Gall, 1809; Spurzheim, 1815) claimed that specific aspects of human behaviour were regulated in particular areas of the cortex. Broca (1861) followed this model, locating the seat of language in a frontal region of the brain. Broca had observed the speech production deficits that occurred in a stroke patient when this region of cortex was damaged along with other regions of the brain. The standard, Broca's-Wernicke's area, model most often cited in recent years was proposed by Lichtheim (1885); Broca's area of the cortex, hypothetically, regulates speech production, while Wernicke's area, a posterior region located near cortical regions associated with auditory and visual perception, is, hypothetically, concerned with language comprehension. Many recent versions of the standard theory (e.g., Caplan, 1987), which take into account the difficulties that Broca's aphasics have in comprehending distinctions in meaning conveyed by syntax, claim that syntactic and other rule-governed processing occur in Broca's area, Wernicke's area is viewed as part of a system concerned with lexical access. However, it is becoming apparent that these locationist models are, at best, incomplete.

Neurobiological studies of humans and other species show that complex behaviours, such as preventing an object from hitting the eye, are regulated by 'functional neural systems' that link activity in many different neuroanatomical structures. A class of functional neural systems rapidly integrates sensory information with the present state of the organism and past experiences to enhance biological fitness through timely motor responses. For example, a monkey's brain has a functional neural system that is adapted to keeping foreign objects from hitting the monkey's eyes. Visual and tactile signals are channelled to the putamin, a subcortical basal ganglia structure, which interrupts ongoing motor activity to cause the monkey's arms immediately to deflect objects that move towards its eyes. The system is activated only when objects approach close to the monkey's eyes (Graziano, Yap & Gross, 1994). The monkey 'functional close-intercept-system' is not localised in a part of the monkey brain dedicated to this activity.

The monkey putamen is implicated in many other activities; populations of putamenal neurons form part of neural systems regulating other aspects of motor control, as well as emotion and cognition (Alexander, Delong & Strick, 1986; Parent, 1986; Cummings, 1993). A particular part of the brain may perform a similar 'computation' such as interrupting an ongoing activity in many different aspects of behaviour. In the case of the putamen, the ongoing activity can be either a 'simple' motor act or a thought process. Different populations of neurons in the primate putamen project to cortical regions concerned with motor control or cognition (Marsden & Obeso, 1994). A particular neural structure is usually implicated in different aspects of behaviour by means of different pathways, or 'circuits', linking activity in neuroanatomical structures distributed throughout the brain.

I have proposed a model for the neurological bases of human language that is consistent with present neurobiological data (Lieberman, 1998, 2000). My major premise is that the human brain contains a 'Functional Language System' (FLS) that evolved to regulate the production and comprehension of spoken language. Like other functional neural systems, it evolved to produce timely responses to environmental challenges and opportunities. The particular 'function' executed by the FLS is that it uses speech rapidly to transmit information and concepts coded as words and syntax.

Vocal language (or alternate forms such as manual sign language or tactile stimulation) allows humans to act or think rapidly, transcending the limits on information flow imposed by the auditory and visual systems. Articulatory rehearsal, a process of 'silent-speech,' also maintains the information and concepts represented by words in verbal working (short-term) memory (Baddeley, 1986; Awh *et al.,* 1996).

The architecture of the human FLS can be understood by considering two aspects of the organisation of the brain. Although various areas of the cortex and particular subcortical structures can be identified that perform particular 'computations', such as storing visual information for a brief period or sequencing motor commands, neurophysiologic studies show that complex behaviours generally are not regulated in one part of the brain. i) A particular neuroanatomical structure often is implicated in different aspects of behaviour. ii) Neuroanatomical structures support many different neural circuits that each transmit information to other neuroanatomical structures. A neural circuit is formed by a segregated neuronal population in one neuroanatomical structure that projects to a neuronal population in another neuroanatomical structure. Complex behaviours generally are regulated by distributed networks consisting of neural circuits linking many neuroanatomical structures throughout the brain (*cf.* Alexander *et al.,* 1986; Mesulam, 1990; Cummings, 1993).

The evolution of the functional language system

The ability to talk is, as noted above, a derived property of human language and a neural substrate that is present today only in *Homo sapiens.* However, converging behavioural and neuro-biological data suggest a probable basis for the evolution of the FLS. As is the case for other aspects of human morphology, such as the bones of the middle ear which derive from the hinged mandibles of reptiles (Mayr, 1982), the proximate logic of evolution is evident when we examine the human brain. The neuroanatomical structure of the human FLS traditionally associated with motor control undoubtedly reflects the proximate logic (Mayr, 1982) and continuity of evolution. The basal ganglia, subcortical structures that regulate many other aspects of motor control, are key elements of the human FLS. The basal ganglia and circuits to the thalamus, cerebellum and cortex integrate sensory information and the knowledge stored in the brain's lexicon to regulate ongoing motor and cognitive activity. The FLS, in all likelihood, derives from natural selection that enhanced biological fitness through rapid motor responses to environmental challenges and opportunities (Lieberman, 1984, 1985, 1991, 1998, 2000). This premise is not particularly novel, Lashley (1951) suggested that a common neural substrate may regulate the 'syntactic organisation' of motor behaviour and thought. In short, the FLS appears to derive from the evolution of the ability to produce timely motor responses in response to changing environmental challenges and opportunities.

Data supporting the evolutionary role of motor control

The cortical and subcortical structures of the brain that regulate motor control play a crucial part in the human FLS. Present comparative studies of subcortical basal ganglia provide some clues to the probable evolution of the FLS. Aldridge *et al.* (1993), determined the role of basal ganglia in rodent grooming patterns. The grooming movements of rats are innately determined. The 'syntax' of the grooming sequence is regulated in basal ganglia; damage to the cortex or cerebellum does not affect the grooming sequence. In contrast, destruction of basal ganglia disrupts these grooming sequences, but does not affect the gestures that make up a grooming sequence. Aldridge *et al.* (1993) conclude that: "*Hierarchical modulation of sequential elements by the neostratum may operate in essentially similar ways for grooming actions and thoughts, but upon very different classes of elements in the two cases... Our argument is that very different behavioural or mental operations might be sequenced by essentially similar neural processes*" (p. 393).

While basal ganglia regulate innate behaviour in rodents, in non-human primates they are elements of neural systems that acquire and regulate learned sequential motor responses. Kimura *et al.* (1993) showed that basal ganglia interneurons in monkeys were implicated in learning conditioned motor tasks. Learned motor activity in response to an external arbitrary stimuli is a cognitive act.

Independent studies of basal ganglia activity in humans and other animals (e.g., Alexander *et al.*, 1986; Middleton & Strick, 1994; Cunnington *et al.*, 1995) show that circuits supported in basal ganglia regulate cognition, projecting to prefrontal cortical areas implicated in 'executive control' and dual-task performance. Similar 'computations' are performed in basal ganglia in motor control and in cognition.

Cunnington *et al.* (1995) conclude that basal ganglia: "*provide an internal cue to terminate supplementary motor area activity following movement, and to activate the preparatory phase for the next submovement, thereby switching between components of a motor sequence.*" (p. 948).

Marsden & Obeso (1994) reviewing studies of human subjects after basal ganglia surgery conclude that: "*... the role of the basal ganglia in controlling movement must give insight into their other functions, particularly if thought is mental movement without motion. Perhaps the basal ganglia are an elaborate machine, within the overall frontal lobe distributed system, that allows routine thought and action, but which responds to new circumstances to allow a change in direction of ideas and movement. Loss of basal ganglia contribution, such as in Parkinson's disease, thus would lead to inflexibility of mental and motor response...*" (p. 893).

Linguistic deficits deriving from impaired basal ganglia activity

Deficits in the comprehension of syntax due to impaired basal ganglia activity were noted in Parkinson's Disease (PD) subjects by Lieberman, Friedman & Feldman (1990), Grossman *et al.* (1991, 1993) and Natsopoulos *et al.* (1993). Cognitive tests were also administered in Lieberman *et al.* (1992). Moderate and severe PD subjects who were more impaired made significantly more errors than relatively unimpaired PD subjects on the Odd-Man-Out test (Flowers & Robertson, 1985), a sorting test that measures the ability to derive an abstract criterion necessary to solve a problem and then shift to a new criterion. The Odd-Man-Out test can be regarded as a probe of both visual and verbal working-memory since it involves sorting geometrical figures that differ in size and shape, and upper and lower case letters of the alphabet that appear to be represented and phonetically rehearsed in verbal working memory (Awh *et al.,* 1996). Moderate and severe PD subjects also made significantly more errors than mild PD subjects on other tests involving working memory, i.e., tests of short term and long term recall, delayed recognition and the Digit span backwards test.

The data of Lieberman *et al.* (1992) showed that the pattern of speech production deficits and syntax comprehension deficits in non-demented Parkinson's Disease subjects was similar in nature to that noted for Broca's aphasia. Acoustic analysis of the speech of 40 PD subjects showed a breakdown in some PD subjects' ability to sequence the motor commands that control the production of stop consonant-vowel sequences. The acoustic parameter that differentiates the stop consonant [*b*] from [*p*] before a vowel or continuant is 'voice onset time' (VOT), the interval between the time at which the lips open and the start of phonation generated by the larynx when these consonants are produced before a vowel or continuant. VOT differentiates these sounds as well as stop consonants such as [*d*] from [*t*] and [*g*] from [*k*] (Lisker & Abramson, 1964). Short VOTs occur for [*b*], [*d*] and [*g*], long VOTs for [*p*], [*t*] and [*k*]. Broca's aphasics lose the ability to control the sequence of motor commands that yield the VOTs that differentiate voiced from unvoiced stop consonants; the deficit involves sequencing rather than the ability to control duration, since they preserve intrinsic vowel durations and other temporal cues, as well as formant frequencies and transitions (Katz, 1988). Broca's aphasics also typically show deficits in the comprehension of syntax (Blumstein *et al.,* 1980). It is significant that the speech production and syntax comprehension deficits associated with Broca's aphasia do not occur in the absence of extensive subcortical damage to the brain (Stuss & Benson, 1986; Dronkers *et al.,* 1992; Mega & Alexander, 1994). In fact, subcortical damage that leaves Broca's area intact can result in Broca-like speech production deficits (Stuss & Benson, 1986; Alexander, Naeser & Palumbo, 1987).

Further evidence for the role of basal ganglia in the FLS is provided by Pickett *et al.* (1998) for a subject who had damage restricted to bilateral damage to the anterior caudate nucleus and putamen. The subject's deficits included impairment of the timing of articulatory components of motor programmes and the inability to switch from one pattern of cognitive or motor activity when appropriate external cues existed. The subject's speech was degraded due to inappropriate sequencing of articulatory gestures (nasalis-ation, laryngeal activity and the co-ordination of intercostal muscles regulating alveolar air pressure with upper airway articulation). The subject also had difficulty comprehending distinctions in meaning conveyed by syntax in English sentences. The subject's errors appear to reflect an inability to terminate syntactic-semantic processing of embedded clauses, where it is necessary to switch to the analysis of new material at clause boundaries. Cognitive deficits, involving impaired sequencing, also occurred for this severely compromised subject; the subject had a 70 percent error rate on the Odd-Man-Out test, which involves forming conceptual categories, when making decisions within a single category. Cognitive preservation occurred when the subject was asked to shift categories; the subject was unable to shift from one thought process to another. In contrast, performance was within normal ranges in tests of lexical access and memory. Correlations between speech motor control deficits and the comprehension of distinctions of meaning conveyed by syntax can occur in otherwise intact individuals. A study of climbers ascending Mount Everest showed correlated decrements in their ability to sequence stop-consonant VOTs and the time that it took to comprehend simple English sentences, similar in nature to, but not as extreme as, that found in PD patients (Lieberman *et al.*, 1994, 1995). The ascent of Mount Everest takes about three months as the climbers occupy a series of camps at successively higher altitudes. Tests of the comprehension of distinctions in meaning conveyed by syntax, tests of cognition and acoustic analyses of the climbers' speech, similar to those used to assess deficits in PD (Lieberman *et al.*, 1992), were performed. The regulation of laryngeal activity with respect to lip and tongue gestures deteriorated as the climbers ascended. The time needed to comprehend spoken English sentences also increased. Response times were 54 percent longer at higher altitudes for simple sentences that are readily comprehended by six-year-old children. In contrast, other cognitive processes, including long-term memory (Nelson *et al.*, 1990) were preserved. These effects were, in all likelihood, the result of impaired basal ganglia activity. Independent studies show that oxygen deprivation impairs *globus pallidus*, the principal output structure of basal ganglia, before damage to the cortex occurs (Laplane, Baulac & Widlocher, 1984; Cummings, 1993).

The test results are significant since, compared to PD or stroke patients, the brain mechanisms implicated in motor control were lightly stressed. The subjects were in peak physical condition and were able to ascend to the summit of Mount Everest, whereas locomotion and balance are severely compromised when basal ganglia deteriorate in Parkinson's Disease (Hohn & Yahr, 1967). Under these conditions, a strong correlation between speech production and the comprehension of syntax was evident.

On the limits of present knowledge of the brain

Although it is clear that the human FLS is unique, the nature of the distinction is still a mystery. It is becoming apparent that gross qualitative anatomical distinctions do not differentiate the brains of human beings and living non-human apes. The frontal regions of the human cortex, for example, stand in the same proportion to total brain volume in humans and non-human apes (Semendeferi *et al.,* 1997). Therefore, it is most unlikely that, as Deacon (1988, 1997) proposed, a disproportionate enlargement of the prefrontal cortex of the human brain in itself confers human linguistic and cognitive ability. If the prefrontal cortex were disproportionately larger in humans, the relative proportions of other frontal regions of the human brain would be much smaller than in non-human apes, which is not the case (Stephan, Frahm & Baron, 1981). Since the volume of the hominid brain gradually increased in the course of human evolution (Jerison, 1973), one possible inference is that the derived properties of human language, speech and syntax also gradually evolved. Increases in computational power affecting motor control and cognition, deriving from increases in scale, may account for the qualitatively different functional 'power' of the human brain. However, the question can not presently be resolved, since the detailed circuitry of neither human nor non-human primate brains is not known. One possibility that fits the close relationship that holds between neural structures regulating voluntary speech and thinking in humans, is that natural selection that was directed at 'freeing' vocal signals from their emotional context was the preadaptive basis for human 'free will', i.e., the ability of humans freely to compose new thoughts (Lieberman, 1994c).

The anatomy of speech production

Although the soft tissue of the tongue, lips and other anatomical structures that are necessary to produce speech are not preserved in the fossil record, the skeletal features that are associated with these structures can be discerned. Over the past 30 years, inferences concerning the evolution of human speech anatomy have been made which also shed some light on the possible evolution of the FLS. The physiology of speech production has been studied since the time of Johannes Muller (1826). The lungs power speech production. The outward flow of air from the lungs is converted to audible sound by the action of the larynx, which during 'phonation' generates a series of quasi-periodic puffs of air as the vocal cords rapidly open and close. The larynx operates in much the same manner as the diaphragm of a harmonica. Acoustic energy can also be generated by air turbulence at a constriction, in much the same manner as the source of acoustic energy in a flute or organ. The airway above the larynx filters the acoustic energy produced by the larynx, in the same manner as the different air passages of an harmonica. The airway above the larynx, termed the 'supralaryngeal vocal tract' (SVT), can continually change its shape in proficient normal human speakers. The human tongue, which extends down into the pharynx, can be depressed or elevated backwards or forwards to change dramatically the shape of the SVT. The position and degree of constriction of the lips and vertical position of the larynx, which can move up or down about 25mm, can also change the SVT configuration. However, tongue manoeuvres produce the greatest SVT shape changes (Nearey, 1979). The filtering properties of the SVT are determined by its shape and overall length (Chiba & Kajiyama, 1941; Fant, 1960; Stevens, 1972). Peak energy can potentially be transmitted through the SVT at particular 'formant frequencies.' Systematic research since the end of the eighteenth century (Hellwag, 1781) shows that the phonetic properties of many speech sounds are determined by these formant frequencies. The vowel [i] of the word **see**, for example, differs from the vowel [a] of the word **ma** solely because of its different formant frequencies. The pitch of a person's voice, which is determined by the rate at which the vocal cords of the larynx open and close, is irrelevant.

The rapid transmission rate of human speech follows from the 'encoding' of formant frequencies. As a person talks, the SVT changes its shape for different speech sounds, thereby changing the formant frequencies. Since the tongue, lips and larynx must move gradually, the formant frequency pattern also changes gradually. Thus, the pattern of formant frequencies generated as a syllable is produced changes at a slower rate than the individual sounds of speech. Human listeners make use of this property. The flow of speech sounds generally exceeds 15 per second, which exceeds the temporal resolving power of the human auditory system (the sounds would merge into a buzz at that rate). However, the 'encoded' syllabic rate is much slower; human listeners derive the sounds that make up syllables by means of a process that involves an implicit neural representation or knowledge of the constraints of speech production (Liberman *et al.,* 1967).

In other words, we perceptually 'decode' the syllables to recover the sounds of speech using some knowledge of speech production. The decoding process must take into account the length of the SVT that produced a speech sound (Nearey, 1979). This complex process allows us to communicate the sounds that convey words at a rate of up to 20 sounds per second. We otherwise would be limited to rates of 5 to 7 sounds per second.

The adult human tongue and SVT differ from those of all other living animals (Negus, 1949). In other species, the body of the tongue is long and relatively flat and fills the oral cavity. During swallowing, the tongue propels food through the oral cavity. The non-human larynx is positioned high and can lock into the nasopharynx, forming an air pathway sealed from the oral cavity, thereby enabling an animal to simultaneously breath and drink or swallow small food particles. In contrast, the posterior portion of the human tongue in a midsaggital view is round and the larynx is positioned low. The resulting human supralaryngeal airway has an almost right angle bend at its midpoint. As we talk, extrinsic tongue muscles can move the tongue upwards, downwards, forwards or backwards, yielding abrupt and extreme changes in the cross-sectional area of the human supralaryngeal airway at its midpoint

(Chiba & Kajiyama, 1941; Fant, 1960; Nearey, 1979). The vowel sounds that occur most often in the languages of the world (Jakobson, 1940; Greenberg, 1963), [*i*], [*u*] and [*a*] – the vowels of the words *see*, *do* and *ma* – can be formed only by the extreme midpoint area function discontinuities of the human supralaryngeal vocal tract (Stevens, 1972; Carré, Lindblom & MacNeilage, 1995).

These vowels have superior qualities for speech perception and production. They are 'quantal', yielding spectral peaks analogous to saturated colours and are inherently resistant to small errors in speech articulation (Stevens, 1972; Beckman *et al.,* 1995). These vowel sounds delimit the acoustic 'space' which all human languages use to produce meaningful phonetic distinctions (Lindblom, 1990). Moreover, the constraints of speech production and the vocal tract appear to be internally modelled when humans perceive speech (Liberman *et al.,* 1967; Lindblom, 1996). Many studies have shown that [*i*], in particular, is the 'supervowel' of human speech. It is less often confused with other sounds (Peterson & Barney, 1952) and, most importantly, yields an optimal reference signal from which an human listener can determine the length of the supralaryngeal vocal tract of a speaker's voice (Nearey, 1979; Fitch, 1994, 1997). It is clear that human infants begin life with a non-human tongue, laryngeal position and supralaryngeal vocal tract (Negus, 1949; Lieberman & Crelin, 1971).

The debate concerning the evolution of the human vocal tract has centred on the question of whether the human larynx lowered its position relative to the mandible and basicranium to allow swallowing in upright bipedal hominids, or whether the driving force was enhanced speech. The answer seems to be speech. Falk (1975) argued that the lower position of the human larynx was a consequence of the manoeuvres necessary for swallowing in an upright position rather than enhancing speech production. Falk's argument hinged on the swallowing manoeuvres of the hyoid bone, which supports the larynx. Available radiographic studies seemed to show that the human hyoid bone executed different manoeuvres during swallowing compared to other pongids. In brief, Falk's argument was that since the human hyoid seemed to move upwards, it would have to be positioned low in the neck. A low hyoid would reshape the human tongue in order to swallow. However, recent studies show that hyoid movement during normal human swallowing is similar to that seen in other mammals (Palmer & Hiiemae, 1997). The earlier data were an artifact of the procedure used in past radiographic studies of swallowing. In fact, human children under the age of six years can swallow food though their hyoid bones are positioned closer to those of newborn infants and non-human primates than adult humans (Lieberman D, & McCarthy 1999). In this regard, Houghton's (1993) reconstruction of a Neanderthal vocal tract with a small tongue that would be incapable of swallowing is obviously incorrect (Lieberman, 1994b). Houghton placed a tongue on the La Chapelle-aux-Saints Neanderthal fossil that would be incapable of propelling food to the back of the hominid's mouth, a necessary part of normal swallowing.

As Darwin (1859) first noted, the morphology of the human supralaryngeal airway is maladapted for swallowing since solid objects can be forcefully propelled downwards by the pharyngeal constrictor muscles and lodge in the larynx, causing asphyxiation. Other maladaptive features of the human supralaryngeal vocal tract include a reduction in chewing efficiency and crowding of teeth which can result in impaction and infection (Lieberman, 1975, 1984, 1991, 1998). The non-human supra-laryngeal airway, which is better adapted for swallowing and has sufficient space for teeth (Negus, 1949), can not produce the human quantal vowels [*i*], [*u*] and [*a*] (Lieberman, 1968; Lieberman, Klatt & Wilson, 1969; Lieberman, Crelin & Klatt, 1972; Carré *et al.,* 1995). Since swallowing in upright bipedal hominids does not depend on having a low larynx, we can conclude that the human supralaryngeal vocal tract is adapted to enhance speech production.

Although the starting and end points of the evolution of the human supralaryngeal vocal tract configurations can readily be observed, its evolution must be inferred from basicranial skeletal morphology since the soft tissue of the vocal tract does not survive. Lieberman & Crelin (1971) studied the basicranial skeletal morphology of the classic La Chapelle-aux-Saints Neanderthal, which resembles that of a newborn human infant, which has non-human vocal tracts similar to that of apes and other mammals. They concluded that the fossil's larynx was positioned close to the skull base, similar to a newborn human infant's larynx. The Neanderthal fossil's SVT thus would have had the same speech limitations as a human newborn's SVT. However, it has become clear that the position of the Neanderthal larynx can not be determined with certainty from the skull base (Lieberman D & McCarthy, 1999). Nonetheless, the classic Neanderthal SVT would most likely not have been able to produce quantal speech sounds. The long oral cavity determined by the palate and long span between the end of the palate and spinal column precludes the La Chapelle-aux-Saints and similar hominids having the ability to produce the midpoint area function variations necessary to produce 'quantal' [*i*] vowels (Lieberman, 1998).

The claim that a humanlike Neanderthal hyoid bone shows that it occupied the same low position as that of a normal contemporary human adult (Arensburg *et al.,* 1989, 1990) is refuted by the fact that the human hyoid descends during the course of ontogenetic development without any systematic change in its shape (Lieberman, 1994a). The human supralaryngeal vocal tract reaches an adult-like configuration, in which the oral and pharyngeal cavities have equal lengths thereby permitting quantal speech production, at age six years. It subsequently maintains those proportions by means of co-ordinated oral cavity and pharyngeal growth (Lieberman D & McCarthy, 1999). The growth pattern necessary to achieve these proportions appears to be a derived human feature absent in certain Neanderthals (Lieberman, D. 1998).

In contrast, the derived skeletal features of the human basicranium can not support a non-human supralaryngeal vocal tract because the reduced length between the posterior margin of the palate and basion do not leave enough room for a larynx positioned *before* the pharynx, close to the basicranium (Lieberman, 1984). Consequently, we can conclude that early fossil anatomically modern humans such as Skhul V possessed human speech producing anatomy.

However, the absence of a human supralaryngeal vocal tract in a fossil hominid is *not* a sign that speech was totally absent. As Lieberman & Crelin (1971) pointed out, the archaeological record shows that classic Neanderthals surely must have possessed the neural substrates that confer language and speech. While archaeologists continue to debate whether Neanderthal culture was as complex and innovative as that of anatomically modern humans, it is clear that Neanderthals made complex tools, cared for the infirm and hunted large animals (Mellars, 1996). We can be certain that some form of speech was present in Neanderthals and in the hominid species ancestral to Neanderthals and modern human beings. There would be no selective advantage for enhanced speech unless speech was present already. Also, as noted above, a necessary condition for the production of human speech is the neural circuitry of the Functional Language System. Hence, we can be certain that early anatomically modern *Homo sapiens,* such as Skhul V, possessed human speech and syntax.

Speech, nonetheless, may have played a part in Neanderthal extinction. Given the fact that differences in dialect are a genetic isolating mechanism in modern human populations (Barbujani & Sokal, 1990, 1991), it is reasonable to suppose that the profound dialect distinctions conferred by human, versus not fully human, supralaryngeal vocal tracts would have minimised gene flow between early anatomically modern humans and contemporary *erectus* grade and certain Neanderthal hominids. However, all the fossils presently classified as 'Neanderthal' may not have had similar supralaryngeal vocal tracts (Lieberman, 1984). Further study is necessary to determine the chronology of the evolution of the human supralarygeal vocal tract. In short, the derived features of the human vocal tract were shaped by selection for enhanced phonetic ability, but speech is possible with a non-human vocal tract.

Concluding comments

To conclude, comparative studies show that apes can not talk. Studies of human speech show that it is a central component of language, yielding a high data-transmission rate as well as playing a part in allowing humans to comprehend distinctions in meaning conveyed by syntax. Neurobiological studies of the human brain show that subcortical structures that regulate speech motor control play a part in comprehending sentences and in abstract reasoning. Studies of the evolution of human speech anatomy provide some insights on the time course of the evolution of human language as well as the extinction of archaic hominid species. It is evident that present day humans have specialised anatomy and brain mechanisms that allow us to talk, transmitting the conceptual information coded as words and integrating sensory information with the knowledge coded in the words of our internal lexicon. Words are powerful conceptual as well as communicative elements. When we think of the word '*tree*' it doesn't necessarily refer to a particular tree or even a species of tree. *Tree*, furthermore, codes a concept. The conceptual information coded in the brain's lexicon appears to recruit information represented in structures of the brain concerned with sensation and motor control. For example, when we say or think of the word '*pencil*' we are activating the shape and colour information stored in the visual cortex (Martin *et al.*, 1995). Therefore, linguistic knowledge is knowledge of the outside world, stored within as words that are accessed vocally and subvocally by the sounds of human speech.

However, comparative studies of humans and chimpanzees show that the lexicon is a primitive feature of human language and thought. And so the neural bases of lexical ability and thought, which exist in present day pongids, must have been present in early hominids. The derived properties of human language, speech and syntax, entail the presence of the Functional Language System of the human brain, a distributed neural system adapted to regulate spoken language. The FLS contributes to biological fitness by rapidly integrating sensory information and conceptual information with prior knowledge, represented by means of words (or their visual representation) to effect appropriate motor or mental responses to the outside environment or an internal mental state. In a sense, human language and thought can be regarded as neurally 'computed' motor activity, ultimately deriving from neuroanatomical systems that generate overt motor responses to environmental challenges and opportunities.

REFERENCES

Alexander GE, Delon MR, Strick PL. 1986. Parallel organization of segregated circuits linking basal ganglia and cortex. *Annual Review of Neuroscience.* **9:** 357-381.

Alexander MP, Naeser MA, Palumbo CL. 1987. Correlations of subcortical CT lesion sites and aphasia profiles. *Brain.* **110:** 961-991.

Aldridge JW, Berridge KC, Herman M, Zimmer L. 1993. Neuronal coding of serial order: Syntax of grooming in the neostratum. *Psychological Science.* **4:** 391-393.

Arensburg B, Tiller AM, Vandermeersch B, Duday H, Schepartz LA, Rak Y. 1989. A Middle Paleolithic human hyoid bone. *Nature.* **338:** 758-760.

Arensburg B, Schepartz LA, Tiller AM, Vandermeersch B, Duday H, Rak Y. 1990. A reappraisal of the anatomical basis for speech in middle palaeolithic hominids. *American Journal of Physical Anthropology.* **83:** 137-146.

Awh E, Jonides J, Smith RE, Schumacher EH, Koeppe RA, Katz S. 1996. Dissociation of storage and rehearsal in working memory: evidence from positron emission tomography. *Psychological Science.* **7:** 25-31.

Baddeley AD. 1986. *Working Memory.* Oxford: Clarendon Press.

Barbujani G, Sokal RR. 1990. Zones of sharp genetic change in Europe are also linguistic boundaries. *Proceedings of National Academy of Sciences, USA.* **187:** 1816-1819.

Barbujani G, Sokal RR. 1991. Genetic population structure of Italy. II. Physical and cultural barriers to gene flow. *American Journal of Human Genetics.* **48:** 398-411.

Beckman ME, Jung T-P, Lee S-H, de Jong K, Krishnamurthy AK, Ahalt SC, Cohen KB, Collins MJ. 1995. Variability in the production of quantal vowels revisited. *Journal of the Acoustical Society of America.* **97:** 471-489.

Benda C E. 1969. *Down's Syndrome: Mongolism and its Management.* New York: Grune and Stratton.

Blumstein SE, Cooper W, Goodglass H, Statlender H, Gottleib J. 1980. Production deficits in aphasia: a voice-onset time analysis. *Brain and Language.* **9:** 153-170.

Broca P. 1861. Remarques sur le siège de la faculté de la parole articulée, suivies d'une observation d'aphemié (perte de parole). *Bulletin de la Societé d'Anatomie (Paris).* **36:** 330-357.

Calvin WH, Bickerton D. (in press). *Lingua ex machina: Reconciling Darwin and Chomsky with the Human Brain.* Cambridge Massachusetts: MIT Press.

Caplan D. 1987. *Neurolinguistics and Linguistic Aphasiology: An Introduction.* Cambridge: Cambridge University Press.

Carré R, Lindblom B, MacNeilage P. 1995. Acoustic factors in the evolution of the human vocal tract. *C. R. Academie des Sciences Paris.* **t 320,** Serie IIb: 471-476.

Chiba T, Kajiyama J. 1941. *The Vowel: Its Nature and Structure.* Tokyo: Tokyo-Kaisekan Publishing Co.

Cummings J L. 1993. Frontal-subcortical circuts and human behavior. *Archives of Neurology.* **50:** 873-880.

Cunnington R, Iansek R, Bradshaw JL, Philips JG. 1995. Movement-related potentials in Parkinson's disease: Presence and predictability of temporal and spatial cues. *Brain.* **118:** 935-950.

Darwin C. 1859. *On the Origin of Species.* Facsimile ed. 1964. Cambridge Massachusetts: Harvard University Press.

Deacon TW. 1988. Human brain evolution II. Embryology and brain allometry. In: Jerison HJ, Jerison I. eds. *Intelligence and Evolutionary Biology.* NATO ASI Series, Berlin: Springer. 383-416.

Deacon TW. 1997. *The Symbolic Species: The Coevolution of Language and the Brain.* New York: W.W. Norton.

Dronkers NF, Shapiro JK, Redfern B, Knight RT. 1992. The role of Broca's area in Broca's aphasia. *Journal of Clinical and Experimental Neuropsychology.* **14:** session 8, Language and Aphasia.

Falk D. 1975. Comparative anatomy of the larynx in man and the chimpanzee: implications for language in Neanderthal. *American Journal of Physical Anthropology.* **43:** 123-132.

Fant G. 1960. *Acoustic Theory of Speech Production.* The Hague: Mouton.

Fernald AT, Taeschner J, Dunn M, Papousek B, de Boysson-Bardies, Fukui I. 1989. A cross-language study of prosodic modifications in mothers' and fathers' speech to preverbal infants. *Journal of Child Language.* **16:** 477-501.

Fitch WT III. 1994. Vocal Tract Length and the Evolution of Language. [Unpublished PhD thesis], Brown University.

Fitch WT III. 1997. Vocal tract length and formant frequency dispersion correlate with body size in macaque monkeys. *Journal of the Acoustical Society of America.* **102:** 1213-1222.

Flowers KA, Robertson C. 1985. The effects of Parkinson's disease on the ability to maintain a mental set. *Journal of Neurology, Neurosurgery, and Psychiatry.* **48:** 517-529.

Gall FJ. 1809. *Recherches sur le Systeme Nerveux.* Paris: B. Bailliere.

Gardner RA, Gardner BT. 1969. Teaching sign language to a chimpanzee. *Science.* **165:** 664-672.

Gardner RA, Gardner BT. 1971. Two-way communication with an infant chimpanzee. In: Schrier A, Stollnitz F. eds. *Behavior of Nonhuman Primates, Vol 4.* New York: Academic Press

Gardner RA, Gardner BT. 1984. A vocabulary test for chimpanzees (*Pan troglodytes*). *Journal of Comparative Psychology.* **4:** 381-404.

Gardner RA, Gardner BT. (in press). Ethological roots of language. In: Gardner RA, Gardner BT, Chiarelli B, Plooj R. eds. *The Ethological Roots of Culture.* Kluwer: Academic Publishers.

Goodall J. 1986. *The Chimpanzees of Gombe: Patterns of Behaviour.* Cambridge Massachusetts: Harvard University Press.

Graybiel AM, Aosaki T, Flaherty AW, Kimura M. 1994. The basal ganglia and adaptive motor control. *Science,* **265:** 1826-1831.

Graziano MSA, Yap GS, Gross CG. 1994. Coding of visual space by premotor neurons. *Science,* **266:** 1054-1057.

Greenberg J. 1963. *Universals of Language.* Cambridge Massachusetts: MIT Press.

Grossman M, Carvell S, Gollomp S, Stern MB, Vernon G, Hurtig HI. 1991. Sentence comprehension and praxis deficits in Parkinson's disease. *Neurology.* **41:** 1620-1628.

Grossman M, Carvell S, Gollomp S, Stern MB, Reivich M, Morrison D, Alavi A, Hurtig HL. 1993. Cognitive and physiological substrates of impaired sentence processing in Parkinson's Disease. *Journal of Cognitive Neuroscience.* **5:** 480-498.

Hayes K J, Hayes C. 1951. The intellectual development of a home-raised chimpanzee. *Proceedings of the American Philosophical Society.* **5:** 105-109.

Hellwag C. 1781. De Formatione Loquelae. [Dissertation] Tubingen.

Hoehn MM, Yahr MD. 1967. Parkinsonism: onset, progression and mortality. *Neurology.* **17:** 427-442.

Houghton P. 1993. Neanderthal supralaryngeal vocal tract. *American Journal of Physical Anthropology.* **90:** 139-146.

Jakobson R. 1940. Kindersprache, Aphasie und allgemeine Lautgesetze. In: Jakobson R. ed. *Selected Writings* The Hague: Mouton. Also translated by Keiler RA. 1968. *Child Language, Aphasia, and Phonological Universals.* The Hague: Mouton.

Jerison HJ. 1973. *Evolution of the Brain and Intelligence.* New York: Academic Press.

Katz WF. 1988. Anticipatory coarticulation in aphasia: Acoustical and perceptual data. *Brain and Language.* **35:** 340-368.

Kimura M, Aosaki T, Graybiel A. 1993. Role of basal ganglia in the acquisition and initiation of learned movement. In: Mano N, Hamada I, DeLong MR. eds. *Role of the Cerrebellum and Basal Ganglia in Voluntary Movements.* Amsterdam: Elsevier. 71-75.

Laplane D, Baulac M, Widlocher D. 1984. Pure psychic akinesia with bilateral lesions of basal ganglia. *Journal of Neurology, Neurosurgery and Psychiatry.* **47:** 377-385.

Lashley KS. 1951. The problem of serial order in behavior. In: Jefress L A. ed. *Cerebral Mechanisms in Behavior.* New York: Wiley. 112-146.

Liberman AM, Cooper FS, Shankweiler DP, Studdert-Kennedy M. 1967. Perception of the speech code. *Psychological Review,* **74:** 431-461.

Lichtheim L. 1885. On aphasia. *Brain.* **7:** 433-484.

Lieberman DE. 1998. Sphenoid shortening and the evolution of modern human cranial shape. *Nature.* **393:** 158-162.

Lieberman DE, McCarthy RC. 1999. The ontogeny of cranial base angulation in humans and its implications for reconstructing pharyngeal dimensions. *Journal of Human Evolution.* **34:** 487-517.

Lieberman P. 1968. Primate vocalizations and human linguistic ability. *Journal of the Acoustical Society of America.* **44:** 1157-1164.

Lieberman P. 1975. *On the Origins of Language: An Introduction to the Evolution of Speech.* New York: Macmillan.

Lieberman P. 1984. *The Biology and Evolution of Language.* Cambridge, Massachusetts: Harvard University Press.

Lieberman P. 1985. On the evolution of human syntactic ability: Its pre-adaptive bases – motor control and speech. *Journal of Human Evolution.* **14:** 657-668.

Lieberman P. 1991. *Uniquely Human: The Evolution of Speech, Thought, and Selfless Behavior.* Cambridge Massachusetts: Harvard University Press.

Lieberman P. 1992. On Neanderthal speech and Neanderthal extinction. *Current Anthropology.* **33:** 409-410.

Lieberman P. 1994a. Hyoid bone position and speech: Reply to Arensburg *et al.* (1990). *American Journal of Physical Anthropology.* **94:** 275-278.

Lieberman P. 1994b. Functional tongues and Neanderthal vocal tract reconstruction: A reply to Houghton (1993). *American Journal of Physical Anthropology.* **95:** 443-452.

Lieberman P. 1994c. Biologically bound behavior, free-will, and human evolution. In: Casti JI. ed. *Conflict and Cooperation in Nature.* New York: John Wiley and Sons. 133-163.

Lieberman P. 1998. *Eve Spoke; Human Language and Human Evolution.* New York: WW. Norton.

Lieberman P. 2000. *Human language and our reptilian brain: The subcortical bases of speech, syntax, and thought.* Cambridge Mass: Harvard University Press.

Lieberman P, Klatt DH, Wilson WH. 1969. Vocal tract limitations on the vowel repertoires of rhesus monkey and other nonhuman primates. *Science.* **164:** 1185-1187.

Lieberman P, Crelin ES. 1971. On the speech of Neanderthal man. *Linguistic Inquiry.* **2:** 203-222.

Lieberman P, Crelin ES, Klatt DH. 1972. Phonetic ability and related anatomy of the newborn, adult human, Neanderthal man, and the chimpanzee. *American Anthropologist.* **74:** 287-307.

Lieberman P. Friedman J, Feldman LS. 1990. Syntactic deficits in Parkinson's disease. *Journal of Nervous and Mental Disease.* **178:** 360-365.

Lieberman P, Kako ET, Friedman J, Tajchman G, Feldman LS, Jiminez EB. 1992. Speech production, syntax comprehension, and cognitive deficits in Parkinson's disease. *Brain and Language.* **43:** 169-189.

Lieberman P, Kanki BG, Protopapas A, Reed E, Youngs JW. 1994. Cognitive defects at altitude. *Nature.* **372:** 325.

Lieberman P, Kanki B G, Protopapas A. 1995. Speech production and cognitive decrements on Mount Everest. *Aviation, Space and Environmental Medicine.* **66:** 857-864.

Lindblom B. 1990. Explaining phonetic variation : A sketch of the H and H theory. In : Hardcastle W, Marchal A. eds. *Speech Production and Speech Modelling.* Dordrecht: Kluwer. 403-439.

Lindblom B. 1996. Role of articulation in speech perception; Clues from production. *Journal of the Acoustical Society of America.* **99:** 1683-1692.

Lisker L, Abramson AS. 1964. A cross language study of voicing in initial stops: acoustical measurements. *Word.* **20:** 384-442.

Marsden CD, Obeso JA. 1994. The functions of the basal ganglia and the paradox of sterotaxic surgery in Parkinson's disease. *Brain.* **117:** 877-897.

Martin A, Haxby JV, Lalonde FM, Wiggs CL, Ungerleider LG, 1995. Discrete cortical regions associated with knowledge of color and knowledge of action. *Science.* **270:** 102-105

Mayr E. 1982. *The Growth of Biological Thought.* Cambridge, Massachusetts: Harvard University Press.

Mega MS, Alexander MF. 1994. Subcortical aphasia: The core profile of capsulostriatal infarction. *Neurology.* **44:** 1824-1829.

Mellars P. 1996. *The Neanderthal Legacy: an Archaeological Perspective from Western Europe.* Princeton, New Jersey: Princeton University Press.

Mesulam MM. 1990. Large-scale neurocognitive networks and distributed processing for attention, language, and memory. *Annals of Neurology.* **28:** 597-613.

Middleton FA, Strick PL. 1994. Anatomical evidence for cerebellar and basal ganglia involvement in higher cognition. *Science.* **266:** 458-461.

Müller J. 1848. *The Physiology of the Senses, Voice and Muscular Motion with the Mental Facilities.* Translated by W. Baly. London: Walton and Maberly.

Natsopoulos D, Grouios G, Bostantzopoulou S, Mentenopoulos G, Katsarou Z, Logothetis J. 1993. Algorithmic and heuristic strategies in comprehension of complement clauses by patients with Parkinson's Disease. *Neuropsychologia.* **31:** 951-964

Nearey T. 1979. *Phonetic Features for Vowels.* Bloomington: Indiana University Linguistics Club.

Negus VE. 1949. *The Comparative Anatomy and Physiology of the Larynx.* New York: Hafner.

Nelson TO, Dunlosky J, White DM, Steinberg J, Townes BD, Anderson D. 1990. Cognition and metacognition at extreme altitudes on Mount Everest. *Journal of Experimental Psychology, Genera.* **119:** 367-374.

Palmer J B, Hiiemae KM. 1997. Integration of oral and pharyngeal bolus propulsion: A new model for the physiology of swallowing. *Journal of Diet, Eating and Swallowing Rehabilitation (Japan).* **1:** 15-30.

Palmer J B, Rudin NJ, Lara G, Crompton AW. 1992. Coordination of mastication and swallowing. *Dysphagia.* **7:** 187-200.

Parent A. 1986. *Comparative Neurobiology of the Basal Ganglia.* New York: John Wiley.

Peterson GE, Barney HL. 1952. Control methods used in a study of the vowels. *Journal of the Acoustical Society of America.* **24:** 175-184.

Pickett ER, Kuniholm, Protopas A, Friedman J, Lieberman P. 1998. Selective speech motor, syntax and cognitive deficits associated with bilateral damage to the head of the caudate nucleus and the putamen. A single case study. *Neuropsychologia.* **36:** 173-188.

Savage-Rumbaugh ES, Rumbaugh D. 1993. The emergence of language. In: Gibson KR, Ingold T. eds. *Tools, Language and Cognition in Human Evolution*. Cambridge: Cambridge University Press. 86-100.

Semendeferi K, Damasio H, Frank R, Van Hoesen GW. 1997. The evolution of the frontal lobes: a volumetric analysis based on three-dimensional reconstructions of magnetic resonance scans of human and ape brains. *Journal of Human Evolution*. **32:** 375-378.

Spurzheim JK. 1815. *The Physiognomical System of Gall and Spurzheim.* London.

Stephan H, Frahm H, Baron G. 1981. New and revised data on volumes of brain structures in insectivores and primates. *Folia Primatologia*. **35:** 1-29.

Stevens KN. 1972. Quantal nature of speech. In: David EE Jr., Denes PB. eds. *Human Communication: A Unified View*. New York: McGraw Hill. 51-66.

Stuss DT, Benson DF. 1986. *The Frontal Lobes*. New York: Raven.

Tool-use, manipulation and cognition in capuchin monkeys (*Cebus*)

J. R. ANDERSON

Introduction

Capuchin monkeys *Cebus* spp., have become increasingly popular as research subjects for behavioural scientists. Visalberghi (1997) has charted the increase in publications devoted to the genus over the last two decades. The upsurge in studies of captive capuchins is partly because these New World monkeys are hardy and relatively easy to maintain; with few special dietary requirements, they thrive well in captivity if their psychological and social needs are met (Visalberghi & Anderson, 1999). However, the intensifying attention on the genus *Cebus* has more to do with the fact that capuchins present a particularly interesting array of biological and behavioural traits among primates. For example, capuchins are slow developers in terms of early neuro-behavioural functions, locomotor behaviour, and basic object manipulation (compared to other species of New World monkeys: see, for examples, Elias, 1977; Fragaszy, 1990; Fragaszy, Baer & Adams-Curtis, 1991). Reproduction begins relatively late in capuchins (first conception occurs after 5 years of age, which is later than in macaques, see Fragaszy & Bard, 1997), and birth rate is low compared to other monkeys (Ross, 1991), also, in captivity at least, capuchins may outlive other monkeys. Whereas macaques rarely reach 40 years of age, at least one capuchin has survived to over 50 years of age (R. Bartus, *pers. comm.*); this capuchin served as a subject in experiments on the cognitive effects of aging until shortly before his death (Bartus *et al.*, 1982). Some recent social behavioural studies have revealed that capuchin monkeys show relatively high levels of interindividual tolerance, which favours the non-aggressive transfer of food between adults and immatures as well as between adults (Perry & Rose, 1994; de Waal, 1997; Fragaszy, Feuerstein & Mitra, 1997). Peaceful transfers of inanimate objects (Thierry, Wunderlich & Gueth, 1989) and tools (Westergaard & Suomi, 1997) between unrelated individuals have also been reported.

In summary, capuchins stand out among monkeys because, in many biological and behavioural respects, they appear to have more in common with the nearest evolutionary relatives of humans, chimpanzees *Pan* spp., than with other monkeys. This remarkable parallelism between the two genera has led to recent focused comparisons of several aspects of their cognition, laterality, development, life-history, and social behaviour (Anderson, 1996; Fragaszy & Bard, 1997; Manson, Perry & Parish, 1997; McGrew &

Marchant, 1997; Visalberghi, 1997). The present chapter focuses on object manipulation, tool-use and cognition. These topics are of enduring interest for debates about the ontogeny and phylogeny of higher mental activity, often with reference to the most successful tool-using species of all, our own. By analysing how capuchin monkeys manipulate objects and respond to tasks in which tool-mediated solutions are possible, and also by comparing their behaviour in such situations with that of other nonhuman primates and with humans, researchers are gaining new insights and refining methods of inquiry into the emergence of advanced cognitive processes at both individual and species (or genus) levels.

Object manipulation in capuchins

Compared to other species of monkeys, capuchins show an impressively wide range of manipulatory acts with objects. Their facility and inventiveness with objects is amply illustrated by Torigoe's (1985) assessment of responses to objects in individuals belonging to over 70 species of primates. Torigoe recorded the primates' contacts with and manipulations of two inanimate objects, namely a piece of nylon rope with two knots at each end, and a small wooden cube. Manipulation patterns were distinguished on the basis of actions done, body-parts used and any relations between objects, such as hitting the object against a substrate or bringing it into contact with another object. An inter-species group comparison resulted in the three groups shown in Table 1.

In the first group of species, containing lemurs, callitrichids, spider monkeys and Old World leaf-eating species such as colobus monkeys and langurs, the object-directed behavioural repertoire was largely limited to simple actions as 'pick-up', 'mouth' and 'transport'. In the second group of species, containing baboons, guenons, mangabeys and macaques, some more varied actions were added, such as rolling or rubbing the objects. Capuchin monkeys were in the third group, which otherwise included only the great and the lesser apes. This group showed all of the lower-level patterns seen in other species, but also engaged in more complex actions such as draping, dropping, striking, swinging and throwing the objects.

With the exception of gibbons and siamangs, the species in the third group in Torigoe's (1985) study also showed secondary or combinatorial manipulations; that is, they manipulated the object in relation to another object, either fixed or detached. This is an important category of object-related behaviour, which has been linked with the emergence of tool-use in capuchins; indeed, tool-use is commonly defined as using one object to effect a change in another object. Natale (1989) emphasised capuchin monkeys' superiority to macaques in terms of the richness of object manipulations observed, particularly in relation to combinatorial acts and the investigation of object-object relations. In a larger study of captive *C. apella*, Fragaszy & Adams-Curtis (1991) reported that capuchins perform object-to-object actions from an early age. Combinatorial acts with objects appeared towards the end of the first year of life, before tool-use appeared. Westergaard & Suomi (1994) found considerable, but not total, overlap in the use of probing tools and performance of combinatorial object manipulation in juvenile and adult *C. apella* (see also Jalles-Filho, 1995).

Table 1 Species groupings based on manipulatory acts with objects (after Torigoe, 1985).

	Examples of manipulations
Group 1 Lemurs Callitrichids Spider monkeys Leaf-eaters	Pick up, mouth, transport
Group 2 Guenons Mangabeys Baboons Macaques	Pick up, mouth, transport, pull, push, rub, slide/stroke, transfer
Group 3 Capuchins Lesser apes Great apes	Pick up, mouth, transport, pull, push, rub, slide/stroke, transfer, drop, drape, swing, throw

However, neither combinatorial acts with objects, nor tool-use are limited to capuchins among monkeys. Torigoe (1985) recorded some combinatorial acts in Old World monkeys as well as capuchins and great apes, and there are many accounts of tool-use in Old World monkeys (Beck, 1980). Westergaard (1992) has related the use of objects as tools in young captive baboons to combinatorial manipulation of objects in the context of play. However, tool-use in Old World monkeys is mostly 'idiosyncratic' (in McGrew & Marchant's, 1997 terms), limited in range and performed by one or, at best, a few individuals in a group. In contrast, capuchin monkeys, in captivity at least, often have a tool-using repertoire, which includes several different modes, tool-use is 'customary', and a given form of tool-use may be shown by several, or by most, members of the group.

Spontaneous manipulation of objects can also be used to assess an individual's classificatory tendencies when the objects can be grouped according to one or more features. For example, Spinozzi & Natale (1989) analysed macaques' and capuchin monkeys' spontaneous groupings of six objects drawn from a pool of four different forms (cups, rings, crosses, sticks) made of four different materials (plexiglass, PVC, wood, plastic). The macaques' classificatory tendencies reflected minimal selections and groupings of two objects, with little development throughout the yearlong period of testing. In contrast, while the capuchins started with minimal two-object collections at 16 months of age, by the age of four years they classified larger collections and could flexibly switch among the criteria for class inclusion. Finally, when given a set of nesting cups and objects to manipulate, capuchin monkeys sometimes produced the most complex combination possible (known as a 'subassembly'), but their productions consisted mainly of the simplest combinations, known as 'pairings' (Westergaard & Suomi, 1994), suggesting simpler organisational aspects of object combinations than those observed in chimpanzees and young children (Greenfield, 1991; Matsuzawa, 1991).

Tool-use in capuchins

Not only do capuchin monkeys appear to surpass other monkeys in terms of diversity and complexity of manipulatory acts and spontaneous sorting of objects into categories, no other monkey genus approaches *Cebus* in the range of tool-using behaviours that have been reported. Visalberghi (1990a) describes some of the characteristics of capuchins, which probably contribute to the emergence of their tool-using exploits. Among these are curiosity and exploration of the environment and novel objects, considerable manual dexterity and manipulatory prowess, including the ability to perform several types of precision grips (Costello & Fragaszy, 1988). McGrew & Marchant (1997) list modes of tool use observed in *Pan* and *Cebus,* and state that wild chimpanzees show over 20 of 27 modes listed, while wild capuchins have shown seven: brandish/flail, club, drop, hammer/pound, probe, prod/jab and aimed throw. Observations of tool-use by wild capuchins are largely anecdotal. Chevalier-Skolnikoff (1990) recorded eight different types of tool-use in a group of *C. capucinus*, mostly in the context of aggression, e.g., flailing, dropping, throwing, poking or hitting. In captivity, however, the gap between chimpanzees and capuchins in modes of tool-use narrows considerably. In addition to the modes mentioned above, captive capuchins have shown the following: absorb/sponge, bait, balance/climb, contain, dig, ladder, pry/lever, reach/rake, stack, wipe, groom, cut/pierce, chisel and grind. It is not clear whether the 'wipe' category incorporates reports of capuchins rubbing certain substances into their pelage; this behaviour has been observed in both captivity and the wild (Ludes & Anderson, 1995; Baker, 1996), and it may represent another mode.

How do the known modes of tool-use by capuchins translate into concrete examples? In the recent literature, captive capuchins have been described using stones and pieces of wood as hammers to crack open nuts (Antinucci & Visalberghi 1986; Anderson, 1990), using sticks and other long thin objects as probes to dip into and extract syrup or honey (Westergaard & Fragaszy, 1987a; Visalberghi, 1990b; Anderson & Henneman, 1994), inserting sticks to push edible items out of a tube (Visalberghi & Trinca, 1989, Visalberghi & Limongelli, 1994) and using a stick to rake in out-of-reach objects (Parker & Poti, 1990). One captive adult female capuchin monkey used sticks to groom her own and her infant's wounds (Westergaard & Fragaszy, 1987b; Ritchie & Fragaszy, 1989). The female prepared the tools before use by chewing the end to be applied to the wound. Capuchins have also used sharp-edged objects to penetrate an acetate cover to extract peanut butter from a container (e.g., Westergaard *et al.*, 1996), and they have used soft materials such as crumpled paper as sponges, and cups to collect liquids or small objects (Westergaard & Fragaszy, 1985, 1987a; Chevalier-Skolnikoff, 1989).

In the wild, 18 of the 31 records made by Chevalier-Skolnikoff (1990) were of branches being broken and dropped in the direction of the observer; also, one individual poked a stick into a hole in a branch and then put it in his mouth. Adult male *C. capucinus* use sticks as weapons against snakes (Chapman, 1986; Boinski, 1988), and a male *C. apella* was observed opening oysters by striking them with a hand-held object, probably an oyster shell (Fernandes, 1991). Overall, in terms of the frequency and range of tool-using acts described, capuchin monkeys come closer to chimpanzees than do any other species of nonhuman primates (Anderson, 1996; Visalberghi & Limongelli, 1996), although there are some important differences between capuchins' and chimpanzees' tool-use (e.g., McGrew, 1993; McGrew & Marchant, 1997; Visalberghi, 1997; see below).

In order to set the scene for exploring the cognitive implications of object manipulation and tool-use by capuchins, one mode will be described in more detail. Possibly the best known form of tool-use by these monkeys is the use of hard objects to hammer open nuts or other foods with a hard protective outer coating. Antinucci & Visalberghi (1986) conducted the first systematic study of 'nut-cracking', comparing a captive, tool-using *C. apella*'s actions with hazelnuts and walnuts with those of a non-tool-using conspecific and with its own behaviour in the absence of any tools. The tool-user showed a distinct order of preference among the three potential tools, namely a stone, a wooden block, then an empty plastic container, corresponding to their relative efficacy as tools, i.e. their hardness. The tool-user started eating the nuts much sooner when he used a tool than when he did not, and much sooner than the other capuchin.

Although the tool-user lived in a group, none of the other group members engaged in tool-aided nut cracking.

Anderson (1990) replicated and extended Antinucci & Visalberghi's (1986) findings by comparing nut-processing time in a group of captive capuchin monkeys given three kinds of hard-shelled nuts and in the presence or absence of stones which could be used as hammers. The group consisted of a wild-born adult male and adult female, and their five captive-born offspring: two adult males, an adolescent male and a juvenile female (a 1-year-old male was not included in the study). The stones weighed between 375 and 660 g.

Of all the group members, only the adult female was never observed to use a tool for nut cracking. All four males regularly used tools when they were available, as did the juvenile female once she had learned the technique during the course of the study (the unstudied, youngest male also eventually became a regular tool-user). The tool-users used the hammer-stones most frequently to open hazelnuts (on approximately 75% of trials), and less frequently to open walnuts (50%) and almonds (41%). A nut-cracking sequence typically consisted of a capuchin picking up a nut and carrying it to the stone, placing the nut on the ground beside the stone, then lifting the stone with both hands and bringing it down on the nut. Sometimes nut and stone were both carried to another part of the enclosure before hammering started; this often required bipedal locomotion.

Individual variations in tool-use technique were notable. For example, the juvenile male typically swept the ground clean with one hand before placing the nut to be cracked, and he preferred to lift the stone and bring it down with one hand while the other hand acted as a screen to prevent the nut from shooting away upon impact. Both immature tool-users habitually touched the nut lightly against the stone before placing it on the ground for cracking; adults never did this. There were also individual variations in the amount of force used to crack the nuts. The two young adult males typically delivered a few light hits with the hammer-stone until the shell cracked, finishing by prising the shell apart with the teeth or hands. They generally used the sound of the shell cracking to know when to stop hammering, but sometimes they looked at the nut between hits. Hammering by the oldest male and the immature monkeys was less controlled, sometimes they need so much force that the nut was pulverised with one blow (although it was always eaten).

In terms of effectiveness of tool-use, in all cases tool-users gained access to the kernel of the nut in less time when they used a tool compared to when they had to open nuts without tools (Figure 1). Furthermore, the reduced processing time was significant for almost all the individual comparisons. For example, the oldest adult male sometimes required more than 1 minute to gain access to the kernel of an almond when no tool was available. Typically he held the almond in one hand and repeatedly tapped it against a hard substrate (the ground or a log), in between biting and gnawing at the shell until the shell gave. In contrast, when a hammer-stone was used, he was usually able to start eating the kernel after less than 10 seconds from the start of the trial. An even greater difference was observed in the juvenile female, who was unable to break into a hazelnut after 30 minutes of biting and tapping the nut against the ground, walls, metal parts of the cage, etc. When given a hazelnut in the presence of a hammer-stone, she required only 5 seconds to break into it.

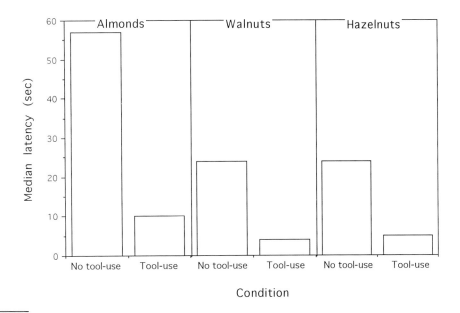

Figure 1
Latencies to open nuts. Without a tool and with a tool. (After Anderson, 1990).

The effectiveness of tool-use for nut-cracking is further illustrated by the fact that nuts which proved too difficult to open with the teeth and/or tapping against a substrate were eventually abandoned if no tools were present. Thus, when no stones were available, all members of the group abandoned nuts after persistent, but failed attempts to open them. In stark contrast, no tool-user ever abandoned a nut in the presence of a tool; all hard nuts could be cracked by using a tool. Only the female with no aptitude for tool-mediated nut-cracking abandoned nuts in both conditions.

Ontogeny and phylogeny of capuchin tool-use

As has already been mentioned, tool-use by capuchin monkeys probably emerges from a tendency to engage in object-object combinatorial or 'generative' acts from a relatively early age (see Fragaszy & Adams-Curtis, 1991). The likelihood of any given capuchin monkey developing tool-use depends upon several factors, including individual predisposition, early experience, environmental contingencies and social constraints, factors which interact in ways that are far from being fully understood. It is usual for reports to indicate that a particular form of tool-use was not in the repertoire of all members of a group (e.g., Antinucci & Visalberghi, 1986; Fragaszy & Westergaard, 1987a; Anderson, 1990; Anderson & Henneman, 1994; Jalles-Filho, 1995; Visalberghi & Limongelli, 1996), and tool-use may not be facilitated by seeing other group-members perform competently, even if the act is modeled repeatedly (Visalberghi, 1993; Visalberghi & Fragaszy, 1990). In some captive groups, tool-use has not appeared even after months of apparently favourable environmental conditions (*personal observations*). Groups housed in indoor cages were more likely to manipulate objects than groups in outdoor runs, where there was more alternative stimulation (Byrne & Suomi, 1996). Westergaard *et al.* (1998) reported that almost 60% of 36 capuchins housed in eight groups used probing tools, with no difference between the sexes. However, whereas almost all individuals below 10 years of age used tools, only around 10% of older monkeys did so, suggesting a sensitive period in development for the acquisition of tool-mediated acts. The authors also found no effect of whether juveniles' mothers used tools on the likelihood of tool-use by juveniles, but if their mothers died when the juveniles were less than 3 years of age, the juveniles were significantly less likely to show tool-use.

Although no strong statements can be made about the likelihood of tool-use appearing in a given individual or group of capuchins, it seems safe to suggest that tool-use is most likely to be seen in an appropriately object-rich environment, especially in captivity where the monkeys have a lot of 'free' time on their hands and conditions may be favourable to the development of innovative behaviours (Kummer & Goodall, 1985).

As far as the evolution of capuchins' tool-using abilities is concerned, the consensus view is that they originate in these monkeys' foraging adaptations. Capuchins are omnivorous primates with a strong tendency to engage in what Terborgh (1983) terms a 'destructive' foraging strategy. As well as including easily processed fruits, leaves, flowers, etc. in their diet, capuchins make heavy use of food sources that require considerable, and sometimes forceful, processing before the edible component is exposed or extracted. These include hard-husked nuts (pounded against branches), snails (also pounded) or insects found under bark (torn off) or housed in other plant parts (broken apart). Such difficult-to-access foods require special anatomical adaptations (robust capuchins have extremely strong masticatory apparatus) as well as behavioural adaptations (see Janson & Boinski, 1992). In this light, capuchins' propensity for varied, vigorous and persistent manipulation of objects, often leading to the destruction of the latter, can be seen as part of a repertoire which in a natural setting might ultimately result in an embedded food item being exposed and made ready for eating. The following kinds of manipulations are described for capuchins feeding on natural foods (Fragaszy & Boinski, 1995): 'strenuous' actions, including dig, rip, bite, bang, grab, break, carry, tap, roll, scrape, chase, as well as 'quiet' actions, including pick, visually examine, lick, mouth, sniff, manually examine, sift, take, feel, scoop, turn over, masticate, open by peeling. Thus, many of the diverse manipulatory patterns and varied modes of *Cebus* tool-use can be seen as extensions of this foraging-based repertoire.

Parker & Gibson (1977) proposed that there was a direct evolutionary relationship between extractive foraging and tool-using ability by capuchins. These authors further suggested that the similarity between capuchins and chimpanzees in their capacity for tool-use was a case of convergent evolution, both species evolving the capacity for true tool-use as one feature of a combined mental and behavioural adaptive complex for solving the problem of getting access to 'embedded' food sources. Several aspects of Parker & Gibson's (1977) general hypothesis of a direct link between extractive foraging and tool-use/advanced cognition are problematical (Tomasello & Call, 1997). Byrne (1997) has challenged it on the basis that the cognitive processes involved in tool-use by chimpanzees and capuchins may be fundamentally different, the major issue discussed in the remainder of this chapter.

Tool-use and cognition in capuchins

Some authors have interpreted capuchins' facility with tools as evidence for these monkeys reaching more advanced stages of Piagetian sensorimotor development than other species of monkeys. This view formed part of Parker & Gibson's (1977) account of tool-use in *Pan* and *Cebus*, and it was stated most strongly by Chevalier-Skolnikoff (1989), who compared zoo-housed spider monkeys with capuchin monkeys, testing their object manipulations and tool-use. Only capuchins showed tool-use. Although Chevalier-Skolnikoff reported 14 different types of 'tool-use' by the capuchins (including throwing an object in aggression or play, flailing, hitting, probing, banging and containing), some of the cases may be more appropriately labeled as 'proto-tool-use' (*cf.* Parker & Gibson, 1977) rather than true tool-use. Even so, spider monkeys showed no tool-use, nor did they show anything like the same variety or sophistication of object-related acts as the capuchin monkeys. In terms of higher-stage sensorimotor schemes, 13% of spider monkeys' object manipulations were ascribed to Stage 3 secondary circular reactions and 87% to Stage 4 co-ordinations. In contrast, 5% of capuchins' object manipulations were at Stage 3, 44% at Stage 4, 42% at Stage 5 tertiary circular reactions and 8% at Stage 5 or Stage 6 ('insightful behaviour').

Chevalier-Skolnikoff's (1989) analysis has been criticised on several fronts, including her definitions of tool-use and 'insightful' acts, her classification of behaviours in terms of Piagetian stages, the uncontrolled nature of the environments and her interpretation of the origins or discovery of tool-use acts observed (for the most pertinent criticisms see Anderson, 1989; Bard & Vauclair, 1989; Bernstein, 1989; Fragaszy, 1989; Parker, 1989; Visalberghi, 1989). Other researchers have assessed sensorimotor intelligence in *Cebus* using more systematic and controlled tasks. The results emerging from these studies present an uneven picture: some have concluded that capuchins may indeed surpass other monkeys, for example by being able to solve object-concept problems involving invisible displacement by means of Stage 6 mental representation (Mathieu *et al.*, 1976; Schino, Spinozzi & Berlinguer, 1990), but other studies have failed to find evidence for this (Natale & Antinucci, 1989; Dumas & Brunet, 1994).

There is also a rather fragmented literature concerning capuchin monkeys' performances on more traditional tasks of learning and memory, including object discrimination learning sets, reversal learning, cross-modal recognition, auditory short-term memory and serial learning. No overall picture of superiority of capuchins compared to other monkeys emerges from this literature, but it contains some tantalising glimpses of excellence by capuchins, justifying new research efforts and attempts to relate species differences to other domains, including social and neurological. In this context, it is noteworthy that capuchins score higher than other monkeys on indices of brain development related to cognitive potential (see Adams-Curtis, 1990; Anderson, 1996; Fragaszy & Bard, 1997 for comparative behavioural and neurological perspectives).

Cognition assessed through controlled tool-use tasks

Over the last decade, experiments have been carried out to take a closer look at tool-use in capuchin monkeys, with emphasis on the degree to which their deployment of tools is based on representational cognitive processes similar to those inferred in human and chimpanzee tool-users. As described earlier, when they use tools to crack open hard nuts, capuchins are selective in the materials they use, and by using a tool they reduce processing time per item consumed, reduce wear and tear on teeth and, thus, improve overall feeding efficiency. When they use tools for dipping, they are also selective and they may modify the tools before use (see below). However, Visalberghi (1993, 1997) has cautioned that when it comes to understanding tool-use by capuchins it is essential to distinguish between their successful performances and their comprehension. There is no doubt that capuchins are excellent performers, quick to learn to repeat sequences of object-mediated acts that have led to desirable outcomes. Thus, they may become skilled tool-users through trial and error, but this does not mean that capuchins have any real understanding of the cause-effect relations involved in tool-use.

It is their performances on another type of tool-use task that appear to betray capuchins' lack of understanding of cause-effect relations. In the first of a series of studies leading to this conclusion, Visalberghi & Trinca (1989) established that three members of a captive capuchin group could reliably push a stick into one end of a 30 cm transparent tube in order to expel a peanut from the other end; performance was stabilised at around 100% success. However, when more complex conditions were introduced, in which the monkeys had to combine or modify the tool, they made a variety of errors, which were not consistent with an understanding of the task. For example, although they eventually solved the problem each time, the monkeys frequently inserted splinters which they detached from a bundle of sticks and which were much too short to be effective. Another condition consisted of presenting the tool with a smaller stick inserted through each end in such a way as to impede the tool's entrance into the tube (the so-called H-stick problem). A frequent error in this case consisted of first removing a small stick from one end of the tool, but then inserting this small stick instead of the now ready-to-use tool. There was no significant decrease in such errors across repeated trials (see also Visalberghi, Fragaszy & Savage-Rumbaugh, 1995), which suggested to the authors that the capuchins did not have an abstract representation of the physical characteristics of a good tool.

Visalberghi & Limongelli (1996) have reviewed studies that use several modifications of the basic stick and tube task. In one variant, called the trap-tube task, the tube had a trap-hole in the middle so that if the reward was pushed from the wrong side it fell into the trap and was no longer available to the subject. Three of four capuchins tested solved the trap-tube task only at chance levels, i.e., they did not anticipate the consequences of inserting the stick from the wrong end. Further testing of the single capuchin that successfully solved the trap-tube task revealed that she used a spatial strategy rather than a true comprehension of the task. For example, when the apparatus was turned upside down so that the trap no longer presented a hazard, the monkey persisted in attentively monitoring the progress of the stick in the tube in a stereotyped manner. Also, by rendering the tube opaque and observing how the monkey approached this variant of the problem, it was possible to show that the capuchin had simply adopted the rather rigid rule of 'push from the end furthest from the reward' (for details, see Visalberghi & Limongelli, 1994). Thus, it would appear that capuchins, though skilful tool-users, might in fact have a relatively limited understanding of the cause-effect relations that would underlie truly insightful or representational tool-use. Chimpanzees perform better on the tube-tasks (although some do not; see Visalberghi & Limongelli, 1996).

In another analysis of the flexibility of capuchins' tool-use, Anderson & Henneman (1994) presented a pair of adult, wild-born capuchins with a series of eight tasks, loosely based on some of Klüver's (1937) classic experiments with an adult female capuchin. The basic task consisted of inserting long and thin sticks into an opaque box to extract honey, which adhered to the end of the sticks.

Table 2 summarises the results of this study. Although there were some clear failures in the series, there were some notable successes. For example, when given a stick which was too thick to be used as a probe, the male would bite and gnaw at it until a splinter was broken off which could be used, or until the stick was sufficiently reduced in width for it to be used effectively. Unlike the error-laden performances described by Visalberghi & Trinca (1989), this capuchin's tool-using contained very few 'erroneous' responses, and any that did occur did so only when the solution was not immediately obvious. When given a choice between thick and thin sticks, both monkeys selected in advance a stick of appropriate width for the task. The most striking finding, however, was that the adult male rapidly, purposefully and consistently used a stick, which was too thick for dipping, as a raking tool to obtain another stick which was out of reach, but was more appropriate for the honey-dipping task (see Anderson, 1996 for illustrations). Not only does the first instance of this behaviour represent a strong candidate for an 'insightful' tool-using act, it is also an example of use of a tool-set, i.e., the use of one tool to prepare the way for another form of tool-use.

Until Westergaard & Suomi's (1993) experimental demonstration of nut-cracking (using a stone) followed by levering out fragments of the nut kernel (using a stick) in capuchins, chimpanzees had been the only nonhuman primates observed using a tool-set (Brewer & McGrew, 1990). Visalberghi & Limongelli (1996) point out that in Westergaard & Suomi's (1993) study the capuchins' performance on the tool-set problem contained many instances of inappropriate behaviour, such as applying sticks to uncracked nuts (which were held in an apparatus) and using to stones to hit already opened nuts. In contrast, use of a tool-set by the male capuchin in the study by Anderson & Henneman (1994) was virtually error-free. Westergaard *et al.* (1995) described combinations of tools (pestles and sponges) used to extract juice from sugarcane and, more recently, Westergaard *et al.* (1996) have described a 'hammer and chisel' action by an adult male *Cebus apella.* This monkey placed a sharp-edged object on the acetate cover of a food-well and then struck the object with a stone, thus penetrating the acetate. The performance was consistent across trials. In both of these reports, however, there is no information on similar combinations of 'tools' in nonfunctional contexts, i.e. there is no comparison of frequency or form of such acts when they lead to food and when they do not. Use of tool-sets by nonhuman primates in the wild remains limited to chimpanzees (Matsuzawa, 1991; McGrew, 1993)

Conclusions

What can be concluded about the cognitive abilities involved in tool-use by capuchin monkeys? At this stage, we can conclude very little with any certainty, given the extremely fragmentary nature of

Table 2 Summary of performances of two adult capuchin monkeys on eight tool-related tasks (after Anderson & Henneman, 1994).

Task name	Task description	Performance
Honey dipping	Thin sticks to be inserted into holes in a honey container	**Male:** Successful dipping on 20 of 20 trials **Female:** Successful dipping in 19 of 20 trials
Thick stick	The stick must be modified before it or part of it can be used	**Male:** Successful modification on 9 of 10 trials **Female:** Failure, with some repetition of inappropriate acts and scrounging*
Stick selection	Choice between thin (tool) sticks and thick sticks	**Male:** Appropriate choice on 13 of 15 trials **Female:** Appropriate choice on 8 of 10 trials
Rake task	A thick stick must be used to rake in a honey-dipping stick	**Male:** Successful raking in 15 of 15 sessions **Female:** Failure, with no attempts and scrounging
Tool construction	Two thick 'sticks' must be joined to form a raking tool	**Male:** Joined sticks in 9 sessions, but did not use as tool **Female:** Failure, with attempts to insert other objects
Telescopic tool	A telescopic aerial must be extended and used as a rake	**Male:** Successful use in 9 of 10 sessions (12 of 20 trials) **Female:** Failure, with no attempts; scrounges from male
Folding tool	A folding ruler must be opened out and used as a rake	**Male:** Failure on 8 of 10 sessions **Female:** Failure, with no attempts
Bent wire tool	A loop of bent soldering wire must be straightened out and used to honey-dip	**Male:** Success on 10 of 10 trials **Female:** failure, with no attempts

* The female was subsequently observed to break off and modify a twig for dipping.

the data. For example, almost all detailed studies of tool-use by capuchins in captivity have involved limited numbers of sessions and relatively few subjects. Furthermore, the subjects are often immature individuals or relatively young adults. Not all chimpanzees perform well on the trap-tube task on which at least one capuchin performed well, albeit by associative rather than representational processes (Visalberghi & Limongelli, 1996).

Individual differences in innovative tendencies are no doubt important in capuchin monkeys. The apparently insightful use of a tool-set described by Anderson & Henneman (1994) was seen in a post-prime adult of almost thirty years of age, with a long lifetime of experience with the properties of objects. (Following capture as a juvenile, this male lived for years on an island in a zoo before arriving at the laboratory where the study was conducted). Tomasello & Call (1997) have also pointed out that in studies in which capuchin monkeys have failed to reach Stage 6 representational performance on Piagetian tasks, the subjects have typically been immature, whereas in the best controlled study with a positive result the subject was an adult (Schino *et al.*, 1990). Thus, a greater range of ages and experience with objects needs to be incorporated into the study of tool-use and cognition.

What appears clear is that if we limit studies to what are essentially extremely brief snapshots of behaviours shown by a small number of individuals in contrived experimental conditions requiring complex solutions, we might be able to estimate what capuchin monkeys (or indeed any species) are capable of, but we also run the risk of forming a misleading picture of the cognitive potential of the species. As an example of how an experiment designed to facilitate tool-use was inadequate, Anderson & Henneman's (1994) adult female capuchin monkey formally failed the 'thick stick' task, i.e., she never fashioned any of the sticks presented into a tool (see Table 2). At a later date, however, when her male companion was not present and she could not obtain any honey by scrounging (licking honey left on the apparatus after the male's tool-use), she promptly climbed to the top of the cage, broke off a piece of overhanging vegetation, modified this tool by biting and then used it to dip for honey. Thus, both the acquisition and expression of an individual's skills may be influenced by social factors and the use of alternative strategies in ways which mask individual potential (see Anderson *et al.*, 1992, 1994; for striking examples of inhibitory social influences on innovative behaviour in other primate genera).

There is some, albeit limited, information available regarding social influences on tool-use and proto-tool-use (i.e. food washing) by capuchins (Fragaszy & Visalberghi, 1989, 1990; Visalberghi, 1990b; Jalles-Filho, 1995; Visalberghi & Fragaszy, 1995). These studies have drawn attention to the roles of stimulus and local enhancement in the dissemination of new behaviours. However, more data are needed, observational and experimental, from natural settings and captivity, from individuals and group settings, with more attention being paid to experiential factors. Also, data from tool-use studies need to be complemented with other lines of evidence. Information from one domain can legitimately be used to supplement, corroborate or to challenge positions based on findings from other approaches. Some of the pertinent information is mentioned elsewhere in this chapter, but again there is ample scope for more and for new data. For example, it is known that capuchin monkeys typically fail to learn tool-use through imitation (e.g. Visalberghi & Fragaszy, 1990), they did not show co-ordination or collaboration in an operant task requiring co-operation between two individuals (Chalmeau, Visalberghi & Gallo, 1997) and they do not show any signs of mirror self-recognition (Anderson & Marchal, 1994). In all of these domains, capuchin monkeys appear inferior to the great apes, but new data may modify this view. There is also a growing literature on laterality of hand function in the context of tool-use by capuchins (reviewed by McGrew & Marchant, 1997), which might also feed into debate about cognitive organisation. As McGrew & Marchant (1997) point out, in terms of modes, frequency and context there are many differences between tool-use by chimpanzees and capuchins, but it is surely only through continuing developments in the study of tool-use and other domains, including social behaviour and behavioural ecology, that we can hope to arrive at a satisfactory understanding of the evolution of capuchins' cognitive tool-kit.

References

Adams-Curtis L. 1990. Conceptual learning in capuchin monkeys. *Folia Primatologica.* **54:** 129-132.

Anderson JR. 1989. On the contents of capuchins' cognitive tool-kit. *Behavioral and Brain Sciences.* **12:** 588-589.

Anderson JR. 1990. Use of objects as hammers to open nuts by capuchin monkeys (*Cebus apella*). *Folia Primatologica.* **54:** 138-145.

Anderson JR. 1996. Chimpanzees and capuchin monkeys: Comparative cognition. In: Russon AE, Bard KA, Parker ST. eds. *Reaching into Thought: The Minds of the Great Apes.* Cambridge: Cambridge University Press. 23-56.

Anderson JR, Degiorgio C, Lamarque C, Fagot J. 1996. A multi-task assessment of hand lateralization in capuchin monkeys (*Cebus apella*). *Primates.* **37:** 97-103.

Anderson JR, Fornasieri I, Ludes E, Roeder J-J. 1992. Social processes and innovative behaviour in changing groups of *Lemur fulvus*. *Behavioural Processes.* **27:** 101-112.

Anderson JR, Henneman M-C. 1994. Solutions to a tool-use problem in a pair of *Cebus apella*. *Mammalia.* **58:** 351-361.

Anderson JR, Marchal P. 1994. Capuchin monkeys and confrontations with mirrors. In: Roeder JJ, Thierry B, Anderson JR, Herrenschmidt N. eds. *Current Primatology, Vol. 2: Social*

Development, Learning and Behaviour. Strasbourg: Université Louis Pasteur. 371-380.

Anderson JR, Peignot P, Adelbrecht C, Fontaine S, Peugeot C. 1994. Social correlates of performance on an underwater foraging task in rhesus monkeys. In: Roeder JJ, Thierry B, Anderson JR, Herrenschmidt N. eds. *Current Primatology, Vol. 2: Social Development, Learning and Behaviour.* Strasbourg: Université Louis Pasteur. 355-362.

Antinucci F, Visalberghi E. 1986. Tool use in *Cebus apella*: A case study. *International Journal of Primatology.* **7**: 351-350.

Baker M. 1996. Fur rubbing: Use of medicinal plants by capuchin monkeys (*Cebus capucinus*). *American Journal of Primatology.* **38**: 263-270.

Bard KA, Vauclair J. 1989. What's the tool and where's the goal? *Behavioral and Brain Sciences.* **12**: 590-591.

Bartus RT, Dean RL III, Beer B, Lippa AS. 1982. The cholinergic hypothesis of geriatric memory dysfunction. *Science.* **217**: 408-417.

Beck BB. 1980. *Animal Tool Behavior: The Use and Manufacture of Tools by Animals.* New York: Garland STPM Press.

Bernstein IS. 1989. Cognitive explanations: Plausibility is not enough. *Behavioral and Brain Sciences.* **12**: 593-594.

Boinski S. 1988. Use of a club by a wild white-faced capuchin (*Cebus capucinus*) to attack a venomous snake (*Bothrops asper*). *American Journal of Primatology.* **14**: 177-179.

Brewer SM, McGrew WC. 1990. Chimpanzee use of a tool-set to get honey. *Folia Primatologica.* **54**: 100-104.

Byrne G, Suomi SJ. 1996. Individual differences in object manipulation in a colony of tufted capuchins. *Journal of Human Evolution.* **31**: 259-267.

Byrne RW. 1997. The Technical Intelligence hypothesis: An additional evolutionary stimulus to intelligence? In: Whiten A, Byrne RW. eds. *Machiavellian Intelligence II: Extensions and Evaluations.* Cambridge: Cambridge University Press. 289-311.

Chalmeau R, Visalberghi E, Gallo A. 1997. Capuchin monkeys, *Cebus apella*, fail to understand a cooperative task. *Animal Behaviour.* **54**: 1215-1225.

Chapman CA. 1986. Boa constrictor predation and group response in white-faced cebus monkeys. *Biotropica.* **18**: 171-172.

Chevalier-Skolnikoff S. 1989. Spontaneous tool use and sensorimotor intelligence in *Cebus* compared with other monkeys and apes. *Behavioral and Brain Sciences.* **12**: 561-627.

Chevalier-Skolnikoff S. 1990. Tool use by wild cebus monkeys at Santa Rosa National Park, Costa Rica. *Primates.* **31**: 375-383.

Costello MB, Fragaszy DM. 1988. Prehensive grips in capuchins (*Cebus apella*). *American Journal of Primatology.* **15**: 235-245.

de Waal FBM. 1997. Food transfers through mesh in brown capuchins. *Journal of Comparative Psychology.* **111**: 370-378.

de Waal FBM, Berger M. 2000. Payment for labour in monkeys. *Nature.* **404:** 563.

Dumas C, Brunet C. 1994. Permanence de l'objet chez le singe capucin (*Cebus apella*): étude des déplacements invisibles. *Canadian Journal of Experimental Psychology.* **48:** 341-358.

Elias MF. 1977. Relative maturity of cebus and squirrel monkeys at birth and during infancy. *Developmental Psychobiology.* **10:** 519-528.

Fernandes MEB. 1991. Tool use and predation of oysters (*Crassotrea rhizophorae*) by the tufted capuchin, *Cebus apella apella*, in brackish water mangrove swamp. *Primates.* **32:** 529-531.

Fragaszy DM. 1989. Tool-use, imitation, and insight: Apples, oranges, and conceptual pea soup. *Behavioral and Brain Sciences.* **12:** 596-598.

Fragaszy DM. 1990. Early behavioral development in capuchins (*Cebus*). *Folia Primatologica.* **54:** 119-128.

Fragaszy DM, Adams-Curtis LE. 1991. Generative aspects of manipulation in tufted capuchin monkeys (*Cebus apella*). *Journal of Comparative Psychology.* **105:** 387-397.

Fragaszy DM, Baer J, Adams-Curtis LE. 1991. Behavioral development and maternal care in tufted capuchins (*Cebus apella*) and squirrel monkeys (*Saimiri sciureus*) from birth through seven months. *Developmental Psychobiology.* **24:** 375-393.

Fragaszy DM, Bard KA. 1997. Comparison of development and life history in *Pan* and *Cebus*. *International Journal of Primatology.* **18:** 683-701.

Fragaszy DM, Boinski S. 1995. Patterns of individual diet choice and efficiency of foraging in wedge-capped capuchin monkeys (*Cebus olivaceus*). *Journal of Comparative Psychology.* **109:** 339-348.

Fragaszy DM, Feuerstein JM, Mitra D. 1997. Transfers of food from adults to infants in tufted capuchins (*Cebus apella*). *Journal of Comparative Psychology.* **111:** 194-200.

Fragaszy DM, Visalberghi E. 1989. Social influences on the acquisition of tool-using behaviors in tufted capuchin monkeys (*Cebus apella*). *Journal of Comparative Psychology.* **103:** 159-170.

Fragaszy DM, Visalberghi E. 1990. Social processes affecting the appearance of innovative behaviors in capuchin monkeys. *Folia Primatologica.* **54:** 155-175.

Greenfield PM. 1991. Language, tools, and the brain: The ontogeny and phylogeny of hierarchically organised sequential behavior. *Behavioral and Brain Sciences.* **14:** 531-595.

Jalles-Filho E. 1995. Manipulative propensity and tool use in capuchin monkeys. *Current Anthropology.* **36:** 664-667.

Janson CH, Boinski S. 1992. Morphological and behavioral adaptations for foraging in generalist primates: The case of the cebines. *American Journal of Physical Anthropology.* **88:** 483-498.

Klüver H. 1937. Re-examination of implement-using behavior in a cebus monkey after an interval of three years. *Acta Psychologia.* **2:** 347-397.

Kummer H, Goodall J. 1985. Conditions of innovative behaviour in primates. *Philosophical Transactions of the Royal Society of London.* **B308:** 203-214.

Ludes E, Anderson JR. 1995. 'Peat-bathing' by captive white-faced capuchin monkeys (*Cebus capucinus*). *Folia Primatologica.* **65:** 38-42.

Manson JH, Perry S, Parish AR. 1997. Nonconceptive sexual behavior in bonobos and capuchins. *International Journal of Primatology.* **18:** 767-786.

Mathieu M, Bouchard MA, Granger L, Herscovitch J. 1976. Piagetian object-permanence in *Cebus capucinus, Lagothrica flavicauda* and *Pan troglodytes. Animal Behaviour.* **24:** 585-588.

Matsuzawa T. 1991. Nesting cups and metatools in chimpanzees. *Behavioral and Brain Sciences.* **14:** 570-571.

McGrew WC. 1993. The intelligent use of tools: Twenty propositions. In: Gibson KR, Ingold T. eds. *Tools, Language and Cognition in Human Evolution.* Cambridge: Cambridge University Press. 151-170.

McGrew WC, Marchant LF. 1997. Using the tools at hand: Manual laterality and elementary technology in *Cebus* spp. and *Pan* spp. *International Journal of Primatology.* **18:** 787-810.

Natale F. 1989. Patterns of object manipulation. In: Antinucci F. ed. *Cognitive Structure and Development in Nonhuman Primates.* Hillsdale, NJ: Lawrence Erlbaum. 97-112.

Natale F, Antinucci F. 1989 Stage 6 object-concept and representation. In: Antinucci F. ed. *Cognitive Structure and Development in Nonhuman Primates.* Hillside NJ: Lawrence Erlbaum Associates. 97-112.

Parker ST. 1989. Imitation and derivative reactions. *Behavioral and Brain Sciences.* **12:** 604.

Parker ST, Gibson KR. 1977. Object manipulation, tool use and senorimotor intelligence as feeding adaptations in cebus monkeys and great apes. *Journal of Human Evolution.* **6:** 623-641.

Parker ST, Poti P. 1990. The role of innate motor patterns in ontogenetic and experiential development of intelligent use of sticks in cebus monkeys. In: Parker ST, Gibson KR. eds. *'Language' and Intelligence in Monkeys and Apes: Comparative Developmental Perspectives.* New York: Cambridge University Press. 219-243.

Perry S, Rose L. 1994. Begging and transfer of coati meat by white-faced capuchin monkeys, *Cebus capucinus. Primates.* **35:** 409-415.

Ritchie B, Fragaszy DM. 1989. A capuchin monkey (*Cebus apella*) uses tools on her infant's wound. *American Journal of Primatology.* **16:** 345-348.

Ross C. 1991. Life history patterns of New World monkeys. *International Journal of Primatology.* **12:** 481-502.

Schino G, Spinozzi G, Berlinguer L. 1990. Object concept and mental representation in *Cebus apella* and *Macaca fascicularis. Primates.* **31:** 537-544.

Spinozzi G, Natale F. 1989. Classification. In: Antinucci F. ed. *Cognitive Structure and Development in Nonhuman Primates*. Hillsdale, New Jersey: Lawrence Erlbaum. 163-187.

Terborgh JW. 1983. *Five New World Primates: A Study in Comparative Ecology*. Princeton: Princeton University Press.

Thierry B, Wunderlich D, Gueth C. 1989. Possession and transfer of objects in a group of brown capuchins (*Cebus apella*). *Behaviour.* **110:** 294-305.

Tomasello M, Call J. 1997. *Primate Cognition*. New York: Oxford University Press.

Torigoe T. 1985. Comparison of object manipulation among 74 species of non-human primates. *Primates.* **26:** 182-194.

Visalberghi E. 1989. Primate tool use: Parsimonious explanations make better science. *Behavioral and Brain Sciences.* **12:** 608-609.

Visalberghi E. 1990a. Tool-use in *Cebus. Folia Primatologica.* **54:** 146-154.

Visalberghi E. 1990b. Influences of aversive processes on innovative behaviors in primates. In : Brain P, Parmigiani S, Blanchard RJ, Mainardi D. eds. *Fear and Defense*. Harwood Academic Publishers. 309-328.

Visalberghi E. 1993. Capuchin monkeys: A window into tool use in apes and humans. In: Gibson KR, Ingold T. eds. *Tools, Language and Cognition in Human Evolution*. Cambridge: Cambridge University Press. 138-150.

Visalberghi E. 1997. Success and understanding in cognitive tasks: A comparison between *Cebus apella* and *Pan troglodytes*. *International Journal of Primatology.* **18:** 811-830.

Visalberghi E, Anderson JR. 1999. Capuchin monkeys. In: Poole T. ed. *The UFAW Handbook on the Care and Management of Laboratory Animals, 7th ed. Vol.1: Terrestrial Vertebrates*. London: Blackwell Science. 601-610.

Visalberghi E, Fragaszy DM. 1990. Do monkeys ape? In: Parker ST, Gibson KR. eds. *'Language' and Intelligence in Monkeys and Apes: Comparative Developmental Perspectives*. New York: Cambridge University Press. 247-273.

Visalberghi E, Fragaszy DM. 1995. Food washing behaviour in tufted capuchin monkeys (*Cebus apella*) and crabeating macaques (*Macaca fascieularis*). *Animal Behaviour.* **40:** 829-836.

Visalberghi E, Fragaszy DM, Savage-Rumbaugh ES. 1995. Comprehension of causal relations in a tool using task by chimpanzees (*Pan troglodytes*) and capuchins (*Cebus apella*). *Journal of Comparative Psychology.* **109:** 52-60.

Visalberghi E, Limongelli L. 1994. Lack of comprehension of cause-effect relations in tool-using capuchin monkeys (*Cebus apella*). *Journal of Comparative Psychology.* **108:** 15-22.

Visalberghi E, Limongelli L. 1996. Acting and understanding: Tool use revisited through the minds of capuchin monkeys. In: Russon AE, Bard KA, Parker ST. eds. *Reaching into Thought: The Minds of the Great Apes*. Cambridge: Cambridge University Press. 57-79.

Visalberghi E, Trinca L. 1989. Tool use in capuchin monkeys: Distinguishing between performing and understanding. *Primates*. **30:** 511-521.

Westergaard GC. 1992. Object manipulation and the use of tools by infant baboons (*Papio cynocephalus anubis*). *Journal of Comparative Psychology*. **106:** 398-403.

Westergaard GC, Fragaszy DM. 1985. Effects of manipulatable objects on the activity of captive capuchin monkeys (*Cebus apella*). *Zoo Biology*. **4:** 317-327.

Westergaard GC, Fragaszy DM. 1987a. The manufacture and use of tools by capuchin monkeys (*Cebus apella*). *Journal of Comparative Psychology*. **101:** 159-168.

Westergaard GC, Fragaszy DM. 1987b. Self-treatment of wounds by a capuchin monkey (*Cebus apella*). *Human Evolution*. **2:** 557-562.

Westergaard GC, Greene JA, Babitz MA, Suomi SJ. 1995. Pestle use and modification by tufted capuchins (*Cebus apella*). *International Journal of Primatology*. **16:** 643-651.

Westergaard GC, Greene JA, Menuhin-Hauser C, Suomi SJ. 1996. The use of naturally occurring copper and iron tools by monkeys: Possible implications for the emergence of metal-tool technology in hominids. *Human Evolution*. **11:** 17-25.

Westergaard GC, Lundquist AL, Haynie MK, Kuhn HE, Suomi SJ. 1998. Why some capuchin monkeys (*Cebus apella*) use probing tools (and others do not). *Journal of Comparative Psychology*. **112:** 207-211.

Westergaard GC, Suomi SJ. 1993. Use of a tool-set by capuchin monkeys (*Cebus apella*). *Primates*. **34:** 459-462.

Westergaard GC, Suomi SJ. 1994. Hierarchical complexity of combinatorial manipulation in capuchin monkeys (*Cebus apella*). *American Journal of Primatology*. **32:** 171-176.

Westergaard GC, Suomi SJ. 1997. Transfer of tools and food between groups of tufted capuchins (*Cebus apella*). *American Journal of Primatology*. **43:** 33-41.

CHAPTER EIGHT # Apes, hominids and technology

J. A. J. GOWLETT

Introduction

In the study of apes and humans, technology provides one of the firmest links between different species, through its nature as *process*. This is because it is external or *extrasomatic* in its expression. When an ape, a human being, or even a bird, employs a stick in a similar task, the tool is not merely the same in concept, it may be actually the same, and therefore presents the same physical challenges of management.

Technology is useful in research for at least three reasons:

- its intrinsic indication of certain abilities,
- the continuity in behaviour that it can establish between species,
- the concrete mapping of behaviour which it makes possible through space and time.

Among the hominoids, technology is commonly employed by only humans and chimpanzees, *Pan troglodytes*, but the processes that underpin it and which it overlays probably have a much broader currency – that would help to explain why flashes of similar behaviour are seen in other species. Thus these processes – whatever they are – are an important issue for study in all the hominoids. They seem to represent a substrate of complex behaviour, which may have a long evolutionary history in the apes, and can be approached through various lines of study.

Technology is here taken to be the regular manufacture and use of tools. Attempts at closer definition seem counter-productive given the complexity of the issues (Ingold, 1993), and it is natural for authors to give different emphases to design content, focusing of energy, or the nature of process. This chapter aims to consider how study of technology can best be applied in cross-fertilisation between primatological and palaeoanthropological research (McGrew, 1992 has commented on a frequent reluctance to achieve such links, although there are notable exceptions including Toth *et al.*, 1993 and Joulian, 1996). It is plain that we can go further in seeking out common ground. If comparisons are to be made across species, then one of the problems is that technology is not always present – there is discontinuity. Another factor is that creatures of the past are gone, so their behaviour needs to be studied by a specialised methodology concentrating on material traces. We can certainly link this more extensively with observations of living animals. Even where technology is present (Figure 1a), its physical similarities across species do not necessarily indicate similar social contexts or basis of learning. Hence a second aim is to consider how technology can be related to questions of current interest in social behaviour, such as theories of social structure and violence (Wrangham & Peterson 1996).

Throughout, there is some risk of restating the obvious. But it is not so clear what is obvious, when there are several focuses of debate, and participants in one may not be aware of concerns in another. Students of early hominid behaviour are predisposed to see something new and distinctive in that behaviour. We need to debate with colleagues studying great apes, especially, because they can often show us where this is not so, or provide a better context. But we also have to negotiate with archaeologists of later periods who focus on major changes of ability that seem to come with modern humans. Their models tend to deny these abilities in earlier humans. It should be stimulating to have more exchange along the line.

In the case of humans and apes, which are closely related, technological comparisons can certainly cast some light on the activities of earlier apes or hominids. The relationships between hominids and the various apes are far better explored than a generation ago, at all levels – physically, genetically, and behaviourally (Chamberlain, 1991; Jeffreys, 1989; Goodman *et al.*, 1989; McGrew, 1992). This does not make it easier to understand them intuitively, exactly because research has established a complex matrix of similarities and differences. Numerical taxonomy was devised to handle such complicated positions, but it cannot sensibly extend to situations where one species has quite enormous development of some faculty only incipient in the others, such as communication via symbols.

Some framework with time-depth can be established by suggesting that present-day chimpanzees may be very similar to the last common ancestor (LCA) of hominids and chimpanzees, and can be used as models for the earliest stages of hominisation. This is useful for modelling, but there is cause to be wary. At a simple physical level, for example, the gorilla foot is more like a human foot than is a chimpanzee foot – even though humans and chimpanzees are the more closely related. Other characters may also fail to vary according to the pattern of relationships. Since the behavioural complexes of a living species reflect a set of ecological relations as well as ancestry (Dunbar, 1995) there is no room for naivety in making comparisons as if by rule book. Even a change in diet could well affect tool-use amongst other aspects of behaviour, and reduce or increase the apparent usefulness of an extant species as a comparator.

Nevertheless, there are huge benefits in taking the best living models available when looking at the past. From the time of the earliest mammals the proportion of ancestry shared between, say, humans and chimpanzees amounts to at least 97% by time (Figure 1b).

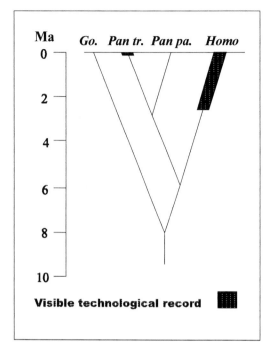

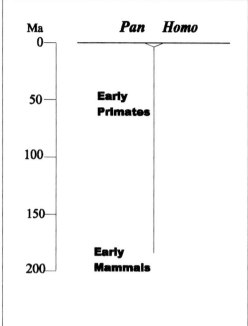

Figure 1
Scales of continuity
and difference in
hominoid evolution.
1a: The known extent
of technology shown
on a tree of
relationships of great
apes and humans.
Although the pattern
of presence and
absence remains
puzzling, recent
studies of bonobos
and gorillas reinforce
the idea that hominids
share a substrate of
complex routine-
based behaviour
which only leads to
technology in
particular circum-
stances (*cf.* Byrne
1996; Ingmanson
1996).
1b: For comparison,
the long common
heritage of humans
and chimpanzees.
All divergence dates
are approximate.

On this perspective, there is good cause for the statement that we are 'in the same world' (Mason, 1979). The brain has had a common development through such a length of time that it must operate on the same fundamental principles in the various species, even though human brains have developed enormously in the last two million years. For this reason, it is justifiable to look for a shared basis for similar phenomena, and chimpanzees may also remain the best available model for early stages of hominisation.

What do we share, and what do we not share with the apes? Sexual signals are highly specific, usually valid only within-species. Much other social behaviour is more widely shared (Goodall, 1976). Language is an instance where dramatically different views are encountered. Some, like Savage-Rumbaugh and colleagues argue strongly that chimpanzees can master the use of symbols, in effect language without the spoken word (Savage-Rumbaugh, 1986). In an extreme view, Pinker argues vehemently that chimpanzees are completely lacking in these abilities, and that scientists have leant over backwards to find them (Pinker, 1994). On another axis of variation, some scholars argue for very early evolution of language (Tobias, 1991; Dunbar, 1996), while others delay it to the appearance of modern humans (Davidson, 1991; Davidson & Noble, 1993).

Technology should be much more straightforward for study, because of the much clearer continuity displayed between humans and apes (Wynn, 1993; Gowlett, 1990, 1996). It is also solid and visible, and can be analysed in mechanical terms (work, effort, efficiency). But what does it show?

Review of evidence for technology

This section seeks common points. Technology – however defined – occurs in very few species. This must be partly a matter of preconditions being rarely met. Most animals are adapted to their environment such that they can meet their needs. Some tool-use appears in birds, especially corvids. They may use sticks as probes. So many experiments have been conducted with primates, that it is easy to get the impression that tool-use is widespread. In fact it is not (e.g. McGrew, 1993). The impression seems to stem from confusion with examples of cultural behaviour that do not involve tools and with more common examples of tool-use in captivity. Tool-use very rarely occurs in monkeys, and is also rare among apes in the wild, except the chimpanzee, *Pan troglodytes*, in which it occurs in all three principal varieties or subspecies.

Of interest is the paucity or absence of technology in other closely related apes (see Byrne, 1996; Ingmanson, 1996; Zihlman, 1996 for reviews of the issues). Among the other examples of cultural behaviour, only the chimpanzee and humans show two important features:

- regular use of a variety of technology,

- regional variation in the technology employed.

Chimpanzee technology

Chimpanzee technology includes use of plant stems, use of sticks, use of leaf sponges, and use of bone tools, with distinct local variation in tool-kits (Goodall, 1976; McGrew, 1992; Boesch & Boesch, 1989; Boesch, 1993, 1996; Matsuzawa & Yamakoshi, 1996). The behavioural matrix is chiefly that of subsistence. Other uses of technology can be seen as 'domestic' – including the use of leaf sponges for personal hygiene and health. In one case at least, the behaviour can be seen as symbolic – the use of plants for presentation (leaf-clipping: McGrew, 1992). In general, however, tools are used largely for extracting resources. Thus there are parallels in the procedures employed, although it is not immediately apparent whether the tool-users appreciate this: using a plant stem to extract a termite; using a leaf sponge for extracting water. But there are contrasts in approach: hammering is not the same as probing, either in the primary action, the preparatory work, or the mode of feeding. The points in common are the selection of a tool, and the fact of feeding, but most other elements of the process are different.

Most chimpanzee tools are made *ad hoc*, for what Woodburn calls 'immediate-return' in the case of hunter-gatherers (e.g. Woodburn, 1988). Yet tools are also reused, sometimes many times in the case of hammerstones, or during a series of feeding events in the case of a fishing stick (McGrew, 1974). There are both sex differences and regional differences in the use of tools. Although chimpanzees make tools, the degree of preparation is basic, and has not been seen to extend to shaping stone, other than by the battering of anvils over time. They do, however, select *suitable* materials or items, which must imply a mental process of comparison with some list of necessary characteristics, on the basis of past experience or observation. For ant or termite dipping, plant stems are broken to an appropriate length, and side shoots are trimmed off.

Hominid technology

Hominids probably evolved 6-8 million years ago, as inferred from genetic evidence and the fossil record (Jeffreys, 1989; Goodman *et al.*, 1989; Hill & Ward, 1988; White, Suwa & Asfaw, 1994). Recent discoveries point towards a rather dense evolutionary bush of early hominid species (Asfaw *et al.*, 1999), in which *Homo* may be a relatively late arrival (Wood & Collard, 1999). Even now the picture of the earliest hominids remains hazy, whether assessed from fossil evidence, genetic evidence or a comparative approach. Of the living primate species most closely related to humans, three have little or no technology, so it must remain uncertain whether the LCA of chimpanzees and humans possessed any simple technology (Figure 1a). It seems likely, however, that among some hominids some technical threshold was passed as much as 3 million years ago, since well-made stone tools appear around 2.5 Myr, as do bone fractures caused by stones (Harris, 1983; Kibunjia, 1994; de Heinzelin *et al.*, 1999).

So far, the simple stone technology of the million years from 2.5 to 1.5 million years ago all shares enough similarities that it can be put in a single tradition, the *Oldowan*. There is little evidence of preferences that amount to stylistic choice, except perhaps in the very latest stages of the Developed Oldowan (Leakey, 1971).

The Oldowan is plainly functional: it provides sharp edges in the form of flakes, and 'mass with edge' in its core tools, which have an average weight of about 0.5 kg. The tools would be useful in butchery. The common association with bone on sites that are far-separated indicates such a focus from earliest times, and cutmarks on bone bear out the inference (e.g. Villa, 1990; de Heinzelin *et al.*, 1999). Other evidence points to a variety of functions, including probably the processing of plant foods and working of wood. Selection of particular raw materials for heavy or light-duty elements of the assemblage shows that their functional properties were individually appreciated (as at Olduvai and Ubeidiya: Leakey, 1971; Bar-Yosef & Goren-Inbar, 1992).

From about 1.5 million years ago, far more design-form appears in the record. The hand-axes of the Acheulean typify this, with their long axes, and stereotyped appearance of symmetry. Acheulean toolkits vary from region to region, and even within site, although there are few signs of directional change through a very long period – as much as a million years. Hand-axes have often been regarded as an enigma (e.g. Wynn, 1995), but compared with Oldowan choppers, they provide numerous advantages for the same weight – including far longer edge length, reduced (sharper) edge angle and greater leverage. Indeed it would be hard to apply any Oldowan stone tool as a lever, whereas Acheulean bifaces are well suited to the purpose. They are effective in butchery, and on some sites associations again point to this use, but other contexts suggest general-purpose use (butchery contexts: e.g. Boxgrove, Aridos; large accumulations suggesting multiple uses: e.g. Kalambo Falls, Olorgesailie – refs: Pitts & Roberts, 1997; Villa, 1990; Clark, in press; Isaac, 1977).

Other developments occur within the later stages of Acheulean. Early *Homo sapiens* or *Homo heidelbergensis* appears perhaps half a million years ago (Rightmire, 1996). Whether we should expect new behaviour to accompany these new forms is an open question, but there is some evidence of innovations, which could greatly help in gaining subsistence. Wooden tools were clearly present from early times, seen first indirectly from wear traces on stone tools at East Turkana (Keeley & Toth, 1981), but now also attested directly in the first preserved wooden spears at about 400,000 (Thieme, 1996), and other occasional artefacts of comparable date (e.g. Belitzky, Goren-Inbar & Werker, 1991). Composite tools can now be seen to date back to 400,000 years or more. Hafting was certainly accomplished at 100,000 (Anderson-Gerfaud, 1990), and may go back as far as 400,000 (Bosinski, 1992).

Archaeologists have strongly discouraged students from any interpretation of early stone tools as weapons. They have been swayed by caution and a reaction to Robert Ardrey, whose scenarios of early hominids 'killing for a living' drew much adverse reaction (Ardrey, 1967, 1976). Just as the extent of chimpanzee violence is being fully recognised, it is ironic to find that the first known wooden tools made by hominids include clear weapons.

In the study of modern chimpanzees, there is no difficulty in discriminating between hunting of other species as prey and cases of intra-species violence, but for early hominids the evidence is likely to remain slight and equivocal. Traditional names such as Oldowan or Acheulean can be a hindrance in the understanding of behaviour. Imposed in a blanket way across great zones of space and time, they have uses in classification, but they need not even indicate shared cultural values. It is certainly inappropriate to talk of 'Oldowans' or 'Acheuleans'.

Figure 2 attempts an alternative approach of giving a timeframe for the adoption of some cultural traits. The record does not allow high resolution, but it gives an indication of cultural complexity.

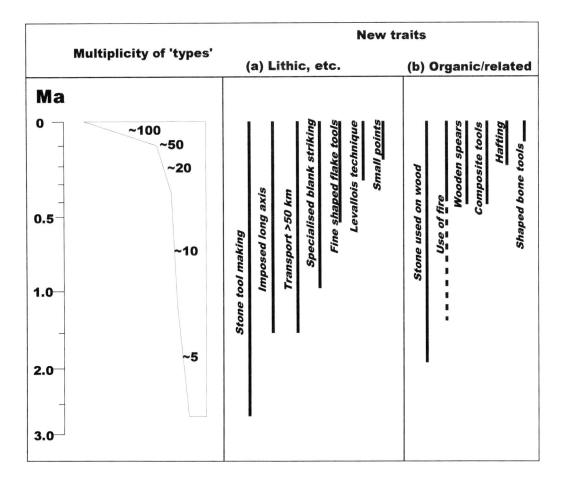

Figure 2
Accumulation of cultural traits in hominids through time. The diagram shows appearance of new traits, and multiplication of artefact 'types' in the record (numbers of types are based approximately on the typologies of Leakey (1971), Kleindienst (1962) and Bordes (1961)). It is a simplification as it does not indicate regional variation, nor the possibility that traits come and go through time.

Some of the characters listed do not simply chart complexity or skills, but offer a fairly direct indication of the harnessing and focusing of energy on the background of landscapes. This mapping of activity across landscapes has become a central interest in archaeology and also a prime contact point with questions of current interest in the social structure of apes (see below).

Artefact transport distances can be taken to indicate that distances of 5-10 km were regularly covered two million years ago, but this is an area where more debate is needed. For chimpanzees, we learn that territorial ranges for groups are usually no more than 4-6 km across (e.g. Yamagiwa *et al.*, 1996), and daily treks usually no longer than 2-3 km (e.g. Wrangham, 1979), although chimpanzees sometimes make far longer journeys. Can archaeologists tell whether the hominid artefact transport was planned or incremental? Transport ranges undoubtedly became much greater about 1.5 million years ago: in the Acheulean, most bifaces come from sources up to 10km from the site, but others were sometimes transported more than 100 km (Clark, 1980; Hay, 1976).

Most archaeological literature assumes that such distances appear only in the last 100,000 years, missing this rare but definite evidence – which we do not fully understand. Such movements do however emphasise the aspect of energetics in technology. Large quantities of stone were moved around the landscape. Logically, such big investments must have had big returns, or natural selection should have eliminated the behaviour. Here there must be much more to emerge from comparative studies (see below). Within the last 100,000 and especially 50,000 years there are further leaps in cultural complexity – in the refinement of artefacts, in elaboration of design, in multiplicity of designs. This is the starburst of modern human behaviour, but its outward manifestations were never universal nor compulsory: simple toolkits have survived as evidence of human cultural variability.

Implications of technology: questions posed

Technology can be seen as a means of focusing energy outside the body, through investment in a tool, so that some greater return can be achieved. It is thus a lever on the environment. Most creatures do not have technology, and have to be self-sufficient in their relations with their environment. Technology could be held to arise from some deficiency of basic adaptation, but it seems more likely that it stems from the seizing of new opportunities in particular evolutionary contexts. These would be contexts where historical trajectory has given a species the necessary abilities as preconditions; where new niches are available and obvious; and where natural selection favours take-up.

It is, then, well established that certain behaviour appears in certain contexts. An extension is to say that it has a particular place in particular routines – e.g. a bird having caught a snail takes it to a stone to drop it. Routines are studied especially in branches of psychology drawing from a systems approach (e.g. Connolly & Dalgleish, 1989). How is the information passed on? The routines are clearly learnt. How they are learnt is evidently not a simple matter. There is widespread agreement now that to posit 'copying' or 'imitation' as an easy route to learning is a major oversimplification (Visalberghi & Fragaszy, 1990; Byrne, 1994), but equally the existence of imitation cannot be dismissed (Boesch, 1993; Whiten, 1996). The study of routines, both in the acquisition of skills and in the operation of skills, is an aid to analysis, which was long underplayed. Now it offers one of the best approaches to comparison across species (Byrne, 1996; Gowlett, 1996) (see below).

Technology is usually agreed to be cultural, because otherwise it would have to be reinvented all the time (not an aspect to be dismissed totally – see Tomasello, 1990). It is essential to the notion of culture that ideas are passed on regularly – though not necessarily by all individuals and to all individuals (another point of contention: see McGrew, 1998). For a cultural transmission system to begin, it can be argued that the disposition to learn must be widespread, and the selective advantage of particular behaviour must be sufficient to set up a feedback system. Although the arguments for 'chimpanzee culture' are persuasive (e.g. McGrew, 1992), Tomasello (1990) points out that the system is a somewhat faltering one, in which young individuals struggle to achieve the skills of an older generation.

This may have two implications: one, that in the context of living chimpanzees selection pressures are not high enough to ensure survival of cultural behaviours; two – perhaps – that cultural behaviour becomes reasonably secure only when it swims in a medium – the context of language. Otherwise, such cultural behaviour consists only of a series of traits, each of which has to struggle for survival, without there being any generalising force to emphasise links (this is not to deny that non-verbal animals can match across the senses, but language greatly facilitates the process: *cf*. Glucksberg, 1988:223).

Beyond reasonable doubt, then, at some point in the hominid line a bridge has been crossed from a world of single cultural traits, surviving piecemeal, to a cultural world in which all is knit together. The process probably defies definition in terms of modern culture, but one question is whether archaeology can use technology to cast light on the events.

I would like to summarise, then, several points or questions that seem pivotal in the search for an evolutionary framework:

- how to relate present and past evidence across species so as to maximise continuity,
- how to explore the idea of relationship between 'a culture' and a single cultural trait, reconsidering at the same time how accurately we distinguish cultural behaviour from 'ordinary' learned behaviour,
- how far we can use the overall information content of technology as an index to other behaviours,
- how to evaluate technology across species in relation to investment and return, and commitment through time,
- how to use technology in evaluating social structure and use of landscape,
- how, in the context of these last, to reassess the importance of tools as weapons.

Analysis: interlinking of routines

I will argue the importance of routines, as made evident in technology, as a way of binding these issues. My analysis follows the headings set out above.

Continuity in routines

Technology is often studied in isolation, but it provides a continuum with other behaviour – through the use of problem-solving routines. Thus a baby who has mastered the use of a spoon is paralleling the simpler process of dipping fingers into food, and raising them to the mouth. That apparently simple operation is also a routine made up of at least three subroutines. An ape pulling apart a seedpod, or cracking a nut, or a monkey peeling a fruit, is also operating a routine. Byrne (1996) analyses, for example, the routines used by gorillas in feeding. As with technology, there is also choice in such behaviour: one individual does it this way, another that. McGrew (1992) emphasises differences in the ways chimpanzees process palm nuts in different areas. For future studies of hominids and apes, the point to draw is that comparisons need not be restricted to, say, social behaviour on the one hand and technology on the other. Technology is always embedded in other routines. There is far more scope for comparisons if the technology can be related to other common routines.

The question of imitation – which has recently exercised primatologists – can also be analysed in terms of assembly of routines. Often it is difficult for a human apprentice to take in the details of an unfamiliar skill, to appreciate fully what is going on, and to grasp 'the knack' of it. It cannot be achieved by simple copying, because there is no simple task to copy: rather there are sets of procedures to master, with complex interrelations between them, and the brain has to manage all this. Then, as they are mastered such tasks are passed largely from cortical control to subcortical function, and even humans have no conscious awareness of how this is done.

For the great apes, it would seem that doubts about imitation (e.g. Tomasello, 1990) have been countered by other observations (e.g. Boesch, 1993; Whiten, 1996). Yet the point remains, that the more complex a task, the harder it is to imitate. To do so successfully, you must break the task down into components, and learn the subroutines. This interpretation may explain some discrepancies in the literature, and also emphasises the great importance of facilitation. Can we learn anything more from such routines? Probably so, because little has been done to explore the overlap between human and chimpanzee abilities, save in stone tool making (Toth *et al.*, 1993), although chimpanzees have learnt many human skills (such as bicycling). At what point then does discontinuity arise? In his classic paper Holloway (1969) linked the increase in human brain size with ability to concentrate. Overall the picture appears to be that some components of cognitive abilities are shared (e.g. Matsuzawa, 1990, 1996), and that it is increasingly hard to characterise those that are not shared except by their *complexity*. In this complexity, I will argue that most, if not all, of the archaeological record indicates behaviour outside the range of other primates, but many of the operations within it fall within the shared range.

Cultural traits and culture

This analysis suggests that there are actually gradients between ordinary manual routines and tool-using routines. Does this mean that there are also gradients between cultural and non-cultural routines? McGrew (1992) has offered discussion of points that amount to cultural behaviour, deriving most of his criteria from Kroeber (1928). They include *innovation, dissemination, standardisation, durability, diffusion*, and *tradition*. To these McGrew added *non-subsistence* and *naturalness* as extra tests for chimpanzee behaviour.

McGrew sought an operational definition, in effect one which ought to withstand the scrutiny of social/cultural anthropologists. Thus the starting point is that there is human culture, and the test is whether another species can conform to the basic elements of this. That approach is enforced by modern cultural anthropology, but perhaps it should not be. There are two species in parallel that have somewhat similar patterns of behaviour – just so. The length of the list comes from having to interpret one by the standards of the other. Thus 'naturalness' simply eliminates human interference. 'Non-subsistence' simply adds a test that the chimpanzees can pass, in the case of the Mahale grooming-hand-clasp (McGrew, 1992:68). 'Innovation' is inevitable, or there would be nothing to study. Dissemination, diffusion and tradition can be argued to be different guises of the same thing.

One can argue that there is continuity in a basic pattern of behaviour handed on by learning across the range from 'ordinary' learning to tool-making/using behaviour. According to Kroeber (1948) the next step is abstraction, but others have found difficulty with this (e.g. White, 1959). For White, a culturalist, the great step was 'symboling'. But this is not the symbolism which later-period archaeologists often deny to early hominids (or living apes). If it is to 'make special' – White's 'symboling' – then this specialness is also imbued to a tool by a chimpanzee. Another chimpanzee might well recognise that the tool is a tool (as when several individuals re-use an ant dipping stick: McGrew, 1974). Wrangham's case of a 'doll' is another instance (Wrangham & Peterson, 1996:253-5). So, technology attaches meaning to certain objects – or the attachment of meaning to objects is instrumental in creating a technology. If there is an additional factor that can be documented as human behaviour emerges, it is surely 'constructional complexity' – Gibson's *hierarchical constructs* (Gibson, 1990). Here, archaeology can document the outward expression, and perhaps disentangle the underlying components.

Information content

How many ideas underlie the use of a tool? Those schemes which measure complexity of material culture, such as Oswalt's (1976) tend not to examine the possible multiplicity of ideas and contained complexity *within* a single element of design (a tech-nounit).

A hand-axe is a technounit: but to make one involves hierarchical constructs, operated through an extended time of manufacture, and involving manipulation of an instruction set in three-dimensional space. Gowlett (1996) attempted to chart the numbers of learned parameters in an early Acheulean industry, and concluded that there were at least seven or eight in a biface, and 25-50 in the whole assemblage.

Archaeology is well suited to such documentation, but cannot fully employ the results. Do they, for example, imply use of language? As we continue to debate whether or how far early artefact sets extend beyond the range of overlap with ape behaviour (*cf.* Wynn & McGrew, 1989), a routine-based exploration of chimpanzee tool manufacture and use, aimed to measure numbers of parameters, might establish greater continuity.

Technology in a functioning society: investment, and timescale of return.

Even in simple technology, routines may be strung together, particularly those of manufacture and use. Thus for a chimpanzee, the making of an ant-fishing stick is followed by its use. It is a fair surmise that the maker decides to make it *so as to* use it. Similar processes incontrovertibly underlie modern human tool-use (Ingold, 1993). Such levels of planning are however sometimes denied by archaeologists to the early hominids, on grounds of their primitive-ness, and our lack of evidence of such intentions.

Surely it is a reasonable inference that the same principle works for early hominids: they made tools so as to use them. Yet the timescale of operation can vary, both for pongids and hominids. If you stop for lunch, and then start work again, this can be called 'segmentation'. Segmentation also occurs if a chimpanzee finishes termite fishing at one nest, and carries its probe while looking for the next one.

In the grand sweep of time, hominid technology has indisputably acquired far more segmentation of manufacturing routines and use routines. There are also many exceptions, because simple immediate technology often suffices to do a job. Modern humans curate *par excellence*, but then so, it can be argued, do some chimpanzees.

Here there are several ideas that can come together in analysis:

- levels of planning, as investigated by Parker & Milbrath (1993),

- operations in the structure of planning (Sacerdoti, 1977; Hoc, 1988),

- immediacy of return, as described by Woodburn (1980, 1988),

- curation of artefacts (Binford, 1973; Toth, 1987; Shott, 1996).

The point of hanging on to the tool has intrigued archaeologists, who have debated the significance of 'curation' (e.g. Binford, 1973, 1979; Shott, 1996). Looking at both chimpanzee and human technology, there are several different possibilities of curation:

- a tool is made for immediate use and discarded (e.g. a stone flake made on the spot for butchery),

- a tool is made for immediate use, and then casually conserved while opportunities for further use crop up (e.g. a chimp preparing a stem for termite-dipping),

- a tool is made for immediate use and discarded, but remains visible, and is reused on future occasions (perhaps by different individuals, e.g. a stone anvil),

- a tool is made for prolonged personal use in the context of travelling for foraging (e.g. a spear; possibly a fine hand-axe),

- a tool is made for general use in the context of a particular task, which recurs (e.g. a modern hammer).

There is far more overlap here between human and chimpanzee behaviour than anybody could glean from the archaeological literature, which usually fails to consider chimpanzees altogether. Discontinuity is perhaps concentrated more in procurement strategy – hominids go to much greater lengths to get materials (Binford, 1979). Unfortunately, archaeology finds an entirely objective analysis difficult, and has tended to classify early hominids as unable to curate (lacking foresight), while permitting modern humans far greater abilities on often similar evidence. Shott defines curation as 'extracting utility' from a tool (Shott, 1996). This can clearly be accidental or deliberate, happenstance or foreseen.

Woodburn has classified modern hunter-gatherers into those who have immediate-return and those who have delayed-return economies, arguing that this makes or reflects distinctions in technology, storage, and even social structure (e.g. Woodburn, 1980, 1988). Pedersen & Waehle (1988) suggest a less rigid distinction, asserting that elements of both patterns co-exist in a single society. Although apes fall into the pattern of immediate-return by all Woodburn's criteria, it could be said that any technology, including chimpanzee technology, implies a slightly delayed return. Stones re-used as hammerstones and anvils perhaps do not qualify, because they provide immediate return, and then delayed return without further investment.

On the other hand, early hominids are clearly involved in delayed returns, even if some modern hunter-gatherers are not. In some instances, hundreds of kilograms of material is transported 5-10 km across the landscape. Even if one is not completely convinced by Potts's stone cache hypothesis (Potts, 1988), it would surely be naive to suggest that the material was carried for nothing or out of some form of stupidity. Better to have no artefacts than to misuse them, because the energetic costs of the system were high.

Landscape, technology and group structure

We come now to one of the most significant areas of difference between modern apes and humans – social structure as imposed on landscape. Use of a landscape approach, and documentation of activities across landscape, may be important for elucidating one of the most important remaining distinctions between apes and humans – size of local group. This in turn has a bearing on studies of language origin (e.g. Dunbar, 1996) and violence (Wrangham & Peterson, 1996).

Technology is a prime source of evidence: in the hominids, at least, it provides maps of activities, limited but vitally useful. Behavioural differences between present day species seem plainly defined: apes operate in far smaller territories than modern hunter-gatherers (with the exception of chimpanzee ranges in savannah: Baldwin, McGrew & Tutin, 1982; Moore, 1996). Most important, they seem to have only one major unit, a local band. Human groups, however fluid the structure, appear always to have two organisational tiers: local band and maximum band. In Australia, this maximum band may coincide with a dialect, but in Africa and elsewhere, the language may extend further than a group, which recognises a common identity.

Comparative observations of ape societies have led to the 'theory of human violence' (Wrangham & Peterson, 1996). This is founded on the basic premise that males compete, singly or in alliances, to control and dominate groups of females, extending their territory as far as possible. In the case of chimpanzees and gorillas, the pattern is marked by pronounced sexual dimorphism, large males, and large canines. If hominids are seen as 'dry country apes', it becomes possible to argue that the great expansion of territories or ranges would have modified this pattern. Not only is this extended range seen in modern hunter/gatherers, but there is also a buffering of land-use, such that there are almost always reserve areas used only at certain times (e.g. Nunamiut; Efe; San: Binford, 1983; Turnbull, 1972; Yellen, 1977).

Among the consequences of range expansion could be 'breaking' of the continuous spatial networks of females apparently found in chimpanzees and gorillas, and strengthening of bonds between females within groups. Overall, males and females might be forced to work and travel on a more equal basis, finding pair bonds useful when resources dictate dispersion. These factors militate towards a reduction in male control and sexual dimorphism. Yet it also has to be conceded that these features characterise the bonobo, *Pan paniscus*, in which range expansion cannot be the explanation.

Archaeology in Africa has documented this change in hominid ranging from at least 1.5 to 2.0 million years ago. How do we know that the artefact movement distances indicate intentional transport, rather than increments of small journeys (non-purposive tool migration: McGrew, 1992, 1993)? One indication is the preferential movement of prepared blanks, for which there appears to be a consistent pattern from the early to late Pleistocene (Toth, 1987; Geneste, 1991). Another is evidence from Olduvai Gorge Bed II, dating to c. 1.5 Myr, of two neighbouring Acheulean sites each taking its raw material almost exclusively from one source – quartz for DK-EE and lava for EF-HR (Hay, 1976; Leakey, 1971). There is not the mix which might be expected if materials were drifting incrementally across the landscape.

Recently Steele (1996) has added to the comparative data of Grant, Chapman & Richardson (1992) to show that the large ranges of later *Homo* match those of carnivores rather than other primates. Archaeology in general, however, has not yet assimilated the evidence showing that vastly extended transport distances of artefact go back to the early Acheulean a million years ago, as mentioned above. The documentation is imperfect, but at sites such as Gadeb in Ethiopia and Khor Abu Anga in Sudan, the transport distances of rare artefacts appear to be 80-100 km (Clark, 1980; Arkell, 1949). Hay remarks, surveying the Olduvai evidence, that almost every sizeable site incorporates a small proportion of highly exotic material (Hay, 1976).

Our problem is that, even granting the deliberate nature of transport, there are alternative interpretations. The transported artefacts could indicate periodic excursions to far distant sources. They could be telltale evidence of a long-distance ranging pattern; or they could indicate exchange of specimens (a social/economic explanation which is an attested factor in some recent long distance movements: White & Modjeska, 1978). Hodder (1978) showed how difficult it is to distinguish between different forms (and explanations) of fall-off curves, even when dealing with modern humans. Simulation has some potential for showing how the distributions might arise (e.g. Steele, 1994), but the scarcity of finds (e.g. three exotic handaxes on a site) makes it very hard to test the evidence. Is this defeat? What would help? Studies of recent long-distance movements of stone tools certainly help (Gamble, 1995). But we archaeologists might learn a great deal also from studies based not on average but on maximum chimpanzee ranges – those of the West African savannah.

Last on this theme, is the issue of spatial structure 'within site'. It is surely time for archaeology to reconsider one of its prevailing implicit tenets: that 'modern = able, ancient = primitive and deficient' – held even when this means denying to early hominids abilities which are plainly present in their nearest living relatives. For example, a lack of 'structured organisation of living areas' in pre-*sapiens* humans is widely taken to imply some lack of structure in behaviour (see discussion in Stringer & Gamble, 1993; Pettitt, 1997).

This is a 'safe' view – although even a short observation of extant relative species suggests that their behaviour is highly organised in spatial terms. Often the comparative evidence is available, but not focused from one field to another. Building of nest 'structures' has already been considered (Sept, 1992; Fruth & Hohmann, 1996); a next step would be to map the local activities of apes spatially in a way that allows comparison with archaeological evidence. Plots of lithic refits now allow this on extents of 1-40 metres (e.g. Tuffreau, Lamotte & Marcy, 1997).

Tools as weapons

Ardrey's work led to a reaction (e.g. Lewis & Towers, 1969). We were not to see human beings as killing for a living; but it is now plain that chimpanzees sometimes do. Yet there is a contrast. Chimpanzees use tools, and are recorded as using branches or sticks in defence, in experiments and in the wild (Boesch, 1991; Kortlandt, 1965). But in fighting they appear to use only their own natural equipment – formidable strength and shearing teeth.

In human evolution there was an old framework belief that bipedalism and reduction of canines were linked with freeing of the hands for tool-use, and adoption of weapons for hunting (e.g. Read, 1920). The new credo has become that there is no link: that bipedalism arose far earlier than tool-use. Now we know from chance finds in archaeology that wooden weapons go back 400,000 years, it should serve the warning that archaeological methodology has no control whatsoever over the relative preservation of wood and stone.

Perhaps wooden staves go back twice as far as stone tools. They could well have played a part in opening up the savannah. Well-developed thumbs in the early hominids could be a key indicator. Archaeology's response to areas where preservation fails us is to make them taboo. Better to deny than to infer. The same principle applies to questions of early colonisations, or the introduction of new technology. Even so, it is time to state the heresy: early tools may have included weapons, and wooden ones may have been the earliest.

Conclusions

In the last few years I have worked with colleagues on a site which is yielding very precise evidence of early human behaviour at moments in time 400,000 years ago (Beeches Pit: Gowlett et al., 1998). Something like 20,000 pieces have been recorded, yielding so far a maximum set of 25 that record linked actions by one individual – active for perhaps as little as ten minutes! It is frustratingly difficult to relate such data to a broader framework, even between archaeological sites; and far more so to extend the framework to species, modern and ancient, whose technology is ephemeral. Yet the necessity of a comparative approach is plain, and the documentation achieved by primatologists is at least as detailed. Archaeologists can benefit from the injection of real life, primatologists perhaps from the linking of methodologies.

Slowly, the data points are on the way to building patterns. The conundrum in building any bridging framework is that apes and humans are closely related to the point of behaving almost identically in some ways, but being remarkably different in others.

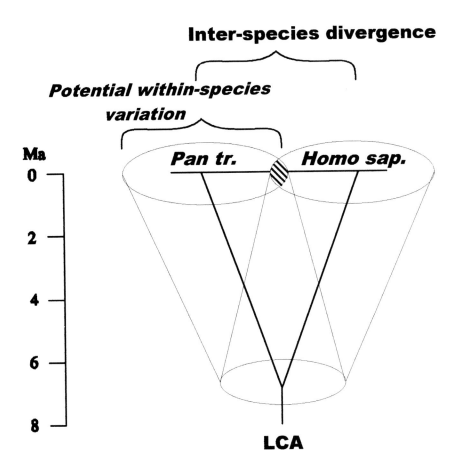

Figure 3
Evolution from the time of a common ancestor of hominids and chimpanzees, seen in terms of divergence and overlap: as the *range* of behaviour in both living species is tested, overlaps have tended to become more apparent.

There are two reasons for studying them in a framework: one, for their own sake and interest; two, so as to gain a better understanding of the processes of hominisation – especially insights into human behaviour that cannot be obtained from studying humans alone.

The second of these depends on a methodologically sound framework for comparison, but in the nature of evolution, present day gaps are often wider than past gaps. Even so, in the last twenty years great strides have been made towards establishing such continuity through 'modelling in' as if across the prongs of a fork, prongs made up of the diverging species. The test is to see how far the behaviour of chimpanzees (in particular) can be mapped onto humans, and human behaviour onto chimpanzees, as some substitute for seeing whatever behaviour existed in the past.

I have two last points about this. As a general model, we can take a divergence model of chimpanzees and humans, and play them against one another in comparisons (Figure 3). This model has been very successful in showing that 'list the difference' approaches are often in error. Humans and chimpanzees overlap in many characteristics, which were held to distinguish them. But in much comparative work the behaviour of a species is described as if it could be represented by some simple 'average'. It remains of great importance to establish *variability*, because we are still getting caught out.

Assumptions are still made that some factor or other (e.g. territorial range) distinguishes hominids and pongids; and then, we realise that our figures are based on small samples, or particular contexts, and that all may fall down yet again. In the case of transport distances and range size there is no point in asserting that there are major differences in hominids and the great apes, only then to find that this is not really so.

Finally: in this (often tacit) approach there has been much emphasis on how chimps can perform human tasks, frequently in well-structured experiments. There has been much less effort to see how well humans can perform chimpanzee tasks. A good analogy in locomotion is offered by the work of Crompton and colleagues on bipedalism, who have assessed early hominid gait partly by seeing how well modern humans can simulate the bent-knee bipedal walk of chimpanzees (Crompton & Li, 1997). Undoubtedly, more insights can be obtained through using humans to follow ape behaviour patterns. Chimpanzee patterns can be examined as routines, as ethnoarchaeology, or both. For the past, more can be done to use technological evidence of hominid ranging patterns in concert with the most relevant primate evidence – that of animals utilising the most comparable habitats.

Acknowledgements

It is obvious that I am much indebted to Bill McGrew for his explorations of the ideas surrounding chimpanzee technology, and I hope he will pardon my own attempts at re-evaluation. I thank Robin Crompton for stimulating ideas, and Caroline Harcourt for patience. My thanks should extend to co-workers at Beeches Pit, and the AHRB who have funded the work.

References

Anderson-Gerfaud P. 1990. Aspects of behaviour in the Middle Palaeolithic: functional analysis of stone tools from southwest France. In: Mellars P. ed. *The Emergence of Modern Humans: an archaeological perspective.* Edinburgh: Edinburgh University Press. 389-418.

Ardrey R. 1967. *The Territorial Imperative.* London: Collins.

Ardrey R. 1976. *The Hunting Hypothesis.* London: Collins.

Arkell AJ. 1949. *The Old Stone Age in the Anglo-Egyptian Sudan.* Khartoum and Cambridge: Sudan Antiquities Service Occasional Paper No. 1.

Asfaw B, White T, Lovejoy O, Latimer B, Simpson S, Suwa G. 1999. *Australopithecus garhi:* a new species of early hominid from Ethiopia. *Science.* **284:** 629-635.

Baldwin PJ, McGrew WC, Tutin CEG. 1982. Wide-ranging chimpanzees at Mt. Assirik, Senegal. *International Journal of Primatology.* **3:** 367-385.

Bar-Yosef O, Goren-Inbar N. 1992. *The lithic assemblages of the site of Ubeidiya, Jordan Valley.* Jerusalem: Qedem. 34.

Belitzky S, Goren-Inbar N, Werker E. 1991. A Middle Pleistocene wooden plank with man-made polish. *Journal of Human Evolution.* **20:** 349-353.

Binford LR. 1973. Interassemblage variability: the Mousterian and the 'functional' argument. In: Renfrew C. ed. *The Explanation of Culture Change: models in prehistory.* London: Duckworth. 227-245.

Binford LR. 1979. Organization and formation processes: looking at curated technologies. *Journal of Anthropological Research.* **35:** 255-273.

Binford LR. 1983. *In Pursuit of the Past.* London: Academic Press.

Boesch C. 1991. The effect of leopard predation on grouping patterns in forest chimpanzees. *Behaviour.* **117:** 220-242.

Boesch C. 1993. Aspects of transmission of tool-use in wild chimpanzees. In: Gibson KR, Ingold T. eds. *Tools, Language and Cognition in Human Evolution.* Cambridge: Cambridge University Press. 171-183.

Boesch C. 1996. Three approaches for assessing chimpanzee culture. In: Russon AE, Bard KA, Parker ST. eds. *Reaching into Thought: the minds of the great apes.* Cambridge: Cambridge University Press. 404-429.

Boesch C, Boesch H. 1989. Hunting behaviour of wild chimpanzees in the Tai National Park. *American Journal of Physical Anthropology,* **78:** 547-573.

Bordes F. 1961. *Typologie du Paléolithique ancien et moyen. 2 vols.* Bordeaux: Centre Nationale de la Recherche Scientifique.

Bosinski G. 1992. *Eiszeitjäger im Neuwieder Becken. Third Edition.* AMT Koblenz: Archäologische Denkmalpflege.

Byrne RW. 1994. The evolution of intelligence. In: Slater PJB, Halliday TR. eds. *Behaviour and Evolution.* Cambridge: Cambridge University Press. 223-265.

Byrne RW. 1996. The misunderstood ape: cognitive skills of the gorilla. In: Russon AE, Bard KA, Parker ST. eds. *Reaching into Thought: the minds of the great apes.* Cambridge: Cambridge University Press. 111-130.

Chamberlain A. 1991. A chronological framework for human origins. *World Archaeology.* **23 (2):** 137-146.

Clark JD. 1980. The Plio-Pleistocene environmental and cultural sequence at Gadeb, northern Bale, Ethiopia. In: Leakey RE, Ogot BA. eds. *Proceedings of the 7th Panafrican Congress of Prehistory and Quaternary Studies.* Nairobi: TILLMIAP. 189-193.

Clark JD, in press. *Kalambo Falls, Volume III.* Cambridge: Cambridge University Press.

Connolly K, Dalgleish M. 1989. the emergence of a tool-using skill in infancy. *Developmental psychology.* **25 (6):** 894-912.

Crompton RH, Li Yu. 1997. Running before they could walk? Locomotor adaptation and bipedalism in early hominids. In: Sinclair A, Slater E, Gowlett J. eds. *Archaeological Sciences 1995. Proceedings of a conference on the application of scientific techniques to the study of archaeology.* Oxford: Oxbow Monographs 64. Oxbow Books. 406-412.

Davidson I. 1991. The archaeology of language origins: a review. *Antiquity.* **65:** 39-48.

Davidson I, Noble W. 1993. Tools and language in human evolution. In: Gibson KR, Ingold, T. eds. *Tools, Language and Cognition in Human Evolution.* Cambridge: Cambridge University Press. 363-388.

Dunbar RIM. 1995. Neocortex size and group size in primates: a test of the hypothesis. *Journal of Human Evolution.* **28:** 287-296.

Dunbar RIM. 1996. *Grooming, Gossip and the Evolution of Language.* London: Faber and Faber.

Fruth B, Hohmann G. 1996. Nest building behavior in the great apes: the great leap forward? In: McGrew WC, Marchant LF, Nishida T. eds. *Great Ape Societies.* Cambridge: Cambridge University Press. 225-240.

Gamble C. 1995. Raw materials, technology and variability in Middle Pleistocene Europe. In: Bermúdez de Castro JM, Arsuaga JL, Carbonell E. eds. *Evolución humana en Europa y los yacimientos de la Sierra de Atapuerca: Actas, Vol.2.* Valladolid: Junta de Castilla y León. 387-402.

Geneste J. 1991. L'approvisionnement en matieres premieres dans les systems de production lithique: la dimension spatiale de la technologie. In: Mora R, Terradas X, Parapl A, Plana C. eds. *Tecnología y cadenas operativas líticas. Treballs d'Arquelogia.* **1:** 1-35.

Gibson KR. 1990. New perspectives on instincts and intelligence: brain size and the emergence of hierarchical mental constructional skills. In: Parker ST, Gibson KR. eds. *'Language' and Iintelligence in*

Monkeys and Apes. Cambridge: Cambridge University Press. 97-128.

Glucksberg S. 1988. Language and thought. In: Sternberg RJ, Smith EE. eds. *The Psychology of Human Thought.* Cambridge: Cambridge University Press. 214-241.

Goodall J. 1976. Continuities between chimpanzee and human behaviour. In: Isaac GLI, McCown E. eds. *Human Origins: Louis Leakey and the East African evidence.* Menlo Park, California: Benjamin. 80-95.

Goodman M, Koop BF, Czelusniak J, Fitch DHA, Tagle DA, Slighton JL. 1989. Molecular phylogeny of the family of apes and humans. *Genome.* **31:** 316-35.

Gowlett JAJ. 1990. Technology, skill and the psychosocial sector in the long term of human evolution. *Archaeological Review from Cambridge.* **9 (1):** 82-103.

Gowlett JAJ. 1996. The frameworks of early hominid social systems: how many parameters of archaeological evidence can we isolate? In: Steele J, Shennan S. eds. *The Archaeology of Human Ancestry: power, sex and tradition.* London: Routledge. 135-183.

Gowlett JAJ, Chambers J C, Hallos J, Pumphrey TRJ. 1998. Beeches Pit: first views of the archaeology of a Middle Pleistocene site in Suffolk, UK, in European context. In: Ullrich H. ed. *Papers presented at the International Symposium 'Lifestyles and survival strategies in Pliocene and Pleistocene hominids'. Anthropologie (Brno).* **36 (1-2):** 91-97.

Grant JWA, Chapman CA, Richardson KS. 1992. Defended versus undefended home range size of carnivores, ungulates and primates. *Behavoural Ecology and Sociobiology.* **31:** 149-161.

Harris JWK. 1983. Cultural beginnings: Plio-Pleistocene archaeological occurrences from the Afar, Ethiopia. *African Archaeological Review.* **1:** 3-31

Hay RL. 1976. *Geology of the Olduvai Gorge.* California: University of California Press.

Heinzelin J de, Clark JD, White T, Hart W, Renne P, Woldegabriel G, Beyene Y, Vrba E. 1999. Environment and behavior of 2.5million-year-old Bouri hominids. *Science.* **284:** 625-629.

Hill A, Ward S. 1988. Origin of the Hominidae: the record of African large hominoid evolution between 14My and 4My. *Yearbook of Physical Anthropology.* **31:** 49-83.

Hoc J-M. 1988. *Cognitive Psychology of Planning.* London: Academic Press.

Hodder I. 1978. Some effects of distance on patterns of human interaction. In: Hodder I. ed. *The Spatial Organization of Culture.* London: Duckworth. 155-178.

Holloway RL. 1969. Culture: a human domain. *Current Anthropology.* **10 (4):** 395-412.

Ingmanson EJ. 1996. Tool-using behavior in wild *Pan paniscus*: social and ecological considerations. In: Russon AE, Bard KA, Parker ST.

eds. *Reaching into Thought: the minds of the great apes.* Cambridge: Cambridge University Press. 190-210.

Ingold T. 1993. Technology, language, intelligence: a reconsideration of basic concepts. In: Gibson KR, Ingold T. eds. *Tools, Language and Cognition in Human Evolution.* Cambridge: Cambridge University Press. 449-472.

Isaac GLl. 1977. *Olorgesailie: Archaeological studies of a Middle Pleistocene lake basin.* Chicago: University of Chicago Press.

Jeffreys AJ. 1989. Molecular biology and human evolution. In: Durant JR. ed. *Human Origins.* Oxford: Clarendon Press. 217-252.

Joulian F. 1996. Comparing chimpanzee and early hominid techniques: some contributions to cultural and cognitive questions. In: Mellars P, Gibson K. eds. *Modelling the Early Human Mind.* Cambridge: McDonald Institute for Archaeological Research. 173-189.

Keeley LH, Toth N. 1981. Microwear polishes on early stone tools from Koobi Fora, Kenya. *Nature.* **293:** 464-465.

Kibunjia M. 1994. Pliocene archaeological occurrences in the Lake Turkana basin. In: Oliver JS, Sikes NE, Stewart KM, eds. *Early Hominid Behavioural Ecology. Journal of Human Evolution.* **27:** 159-171.

Kleindienst MR. 1962. Components of the East African Acheulian assemblage: an analytic approach. In: Mortelmans C, Nenquin J. eds. *Actes du IVe Congres panafricain de Préhistoire et de l'étude du Quaternaire.* Tervuren: Belgium. 81-105.

Kortlandt A. 1965. How do chimpanzees use weapons when fighting leopards? *Yearbook of the American Philosophical Society.* 327-332.

Kroeber AL. 1928. Sub-human cultural beginnings. *Quarterly Review of Biology.* **3:** 325-342.

Kroeber AL. 1948. *Anthropology.* London: Harrap.

Leakey MD. 1971. *Olduvai Gorge. Vol. III: excavations in Beds I and II, 1960-1963.* Cambridge: Cambridge University Press.

Lewis J, Towers B. 1969. *Naked Ape or* Homo sapiens? London: Garnstone Press.

McGrew WC. 1974. Tool use by wild chimpanzees in feeding upon driver ants. *Journal of Human Evolution.* **3:** 501-508.

McGrew WC. 1992. *Chimpanzee Material Culture: implications for human evolution.* Cambridge: Cambridge University Press.

McGrew WC. 1993. The intelligent use of tools: twenty propositions. In: Gibson KR, Ingold T. eds. *Tools, Language and Cognition in Human Evolution* Cambridge: Cambridge University Press. 151-170.

McGrew WC. 1998. Culture in nonhuman primates? *Annual Review of Anthropology.* **27:** 301-328.

Mason WA. 1979. Environmental models and mental modes: representational processes in the great apes. In: Hamburg DA, McCown ER. eds. *The Great Apes.* Menlo Park, California: Benjamin. 277-293.

Matsuzawa T. 1990. Spontaneous sorting in humans and chimpanzees. In: Parker ST, Gibson KR. eds. *'Language' and Intelligence in Monkeys and Apes.* Cambridge: Cambridge University Press. 451-468.

Matsuzawa T. 1996. Chimpanzee intelligence in nature and in captivity: isomorphism of symbol use and tool use. In: McGrew WC, Marchant LF, Nishida T. eds. *Great Ape Societies.* Cambridge: Cambridge University Press. 1196-209.

Matsuzawa T, Yamakoshi G. 1996. Comparison of chimpanzee material culture between Bossou and Nimba, West Africa. In: Russon AE, Bard KA, Parker ST. eds. *Reaching into Thought: the minds of the great apes.* Cambridge: Cambridge University Press. 211-232.

Moore J. 1996. Savanna chimpanzees, referential models and the last common ancestor. In: McGrew WC, Marchant LF, Nishida T. eds. *Great Ape Societies.* Cambridge: Cambridge University Press. 275-292.

Oswalt WA. 1976. *An Anthropological Analysis of Food-getting Technology.* New York: Wiley.

Parker ST, Milbrath C. 1993. Higher intelligence, propositional language and culture as adaptations for planning. In: Gibson KR, Ingold T. eds. *Tools, Language and Cognition in Human Evolution.* Cambridge: Cambridge University Press. 314-333.

Pedersen J, Waehle E. 1988. The complexities of residential organisation among the Efe (Mbuti) and the Bagombi (Baka): a critical view of the notion of flux in hunter-gatherer societies. In: Ingold T, Riches D, Woodburn J. eds. *Hunters and Gatherers: history, evolution and social change.* Oxford: Berg. 75-90.

Pettitt PR. 1997. High resolution Neanderthals? Interpreting Middle Palaeolithic intrasite spatial data. *World Archaeology.* **29 (2):** 208-224.

Pinker S. 1994. *The Language Instinct.* New York: Morrow.

Pitts M, Roberts M. 1997. *Fairweather Eden.* London: Century Books.

Potts R. 1988. *Early Hominid Activities at Olduvai.* New York: Aldine de Gruyter.

Read C. 1920. *The Origin of Man and of his Superstitions.* Cambridge: Cambridge University Press.

Rightmire GP. 1996. The human cranium from Bodo, Ethiopia: evidence for speciation in the Middle Pleistocene? *Journal of Human Evolution.* **31:** 21-39.

Sacerdoti ED. 1977. *A Structure for Plans and Behaviour.* New York: Elsevier.

Savage-Rumbaugh ES. 1986. *Ape Language: from conditioned response to symbol.* Oxford: Oxford University Press.

Sept J. 1992. Was there no place like home? A new perspective on early hominid archaeological sites from the mapping of chimpanzee nests. *Current Anthropology.* **33 (2):** 187-207.

Shott MJ. 1996. An exegesis of the curation concept. *Journal of Anthropological Research.* **52:** 259-280.

Steele J. 1994. Communication networks and dispersal patterns in human evolution: a simple simulation model. *World Archaeology.* **26 (2):** 126-143.

Steele J. 1996. On predicting hominid group sizes. In: Steele J, Shennan S. eds. *The Archaeology of Human Ancestry.* London: Routledge: 230-252.

Stringer C, Gamble C. 1993. *In Search of the Neanderthals.* London: Thames and Hudson.

Thieme H. 1996. Altpaläolithische Wurfspeere aus Schöningen, Niedersachsen – ein Vorbericht. *Archäologisches Korrespondenzblatt.* **26 (4):** 377-393.

Tobias PV. 1991. The emergence of spoken language in hominid evolution. In: Clark JD. ed. *Approaches to Understanding Early Hominid Life-ways in the African Savanna.* Romisch-Germanisches Zentralmuseum Forschungsinstitut fur Vorund Fruhgeschichte in Verbindung mit der UISSP, 11 Kongress, Mainz, 31 August – 5 September 1987, Monographien Band 19. Bonn: Dr Rudolf Habelt GMBH. 67-78.

Tomasello M. 1990. Cultural transmission in the tool use and communicatory signalling of chimpanzees? In: Parker ST, Gibson KR. eds. *'Language' and Intelligence in Monkeys and Apes.* Cambridge: Cambridge University Press. 274-311.

Toth N. 1987. Behavioral inferences from early stone age assemblages: an experimental model. *Journal of Human Evolution.* **16:** 763-787.

Toth N, Schick KD, Savage-Rumbaugh ES, Sevcik RA, Rumbaugh DM. 1993. Pan the tool-maker: investigations into the stone toolmaking and tool-using capabilities of a Bonobo (*Pan paniscus*). *Journal of Archaeological Science.* **20 (1):** 81-91.

Tuffreau A, Lamotte A, Marcy J-L. 1997. Land-use and site function in Acheulean complexes of the Somme Valley. *World Archaeology.* **29 (2):** 225-241.

Turnbull CM. 1972. Demography of small-scale societies. In: Harrison GA, Boyce AJ. eds. *The Structure of Human Populations.* Oxford: Clarendon Press. 283-312.

Villa P. 1990. Torralba and Aridos: elephant exploitation in Middle Pleistocene Spain. *Journal of Human Evolution.* **19:** 299-309.

Visalberghi E, Fragaszy DM. 1990. Do monkeys ape? In: Parker ST, Gibson KR. eds. *'Language' and Intelligence in Monkeys and Apes.* Cambridge: Cambridge University Press. 247-273.

White LA. 1959. The concept of culture. *American Anthropologist.* **61:** 227-251.

White JP, Modjeska N. 1978. Where do all the stone tools go? Some examples and problems in their social and spatial distribution in the Papua New Guinea Highlands. In: Hodder I. ed. *The Spatial Organization of Culture.* London: Duckworth. 25-38.

White TD, Suwa G, Asfaw B. 1994. *Australopithecus ramidus,* a new species of early hominid from Aramis, Ethiopia. *Nature.* **371:** 306-312

Whiten A. 1996. Imitation, pretense, and mindreading: secondary representation in comparative primatology and developmental psychology? In: Russon AE, Bard KA, Parker ST. eds. *Reaching into Thought: the minds of the great apes.* Cambridge: Cambridge University Press. 300-324.

Woodburn J. 1980. Hunters and gatherers today and reconstruction of the past. In: Geller E. ed. *Soviet and Western Anthropology.* London: Duckworth. 95-117.

Woodburn J. 1988. African hunter-gatherer social organisation: is it best understood as a product of encapsulation? In: Ingold T, Riches D, Woodburn J. eds. *Hunters and Gatherers: history, evolution and social change.* Oxford: Berg. 31-64.

Wrangham RW. 1979. Sex differences in chimpanzee dispersion. In: Hamburg DA, McCown ER, eds. *The Great Apes.* Menlo Park, California: Benjamin. 481-489.

Wrangham R, Peterson D. 1996. *Demonic Males: apes and the origins of human violence.* London: Bloomsbury.

Wynn T. 1993. Layers of thinking in tool behaviour. In: Gibson KR, Ingold T. eds. *Tools, Language and Cognition in Human Evolution.* Cambridge: Cambridge University Press. 389-406.

Wynn T. 1995. Handaxe enigmas. *World Archaeology.* **27 (1):** 10-24.

Wynn T, McGrew WC. 1989. An ape's eye view of the Oldowan. *Man (N.S).* **24:** 383-398.

Yamagiwa J, Maruhashi T, Yumoto T, Mwanza N. 1996. Dietary and ranging overlap in sympatric gorillas and chimpanzees in Kabuzi-Biega National Park, Zaire. In: McGrew WC, Marchant LF, Nishida T. eds. *Great Ape Societies.* Cambridge: Cambridge University Press. 82-98.

Yellen J. 1977. *Archaeological Approaches to the Present.* New York: Academic Press.

Zihlman A. 1996. Reconstructions reconsidered: chimpanzee models and human evolution. In: McGrew WC, Marchant LF, Nishida T. eds. *Great Ape Societies.* Cambridge: Cambridge University Press. 293-304.

Social knowledge and social manipulation in monkeys and apes

J. CALL

Introduction

Owing in part to the influential work of Wolfgang Köhler (1925), intelligence in non-human primates is commonly understood as the ability to solve problems. In a typical problem-solving situation, a subject attempts to obtain a goal whose direct access is blocked by an obstacle. Although tool-use is perhaps the best known example, non-human primates have demonstrated a notable ability to solve other problems, including complex discriminations, retrieving hidden food from multiple locations in an efficient manner, and using mathematical concepts to maximise their food intake. All these problems fall under the rubric of ecological or physical cognition the evolution of which was a result of the need to solve various ecological problems related to food foraging (Milton, 1981; Parker & Gibson, 1979). More recently, another explanation for the evolution of intelligence in primates has been suggested. This explanation, which has its roots in the late 1960s and 1970s (Jolly, 1966; Humphrey, 1976), posits that primate intelligence evolved to solve social rather than ecological problems (see papers in Byrne & Whiten, 1988 and Whiten & Byrne, 1997; de Waal, 1982). The demands of social life are particularly high in those species, such as many primates, that have a long life span and live in permanent or semi-permanent aggregations. Social primates face numerous situations throughout their lives in which they have to co-operate and compete with conspecifics, who often belong to their own social groups, to obtain limited resources such as food or mates. Repeated interaction over time promotes the formation of long-term relationships among individuals (Hinde, 1979).

These relationships are useful because they enable animals to anticipate whom is likely to help in case of need and whom is likely not to. In this complex social web, some relationships are classified as friendly while others are classified as unfriendly. Friends are animals who reciprocate grooming, lend support in agonistic interactions with third parties, share food, or exchange one type of service for another, such as grooming for agonistic aiding. Non-friends, and enemies in particular, not only do not help each other in agonistic situations or groom each other, but they also direct aggression toward each other when the opportunity arises. These interactions can become quite complex. For instance, Silk (1992) and de Waal & Luttrell (1988) have shown that male bonnet macaques *Macaca radiata* and chimpanzees, respectively, join aggressors in attacking their former opponents. In other words, if individual A attacks B, B will join C when at a later time C is attacking A. Thus, animals have to co-operate and compete with conspecifics to attain their goals. Such an exercise can become quite a complicated balancing act if we consider that on some occasions even former opponents are approached in seeking help against third parties. The special conditions of social life in primates, with their long-term relationships and complex and changing environment, seems a very suitable ground for the evolution of cognitive mechanisms which provide flexibility. In this chapter, I will explore the social cognition of monkeys and apes. To do so, I will divide social cognition into two complementary components: social knowledge and social manipulation. This division will help to clarify and sort out the complex field of socio-cognitive abilities of monkeys and apes. Social knowledge refers to what animals know about their social environments (i.e., social field, Kummer, 1982). In particular, it refers to their knowledge regarding their own interactions and relationships with others (i.e., dyadic relationships) as well as the interactions and relationships among groupmates (i.e., triadic relationships). It involves, for instance, knowledge about what individual A can expect when B approaches her, who usually grooms A's offspring, or what individual B does when B's offspring is attacked by C. In a sense, social knowledge is a database of the ways groupmates behave in various social situations. But social knowledge may be more than that. Social knowledge can also be used as a tool to guess what others are likely to do in a particular novel situation. On the other hand, social manipulation refers to what animals are capable of doing (or, in some cases, refraining from doing) to manipulate their conspecifics and obtain their goals through them. For instance, this may involve what gestures an adult chimpanzee can use to obtain food from another chimpanzee or what vocalisations an individual can use to request help from a dominant individual against another groupmate. Social manipulation can be dyadic, when only two individuals are involved (e.g. A manipulates B), or triadic, when at least three individuals are involved (e.g. A manipulates B who in turn manipulates C to A's benefit). In the latter part of this chapter, I will discuss how the combination of social knowledge and social manipulation makes primate cognition especially powerful and complex. Finally, I will propose that the cognitive mechanism governing primate social cognition is based on representing behaviours and relationships and generating behavioural rules, rather than representing the mental states of others (i.e., theory of mind).

Social Knowledge

Knowing about behaviour

At the most basic level of social knowledge lies the understanding of others' behaviour. Individuals are capable of predicting the future behaviour of conspecifics based on their past behaviour, and on their own past experiences with them. One obvious behaviour that can be used to predict others' future moves is communicative signals, which have specially evolved for purposes of announcing intentions and impending behaviour to conspecifics. All primates possess communicative signals, which they use to influence the behaviour of their conspecifics, and recipients of those signals know how to interpret them. There are other behaviours, however, which have not evolved for communicative purposes but that individuals may have learned to use to anticipate their groupmates' future behaviour. For instance, Menzel (1973, 1974) described young chimpanzees using the direction of travel of an individual who knew where a pile of food was located to infer the precise location of the food. Thus, chimpanzees were reading the behaviour of conspecifics as if it were a communicative signal to detect the location of food. Coussi-Korbel (1994) described a similar case of behaviour reading in mangabeys.

In her study, a dominant monkey attempted to read the behaviour of a subordinate monkey who knew where food was located in their enclosure. Initially, the dominant animal followed the subordinate to the place where the food was located and took it away from him. After a few trials, however, the subordinate stopped going to the food location while the dominant was watching, instead he waited until the dominant lost interest. On some occasions the subordinate even seemed to send the dominant in the wrong direction in order to obtain the food. Menzel (1973, 1974) also described similar counter-deceptive manoeuvres in which a subordinate chimpanzee changed tactics several times over a period of several months in order to outwit a dominant animal who also kept changing tactics to adapt to the new situation.

Knowing about relationships

Over time, repeated interactions turn into relationships, that is, stable patterns of interaction between individuals. One of the benefits of establishing relationships is that it permits individuals to anticipate and foresee the future behaviour of their conspecifics. Primates possess various kinds of relationships such as friendships, dominance and kinship. From a socio-cognitive point of view, kinship is the kind of social relationship which has been most intensively investigated.

There are two different levels of complexity in knowing about relationships: dyadic and triadic. Let me begin with the dyadic relationships. It is clear that individuals of various species recognise particular individuals. There is also evidence suggesting that individuals recognise the kinship relationship between themselves and other individuals. This recognition is most likely based on perceiving patterns of association rather than on knowledge regarding the genetic relationships between group members. Thus, individuals treat their own kin differently from nonkin. Individuals of various primate species associate with, groom and provide agonistic support for kin more often than nonkin (Bernstein, 1988; Bernstein & Ehardt, 1986; Gouzoules & Gouzoules, 1987). Some studies also show that there is more aggression directed toward kin, although generally there is also a higher frequency of reconciliation, at least in certain species (Aureli, Das & Veenema, 1997; Call, Judge & de Waal, 1996).

With regard to the knowledge of triadic relationships (i.e., among third parties), observational studies have shown that various species of macaque take kin relations into consideration in post-conflict situations. On some occasions, victims of aggression redirect aggression against their opponent's kin (Aureli *et al.*, 1992; Judge, 1982; Cheney & Seyfarth, 1986, 1989). Aureli *et al.*, (1992) found an even more complex situation in Japanese macaques *Macaca fuscata* in which the kin of victims retaliated against the aggressor's kin. In addition to this increase of aggression directed toward the opponent's kin, there is also an increase in affiliation following conflicts toward the opponent's kin in several macaque species, i.e., triadic reconciliation. For example, Judge (1991) found that pigtail macaque aggressors increased their contacts with the kin of their victims. Similarly, Das, Penke & van Hooff (1997) found that female long-tailed macaque aggressors directed affiliation toward their opponent's kin.

Overall, these studies suggest that monkeys recognise the kin relations among group members. However, another possible interpretation is that given that certain individuals (who happen to be kin) have supported each other in the past, individuals could recognise who could be a potential enemy in the near future. In order to prevent the risk of aggression from conspecifics who have joined forces in the past, individuals may use two different strategies. On the one hand, macaques may direct preventive strikes by attacking the likely supporters (i.e., kin) of their victims (i.e., redirected aggression), or, on the other hand, they may adopt a more conciliatory approach by directing affiliative behaviour to prevent the escalation of aggression (triadic reconciliation). Note that this explanation would not require individuals to know about triadic relationships, but simply to remember what each individual in the group did in the past.

Knowledge about kinship relationships also extends to other domains besides post-conflict situations. Using an experimental approach, Cheney & Seyfarth (1980) investigated whether vervet monkey *Cercopithecus aethiops* mothers, recognise their own infant's vocalisations. They recorded the calls of several infants and played each call to a group of vervet mothers, which included the mother, whose infant's call was being played. The authors found that mothers responded more vigorously (as measured by looking time) to their own infant's call compared to the calls of other infants. This indicated that mothers did indeed recognise their own infant's calls. More interestingly, mothers whose infant's call was not being played looked at the infant's mother whose call was being played, suggesting that mothers recognised that the infant whose call was being played was somehow related to that particular mother (even before she had made any overt movement). In other words, vervet monkey mothers may recognise mother-infant relationships.

Finally, Dasser (1988a,b) also examined the ability of long-tailed macaques *Macaca fascicularis* to recognise mother-infant relations using a matching to sample and a simultaneous discrimination paradigm. Two long-tailed macaques were shown pictures of certain mother-infant pairs belonging to their social group. Thus, the slides depicted individuals whom both subjects knew. During the first phase of the experiment, subjects were shown slides of mother-infant pairs. After both macaques were trained on those slides, they advanced into the next phase, in which Dasser presented two other types of slides. The first type consisted of slides depicting new mother-infant pairs who also belonged to the group but which subjects had not seen during the first phase of the experiment. The second type of slides depicted other pairs of groupmates, which did not constitute examples of mother-infant pairs. Pairs in this second type of slides were chosen so that they would resemble the physical appearance of mothers and infants (i.e., adult and immature animals). The question was whether subjects would select those slides depicting the relationship which subjects had experienced during the initial phase of the experiment. Results indicated that both subjects selected the slides depicting a mother-infant pair. In a second experiment, Dasser (1988a,b) extended her results to sibling relationships.

In sum, primates are capable of reading and knowing about the behaviour directed toward themselves and toward others. Moreover, monkeys also have some expertise in recognising the relationships between themselves and others, and among groupmates. At this point, however, it is still not clear what the nature of this knowledge is. One possibility is that primates may base their social knowledge solely on remembering past interactions. That is, individuals are simply capable of remembering 'who did what to whom' in the past and then using that information to predict future interactions. One serious limitation of this alternative is that primates would be incapable of predicting the outcome of novel interactions, for instance, when they had never seen two particular conspecifics interact before, or novel situations such as when a novel item is introduced and individuals have to compete to gain access to it. Yet it is true that even this relatively simple alternative could account for the results of the observational studies and also the experimental findings of Cheney & Seyfarth (1980) since subjects may have responded based on past interactions. This explanation, however, cannot account for the results in the Dasser (1988a,b) experiment, which represents a completely novel situation.

A second possibility is that primates go beyond merely recalling particular behavioural episodes, but, instead, are capable of a more abstract form of knowledge which, although based on past interactions, may allow them to generate hypotheses about who interacts with whom, when and how. This kind of knowledge would be analogous to the formation of rules and categories which primates readily show in the context of (non-social) learning and categorisation problems (Tomasello & Call, 1997). Unlike the previous alternative, this type of knowledge could account for Dasser's (1988a,b) results and would permit prediction and foresight in novel situations because this type of knowledge is not tied to particular exemplars. An example may help to illustrate this point. Let's suppose that individual X has observed that mothers A and B come to the rescue of their respective infants when they scream. In contrast, X has never heard C's infant scream. If X has developed a hypothesis about what mothers do for their infants, she will correctly infer that C will come to the rescue when her infant screams. In contrast, X will not know what to expect if her knowledge of others' interactions and relationships is based merely on past experience of particular cases. Although at this point it is not known to what extent knowledge of relationships is based merely on remembering past interactions as opposed to a more abstract form of knowledge, it would not be surprising if primates do more than simply recall all their past interactions. This is particularly true given the ability of primates to create rules in reversal learning and also their ability to classify stimuli into meaningful categories (Rumbaugh & Pate, 1984; Roberts & Mazmanian, 1988). I will come back to this idea in the final discussion.

Social Manipulation

The ability to move independently (i.e., animacy), is a critical feature which distinguishes animate from inanimate entities. When individuals interact with inanimate objects, the laws of physics determine what problems can and cannot be solved. For instance, to obtain a fruit located at a certain height, all that is needed is a tool that is long enough, applied with sufficient force at the right angle for the required amount of time. In contrast, when individuals interact with animate entities, the laws of physics do not solely determine what social problems can be solved. For instance, in order to remove someone from a particular location, behaviours such as tickling or simply indicating one's desire may suffice. Note that the mechanical force used in tickling or during speech would not be sufficient if the body to be moved did not have the property of animacy. Therefore, animacy opens the door to manipulation in ways that are just not possible in the realm of inanimate objects.

Primates know that their conspecifics can do things for them, and they exploit this feature for their own benefit. There are two sources that determine the complexity of social manipulation. The first source of complexity involves the complexity of behaviours which subjects may use to influence the behaviour of others. The second source of complexity involves the number of individuals involved in the interaction and, more precisely, whether the subject who desires a goal interacts directly or indirectly (through an intermediary) with the individual who has access to the goal. Let's review each of these two types of complexity in social manipulation in turn.

Behavioural complexity

At the most basic level of manipulation, individuals can manipulate others by exerting the necessary mechanical force to obtain their objective. For instance, one individual could push another towards an out-of-reach goal and then climb on top of him as if he were a stool, or could open the jaws of a subordinate animal to obtain the food that she had in her mouth. As noted before, however, this type of manipulation is little different from the kinds of manipulations directed to inanimate entities, and does not really qualify as social manipulation. Instead, social manipulation relies, on the one hand, on communicative signals to convey desired goals, and, on the other hand, on individuals' animacy to independently provide them. Gómez (1990, 1991) has elegantly charted the transition from non-social to social manipulation in an infant gorilla. Gómez observed that the infant gorilla initially treated humans as objects when attempting to obtain goals. For instance, the gorilla would push humans around and use them as stools to climb to high places. Note that if, instead of an human, the gorilla had had a stool, she would have employed the same behaviour. Later on, however, the infant began treating humans as agents, requesting them by means of gestures (instead of pushing them) to move to the appropriate location. Thus, one way to investigate the ability for social manipulation in primates is to study the complexity and flexibility of intentional gestural communication.

Two defining features of communication that is intentional are: response waiting and the use of multiple means to obtain a single goal. Response waiting shows that individuals expect the recipient of their gestures to act after receiving the gesture; that is, it shows an understanding of others as animate because gestures *per se* cannot mechanically achieve the intended goal. The use of multiple means to obtain a single goal shows that individuals have a goal in mind and will only cease their gestural use after their goal has been achieved; it also demonstrates the ability to vary the gestures flexibly until they fulfil their goal. Since most of the studies on intentional communication have been conducted with chimpanzees *Pan troglodytes*, this short review will be heavily based on them.

Chimpanzees have an extensive gestural repertoire. Tomasello and colleagues (Tomasello *et al.,* 1985, 1989, 1994, 1997) have identified around three dozen gestures over a number of years. For instance, chimpanzees extend their arm to beg for food and clap their hands to call attention to themselves, and young chimpanzees touch

Hand-beg

Hand-clap

Arm-on

Figure 1
Three examples of
gestural
communication in
chimpanzees in each
of the sensory
modalities. Hand-beg
and hand-clap are
used to request food,
whereas arm on is
used to solicit
mothers to move to
different locations in
the enclosure.

their mother's side to request travel to a different location (see Figure 1). Chimpanzees can use single gestures or combinations of gestures to obtain their goals. If recipients ignore their requests, they often use other gestures or novel combinations to achieve that particular goal. Gestures are used for a variety of purposes such as requesting food, sex, play, agonistic support or movement.

Most gestures are used in more than one context and multiple gestures are commonly used for one particular context. In addition to the variety of gestures and contexts, chimpanzees also use different gesture sensory modalities depending on the attentional state of the recipient. Visual gestures, that is gestures which only have a visual component and cannot be heard or felt (e.g., hand begging, see Figure 1) are used only when the recipient is potentially capable of perceiving the gesture, that is looking at, or at least facing, the gesturer. In contrast, gestures with auditory or tactile components such as hand clapping or arm on (see Figure 1) are used independently of the attentional state of the recipient. Some apes, macaques *Macaca* spp. and capuchins *Cebus* spp. have even learned to use pointing – a gesture which is not part of their natural behavioural repertoire – to request food from humans (Blaschke & Ettlinger, 1987; Call & Tomasello, 1994; Hess, Novak & Povinelli, 1993; Leavens, Hopkins & Bard, 1996; Mitchell & Anderson, 1997). Enculturated apes (i.e., apes which have been human reared) have also been observed to use pointing gestures to request things other than food (see Call & Tomasello, 1996, for a review). For instance, the bonobo Kanzi used pointing gestures to indicate the location he wanted to travel to with his human companions (Savage-Rumbaugh *et al.,* 1986).

In the studies reviewed earlier, individuals invariably pointed to the goal, which they wanted to obtain. Call & Tomasello (1994) also found that orang-utans *Pongo pygmaeus* were capable of pointing to intermediaries, which were needed to obtain the goal. In particular, Call & Tomasello (1994) found that two orang-utans were capable of using pointing to indicate the location of a hidden tool, which the experimenter needed to obtain the orang-utans' food. These orang-utans first pointed to the location of the hidden tool and then, after the experimenter had retrieved the tool, they pointed to the location of the hidden food. One chimpanzee and one capuchin monkey have even used pointing to consistently direct a human competitor (who would keep the food for himself if he were to find it) toward an empty container (Mitchell & Anderson, 1997; Woodruff & Premack, 1979).

Although other chimpanzees and capuchins in these studies did not use pointing to deceive the competitor, they nevertheless withheld information that may have informed the competitor of the food's location. Recall that one of the skills in social knowledge previously discussed was the ability to read the behaviour of others. Interestingly, individuals who withheld information from the competitor readily pointed in the presence of a human who would give them the food, which he found. In a similar vein, Mitchell (1991) observed two male gorillas using various tactics such as withholding information and using distractions in order to outwit a female gorilla and gain access to her infant.

Number of intermediaries

Most behavioural interactions aimed at manipulating others to obtain goals occur in a dyadic fashion. In these, individual A directly interacts with individual B to obtain a resource whose access is controlled by B. For instance, a chimpanzee may use a begging gesture to request meat from another chimpanzee after a successful hunting episode. Dyadic interactions of this sort, in which individuals use the complex behavioural strategies described in the previous section to attain their goals, are very common.

There are also numerous instances of triadic interactions in which individual A interacts with B, who in turn interacts with C to A's benefit. Let's use an example observed by Toshisada Nishida (1990) in wild chimpanzees (see Figure 2). A male juvenile chimpanzee (KB) was at the stage of being weaned by his mother (CH). At the time this observation took place, CH was engaged in a grooming episode with an adult male, and KB became increasingly frustrated by his mother's refusal to allow him to nurse. Nearby there was an adolescent male (MS) who was sitting on his own away from the group. KB approached MS and started screaming and reaching towards him. When CH and her consort looked up at MS, he quickly stood up and pant-grunted vigorously (a sign of submission), and left the scene. After this incident, CH allowed KB to nurse. This use of others to solve one's problems is commonly referred to as social tool use, and the individual the subject uses instrumentally to solve his problem is known as the 'social tool' (Byrne & Whiten, 1987; Bard, 1990). Triadic manipulations of this kind play a fundamental role when an individual cannot directly interact with, or manipulate, another individual to obtain its goals.

Many primate species, including macaques, chimpanzees, baboons, vervet monkeys and capuchins, engage in these triadic interactions in the form of coalitions. In these interactions, one or more individuals jointly co-operate against a single individual or a group of individuals. Although these interactions usually involve few individuals, there have been cases where entire matrilines have been involved, which, clearly, exponentially increases the complexity of the interactions. Coalitions are usually formed for various purposes, such as defence against attacks from other group members, displacing others from food resources or receptive mates and even, perhaps, to strive for power (de Waal, 1987). Most coalitions are reactive, that is, they are formed after the conflict is under way as opposed to forming before the conflict has erupted, which might have revealed some form of foresight. Another important aspect of these triadic interactions is their duration. Harcourt & de Waal

Figure 2
An example of social tool use from Nishida (1990) and three possible interpretations of the social cognitive skills involved.

1) non-representational

2) representational; and

3) meta-representational

(1992) have distinguished between two types of triadic interactions based on their temporal dimension.

These authors propose using the term coalition for those more temporary or opportunistic interactions, and using the term alliances for more long-term commitments. It is these more long-term commitments which open the door to various bartering strategies such as reciprocity and interchange. In reciprocity, two individuals behave reciprocally toward each other, exchanging the *same* behavioural 'currency' over time. For instance, A grooms B and B grooms A. In interchange, individuals also behave reciprocally toward each other but exchange *different* behavioural currencies over time. For instance, A grooms B and B supports A in agonistic encounters with other group members. Cases of reciprocity and interchange have been reported for both monkeys and apes. For instance, vervet monkeys, macaques, chimpanzees and baboons reciprocate. Observational evidence also suggests that vervet monkeys and chimpanzees also exchange grooming for agonistic support (see Tomasello & Call, 1997, for a review). Seyfarth & Cheney (1984) and Hemelrijk (1994) have also provided experimental evidence reinforcing the notion that animals may tend to support those who have recently groomed them. From a cognitive point of view, reciprocity and interchange are especially relevant because they may imply the use of a 'cognitive tally sheet' (de Waal & Luttrell, 1988) which subjects use to keep track of the favours given and received from other group members.

In summary, monkeys and apes use a variety of communicative signals in dyadic and triadic interactions to manipulate conspecifics. Chimpanzees (but possibly other primates as well) use multiple intentional gestures for one or multiple purposes, which, on some occasions, include deception; they are sensitive to the attentional states of recipients; and they can learn novel gestures to request a number of things. Some studies of monkeys suggest that they may accomplish similar goals with the use of vocalisations (see Tomasello & Call, 1997). These complex signals constitute the building blocks of dyadic and triadic interactions whose complexity is accentuated by the use of cognitively complex processes such as mental score sheets. There is no doubt that monkeys and apes deploy their most complex skills of social manipulation during the course of triadic interactions. One especially interesting feature of these is their indirect nature; that is, targeted individuals are reached indirectly by the subject through another individual. It is easy to establish an analogy between this form of social manipulation and other forms of (non-social) problem solving such as tool-making and tool-using, whose complexity resides precisely in the use of indirect routes which, at first sight, may seem completely irrelevant for obtaining the goal (e.g., stripping pieces of bark to prepare a tool).

Social tool-use, however, is arguably more complex than non-social tool-use because in the former case the subject does not have complete control over the tool. Unlike physical tools, which simply react to the actions of the subject, social tools are capable of behaving independently, and sometimes in ways, which the subject may not have anticipated. A potential disadvantage of this is that on some occasions the social tool may not do what the subject needs, but the opposite. For instance, using Nishida's (1990) example mentioned earlier, the mother chimpanzee may choose to depart from the scene to avoid her offspring's continued tantrums. On the other hand, the social tool's ability to behave independently from the subject also has its advantages since it (the social tool) can come up with social strategies which the subject was not aware of. Using a social tool is equivalent to using a physical tool that can make decisions on its own, independently of the commands given by the subject. Using a warfare analogy, using a physical tool would be equivalent to firing an unguided ballistic cannon shell, whereas social tool-use would be equivalent to firing a target-seeking missile. Therefore the power of social tool-use is greater than physical tool-use, but at the same time, its power may also be more difficult to harness.

Cognitive mechanisms involved in primate social cognition

Three mechanisms

Monkeys and apes possess a great deal of social knowledge and many social manipulative skills. In particular, monkeys and apes know about the behaviour of their conspecifics, their own relationships with others and the relationships among third parties. Furthermore, monkeys and apes are quite skilful in using signals to manipulate others both directly and indirectly (the latter by means of third parties). Social knowledge and social manipulation are two complimentary elements in the social cognition of primates. It is the combination of these two elements that makes the social behaviour and cognition of primates particularly complex and powerful.

It is always a difficult task to determine the cognitive basis of social complexity. Byrne & Whiten (1987, 1992) and Byrne (1997a) have previously explored the various cognitive mechanisms, which may underlie the use of tactical deception in primates. In general, and omitting other explanations such as coincidences (see Byrne, 1997a), Byrne & Whiten classified cases of tactical deception as either representing cases of learning to deceive or cases of mindreading (i.e., mental state attribution). All examples of tactical deception in monkeys were classified as cases of learning, whereas some ape examples, the authors argued, were better explained by processes of mind-reading. In Byrne's own words: *"Whereas monkeys of all taxa can learn subtle tactics of deception, only the great apes sometimes seem to understand the false beliefs involved"* (Byrne, 1997b, p. 176).

In this chapter (and elsewhere, Tomasello & Call, 1997), we provide what we see as a more complete classification, which builds on Byrne & Whiten's previous work but which also presents three important differences. First, the current classification is based on three main mechanisms to explain social complexity instead of the two posited by Byrne (1997a,b) and Byrne & Whiten (1987, 1992). The current account incorporates the learning and mind-reading mechanisms but adds a critical third one which lies in between these other two mechanisms with regard to its cognitive complexity (Tomasello & Call, 1997). Second, the use of representation (or different types of representation) plays a central role in the current classification. In fact, what type of representation primates are likely to use is what defines each of the three mechanisms proposed. One advantage of focusing on representation as a key concept is that it enables a more continuous (as opposed to dichotomous, i.e., learning vs. mind reading) view of the various cognitive mechanisms used in complex social situations. Finally, the present classification has a wider scope of application than Byrne & Whiten's because it can be used to explain not only instances of tactical deception, but other instances of social manipulation as well (e.g., redirected aggression, Aureli *et al.*, 1992; recruitment tactics, de Waal & van Hooff, 1981). Tactical deception is just one particular case of social manipulation.

In the current account of primate social complexity, there are at least three basic mechanisms: non-representational, representational and meta-representational (see Table 1).

Table 1 Hierarchy of possible mechanisms used to explain the social knowledge and social manipulation of monkeys and apes. Complex mechanisms are formed by adding a new cognitive component to existing mechanisms

Mechanism	Type of representation	Example
1. Non-representational		
a. hard-wired response	None	Reflex
b. simple learning	None	Trial-and-error
2. Representational		
a. recalling past experiences		
b. applying past experience to novel situation	Behaviour, relationships, and categories	Insight
c. understanding causal links in the problem		
3. Meta-representational		
attributing mental states to others	Intentions, desires, knowledge, and beliefs	Theory of mind

We can use Nishida's (1990) example presented earlier to explain in more detail each of the three mechanisms (see Figure 2). Recall that in that example, a juvenile chimpanzee wanted to nurse but his mother had refused him repeatedly. In order to obtain his goal, the young chimpanzee used the 'non-existing' threats of an adolescent chimpanzee to make his mother comfort him and thus gain access to the nipple. At least three different interpretations of this scenario are possible:

Non-representational

This mechanism is based on possessing hard-wired responses or forming simple associations through such processes as trial-and-error. For instance, the chimpanzee screaming is a hard-wired response to frustration, which provokes his mother to protect and comfort him. In this case, the juvenile does not understand the connection between screaming and obtaining access to the nipple, or any of the intermediate causal links of the problem (e.g., the adolescent's 'non-existing' threat made the juvenile's mother more likely to protect and comfort him). A second possibility, still within this non-representational framework, involves a greater flexibility based on some form of simple learning (not simply automatically triggered responses), but which still does not require mental representation. That is, screaming may have been reinforced in the past for its positive consequences during the course of other frustrating situations, which the juvenile chimpanzee may have encountered. In this case, screaming would be analogous to learning motor responses through operant conditioning without necessarily having access to a representation of such responses.

Representational

This mechanism is based on imagining possible solutions through such processes as insight. In its simplest form, the juvenile may remember that screaming allowed him to obtain the food in the past, and thus he uses the same strategy again. This explanation would imply that the juvenile understands the relation between screaming and obtaining access to the nipple, but it does not necessarily imply that the youngster understands the intermediate causal links of the problem such as why the adolescent male left when he screamed, or why his mother is more permissive after this incident. A second more complex possibility would be based on recalling past experiences and applying them to *novel* situations. In this case, creative problem solving (as opposed to a long history of reinforcement) is responsible for the solution to the problem. For instance, the juvenile may remember that, in the past, screaming (and his mother's subsequent intervention) saved him from being harassed by an older juvenile, and thus he may use screaming (untested in this novel food situation) to bring about a positive outcome to his problem. Again, note that the juvenile still may not necessarily understand the intermediate causal links in the problem. Finally, the most complex representational strategy would entail some basic knowledge about the intermediate causal links in the problem and the ability to apply them to reach a creative solution. First, the juvenile knows that he has to make his mother willing to comfort him in order to gain access to the nipple. Second, he also knows that: i) if an adolescent threatens him and he screams, his mother will protect and comfort him, and ii) once his mother is comforting him (e.g., by embracing him), he will have access to the nipple. Thus, to solve the problem, the juvenile has to put all those pieces of information together. This explanation makes use of intermediate causal links to solve the problem in a way, which was not used in the other two representational levels. These causal links, however, are based purely on representing behavioural patterns and relationships between individuals, not mental states as in the next mechanism.

Meta-representational

This mechanism is based not only on representing the solutions to problems but also on representing the representations of others, especially those representations relating to intentions, desires, knowledge, and beliefs. In the current example, this would imply that the juvenile knows that: i) if he screams and there is an adolescent male nearby his mother will *believe* that the adolescent male attacked him, ii) if his mother believes that he is being attacked she will come to rescue and comfort him, and this will give him access to the nipple. This account differs from the preceding one on a crucial point. The juvenile is thinking about his mother's beliefs (e.g., she will *believe* that he is under attack), not her behaviour.

Of the three mechanisms proposed, current evidence suggests that primates possess both non-representational and representational levels. It is important to emphasise that both mechanisms may coexist and may be used to solve different problems (Call, in press); there is no *a priori* argument to presuppose that representational mechanisms automatically take over all the functions of non-representational mechanisms once they develop. It is clear that primates are capable of using non-representational mechanisms since numerous studies show that primates both have hard-wired responses to social stimuli (Perret & Mistlin, 1990) and can readily learn through associationistic processes, even in social situations (Rumbaugh & Pate, 1984; Lepoivre & Pallaud, 1986). However, there is mounting evidence that non-representational mechanisms cannot fully account for current findings (Tomasello & Call, 1997, for a review). For instance, Coussi-Korbel (1994) found that mangabeys learned not to retrieve food in the presence of a dominant animal in very few trials – a finding that does not fit well with traditional learning theory.

On the other hand, the evidence for the use of meta-representational mechanisms, although certainly advocated by some authors to explain at least some instances of ape tactical deception (e.g., Byrne & Whiten, 1992; Byrne, 1997a,b) has, currently, received little support from recent studies (see Tomasello & Call, 1994, 1997; Call & Tomasello, in press; Heyes, 1998; Povinelli & Eddy, 1996; but see Call & Tomasello, 1998). Nevertheless, Whiten (1994) has pointed out that mind reading encompasses both a number of different phenomena (e.g., intention, desire, knowledge, beliefs) and different levels of understanding of each of these phenomena.

Whether apes and other primates may possess some forms of mind-reading but not others or different levels of understanding in each form of mind-reading is still an open question which future research should address.

The nature of social representations

A representational understanding of the behaviour of others that does not make any assumption regarding mental state attribution thus accounts well for the sophisticated socio-cognitive complexity of primates. According to this proposal, primate social cognition is based on an understanding of others, which relies on things like remembering, foreseeing and manipulating in complex ways the behavioural patterns of others. Primates mentally represent possible solutions to various social problems and select the most appropriate course of action without incurring costly errors derived from trial-and-error strategies or falling into dead-end behavioural strategies. Furthermore, social cognition in the form of mental representation may even allow mental manipulation and combination of solutions, thus avoiding errors or finding solutions, which would be unlikely to be found just by trial-and-error. This representational proposal is in some ways analogous to the sort of understanding found in insightful problem solving (Köhler, 1925).

Still the question remains regarding the precise nature of primates' social representations. Some of the candidates outlined previously include representing stimuli, behaviours, behavioural rules, relationships and, perhaps, even categories. Unfortunately, the field of primate social cognition is still in its infancy and there is little information about the types of social representation that primates possess. However, we can speculate using the much more numerous findings in the domain of physical cognition and try to find evidence suggesting that primates may represent behaviours and relationships, can imagine novel behavioural outcomes and relationships and generate behavioural rules, and that they are capable of categorising behaviours and relationships.

Studies on identity and oddity learning have shown that primates can represent stimuli (D'Amato & Salmon, 1984), which may translate in social terms as the ability to represent individuals and their behaviours. In turn, the ability to rotate objects mentally (Vauclair, Fagot & Hopkins, 1993) may indicate the ability to imagine novel behavioural outcomes. Likewise, the use of transitive inference (McGonigle & Chalmers, 1977; D'Amato et al., 1986) may suggest the ability to predict behavioural outcomes or relationships (e.g., dominance) between two individuals based on their interactions or relationships with a common third party. Studies on analogical reasoning (e.g., Premack, 1983), that is, perceiving the relation between stimuli relations, may be analogous to representing, and even classifying, relationships between individuals. Studies of learning set formation and reversal learning (Harlow, 1949; Rumbaugh & Pate, 1984) have shown that primates can generate rules of learning, even when novel stimuli are used. This ability may be analogous to learning behavioural rules about individuals. Moreover, some studies of conditional discrimination have shown that monkeys can use discriminative stimuli to select appropriate stimuli relations (Burdyn & Thomas, 1984), which may translate in the social arena as perceiving social relationships between individuals as a function of certain social cues. Note that these relations between stimuli do not correspond to perceptual (i.e., superficial) features such as colour or shape, but involve relations which are abstract. These would be analogous to perceiving relationships between groupmates. Finally, primates are also able to categorise stimuli, even using functional, as opposed to perceptual, features (Savage-Rumbaugh *et al.,* 1980), which may translate into the ability to categorise relationships and use non-perceptual social attributes to classify relationships between individuals.

Despite primates' mastery of these various skills, experiments on the understanding of causality of tool-use also have uncovered some limitations. For instance, capuchins and some chimpanzees fail to prepare an appropriate tool to fit a hole of a certain diameter, or fail to foresee some of the problems associated with using a stick to poke a reward out of a tube (Visalberghi & Limongelli, 1996). Only after failing and trying different solutions, they modify the tool appropriately or take the previously unforeseen problems into consideration. This outcome could be explained if individuals were using a representation of a tool that worked in the past to solve a similar problem. Their understanding of causality is quite crude which may make the management of links (crucial for the last representational mechanism) a difficult task for primates. Call (in press) argued that primates' problem understanding may be limited by their depth of processing. That is, primates may be capable of understanding general relations between problem components (e.g., the tool is needed to solve the problem) but have difficulty with more specific relations (e.g., the tool needs to be inserted in a certain way to solve the problem). Therefore, although primates are capable of mentally representing behaviours and behavioural rules and relationships, and can even categorise those relationships, they may have a special difficulty in understanding specific relations between the components of a problem. In terms of the types of representations used, we may speculate that primates may be able to use the first two representational levels depicted in Table 1, but have difficulty using the last representational level.

Conclusion

The social knowledge and social manipulation of monkeys and apes is based on a representational understanding of the behaviour of others. Primates mentally represent possible solutions to various social problems although they may have special difficulties with representing the causal links between the elements of the problem. Nevertheless, this still leaves primates with a quite sophisticated social cognition, which is based on things like remembering, foreseeing and manipulating the behaviour and relationships of others in complex ways.

Acknowledgements

I thank Malinda Carpenter for her many helpful comments during the preparation of this manuscript. I also thank Dick Byrne for his critical reading of an earlier version of this manuscript, and Tom Lisuey for drawing Figure 2.

References

Aureli F, Cozzolino R, Cordischi C, Scucchi S. 1992. Kin-oriented redirection among Japanese macaques: an expression of a revenge system? *Animal Behaviour.* **44**: 283-292.

Aureli F, Das M, Veenema HC. 1997. Differential kinship effect on reconciliation in three species of macaques (*Macaca fascicularis, M. fuscata,* and *M. sylvanus*). *Journal of Comparative Psychology.* **111:** 91-99.

Bard KA. 1990. 'Social tool use' by free ranging orang-utans: A Piagetian and developmental perspective on the manipulation of an animate object. In: Parker ST, Gibson KR. eds. *'Language' and Intelligence in Monkeys and Apes.* Cambridge: Cambridge University Press. 356-378.

Bernstein IS, Ehardt CL. 1986. Selective interference in rhesus monkey (*Macaca mulatta*) intragroup agonistics episodes by age-sex class. *Journal of Comparative Psychology.* **100:** 380-384.

Bernstein IS. 1988. Kinship and behavior in nonhuman primates. *Behavior Genetics.* **18:** 511-524.

Blaschke M, Ettlinger G. 1987. Pointing as an act of social communication by monkeys. *Animal Behaviour.* **35:** 1520-1523.

Burdyn LE, Thomas RK. 1984. Conditional discrimination with conceptual simultaneous and successive cues in the squirrel monkey (*Saimiri sciureus*). *Journal of Comparative Psychology.* **98:** 405-413.

Byrne RW. 1997a. Machiavellian intelligence. *Evolutionary Anthropology.* **5:** 172-180.

Byrne RW. 1997b. What's the use of anecdotes? Distinguishing psychological mechanisms in primate tactical deception. In: Mitchell RW, Thompson NS, Miles HL. eds. *Anthropomorphism, Anecdotes, and Animals.* Albany, New York: The State University of New York Press. 134-150.

Byrne RW, Whiten A. 1987. The thinking primate's guide to deception. *New Scientist.* **116. 1589:** 54-57.

Byrne R, Whiten A. 1988. *Machiavellian intelligence. Social Expertise and the Evolution of Intellect in Monkeys, Apes, and Humans.* New York: Oxford University Press.

Byrne RW, Whiten A. 1992. Cognitive evolution in primates: Evidence from tactical deception. *Man.* **27:** 609-627.

Call J, in press. Representating space and objects in monkeys and apes. *Cognitive Science.*

Call J, Judge PG, de Waal FBM. 1996. Influence of kinship and spatial density on reconciliation and grooming in rhesus monkeys. *American Journal of Primatology.* **39:** 35-45.

Call J, Tomasello M. 1994. Production and comprehension of referential pointing by orang-utans (*Pongo pygmaeus*). *Journal of Comparative Psychology.* **108:** 307-317.

Call J, Tomasello M. 1996. The effect of humans on the cognitive development of apes. In: Russon AE, Bard KA, Parker ST. ed. *Reaching into Thought. The Minds of the Great Apes.* Cambridge: Cambridge University Press. 371-403.

Call J, Tomasello M. 1998. Distinguishing intentional from accidental actions in orang-utans (*Pongo pygmaeus*), chimpanzees (*Pan troglodytes*), and human children (*Homo sapiens*). *Journal of Comparative Psychology.* **112:** 192-206.

Call J, Tomasello M. in press. A nonverbal theory of mind test. The performance of children and apes. *Child Development.*

Cheney DL, Seyfarth RM. 1980. Vocal recognition in free-ranging vervet monkeys. *Animal Behaviour.* **28:** 362-367.

Cheney DL, Seyfarth RM. 1986. The recognition of social alliances by vervet monkeys. *Animal Behaviour.* **34:** 1722-1731.

Cheney DL, Seyfarth RM. 1989. Reconciliation and redirected aggression in vervet monkeys *Cercopithecus aethiops. Behaviour.* **110:** 258-275.

Coussi-Korbel S. 1994. Learning to outwit a competitor in mangabeys (*Cercocebus torquatus torquatus*). *Journal of Comparative Psychology.* **108:** 164-171.

D'Amato MR, Salmon DP. 1984. Cognitive processes in cebus monkeys. In: Roitblat HL, Bever TG, Terrace HS. eds. *Animal Cognition.* Hillsdale, NJ: Lawrence Erlbaum Associates. 149-168.

D'Amato MR, Salmon DP, Loukas E, Tomie A. 1986. Processing of identity and conditional relations in monkeys (*Cebus apella*) and pigeons (*Columba livia*). *Animal Learning and Behavior.* **14:** 365-373.

Das M, Penke Z, van Hooff JARAM. 1997. Affiliation between aggressors and third parties following conflicts in long-tailed macaques (*Macaca fascicularis*). *International Journal of Primatology*. **18:** 159-181.

Dasser V. 1988a. A social concept in Java monkeys. *Animal Behaviour*. **36:** 225-230.

Dasser V. 1988b. Mapping social concepts in monkeys. In: Byrne RW, Whiten A. eds. *Machiavellian Intelligence. Social Expertise and the Evolution of Intellect in Monkeys, Apes, and Humans*. New York: Oxford University Press. 85-93.

de Waal FBM. 1982. *Chimpanzee politics*. London: Jonathan Cape.

de Waal FBM. 1987. Dynamics of social relationships. In: Smuts BB, Cheney DL, Seyfarth RM, Wrangham RW, Struhsaker TT. eds. *Primate societies*. Chicago: The University of Chicago Press. 421-429.

de Waal FBM, Lutrell LM. 1988. Mechanisms of social reciprocity in three primate species: Symetrical relationship characteristics or cognition?. *Ethology and Sociobiology*. **9:** 101-118.

de Waal FBM, van Hooff JARAM. 1981. Side-directed communication and agonistic interactions in chimpanzees. *Behaviour*. **77:** 164-198.

Gómez JC. 1990. The emergence of intentional communication as a problem-solving strategy in the gorilla. In: Parker ST, Gibson KR. eds. *'Language' and Intelligence in Monkeys and Apes*. Cambridge: Cambridge University Press. 333-355.

Gómez JC. 1991. Visual behaviour as a window for reading the mind of others in primates. In: Whiten A. ed. *Natural Theories of Mind*. Oxford: Blackwell. 195-207.

Gouzoules H, Gouzoules S. 1987. Kinship. In: Smuts BB, Cheney DL, Seyfarth RM, Wrangham RW, Struhsaker TT. eds. *Primate societies*. Chicago: The University of Chicago Press. 299-305.

Harcourt AH, de Waal FBM. 1992. *Coalitions and alliances in humans and other animals*. New York: Oxford University Press.

Harlow HF. 1949. The formation of learning sets. *Psychological Review*. **56:** 51-65.

Hemelrijk CK. 1994. Support for being groomed in long-tailed macaques, *Macaca fascicularis*. *Animal Behaviour*. **48:** 479-481.

Hess J, Novak MA, Povinelli DJ. 1993. 'Natural pointing' in a rhesus monkey, but no evidence of empathy. *Animal Behaviour*. **46:** 1023-1025.

Heyes CM. 1998. Theory of mind in nonhuman primates. *Behavioral and Brain Sciences*. **21:** 101-134.

Hinde RA. 1979. *Towards Understanding Relationships*. London: Academic Press.

Humphrey NK. 1976. The social function of intellect. In: Bateson P, Hinde RA. eds. *Growing Points in Ethology*. Cambridge: Cambridge University Press. 303-321.

Jolly A. 1966. Lemur social behavior and primate intelligence. *Science*. **153:** 501-506.

Judge PG. 1982. Redirection of aggression based on kinship in a captive group of pigtail macaques. *International Journal of Primatology.* **3**: 301.

Judge PG. 1991. Dyadic and triadic reconciliation in pigtail macaques (*Macaca nemestrina*) *American Journal of Primatology.* **23**: 225-237.

Köhler W. 1925. *The Mentality of Apes.* London: Routledge and Kegan Paul.

Kummer H. 1982. Social knowledge in free-ranging primates. In: Griffin DR. ed. *Animal Mind – Human Mind.* Berlin: Springer-Verlag. 113-130.

Leavens DA, Hopkins WD, Bard KA. 1996. Indexical and referential pointing in chimpanzees (*Pan troglodytes*). *Journal of Comparative Psychology.* **110**: 346-353.

Lepoivre H, Pallaud B. 1986. Learning set formation in a group of baboons (*Papio papio*). *American Journal of Primatology.* **10**: 25-36.

McGonigle BO, Chalmers M. 1977. Are monkeys logical? *Nature.* **267**: 694-696.

Menzel Jr EW. 1973. Leadership and communication in young chimpanzees. In: Menzel Jr. EW. ed. *Precultural Primate Behavior.* Basel: Karger. 192-225.

Menzel Jr EW. 1974. A group of young chimpanzees in a one-acre field: leadership and communication. In: Schrier AM, Stollnitz F. eds. *Behavior of Nonhuman Primates.* New York: Academic Press. 83-153.

Milton K. 1981. Distribution patterns of tropical plant foods as an evolutionary stimulus to primate mental development. *American Anthropologist.* **83**: 534-548.

Mitchell RW. 1991. Deception and hiding in captive lowland gorillas (*Gorilla gorilla gorilla*). *Primates.* **32**: 523-527.

Mitchell RW, Anderson JR. 1997. Pointing, withholding information, and deception in capuchin monkeys (*Cebus apella*). *Journal of Comparative Psychology.* **111**: 351-361.

Nishida T. 1990. Deceptive behavior in young chimpanzees: An essay. In: Nishida T. ed. *The Chimpanzees of the Mahale Mountains.* Tokyo: The University of Tokyo Press. 285-290.

Parker ST, Gibson KR. 1979. A developmental model for the evolution of language and intelligence in early hominids. *Behavioral and Brain Sciences.* **2**: 367-408.

Perrett DI, Mistlin AJ. 1990. Perception of facial characteristics by monkeys. In: Stebbins WC, Berkley MA. eds. *Comparative Perception.* New York: John Wiley and Sons. 187-215.

Povinelli DJ, Eddy TJ. 1996. What young chimpanzees know about seeing. *Monographs of the Society for Research in Child Development.* **61(3)**.

Premack D. 1983. The codes of man and beasts. *Behavioral and Brain Sciences.* **6**: 125-167.

Roberts WA, Mazmanian DS. 1988. Concept learning at different levels of abstraction by pigeons, monkeys, and people. *Journal of Experimental Psychology: Animal Behavior Processes.* **14:** 247-260.

Rumbaugh DM, Pate JL. 1984. Primates' learning by levels. In: Greenberg G, Tobach E. eds. *Behavioral Evolution and Integrative Levels.* Hillsdale, NJ: Lawrence Erlbaum Associates. 221-240.

Savage-Rumbaugh ES, Mcdonald K, Sevcik RA, Hopkins WD, Rubert E. 1986. Spontaneous symbol acquisition and communicative use by pygmy chimpanzees (*Pan paniscus*). *Journal of Experimental Psychology: General.* **115:** 211-235.

Savage-Rumbaugh ES, Rumbaugh DM, Smith ST, Lawson J. 1980. Reference: The linguistic essential. *Science.* **210:** 922-925.

Seyfarth RM, Cheney DL. 1984. Gooming, alliances and reciprocal altruism in vervet monkeys. *Nature.* **308:** 541-543.

Silk JB. 1992. The patterning of intervention among male bonnet macaques: reciprocity, revenge, and loyalty. *Current Anthropology.* **33:** 318-325.

Tomasello M, Call J. 1994. Social cognition of monkeys and apes. *Yearbook of Physical Anthropology.* **37:** 273-305.

Tomasello M, Call J. 1997. *Primate Cognition.* New York: Oxford University Press.

Tomasello M, Call J, Nagell K, Olguin R, Carpenter M. 1994. The learning and use of gestural signals by young chimpanzees: A trans-generational study. *Primates.* **35:** 137-154.

Tomasello M, Call J, Warren J, Frost GT, Carpenter M, Nagell K, 1997. The ontogeny of chimpanzee gestural signals: A comparison across groups and generations. *Evolution of Communication.* **1:** 223-257.

Tomasello M, George B, Kruger A, Farrar M, Evans A. 1985. The development of gestural communication in young chimpanzees. *Journal of Human Evolution.* **14:** 175-186.

Tomasello M, Gust D, Frost GT. 1989. The development of gestural communication in young chimpanzees: a follow up. *Primates.* **30:** 35-50.

Vauclair J, Fagot J, Hopkins WD. 1993. Rotation of mental images in baboons when the visual input is directed to the left cerebral hemisphere. *Psychological Science.* **4:** 99-103.

Visalberghi E, Limongelli L. 1996. Acting and understanding: Tool use revisited through the minds of capuchin monkeys In: Russon AE, Bard KA, Parker ST. eds. *Reaching into Thought. The Minds of the Great Apes.* Cambridge: Cambridge University Press. 57-79.

Whiten A. 1994. Grades of mindreading. In: Lewis C, Mitchell P. ed. *Children's Early Understanding of Mind.* Hillsdale, New Jersey: Lawrence Erlbaum Associates. 47-70.

Whiten A, Byrne RW. 1997. *Machiavellian intelligence II. Extensions and evaluations.* Cambridge: Cambridge University Press.

Woodruff G, Premack D. 1979. Intentional communication in the chimpanzee: The development of deception. *Cognition.* **7:** 333-362.

CHAPTER TEN

Individual differences in chimpanzee (*Pan troglodytes*) personality and their implications for the evolution of mind

L. E. MURRAY

Introduction

Personality in non-human primates

While earlier descriptions exist (Yerkes & Yerkes, 1929; Yerkes, 1943; Hebb, 1946), it is only over the past thirty years that the existence of individuality in non-humans has been recognised and acknowledged with any enthusiasm (Schaller, 1963; Bolwig, 1964; Reynolds & Reynolds, 1965; van Hooff, 1967), and such a concept remains controversial within the scientific community. Subjective impressions are another matter, and very few people would dispute the fact that their pet dog, for instance, has a specific personality (Serpell, 1983). Non-human primates are a logical next step from which the layperson can recognise individuality, and this is likely to be based on, and influenced by, empathy and the attribution of our own mental states and emotions. It is perhaps because they are so close to humans, both in genetic and evolutionary terms, that some scientists are opposed to the idea of these animals possessing individual personalities, challenging the uniqueness of humans.

Various researchers have labelled aspects of temperament in their subjects. The volatile temperament and behaviour of chimpanzees was described early on (Köhler, 1925; Yerkes, 1943). While there has until recently been relatively little research into chimpanzees' emotions, subjective impressions of emotions in free-living chimpanzees reveal striking similarities to those of humans, and include pleasure, joy, sorrow, boredom, apprehension, fear, distress, annoyance, anger, rage, enjoyment, and excitement specifically related to either a social or a sexual sphere (Goodall, 1986). Chimpanzees have also been described as 'brash or shy, and sensitive' (Reynolds & Reynolds, 1965), 'curious' (Morris, 1965), and 'self-assured', 'happy', 'proud' and 'calculating' (de Waal, 1982).

There is little doubt that descriptions of, and the recounting of episodes in the lives of, the great apes by human observers are plentiful. They are, however, subjective. While it may be easy to anthropomorphise about animals such as chimpanzees when we watch them as characters in a daily drama, it is harder to find ways of quantifying what we call 'personality', and to go some way to assessing those individual differences which may exist. In 1943, Yerkes stressed the need for quantitative assessment of the individuality he knew undoubtedly existed in the chimpanzees at his research centre. More recently, primate researchers are still suggesting that a greater focus on personality is required (Kano, 1986). Rating scales of personality traits have been extensively employed with human subjects (e.g. Plutchik & Kellerman, 1974), but their use as a means of quantifying the subjective impressions of individuality on the part of those working with animals, such as dolphins *Tursiops truncatus* (Kellerman, 1966) and cats *Felis catus* (Feaver *et al.,* 1986), has been relatively limited.

For the non-human primates, there have been several attempts to apply rating scales: olive baboons *Papio anubis* (Buirski *et al.,* 1973); chimpanzees *Pan troglodytes* (Buirski, Plutchik & Kellerman, 1978; Buirski & Plutchik, 1991); gorillas *Gorilla gorilla gorilla* (Gold & Maple, 1994); vervet monkeys *Cercopithecus aethiops* (Raleigh, McGuire & Brammer, 1989; McGuire, Raleigh & Pollack, 1994); pig-tailed macaques *Macaca nemestrina* (Caine, Earle & Reite, 1983); stumptail macaques *Macaca arctoides* (Mondragon-Ceballos, Santillan-Doherty & Chiappa, 1991); rhesus macaques *Macaca mulatta* (Chamove, Eysenck & Harlow, 1972; Stevenson-Hinde & Zunz, 1978; Stevenson-Hinde, Stillwell-Barnes & Zunz, 1980a, 1980b; Bolig, Price,O'Neill & Suomi, 1992). Such studies examine personality traits in relation to the early experiences and current physiological (usually stress) responses of individuals, and, perhaps most importantly, seek to determine the power of personality traits in predicting actual behaviour.

The general Emotions Profile Index (EPI) method (Plutchik 1965; Kellerman & Plutchik, 1968; Plutchik & Kellerman, 1974) involves the selection of the more appropriate description out of pairs of adjectives; for example, would an animal be described as more 'gloomy' or more 'resentful'? The selections yield eight scores, the relative strength of which represents the eight basic primary emotions (protection, observed as fear; destruction, observed as anger; incorporation, observed as acceptance; rejection, observed as disgust; orientation, observed as surprise; exploration, observed as expectation; reproduction, observed as joy; and deprivation, observed as sadness) according to Plutchik's theory of emotion (Plutchik, 1962, 1970). The thrust of this theory is that all emotional states and behavioural traits, however complex, can be reduced to combinations of two or more of the eight basic primary emotions. For example, the trait of jealousy would have as its component emotions, deprivation and destruction.

The EPI used by Buirski and his co-workers (1973, 1978) is based on personality theory which emphasises the importance of emotions for evolutionary adaptation (see also Gooch, 1973), and their baboon version uses twelve descriptive terms: friendly, affectionate, defiant, assertive, submissive, obedient, belligerent, impulsive, alarmed, cautious, jealous and sullen. The terms 'obedient' and 'sullen', however, were found to be too inferential, and their future use in such scales was not advised. A revised chimpanzee version EPI also found some significant sex differences in personality among twenty-three chimpanzees at Gombe (Buirski *et al.,* 1978). Female chimpanzees were rated as more timid and depressed, but more trustful than males. Males, on the other hand, were rated as being more distrustful than their female conspecifics. Certain other trends were identified, but it was not claimed that these differences were significant. Male chimpanzees were found to be relatively more aggressive, rather than timid, and more sociable and impulsive. This revised scale used 45 sets of paired trait adjectives, thought to be more characteristic of chimpanzees, representing combinations of the following ten trait terms: belligerent, defiant, depressed, dominant, fearful, inquisitive, irritable, playful, sociable and submissive. The selection from the paired adjectives is scored in terms of the following implied basic emotional dispositions: trust versus distrust, timidity versus aggression, gregariousness versus depression, and control versus dyscontrol.

The EPI has accompanied a study of environmental enrichment, and revealed differences in emotionality between the captive chimpanzees when compared with Buirski *et al's.,* (1978) report of their wild counterparts in Gombe (Farmer, 1993). Buirski & Plutchik (1991) suggested comparisons between wild and captive populations could detect the effects of captivity on an individual's psychological state. Chimpanzees in captivity were found to be significantly less trustful, more distrustful, less controlled, less gregarious and more aggressive. No significant sex differences among the captive chimpanzees were found with this method, however. An unnatural group structure, a lack of control over the environment, and the effects of becoming humanised were proposed as the captive conditions leading to these differences (Farmer, 1993). Buirski *et al.,* (1973, 1978) state that there was "*reasonable reliability*" between raters, but they fail to say whether or not the inter-observer correlations were significant. Low inter-rater reliability using the EPI method has been found for individual monkeys (*Papio hamadryas, Macaca fuscata* and two *Saimiri* species) whose social status was changing, which died soon after they were assessed, and for adolescent males, sub-adults and infants (Martau, Caine & Candland, 1985).

To an extent, these findings indicate that discernible personalities exist both in baboons and in chimpanzees. However, the findings do not emphasise the individuality of these species, in the sense that Buirski *et al.,* (1978) found the 'average' profile of a chimpanzee to be very similar to that of a baboon and also to that of a 'college student'. The EPI uses paired trait adjectives, which are hard to differentiate, and these items are used to 'imply' underlying emotions. This method therefore seems open to ambiguity, and it is also founded on an assumption that the same emotional dispositions (determined by the agreement of a group of 'judges') are applicable to all humans and other animals. Use of this method has, at least in one isolated example, detected social deviance (Buirski & Plutchik, 1991). The subsequently infanticidal and cannibalistic adult female chimpanzee, Passion, had in 1973 been rated as more aggressive, depressed and distrustful than other females, and Buirski & Plutchik

(1991) claim that such sensitivity of detection demonstrates the descriptive and diagnostic powers of the EPI instrument.

The present study uses a seven-point rating scale derived largely from Stevenson-Hinde & Zunz's (1978) rating scale for rhesus macaques *Macaca mulatta*. Rather than using pairs of adjectives, this scale requires raters to assign a score of between one and seven to each animal for each of an extensive list of adjectives. Their list comprised twenty-three items, nineteen of which were found to be reliable (following correlations between the two observers: Pearson, p<0.05, one-tailed). Ten new adjectives were added in the third year of the study. A mean rating across observers for each subject on each item was calculated, and this formed the input for a principal components analysis, without rotation. This type of analysis, independent of any theories, yields components uncorrelated to each other, finding linear combinations of orthogonal variables which account for more of the variance in rating scores than do the others – i.e. Component 1 would account for the most variance, C2 would be the next best, and so on until all, or as much as is possible, of the variance is accounted for. A score for each component can be calculated for each individual subject by multiplying their standardised rating on an item by the loading of that item, and then dividing by the eigenvalue of the component, summed over all items. The standardised rating is calculated by dividing the deviation from the mean over all subjects by the standard deviation, and the eigenvalue is the variance accounted for by that component.

Among the rhesus macaques, three main components could be identified, from which scores were calculated to describe the personalities of the individuals in terms of confidence, excitability and sociability. Adult male rhesus macaques were found to be more confident than females, and confident and sociable mothers had infants who were also respectively confident and sociable, while excitable mothers had infants who lacked confidence (Stevenson-Hinde *et al.*, 1980a). Stevenson-Hinde and her co-workers correlated ratings over time as well, but the present study uses only data from one period. A modified version of this ratings system has also been used as a 'Gorilla Behaviour Index', in an attempt by the managers of the Gorilla Species Survival Plan to have behavioural profiles compiled for each of the gorillas held in North America (Gold & Maple, 1994). The identification of four components – named 'Extroverted', 'Dominant', 'Fearful' and 'Understanding' – enables decisions to be made regarding relocations of particular individuals to optimise compatibility.

Personality traits and types, and evolution of mind

Assessment of individual differences may also elucidate the role played by personality in shaping the evolution of mind. With the genetic variation between humans and chimpanzees being only just over one per cent (Sarich & Cronin, 1976), chimpanzees are closer to humans than they are to monkeys or gorillas. They have a similar brain structure, extensive cognitive and perceptual abilities, exhibit many similar behaviours and emotional expressions and share many of our emotional needs. In the wild, the mental skills of chimpanzees are evidenced in tool making and tool-use, co-operation in hunting, deception and in the complexity of their social relationships. Captive animals have been tested on many different mental skills, including reasoning (Gillan, 1981), mirror and video self-recognition (Gallup 1970, 1977, 1979; Menzel, Savage-Rumbaugh & Lawson, 1985; Savage-Rumbaugh & Rubert, 1986), mathematical competence (Pérusse & Rumbaugh, 1990), and language (Gardner & Gardner, 1969).

Personality traits would not be useful if they did not enable prediction of at least some individual variation in behaviour. Although an individual's behaviour in one situation may not necessarily be predictive of its behaviour in other situations (Mischel 1993), greater cross-situational consistency can become more apparent with the correct investigative techniques (Eysenck & Eysenck, 1980), or with meaningful coding of behaviours (Funder & Colvin, 1991). Even an interactionist view, which takes into account both personal and environmental qualities, is one in which behaviour remains largely determined by traits; the causal primacy assumption of traditional trait theories being that causality is mainly in the direction from trait to behaviour (e.g. Allport, 1937; Cattell, 1973). Another basic assumption of such trait theories involves the 'inner locus', assuming that traits describe core qualities of the individual, which may not be obviously manifest. As an example, Deary & Matthews (1993) suggest considering how a latent extravert who happens to be an undertaker might have little opportunity to exhibit his core trait tendencies. This is a good example of how the situation may constrain the expression of traits in behaviour.

What needs to be determined is which specific trait (or group of traits) governs behaviour when it is expressed. Personality 'types', or ratings according to principal components, may enable prediction of expected behaviours, such that one can expect people of a certain type, or with certain traits, to exhibit particular behaviours in their interactions. For example, people termed 'neurotic' are more likely to be shy (Crozier, 1979), withdrawn (McCrae & Costa, 1986), anxious and depressed (Eysenck & Eysenck, 1985), have sexual problems (Eysenck, 1976), and cognitive incompetencies (Matthews, Coyler & Craig, 1990), and they may be more susceptible to certain forms of criminality (Eysenck, 1977) and drug addiction (Gossop & Eysenck, 1983). From such a list of behavioural indices, it is apparent that neuroticism itself can be regarded as both a cause and an effect of such psychological disturbance. Extraverts, on the other hand, are happier (Lu & Argyle, 1991) and are more able to utilise effective coping strategies (Parkes, 1986), performing more favourably under stressful conditions (Corcoran, 1972). They also have superior short-term memory but are poorer at certain other mental skills, such as problem solving (Eysenck, 1982).

Figure 1
The Chester
chimpanzee group.

Row 1 Adult males
Row 2 Young adult
male - Juvenile males
Row 3 Adult females
Row 4 Young adult
females
Row 5 Juvenile
females
Row 6 Infant females

Photos: The author and Chester Zoo

How might non-human primates compare?

One of the most famous distinctions between human individuals is that between 'Type A' coronary-prone and 'Type B' people (Friedman & Rosenman, 1959), and the very label illustrates the way in which certain traits are thought to lead to a physical manifestation of disease. Type A people are typically perfectionistic, impatient, hard to get along with, insecure in social situations, industrious, competitive, aggressive and hurried (Brody, 1980). Type Bs, conversely, are more relaxed and sociable (Glass, 1983). The typical striving for success of Type As provides a good example of how the individual's personality leads them into highly stressful situations, rather than the trait developing due to the situation (Smith & Anderson, 1986). Such people will often freely admit that they thrive under pressure and, while this propels the individual into a circle of never-ending stress, this type of person could be frustrated and unhappy if such situations were avoided. Again, might there be a similar distinction in the ape world, possibly related to status seeking amongst adult males?

Another distinction between humans is that where individuals have either an internal or external locus of control (Rotter & Hochreich, 1975). 'Internals' believe they influence what happens to them, but 'externals' think they are at the mercy of external forces such as fate or luck. Is it possible that chimpanzees may also operate along similar lines?

Method

Study sites and subjects

A total of 59 individuals were studied in 1992 in three zoological collections in England.

Chester Zoo (N=22)

Chester Zoo has the largest social group of chimpanzees in the United Kingdom, containing four adult males, with four generations of families represented, almost exclusively parent-reared, Figure 1. The chimpanzees have a large grass-covered outside island, with an area of approximately 2000 square meters (half an acre) and a circumference of 183 metres, containing sand, a concrete tunnel, a swing-pole and dead oak trees. Their indoor enclosure is 13 metres wide tapering up to a height of 12 metres. This contains a large tubular steel climbing frame, with wooden platforms, ropes and tyres. Ropes are also fastened to various points on the weld-mesh, which covers the walls tapering to the roof point. A water-filled moat inside duplicates the large moat outside which acts as a barrier around the island.

London Zoo (N=11)

The group of eleven chimpanzees at London includes just one adult male, and all infants are parent-reared. The group has a double outside enclosure, comprising two rectangular areas, each of 120 square metres, which have a connecting passage between them. The outside roof areas, approximately 5 metres in height, are covered with space-frame climbing apparatus, from which hang ropes. There are also two indoor on-show areas, accessible from outside or from the back beds.

Twycross Zoo (N=26)

 i) Seven chimpanzees, including two young adult males, are grouped together. They have an indoor cement enclosure with access to an outside dry-moated grass enclosure. When separated in night-beds, some of this group can see or touch through the wire the two infants in (ii).

 ii) Two infants are confined to an extended bed area with no outside access. They are taken into hand-rearers' houses at night.

 iii) Two juveniles are housed together in a small indoor hut with a larger non-grass outside enclosure.

 iv) Two infants are housed together through a wire partition from one infant gorilla, with which they take turns to play in the afternoon, none of them having outside access.

 v – ix) Thirteen adult chimpanzees are split into five groups of two or three, and are housed in the long chimpanzee house indoor enclosures with adjoining partitioned outdoor enclosures.

Table 1 shows the classification of subjects according to age and sex.

Table 1 Subject age and sex classification.

	Males	Females
Infants (0-4 yrs.incl.)	2	10
Juveniles(5-8 yrs.incl.)	5	3
Young Adults (9-20 yrs.)	8	17
Mature Adults (21 yrs+)	5	9
Total Subjects	**20**	**39**

Data collection

Personality ratings questionnaires

 The rating scale contained a list of 28 behaviourally defined adjectives, closely following the scale devised and used by Stevenson-Hinde and her co-workers with rhesus macaques *Macaca mulatta* (Stevenson-Hinde & Zunz, 1978; Stevenson-Hinde *et al.*, 1980a). Raters gave each individual animal a score on a seven point scale, depending on the strength of the manifestation of each particular behaviour, where 1 equals none of the behaviour and 7 represents extreme behaviour. The adjectives and their behavioural definitions appear in Table 2.

Table 2 Personality adjectives and their behavioural definitions.

1.	Active – moves about a lot.
2.	Aggressive – causes harm or potential harm.
3.	Apprehensive – seems to be anxious about everything; fears and avoids any kind of risk.
4.	Confident – behaves in a positive, assured manner; not restrained or tentative.
5.	Curious – readily explores new situations.
6.	Deferential – gives in readily to others.
7.	Eccentric – shows stereotypes or unusual mannerisms.
8.	Effective – gets own way; can control others; leads.
9.	Equable – reacts to others in an even calm way; is not easily disturbed.
10.	Excitable – over-reacts to any change.
11.	Fearful – fear-grins; retreats readily from others or from outside disturbances.
12.	Gentle – responds to others in an easy kind manner.
13.	Insecure – hesitates to act alone; seeks reassurance from others.
14.	Intelligent – clever; tactical; manipulative; inventive.
15.	Irritable – reacts negatively with little provocation.
16.	Maternal/Paternal – warm and receptive to infants.
17.	Opportunistic – seizes a chance as soon as it arises.
18.	Permissive* – could, but does not, interfere with the behaviour of others.
19.	Playful – initiates play and joins in when play is solicited.
20.	Popular – is sought out as a companion by others.
21.	Predictable* – consistent in behaviour.
22.	Protective – prevents harm or possible harm to others.
23.	Sensitive* – responds or reacts with minimal cues to the behaviour of others.
24.	Slow – moves and sits in a relaxed manner; moves slowly and deliberately; not easily hurried.
25.	Sociable – seeks companionship of others.
26.	Solitary – spends time alone.
27.	Strong – depends upon sturdiness and muscular strength.
28.	Tense – shows restraint in posture and movement.

* Adjectives subsequently omitted from analysis due to poor intra-item reliability

Ratings questionnaires were completed by the author for all individuals and by four keepers at Chester, three keepers at London, and one or two keepers (out of a total of six) at Twycross who rated only those apes they worked with. Full details of rating instructions can be found in Murray (1995, 1998). These ratings may be affected by the personalities and biases of the raters themselves. However, after multiple regression analyses of intra-item reliability and correlations of inter-rater reliability were performed, only 3 of the original 28 adjectives had to be rejected because of low correlations between raters. Altogether, over 1000 hours of focal samples of behaviour were observed which were then correlated with the ratings (Murray, 1995).

Data analysis

Variation in ratings

Ratings for adjectives were normally distributed and differences between age, sex, rearing and grouping categories were explored using analysis of variance (ANOVA). Independent categorical variables were age (Immatures: ≤ 107 months; Adults: ≥ 108 months), sex (M or F), rearing (parent- or hand-reared) and grouping (Large: ≥ 4 individuals; Small: 1-3 individuals). Age in months and actual group size were also used in correlational analyses.

Correlation and principal components analyses

In order to identify adjectives which are related, and so that these associations may then be used to aid the inference of underlying personality traits, mean ratings for each subject on each adjective were analysed by Pearson correlation coefficients.

Significance levels were set at $p \leq 0.001$ to minimise type I errors. In an attempt to determine possible underlying factors within the personalities of the chimpanzee subjects, their mean ratings were additionally subjected to principal components analysis. Component scores for each subject provide a valuable means of assessing individual differences, and additional scores representing levels of confidence, sociability and excitability were also calculated from individuals' standardised scores on leading items on the components (Stevenson-Hinde et al., 1980a).

Results & Discussion

Variation in ratings

Individual ratings on the 25 adjectives found to be reliable were determined. Table 3 shows the mean ratings and standard deviations for all chimpanzees on each adjective, while Table 4 presents mean ratings by sex and age. Ratings ranged from 2.8 for 'Tense' to 4.7 for 'Maternal/Paternal'.

Differences in personality ratings according to sex and age

While male chimpanzees were rated as stronger but also more excitable than females, immature chimpanzees appear more active and playful, and are more curious, popular and sociable than adults. Within the immature age-group, individuals tend to become more

Table 3 Mean ratings on personality adjectives for chimpanzees.

Adjective	Mean rating	Standard deviation
Active	4.4	1.0
Aggressive	3.0	1.2
Apprehensive	3.3	1.1
Confident	4.3	0.9
Curious	4.6	0.8
Deferential	3.4	1.5
Eccentric	2.9	1.4
Effective	3.6	1.3
Equable	4.1	0.9
Excitable	3.9	0.9
Fearful	3.3	1.1
Gentle	4.4	0.9
Insecure	3.1	1.1
Intelligent	4.6	0.7
Irritable	3.2	1.1
Maternal/Paternal	4.7	1.3
Opportunistic	4.4	0.8
Playful	4.2	1.2
Popular	4.4	1.0
Protective	3.9	1.0
Slow	3.3	1.2
Sociable	4.4	0.8
Solitary	3.4	1.0
Strong	3.8	1.2
Tense	2.8	1.0

aggressive and excitable as they pass from infancy into the juvenile period, although this transition also marks an increase in ratings for intelligence. The transition to adulthood is notable for increasing slowness, and this is most apparent as young adults move into later adulthood.

Adult chimpanzees are significantly more eccentric, effective, excitable, gentle, protective, slow, solitary and strong than immatures. Such age-related patterns have also been found in other species, such as rhesus macaques (Bolig *et al.,* 1992).

Correlation analysis of chimpanzee ratings

Figure 2 illustrates the correlations between personality ratings adjectives for the chimpanzees. The adjectives which cluster together closely approximate the personality components to be discussed below. The most obvious cluster concerns those adjectives relating to confidence, or lack of it. 'Confident' and 'Effective' are positively associated with each other, and negatively linked to the

Table 4 Mean ratings on personality adjectives for chimpanzees by sex and age.

Adjective	M	F	I	J	YAd	Ad
Active	4.6	4.3	4.7	5.3	4.3	3.8
Aggressive	3.3	2.8	2.3	3.3	3.2	3.1
Apprehensive	3.2	3.3	2.7	3.5	3.5	3.3
Confident	4.3	4.3	4.7	4.2	4.0	4.4
Curious	4.5	4.7	5.2	4.8	4.4	4.5
Deferential	3.3	3.4	3.1	3.5	3.5	3.1
Eccentric	2.8	2.9	2.1	2.7	3.1	3.1
Effective	3.8	3.5	3.1	3.2	3.6	4.3
Equable	4.1	4.1	4.2	3.8	4.1	4.2
Excitable	4.3	3.7	3.0	4.1	4.2	3.9
Fearful	3.4	3.3	3.3	3.8	3.4	3.1
Gentle	4.5	4.4	4.2	4.0	4.6	4.7
Insecure	3.1	3.0	2.9	3.2	3.1	3.1
Intelligent	4.4	4.7	4.4	4.8	4.6	4.6
Irritable	3.0	3.3	2.7	3.5	3.3	3.2
Maternal/Paternal	4.5	4.7	3.8	4.7	4.5	5.4
Opportunistic	4.2	4.5	4.4	4.6	4.3	4.3
Playful	4.3	4.1	5.4	5.3	3.6	3.6
Popular	4.5	4.3	4.9	4.7	4.2	4.1
Protective	3.8	3.9	3.3	4.0	3.9	4.1
Slow	3.1	3.3	2.5	2.1	3.3	4.6
Sociable	4.2	4.4	4.8	4.9	4.1	4.2
Solitary	3.6	3.3	2.7	2.6	3.7	3.9
Strong	4.4	3.5	2.7	3.5	4.3	4.1
Tense	2.7	2.9	2.2	2.9	3.0	2.8

M: Male **F:** Female **I:** Infant **J:** Juvenile **YAd:** Young Adult **Ad:** Adult

inter-related adjectives: 'Apprehensive', 'Deferential', 'Fearful', 'Insecure' and 'Tense'. 'Aggressive' and 'Irritable' are positively associated, the former also being strongly linked to 'Effective'. Another cluster involves the adjectives 'Sociable', 'Playful' and 'Popular' which are positively associated with each other, and negatively correlated with 'Solitary'. Two remaining pairs of adjectives also have strong relationships; these being 'Active' with 'Slow', and 'Intelligent' with 'Opportunistic'.

Certain correlations were unique to specific age/sex classes of chimpanzees, and one of the most interesting points to note is that the more protective and confident a male is, the more popular he appears to be. A negative relationship exists between opportunism and apprehension in males, while 'Opportunistic' and 'Strong' are positively correlated in females. Among immature chimpanzees, there is a positive relationship between greater activity and being more protective, and greater playfulness also relates to a higher degree of protection in this age group. Among adult chimpanzees, there is a positive relationship between 'Maternal/Paternal' and 'Protective' and between 'Confident' and 'Aggressive'.

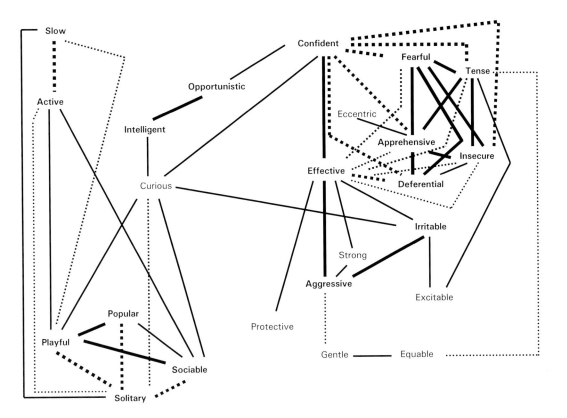

Figure 2
Correlations (significant at p<0.001) between personality ratings adjectives for chimpanzees (N=59). Broken lines denote negative relationships. Associations with coefficients >.60 are shown in bold.

Principal components analysis of chimpanzee ratings

The Principal Components Analysis on mean ratings extracted six components with eigenvalues greater than 1, accounting for 77.5% of the variance in ratings for chimpanzees. Table 5 presents the loadings of the 25 adjectives on each of Components 1, 2 & 3,

Table 5 PCA loading of the twenty five personality ratings on components 1, 2, and 3.

Adjective	C1: Confident/ Apprehensive	C2: Sociable/Solitary	C3: Excitable/Slow
% Variance	23.7%	18.4%	15.4%
Confident	**0.92**	-0.02	-0.05
Effective	**0.73**	-0.46	0.23
Opportunistic	**0.59**	0.08	0.35
Intelligent	**0.47**	-0.01	0.40
Tense	**-0.63**	-0.22	0.57
Deferential	**-0.72**	0.35	0.24
Insecure	**-0.75**	0.09	0.36
Fearful	**-0.76**	0.26	0.33
Apprehensive	**-0.85**	-0.04	0.36
Playful	0.15	**0.83**	0.28
Sociable	0.24	**0.74**	0.35
Popular	0.29	**0.69**	0.16
Curious	0.52	**0.53**	0.21
Equable	0.19	**0.42**	-0.20
Gentle	-0.23	**0.35**	0.02
Strong	0.23	**-0.49**	0.38
Slow	0.07	**-0.51**	-0.33
Solitary	-0.20	**-0.78**	0.07
Maternal/Paternal	0.20	0.14	**0.69**
Protective	0.22	-0.17	**0.60**
Excitable	-0.22	-0.36	**0.60**
Aggressive	0.44	-0.50	**0.52**
Active	0.28	0.37	**0.50**
Irritable	0.34	-0.37	**0.49**
Eccentric	-0.23	-0.15	**0.47**

the major components each accounting for more than 10% of this variance, and these dimensions are represented in Figure 3. Each of these components can be characterised as follows:

CONFIDENT/APPREHENSIVE
The first and most significant component suggests that chimpanzees vary principally along a dimension concerned with how

confident and effective they are in relation to each other, and has much to do with status and leadership. This component has similarities to the basic disposition of 'timidity versus aggression' used in the EPI (Buirski *et al.*, 1978). Relative timidity in female chimpanzees has been reported for free-living individuals, but this – like some other traits found in wild apes – was not evidenced in this study. There were no age or sex differences in chimpanzees' 'Confident' scores. The nomenclature differs between the two studies, but there is no indication from this study that captive female chimpanzees exhibit any behaviours or mood manifestations which could be interpreted as signs of depression, or that the sexes differ in terms of trustfulness, as found by Buirski *et al.* Indeed, depression was used as the opposing term to gregariousness, and was purported to be a basic emotional disposition (Buirski *et al.*, 1978). However, it seems an attribution of human beliefs to contend that an individual who prefers to remain largely on his or her own is necessarily depressed.

Both the dominant male and female of the largest group of chimpanzees at Chester are rated as the most confident chimpanzees of their sex but, since such individuals are regarded as the dominant animals, they may be rated higher on traits associated with that role. Intelligence is an important characteristic of the 'Confident/Apprehensive' component in chimpanzees, and could be the extra attribute which elevates certain individuals above the threshold level of their peers and enables them to acquire alpha status. Intelligence and opportunism can be seen as features of the human 'five-factor' dimensions relating to both conscientiousness, and openness and originality.

SOCIABLE/SOLITARY

The second component concerns how sociable individuals are in relation to each other. Being sociable and being solitary are not necessarily mutually exclusive however, as many individuals spend time both on their own and with certain preferred others. The importance and popularity of immature chimpanzees as primary play partners was evident, even to the extent that, without young to provide the impetus for play, adult chimpanzees grouped together do not engage in this activity at all. In comparison to many captive gorillas for whom play is an extremely rare occurrence (Murray, 1995), male chimpanzees in particular are much more sociable and playful, and this makes them popular group members. Male chimpanzees in the wild have been rated as relatively more sociable than females (Buirski *et al.*, 1978), which is unsurprising given the more gregarious nature of males (Wrangham & Smuts, 1980). While there is no significant difference between the sexes in their 'Sociable' scores here, captive female chimpanzees appear relatively more sociable than their wild counterparts.

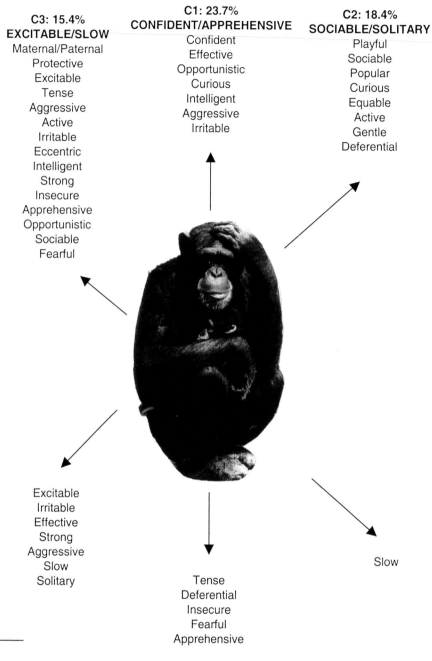

C3: 15.4%
EXCITABLE/SLOW
Maternal/Paternal
Protective
Excitable
Tense
Aggressive
Active
Irritable
Eccentric
Intelligent
Strong
Insecure
Apprehensive
Opportunistic
Sociable
Fearful

C1: 23.7%
CONFIDENT/APPREHENSIVE
Confident
Effective
Opportunistic
Curious
Intelligent
Aggressive
Irritable

C2: 18.4%
SOCIABLE/SOLITARY
Playful
Sociable
Popular
Curious
Equable
Active
Gentle
Deferential

Excitable
Irritable
Effective
Strong
Aggressive
Slow
Solitary

Tense
Deferential
Insecure
Fearful
Apprehensive

Slow

Figure 3
Components
accounting for 10%
or more of the
variance in
chimpanzee
personality ratings.
All adjectives shown
loaded at 0.317 or
more ($=\sqrt{10\%}$).

EXCITABLE/SLOW

The third component is concerned with excitability, parental behaviour, aggression and activity levels. Although an age-related generalisation can be made that immatures are more active and adults more slow, there are exceptions. The biological ageing process may have consequences common to all primates (Picq, 1992). An age-related decrease in social interactions resembles the trend found in humans (Cumming, 1963), and the degree of withdrawal in older apes from a more active social life resembles the 'voluntary disengagement' which can occur with ageing humans.

In non-human primates, this can be related to a decline in social rank (Davis, 1978). However, many elder individuals may simply have less motivation to participate actively in social interactions, and may withdraw while maintaining their rank and attractiveness (Hauser & Tyrrel, 1984). In the great apes, mature individuals are often treated with a great deal of respect, as is the case of the great-grandmother, Meg, in the large multi-generation chimpanzee group at Chester. Such individuals can hold influential positions within groups which are independent of formal rank, but which can be largely based on personality (de Waal, 1982), with similarities to certain human egalitarian societies, such as the !Kung (Lee, 1979).

Describing individuals in terms of how confident they are is an important and indicative facet of personality. Furthermore, sociability and excitability can be considered as revealing descriptors. Individual scores on these components provide a valuable means of assessing individual differences, and additional scores representing levels of confidence, sociability and excitability were also calculated from individuals' standardised scores on leading items on these components. From these, it is evident that immature chimpanzees have higher scores on Component 2, higher 'Sociable' scores, and lower 'Excitable' scores than adults, while those chimpanzees living in larger groups have higher scores on Components 2 and 3.

Personality types in chimpanzees

The existence of individual personalities in chimpanzees is supported both by concordance among raters in the quantitative assessment of behavioural adjective ratings and by validation of these ratings with observed behavioural measures (Murray, 1995). Such personality assessments are thus unlikely to represent merely the anthropomorphic projections of the raters. Subjective impressions are not only supported, but statistically confirmed, enabling the concept of personality in chimpanzees to be objectively assessed and examined. Not only has this provided descriptions of individuals in their social context, but use of this method has enabled identification of five major personality types based on the individuals' pattern of scores calculated as representing levels of confidence, sociability and excitability. This emergence of types has

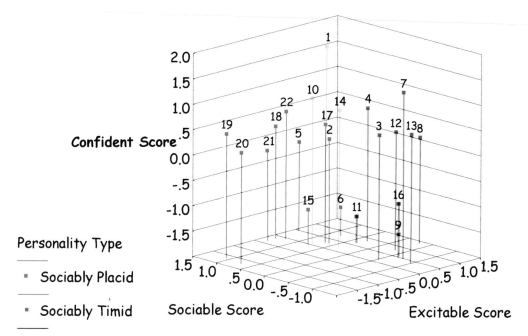

Personality Type

▪ Sociably Placid

▪ Sociably Timid

▪ Excitably Timid

▫ Sociably Confident

▪ Excitably Confident

Figure 4
Classification of individual chimpanzees from the Chester group into 5 personality types based on PCA component scores. (See Figure 1)

Adult males
1 Boris
2 Nicky
3 Wilson

Young adult male
4 Friday

Juvenile males
5 Dylan
6 Rory

Adult females
7 Cleo
8 Gloria
9 Kate
10 Meg

Young adult females
11 Farthing
12 Florin
13 Halfpenny
14 Heidi
15 Mandy
16 Rosie

Juvenile females
17 Kankan
18 Sarah

Infant females
19 Kaylie
20 Layla
21 Sally
22 Wanda

a quantitative basis, and it also provides a more general descriptive power to inter-individual comparisons.

It was possible to identify common patterns shared by several subjects on the basis of individual component scores (Murray, 1995), with six different patterns emerging for chimpanzees. These 'sub-types' were condensed into the five major personality types shown in Figure 4 and described below, one of which can then be used to describe each individual in the study.

Individuals who are EXCITABLY CONFIDENT are confident and excitable rather than sociable, and this group is made up entirely of adults. Many other individuals instead can be considered SOCIABLY CONFIDENT, having the confidence of the previous type but without their excitable nature. This type exists among both adults and immatures. At the opposite end of the spectrum of personalities are those apes described as EXCITABLY TIMID and SOCIABLY TIMID. The Excitably Timid individuals – virtually all adult females – are excitable and lack confidence, whereas the Sociably Timid chimpanzees lack confidence but are nevertheless sociable. Such a lack of confidence is not unusual for the immatures of this type, while the adults who are Sociably Timid do not appear driven to change their status. The final personality type is the one termed SOCIABLY PLACID. These are entirely immatures, whose sociability and calm natures are their most noticeable personality features, rather than a particular timidity. Figure 5 illustrates the relationships between the personality types identified and the dimensions underlying them.

Personality types may prove a useful means of predicting behaviour in chimpanzees, although examination of component scores and especially the actual ratings on adjectives are likely to have greater power for this purpose because they are more discrete measurements. One of the criticisms of placing too much emphasis on scores on the 'Big Five' dimensions is that specificity is increasingly sacrificed for the sake of generality (Buss, 1989; John, 1989; McAdams, 1992). McAdams illustrates this point by suggesting how the general trait of 'extraversion' might subsume a more specific trait such as 'sociability' which, in turn, subsumes the even more specific trait of 'friendliness' (McAdams, 1992).

How do these findings help our understanding of personality and what might they tell us about the evolution of mind? For one, they help elucidate the amalgam of constructs that make up a personality. Consistencies were found among these apes, showing that quantitative assessment of the constructs of personality based on ratings is possible for chimpanzees in captivity. At the same time, this labelling of the subjects should not be taken as undermining the high individuality among these apes, in both their personality and behaviour. Typing here is simply a useful tool for describing individuals.

It is interesting to note that those adjectives which resulted in few correlations with observations of behaviour are the following:

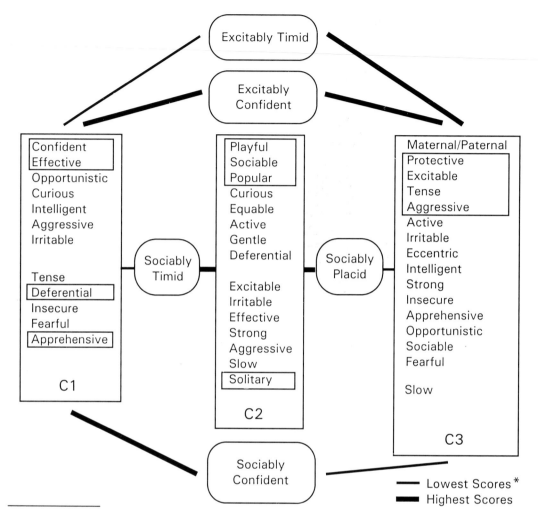

Figure 5
The five major personality types identified for chimpanzees (rounded boxes), showing the two major links each has with 'Confident', 'Sociable, and 'Excitable' scores calculated from the boxed adjectives on each of the principal components or underlying dimension of personality.

* 'Confident', 'Sociable' and 'Excitable' scores ranged from approximately −2.5 to 1.5. Individuals were allocated to specific personality types on the basis of the magnitude of their own three scores in relation to each other, and this is what the 'lowest' and 'highest' scores shown in Figure 5 refer to.

'Eccentric', 'Intelligent', 'Opportunistic' and 'Tense' (Murray, 1995). These adjectives might reflect 'Type A' characteristics, and play an important role in the unique personality of some individuals. Those apes identified as 'Excitably Confident' may share certain characteristics with the Type A human. Such characteristics include aggression, irritability, excitability, activity, curiosity and efficiency. The 'Sociably Placid' personality type, and possibly the 'Sociably Timid' type, bear more resemblances to the Type B person, having characteristics such as sociability and equability.

Can any similarity be seen between humans and chimpanzees in terms of the locus of control distinction (Rotter & Hochreich, 1995) One young adult male chimpanzee, for example, may spend a great deal of time and effort displaying and ingratiating himself with the females of the group even though his gratification (attaining the dominant position within the group) may have to be deferred for some time, whereas another male may show no such drive towards status. In this situation – in fact, the examples relate to two of the adult males at Chester, Friday and Nicky – the former could be classed as an 'internal', believing that hard work pays off now and in the future, whereas the latter individual is perhaps an 'external', perceiving no relationship between expenditure of effort now and what may happen in the future.

Evolutionary personality psychology and the five-factor model

There is growing evidence on inter-generational consistency of personality. Among free-living animals, it has been noted that infant chimpanzees whose mothers were supportive and affectionate grew up to be confident and assertive, and able to achieve higher rank (Goodall, 1986). Macaques have also been found to acquire certain levels of confidence and sociability from their mothers. Significant similarities have been found between chimpanzee mothers and offspring in terms of popularity, playfulness and equability, and also in their scores on the Sociable-Solitary personality component (Murray, *in prep.*). Maternal siblings also have similar scores on this component, and on the 'Excitability' component, and tend to be alike in terms of playfulness, slowness, strength and eccentricity.

Some amount of early experience with the natural mother may make a crucial difference to traits such as sociability and excitability. In this context, Boris – the dominant male of the Chester group – has managed to acquire and maintain his position despite his first few years being spent with a human family in a New York apartment. The Freudian view of the importance of the first six years of an individual's life in the formation of their personality (Freud, 1940) – although arguably only applicable to humans – would suggest that Boris would have missed out on the acquisition of important species-specific attributes and instead become largely humanised, but this is not supported.

The environment can have a major influence on individual differences in personality. Strong correlations have been found between personality ratings and component scores, and the size of the group in which a chimpanzee is kept (Murray, 1998). When chimpanzees are kept in larger groups, as opposed to in pairs or trios for example, they are more maternal/paternal, playful, popular, gentle, protective, sociable, curious, intelligent and irritable; they are less solitary and slow, and they have higher scores on the components related to both sociability and excitability.

It is best then to take an interactionist view of personality, taking into account genetic predispositions, which are then moulded by environmental influences, and expressed as observable traits. One evolutionary model for individual differences contends that heritable differences develop as the adaptive value of characteristics changes over evolutionary time (Buss, 1991). From an evolutionary perspective, traits and behaviours exist to solve specific adaptive problems. Taking the concept of dispositions as strategies, individuals are seen as different because of the various problem-solving strategies they have evolved. What may be the psychological mechanisms, as opposed to physiological responses, that govern how information is processed from the environment, allowing decisions to be made in order to find particular solutions? While others argue that individual differences in personality have no adaptive significance (Tooby & Cosmides, 1990), the theory of mind (Premack & Woodruff, 1978) comes into play, in that it is obviously going to be very useful, if not actually necessary, for one chimpanzee, for example, to know that another is aggressive or is weak, and to be able to attribute a mental state to that other, if not necessarily being able to predict their future actions precisely.

Research in the fields of self-recognition and tactical deception has provided numerous examples of the levels at which chimpanzee minds can work. Large groups may also facilitate the expression of intelligence (Murray, 1998). One way of explaining the evolution of the primate brain and cognition is by selection for social intelligence, rather than by selection for tool-making, co-operation, or food-gathering, for instance (Cheney *et al.,* 1986). Parker & Gibson (1977) contend that it is not social complexity, but tool-assisted foraging, that provided the impetus for the evolution of intelligence. It is to the social arena, however, that most attention is directed. The increase in numbers of individuals brings with it associated levels of complexity, with individuals being faced with dilemmas between their own self-interests and those of their social group. The 'Machiavellian Intelligence' hypothesis (Byrne & Whiten, 1988) suggests that it is the social complexity of primate groups, rather than pure physical needs, that has led to the levels of intelligence seen in some primate species. But, what constitutes social complexity? I have suggested previously (Murray, 1998) that the social complexity arguably responsible for increased primate intelligence may be based not insignificantly on individual personalities, and the ways in which these affect dyadic and polyadic interactions among group members, and that these personalities, as well as being illustrative, are able to be measured to aid in the quantification of such complexity. Individuals are likely to differ in their ability to assess the personality of conspecifics. The amount of experience and information needed to form an accurate perception of another's personality characteristics will vary considerably within any population. Just as certain aspects of intelligence may have evolved to cope with complex interactions among conspecifics, in this way personalities can also have a mutual influence in driving the social complexity of a group.

It has been argued that for species with male dominance hierarchies, females may respond to 'courtship aggression' by selecting more dominant and protective males (Clutton-Brock *et al.,* 1988). According to costs and benefits principles, if the aggression directed at females by males is costly to these females, they should receive overcompensating benefits, potentially in the form of superior fitness qualities (Pomiankowski, 1987). However, determining what that benefit may be, particularly for captive individuals, is difficult. Mate selection for genetic quality has not been demonstrated in female primates (Smuts, 1987), and neither do male apes play a direct role in parental care (Goodall, 1986; Manson, 1994). A female could, therefore, select a male according to perceived traits which are qualities the female would find potentially desirable for her offspring. These traits may be perceived as having contributed to the acquisition of the male's high status, and this would explain preference for the dominant animal. It would also, however, be dependent on the heritability of the particular male's personality traits. The 'individual attributes' model (Chase, 1974) may account for the observed linearity in dominance hierarchies, but this focuses on purely physical attributes, such as weight and age, and how they determine potential fighting ability. It has been argued that the model would be improved if it took into account social factors, such as experience (Landau, 1951a, 1951b; Rothstein, 1992), and I would suggest that it would be even more robust if it also, if not primarily, takes account of the trait attributes of personality, including the aspects of emotion and motivation which may be perceived and responded to in an individual by conspecifics.

The ability to predict behaviour and make decisions, from a greater understanding of individual personalities, has potential not only for the individual animals of a given species but also for those entrusted with their care; for example, in aiding conservation in the wild and captive welfare. Individuals to be housed together can be matched for compatibility, for example, and this is already being used for gorillas in North American zoos (Gold & Maple, 1994).

The components which emerged from this and other studies can be seen as dimensions along which individuals vary. Do these dimensions bear any resemblance to any of the basic motivational forces purported to drive personality in humans? They do. C1 is concerned with confidence and status, or lack of it. Status is indeed argued to be a basic human motivator (Wiggins, 1979, 1990; Peabody & Goldberg, 1989); a necessary requirement for the formation of groups and for reproductive success, and perhaps more evident in males.

Female humans, on the other hand, may strive more for intimacy and affiliation with others, termed 'communion' (Wiggins, 1979, 1990), or 'popularity' (Buss, 1991). Both of these are features of a social domain, and have obvious similarities to C2. Some of the correlations between observed behaviours and personality ratings help us better understand terms such as 'sociability', enabling more precise definition and explanation with reference to personality attributes. For example, there appear to be stronger links between sociability and play behaviour in chimpanzees than between sociability and grooming (Murray, *in prep.*). The quest for status, of course, and even for social fulfilment, can both be regarded as having an even more fundamental drive powering them: the drive for sex. As Buss remarks, *"Not by chance do power and love emerge consistently and cross-culturally as the two most important axes of interpersonal behaviour."* (Buss, 1991, p.470). Now, we can add that these are also found across species.

Factor analyses of personality ratings have yielded a multitude of candidates, but five recurrent and stable factors have been identified and are routinely found: Extraversion (or surgency), Agreeableness (or warmth), Conscientiousness (or will), Neuroticism (or emotional stability) and Openness to experience (or intellect/culture) (Tupes & Christal, 1961; Norman, 1963; Costa & McCrae, 1980; McCrae & Costa, 1987). These personality dimensions are based on the inter-correlations between lower-level traits (or adjectives, for example). A multitude of studies on these factors from the 1980s onwards have confirmed them as fundamental bases of personality, found not only in ratings, but in other forms of assessment (e.g. self-reports). It is argued that a limited information-processing capacity dictates that humans can concisely remember five (±2) chunks of description capturing the essence of an individual character (Digman, 1990).

It is believed that this 'five-factor model' provides an accurate representation of the structure of traits, specifically meaning the patterns of covariation of traits across individuals, rather than to the organisation of attributes within an individual (McCrae & John, 1992). This five-factor model is closely related to and influenced by the 'PEN' system which contends that extraversion (E) and neuroticism (N) are major facets of personality (Eysenck, 1967; Wiggins, 1968), with the P representing the psychotic element (Eysenck & Eysenck, 1985).

Both the C1 and C2 components which emerged for the chimpanzees can be interpreted in terms of the 'Extraversion' dimension in the five-factor model of personality (Eysenck, 1967; McCrae & John, 1992), in that such an 'Extravert/Introvert' dichotomy could reasonably be expressed in terms of confidence or sociability. The distinction between extraversion and introversion is widely regarded as representing the major extremes of the personality spectrum (Wiggins, 1968), and the distinctions between both the 'Confident' and 'Timid' personality types and between sociable versus unsociable individuals may be seen as approximating that between extraversion and introversion. It also has similarities to distinctions of 'brash' or 'shy' previously made in connection with wild chimpanzees (Reynolds & Reynolds, 1965), and of 'bold' or 'shy', with reference to wild gorillas (Schaller, 1963). Immatures, with their higher scores on C2, would be classed as the extraverts in terms of sociability.

The scores representing levels of confidence, sociability and excitability are very similar to those found to be descriptive of the personalities of rhesus macaques (Stevenson-Hinde *et al.,* 1980a). The 'Sociable' scores are also akin to the human trait of 'social attractiveness', while the 'Confident' scores resemble the trait of 'competence' identified for humans (Giles, 1971). They can be seen as similar to the Likert attitudinal scales (Likert, 1932), which are summated rating scales, from which an individual's answers to particular 'pro' and 'anti' questions yield a single attitude score. From this type of methodology, it is reasonable, therefore, to consider 'confidence', 'sociability' and 'excitability' as quantifiable traits in chimpanzees. Specifically, they may be the 'basic traits' of personality in these animals (Eysenck, 1986). C1 can also be related to the 'Conscientiousness' factor, while C3 perhaps has tenuous connections to the factor of 'Agreeableness/Aggression'. The strong links between Intelligence and Opportunism found among both chimpanzees and gorillas (Murray, 1995), could either be related to the 'Openness to Experience' factor, or should be included, as others have suggested (Brand, 1984), as a sixth factor, and another broad trait. Variation in all the factors, except 'Agreeableness', is argued to be moderately heritable (Plomin & Nesselroade, 1990), with individual variation in agreeableness believed to be due to environmental rather than genetic differences (Plomin & Rende, 1991). One theory suggests that it is the presence of one's father in early childhood which determines personality patterns relating to sociosexual activity and co-operation/aggression (Draper & Belsky, 1990). The presence of the father could not be so important, however, in the lives of non-human primates.

The identification of personality components provides information and answers to *one* set of questions with which personality psychology is concerned, that of uncovering more general (perhaps universal) tendencies or structures. However, from the standpoint of individual differences, scores on such components do differentiate between individuals, while ratings on specific trait adjectives provide yet more specific information enabling greater precision in the prediction of behaviour. These factors can thus be seen as representing at least some of the most fundamental and important dimensions governing how non-human, as well as human, primates operate in the social domain in which they are placed (Buss, 1991), a view in accordance with others stressing the importance of the social arena and, in particular, its relation to intelligence (Byrne & Whiten, 1988). More and more evidence is accumulating which emphasises the closeness of the evolutionary connections between humans and great apes, and quantification of individual differences in chimpanzees has now been extended to the determination of personality types, also strikingly similar to those of humans. Conservation efforts in the wild and welfare decisions in captivity

Eysenck MW. 1982. *Attention and Arousal: Cognition and Performance.* London: Springer.

Eysenck MW, Eysenck HJ. 1980. Mischel and the concept of personality. *British Journal of Psychology.* **71:** 191-209.

Farmer KH. 1993. Foraging behaviour and personality in captive chimpanzees (*Pan troglodytes*): implications for welfare. [Unpublished MSc. thesis] University of Edinburgh.

Feaver J, Mendl M, Bateson P. 1986. A method for rating the indivdual distinctiveness of domestic cats. *Animal Behaviour.* **34:** 1016-1025.

Freud S. 1940. An outline of psychoanalysis. In translation: Strachey J, ed. 1964. *The Standard Edition of the Complete Psychological Works (Vol. 23).* London: Hogarth Press.

Friedman M, Rosenman RH. 1959. Association of a specific overt behaviour pattern with increases in blood cholesterol, blood clotting time, incidence of arcus senilis and clinical coronary heart disease. *Journal of the American Medical Association.* **169:** 1286-1296.

Funder DC, Colvin CR. 1991. Explorations in behavioural consistency: Properties of persons, situations and behaviours. *Journal of Personality & Social Psychology.* **60:** 773-794.

Gallup GG Jr. 1970. Chimpanzees: Self-recognition. *Science.* **167:** 86-87.

Gallup GG Jr. 1977. Self-recognition in primates: a comparative approach to the bidirectional properties of consciousness. *American Psychologist.* **32:** 329-338.

Gallup GG Jr. 1979. Self-awareness in primates. *American Scientist.* **67:** 417-421.

Gardner BT, Gardner RA. 1969. Teaching sign-language to a chimpanzee. *Science.* **165:** 664-672.

Giles H. 1971. Patterns of evaluation to RP, South Welsh and Somerset accented speech. *British Journal of Social & Clinical Psychology.* **10:** 280-281.

Gillan DJ. 1981. Reasoning in the chimpanzee II: transitive inference. *Journal Experimental Psychology. Animal Behavour Proceedings.* **7:** 150-164.

Glass DC. 1983. Behavioural, cardiovascular and neuroendocrine responses to psychological stressors. *International Review of Applied Psychology.* **32:** 137-151.

Gold KC, Maple TL. 1994. Personality assessment in the gorilla and its utility as a management tool. *Zoo Biology.* **13:** 509-522.

Gooch S. 1973. *Personality and evolution: The biology of the divided self.* London: Wildwood House.

Goodall J. 1986. *The chimpanzees of Gombe: Patterns of behaviour.* Cambridge, MA: Belknap Press of Harvard University Press.

Gossop MR, Eysenck SBG. 1983. A further investigation into the personality of drug addicts in treatment. *British Journal of Addiction.* **75:** 305-311.

Hauser MD, Tyrrel G. 1984. Old age and its behavioural manifestations: a study of two species of macaque. *Folia Primatologica*. **43:** 24-35.

Hebb DO. 1946. Emotions in man and animals: an analysis of the intuitive process of recognition. *Psychological Review*. **53:** 88-106.

van Hooff JARAM. 1967. The facial displays of the catarrhine monkeys and apes. In: Morris D. ed. *Primate Ethology*. London: Weidenfeld & Nicolson. 7-68.

John OP. 1989. Towards a taxonomy of personality descriptors. In: Buss DM & Cantor N, eds. *Personality Psychology: Recent trends and emerging directions*. New York: Springer-Verlag. 261-271.

Kano T. 1986/1992. *The last ape: Pygmy chimpanzee behaviour and ecology*. Stanford University Press.

Kellerman H. 1966. The emotional behaviour of dolphins (*Tursiops truncatus*): implications for psychoanalysis. *International Mental Health Letters*. **8:** 1-7.

Kellerman H, Plutchik R. 1968. Emotion-trait interrelations and the measurement of personality. *Psychological Report*. **73:** 1107-1114.

Köhler W. 1925. *The Mentality of Apes*. London: Routledge & Kegan Paul.

Landau HG. 1951a. On dominance relations and the structure of animal societies: I. Effect of inherent characteristics. *Bulliten Math. Biophysics*. **13:** 1-19.

Landau HG. 1951b. On dominance relations and the structure of animal societies: II. Some effects of possible social factors. *Bulliten. Math. Biophyics.*. **13:** 245-262.

Lee R. 1979. *The !Kung San: Men, women and work in a foraging society*. Cambridge: Cambridge University Press.

Likert R. 1932. A technique for the measurement of attitudes. *Archives of Psychology*. **No. 140** (6).

Lu L. Argyle M. 1991. Happiness and cooperation. *Personality and Individual Differences*. **12:** 1019-1030.

Manson JH. 1994. Male aggression: a cost of female mate choice in Cayo Santiago rhesus macaques. *Animal Behaviour*. **48:** 473-475.

Martau P, Caine N, Candland D. 1985. Reliability of the Emotions Profile Index, Primate form, with *Papio hamadryas*, *Macaca fuscata*, and two *Saimiri* species. *Primates*. **26:** 501-505.

Matthews G, Coyle K, Craig A. 1990. Multiple factors of cognitive failure and their relationships with stress vulnerability. *Journal of Psychopathology and Behavioural Assessment*. **12:** 49-65.

McAdams DP. 1992. The five-factor model in personality: A critical appraisal. *Journal of Personality*. **60:** 329-361.

McCrae RR, Costa PT Jr. 1986. Personality, coping and coping effectiveness in an adult sample. *Journal of Personality*. **54:** 385-405.

McCrae RR, Costa PT Jr. 1987. Validation of the five-factor model of personality across instruments and observers. *Journal of Personality & Social Psychology*. **52:** 81-90.

McCrae RR, John OP. 1992. An introduction to the five-factor model and its applications. *Journal of Personality.* **60:** 175-215.

McGuire MT, Raleigh MJ, Pollack DB. 1994. Personality features in vervet monkeys: the effects of sex, age, social status, and group composition. *American Journal of Primatology.* **33:** 1-13.

Menzel E, Savage-Rumbaugh ES, Lawson J. 1985. Chimpanzee spatial problem-solving with the use of mirrors and televised equivalents of mirrors. *Journal of Comparative Psychology.* **99:** 211-217.

Mischel W. 1993. *Introduction to Personality.* Fort Worth: Harcourt Brace.

Mondragon-Ceballos R, Santillan-Doherty AM, Chiappa P. 1991. Correlation between subjective assessment of individuality traits and ethological sampling of behaviour in stumptail macaques. In: Ehara A, Kimura T, Takenaka O, Iwamoto M. eds. *Primatology today: Proceedings of the XIIIth Congress of the International Primatological Society, Nagoya and Kyoto, 18-24 July 1990.* Amsterdam: Elsevier Science Publishers. 351.

Morris D. 1965. *The Mammals.* New York: Harper & Row.

Murray LE. 1995. Personality and individual differences in captive African apes. [PhD thesis] University of Cambridge, UK.

Murray LE. 1998. The effects of group structure and rearing strategy on personality in chimpanzees *Pan troglodytes* at Chester, London ZSL and Twycross Zoos. *International Zoo Yearbook.* **36:** 97-108.

Norman WT. 1963. Toward an adequate taxonomy of personality attributes: Replicated factor structure in peer nomination personality ratings. *Journal of Abnormal & Social Psychology.* **66:** 574-583.

Parker S, Gibson K. 1977. Object manipulation, tool use and sensorimotor intelligence as feeding adaptations in cebus monkeys and great apes. *Journal of Human Evolution.* **6:** 623-641.

Parkes KR. 1986. Coping in stressful episodes: The role of individual differences, environmental factors, and situational characteristics. *Journal of Personality & Social Psychology.* **51:** 1277-1292.

Peabody D, Goldberg LR. 1989. Some determinants of factor structures from personality-trait descriptors. *Journal of Personality and Social Psychology.* **57:** 552-567.

Pérusse R, Rumbaugh DM. 1990. Summation in chimpanzees (*Pan troglodytes*): Effects of amounts, number of wells, and finer ratios. *International Journal of Primatology.* **11:** 425-437.

Picq J-L. 1992. Aging and social behaviour in captivity in *Microcebus murinus. Folia Primatologica.* **59:** 217-220.

Plomin R, Nesselroade JR. 1990. Behavioural genetics and personality change. *Journal of Personality.* **58:** 191-220.

Plomin R, Rende R. 1991. Human behavioural genetics. *Annual Review of Psychology.* **42:** 161-190.

Plutchik R. 1962. *The Emotions: Facts, theories and a new model.* New York: Random House.

Plutchik R. 1965. What is an emotion? *Journal of Psychology.* **61:** 295-303.

Plutchik R. 1970. Emotions, evaluation and adaptive processes. In: Arnold M, ed. *Feelings and emotions.* New York: Academic Press. 3-24.

Plutchik R, Kellerman H. 1974. *Emotions Profile Index.* Los Angeles, CA: Western Psychological Services.

Pomiankowski AN. 1987. The costs of choice in sexual selection. *Journal of Theoretical Biology.* **128:** 195-218.

Premack D, Woodruff G. 1978. Does the chimpanzee have a theory of mind? *Behavioural & Brain Sciences.* **1:** 515-526.

Raleigh M, McGuire M, Brammer G. 1989. Subjective assessment of behavioural style: Links to overt behaviour and physiology in vervet monkeys. *American Journal of Primatology.* **18:** 161-162.

Reynolds V, Reynolds F. 1965. Chimpanzees in the Budongo forest. In: DeVore I, ed. *Primate Behaviour: Field studies of monkeys and apes.* New York: Holt, Rinehart & Winston. 368-424.

Rothstein A. 1992. Linearity in dominance hierarchies: a third look at the individual attributes model. *Animal Behaviour.* **43:** 684-686.

Rotter JB, Hochreich DJ. 1975. *Personality.* Glenview, IL: Scott, Foresman.

Sarich VM, Cronin JE. 1976. Molecular systematics of the primates. In: Goodman M, Tashian RE. eds. *Molecular Anthropology.* New York: Plenum Press. 141-1170.

Savage-Rumbaugh ES, Rubert E. 1986. Video representations of reality. In: Savage-Rumbaugh ES, ed. *Ape language: From conditioned response to symbol.* New York: Columbia University Press. 299-323.

Schaller GB. 1963. *The Mountain Gorilla.* Chicago: University of Chicago Press.

Serpell JA. 1983. The personality of the dog and its influence on the pet-owner bond. In: Katcher AH, Beck AM, eds. *New Perspectives on our Lives with Companion Animals.* Philadelphia: University of Pennsylvania Press. 57-63.

Smith TW, Anderson NB. 1986. Models of personality and disease: An interactional approach to Type A behaviour and cardiovascular risk. *Journal of Personality & Social Psychology.* **50:** 1166-1173.

Smuts BB. 1987. Sexual competition and mate choice. In: Smuts BB, Cheney DL, Seyfarth RM, Wrangham RW, Struhsaker TT, eds. *Primate societies.* Chicago: University of Chicago Press. 385-399.

Stevenson-Hinde J, Zunz M. 1978. Subjective assessment of individual rhesus monkeys. *Primates.* **19:** 473-482.

Stevenson-Hinde J, Stillwell-Barnes R, Zunz M. 1980a. Subjective assessment of rhesus monkeys over four successive years. *Primates.* **21:** 66-82.

Stevenson-Hinde J, Stillwell-Barnes R, Zunz M. 1980b. Individual differences in young rhesus monkeys: consistency and change. *Primates.* **21:** 498-509.

Tooby J, Cosmides L. 1990. On the universality of human nature and the uniqueness of the individual: The role of genetics and adaptation. *Journal of Personality.* **58:** 17-67.

Tupes EC, Christal RE. 1961. *Recurrent Personality Factors Based on Trait Ratings (USAF ASD Tech. Rep. No. 61-97).* Lackland Air Force Base, Texas: U.S. Air Force.

de Waal FBM. 1982. *Chimpanzee Politics.* Baltimore: Johns Hopkins University Press.

Wiggins JS. 1968. Personality structure. *Annual Review of Psychology.* **19:** 293-350.

Wiggins JS. 1979. A psychological taxonomy of trait-descriptive terms: The interpersonal domain. *Journal of Personality and Social Psychology.* **37:** 395-412.

Wiggins JS. 1990. Agency and communion as conceptual coordinates for the understanding and measurement of interpersonal behavior. In: Cicchetti D, Grove W. eds. *Thinking Clearly in Psychology, Vol II: Personality and Psychopathology. Essays in honor of Paul E. Meehl.* Minnesota: University of Minnesota Press. 89-113.

Wrangham RW, Smuts BB. 1980. Sex differences in the behavioural ecology of chimpanzees in the Gombe National Park, Tanzania. In: Short RV & Weir BJ, eds. *The Great Apes of Africa.* Cambridge: Journals of Reproduction and Fertility Ltd. 13-31.

Yerkes RM. 1943. *Chimpanzees: A laboratory colony.* New Haven: Yale University Press.

Yerkes RM, Yerkes AW. 1929. *The Great Apes: A study of anthropoid life.* New Haven: Yale University Press.

*New Perspectives in
Behaviour & Ecology*

Bipedal behaviour in captive chimpanzees *(Pan troglodytes).*

S. K. S. THORPE, R. H. CROMPTON & A. CHAMBERLAIN

Introduction

While our close relationship to the African apes has been accepted since the late 19th. century, our self-image continued to be flattered throughout the first half of the twentieth century by the concept of 'Man the Toolmaker'. This image of ourselves as an unique, tool-making, culture-bearing species was shattered when Goodall's (1968) field-studies of common chimpanzees (*Pan troglodytes*) reported not only extensive use of tools, but, in the case of anting-sticks, their manufacture, implying foresight. The same studies provided evidence that common chimpanzees at least share our catholic diet, including our propensity for meat eating, so that dietary adaptations are also unlikely to characterise anthropogenesis. Thus, of all the behaviours, which can be directly reflected by the hard evidence for human origins, only habitual terrestrial bipedalism remains a uniquely hominid attribute. All the apes exhibit bipedalism, and it is, therefore, a reasonable assumption that we should expect bipedalism to have existed in the behavioural repertoire of the protohominid, if not even the common hominoid ancestor. Indeed, it is now generally accepted that early hominids may first be recognised in the fossil record by features of the locomotor system, which are adaptive for bipedality. However, as Fleagle's textbook (1988) reminds us: *"African apes are so similar in their postcranial anatomy (long forelimbs relative to hindlimbs, mobile shoulders, broad thorax with dorsally placed scapula, reduced number of lumbar vertebrae, and the absence of a tail) that some authors consider them as size variants of a single type"*

Thus, chimpanzees have long been used as a living analogue to enhance understanding of the early evolution of mechanical aspects of hominid bipedalism. Jenkins' classic paper (1972) set out the essential kinematic similarities and differences between human and chimpanzee bipedal gait, and more recent papers have examined the similarities and differences in the pattern of muscle recruitment (e.g. Tuttle, Basmajian & Ishida, 1979; Stern & Susman, 1981, Ishida, Kimura & Kondo, 1985) and in external reaction forces (e.g. Ishida, Kimura & Okada, 1974; Kimura, Okada & Ishida, 1977; Kimura 1985).

Most people now accept that humans may be considered as African apes. On the basis of Fleagle's (1988) comments, can we then conclude that human postcranial morphology is to a large extent an allometric adjustment to the morphology of common chimpanzees, bonobos *Pan paniscus* and gorillas *Gorilla gorilla*? Recently Thorpe *et al.* (1999) examined whether chimpanzees have muscle dimensions that allow them to move in a dynamically similar manner to humans, that is whether the skeletal differences are compensated for by changes in joint geometry or muscle architecture. The study found that chimpanzees possessed longer muscle fascicles in all hindlimb muscles, but smaller muscle physiological cross sectional areas, than were predicted for humans of equal body mass. The hypothesis of dynamic similarity was rejected with respect to the variables considered. Their results further suggested that the emphasis for chimpanzees is on joint mobility at the expense of tension production, reflecting a compromise between the demands of arboreal feeding and terrestrial travel. In contrast, human hindlimbs were found to have large physiological cross sectional areas and short fascicles suggesting a demand for exerting large forces in a small range of joint positions. Furthermore, when chimpanzee and human muscles are subject to the same stresses, chimpanzees exert far smaller moments at the joints, particularly in the quadriceps and ankle extensors. These differences in muscle architecture and function indicate that humans are primarily adapted for running, because they are capable of exerting large moments at the joints but their short muscle fascicles limit mobility. In contrast chimpanzees have retained generalised primate adaptations for climbing whilst their small muscle physiological cross sectional areas restrict their ability to walk and particularly to run bipedally.

Work by Taylor & Rowntree (1973) suggested that chimpanzees are not much more energetically effective as quadrupeds than bipeds, and Rodman & McHenry (1980) concluded from the same data that chimpanzees incur 50% greater costs in quadrupedal travel than do typical mammalian quadrupeds. However, studies by Li *et al.* (1996), Crompton & Li (1997) and Crompton *et al.* (1998) showed that the 'bent-hip, bent-knee' (Stern & Susman, 1983) gait typical of chimpanzee bipedalism is highly mechanically ineffective, to a substantial extent because the exchange of potential and kinetic energies which occurs in erect human bipedalism is abolished or greatly reduced.

This raises the question why, if bipedalism is such an expensive mode of locomotion for common chimpanzees, it accounts for approximately 1.5% of a wild chimpanzee's daily locomotor repertoire, as indicated by the excellent field studies of Doran and Hunt (Doran, 1992a, 1992b; Hunt, 1990, 1992, 1994). Goodall (1968), in an extensive ethogram of chimpanzee behaviour, found that bipedalism has a number of roles, particularly for carrying food items, to see over long grass, when it is raining and in aggressive behaviour. Bipedalism has been reported to occur in an aggressive context in most apes (see e.g. Mori, 1984 for pygmy chimpanzees; Carpenter, 1964 for gibbons and Fossey, 1985 for mountain gorillas). Hunt (1994) however recorded that 80% of bipedalism was exhibited in a feeding context, 95% of which was postural rather than locomotory and Susman (1984) found a relationship between the extent of bipedalism and the degree of habituation of *Pan paniscus* in that the more habituated they became the less bipedalism they exhibited.

A variety of explanatory scenarios have also been adduced at one time or another concerning the advantages of human bipedality over quadrupedal locomotion, and many of these are reviewed in Rose (1991). More recently, however, Hunt (1992) combined data on the frequencies of all modes of locomotion, with consideration of the distinctiveness of each locomotor mode and an estimate of the ground reaction forces, to examine which locomotory behaviours have most influenced the musculo-skeletal development of chimpanzees. He concluded that arm hanging and climbing would have placed the greatest selective pressure on the development of functional anatomy and that the rarity of bipedalism argues against any significant anatomical adaptations. Hunt used this argument to support his hypothesis that hominoid, and by extension hominid bipedalism is a foraging adaptation. However, its more broad implication is that bipedalism is not a purely locomotor adaptation, and another recent paper by Jablonski & Chaplin (1993) returns to the idea (suggested earlier by Livingstone (1962) and Wescott (1967)) that bipedalism may have evolved as an adaptation for intraspecific and extraspecific display.

Since the two main contexts of bipedal posture in the literature appear to be food procurement and aggressive behaviour (Goodall, 1968, 1986; Hunt, 1994), it is desirable to know how good the statistical association is between these behavioural contexts and bipedality. Although Hunt's (1994) observations rank feeding as the commonest context for bipedalism, Goodall's (1968, page 376 and 1986, pages 315-316) suggest a much greater role for aggressive behaviour.

The conflicting results of these two studies suggest ecological differences between the two sites may elicit quantitatively different behavioural repertoires: a new study under more controlled conditions may, therefore, be of value. Further, although Table 1 in Hunt (1994) provides a rank ordering of the contexts in which bipedalism occurs, and general frequencies of bipedalism are provided by Goodall (1968 and 1986), neither author presents a detailed statistical treatment of the contexts of bipedalism (for example, contrasting contexts in males and females), and indeed no field studies which do so are known to us. While the association between food procurement and bipedality could be assessed only in the field, under natural conditions of food availability, there is no reason why the association between bipedalism and social display could not be assessed in a captive population.

The aim of this study is thus to establish whether captive chimpanzees do exhibit bipedalism more commonly in the context of aggressive displays than in the other behavioural contexts which can reasonably be investigated in a captive population.

Materials and Methods

The study was conducted on a group of captive chimpanzees at Chester Zoo, for a total observation time of 94 hours during March and April 1994. The group lived on a large open island with ample room and facilities for exercise. The chimpanzees were fed twice daily. The group is an established colony of four generations and at the time of study consisted of 24 individuals. Only data from adult animals, defined as greater than 12 years old, are included in this analysis since chimpanzee locomotor profiles alter during ontogeny (Doran, 1992a). Rank order is generalised since rank may differ according to circumstances.

General Behavioural Repertoire

An assessment of the animals' general locomotor repertoire was conducted to establish the proportion of locomotion, which was bipedal. For this focal animal sampling (in which one animal is exclusively followed for a set period of time) (Altmann, 1974) was used (mean sample length = 180 minutes), in conjunction with locomotor bout sampling with distance (Doran, 1992a). This method records all instances of locomotor behaviour for the study subject and distance (steps) travelled in each bout. One bout is defined as movement from one stationary posture to another, or as a definable segment of a continuous sequence of progression (after Fleagle, 1976). An audiotape was used to record all observations. For each locomotor bout, time, locomotor mode and distance travelled were recorded. Postural and locomotor mode classifications are summarised in Table 1.

When the focal animal exhibited bipedal behaviour the context was also recorded. All observations of bipedal standing, walking, running, jumping, rocking and swaggering were included. The sample of bipedal behaviour also includes some observations of chimpanzees other than the focal animal, recorded when the focal animal was inactive. The contexts in which bipedal bouts were exhibited are: carrying food or infants; preparation for the next loco-motor mode; reach; enhanced vision; aggression; play; grooming; adverse weather (chimpanzees dislike getting their hands wet when it rains) and no obvious context. In cases where one bout exhibited more than one behaviour the predominant behaviour, i.e. that which also occurred in the bout immediately before or after, was recorded.

The role of bipedalism was compared to other forms of locomotion using the χ^2 test by taking a random sample of non-bipedal bouts from the control study. Only quadrupedalism, tripedalism and quadrumanous climbing and scrambling were included in the non-bipedal sample because bimanual suspension and leaping and diving were considered to be reliant on substrates on which bipedalism could not occur.

Table 1 Postural and locomotor mode classifications (modified after Susman, 1984).

Category	Forms
Quadrupedal	Locomotion which employs a definable (usually diagonal sequence) quadrupedal gait. Includes quadrupedal knuckle walk, quadrupedal knuckle run and tripedal knuckle walk.
Bipedal	Locomotion with weight borne by the hindlimbs. The trunk does not have to be vertical. This includes unaided bipedalism, aided bipedalism to provide balance during locomotion and bipedal running.
Climbing	Locomotion, which includes vertical climbing and quadrumanous climbing and scrambling, in which all four limbs are used in varying combinations during unpatterned, diverse gaits on all substrates.
Bimanual suspension	Locomotion in which weight is borne by the forelimbs, the trunk is vertical and suspended below a substrate. This includes armswinging; alternating hand to hand progression beneath substrates, and dropping: hanging beneath one substrate to drop onto another.
Leaping and diving	Locomotion either by leaping feet first with trunk vertical or diving head first with trunk horizontal.
Quadrupedal stand	Posture supported by three or four limbs.
Bipedal stand	Bipedal posture (aided and unaided).
Arm hang	Postural arm hang (aided and unaided).
Squat	Posture in which body weight is borne by the feet but the hip and knee are strongly flexed.
Lie	Posture in which weight is borne by the back, side or stomach on a horizontal substrate.

Aggression

The definition of aggression is traditionally accepted to be when one individual makes physical contact with another, in a behavioural context that does not appear to be friendly and in response to which the recipient typically flees or ceases to perform the activity that triggered the aggression. The recipient may also show a variety of submissive or appeasing gestures, or alternatively may fight back (Goodall, 1986). Goodall (1986) also includes threat in her definition of aggression. This is a non-contact behaviour that elicits a similar response to that of physical attack in the threatened individual. Display is taken to be a ritualised form of the behaviours that are exhibited in aggressive interactions and is, therefore, included in the definition of aggression for the purposes of this investigation.

The purpose of this study was to examine the locomotor modes exhibited in aggressive interactions and the behaviour patterns associated with them. All aggressive interactions were recorded in the form of behavioural bouts using 'behaviour sampling', which samples rare or brief types of behaviour (Martin & Bateson, 1986). This method assigns equal weight to each behaviour within a pattern, regardless of duration. For each aggressive interaction the following were recorded: initiator of the interaction; recipient/s; context; outcome and behavioural pattern. Context classifications were: dominance (direct challenges on dominance rank); competition over food; protection of an infant/subordinate/friend; redirected aggression (chimpanzees often redirect aggression towards lower ranking individuals after they have been attacked or threatened by a superior whom they dare not attack); social excitement; fear of an unknown (e.g. when they were suddenly startled by a strange noise or sudden movement); retaliation and no obvious context.

Table 2 Observed behavioural components of aggressive interactions and associated frequencies.

Behaviour	Description	Freq.
1. Pant hoot	Vocalisation used when the animals are excited, especially during social excitement.	28
2. Bark	Threat vocalisation.	4
3. Hair erect	Often the first indication of an aroused or angry state but underestimated as difficult to detect from a distance.	112
4. Penile erection	Underestimated as difficult to observe from some directions. Includes erection and semi-erection except when exhibited during mating.	28
5. Hunched shoulders	Often exhibited in association with bipedal and quadrupedal swagger.	19
6. Drum	Standing bipedally drumming on another surface with hands or standing quadrupedally drumming on ground with hands or feet.	6
7. Clap	Standing bipedally, clapping hands together.	10
8. Sit rock	Often the first obvious indication of an aggressive interaction, the initiator sits rocking backwards and forwards with increasingly pronounced movements and increasing speed, frequently followed by pant hooting.	20
9. Leap kick	Running towards the windows where the visitors stand or towards the door of the keeper's area, jumping at the window, kicking it with both feet and then running off again. The alpha male, Boris, only exhibited this behaviour.	25
10. Shake rope	Exhibited whilst standing high up on the climbing frame in the inside enclosure. The ropes are attached to the ceiling and hang almost to the floor. Thus when shaken the rope at the bottom flies around.	16
11. Sit	During aggressive interactions chimpanzees sometimes stop and sit and perform normal activities i.e. feeding. After several minutes they resume the interaction.	1

12. Feed	See above.	1
13. Mount	Either from behind or from the front over the head of the recipient, staying in the same position for up to one minute. This behaviour was occasionally aimed at individuals other than those involved in the dominance interaction.	10
14. Pass over	Approaching the recipient as if to attack, but swerving the whole body at the last moment.	6
15. Bluff hit	Approaching to strike the recipient but sweeping the hand away at the last moment.	1
16. Light physical attack	Short, aggressive interactions such as slapping, hitting, and kicking.	29
17. Heavy physical attack	Violent and often prolonged physical attack such as drumming on the recipient, stamping and biting.	3
18. Bs 1	Bimanual suspension using one hand. Generally swinging from one platform of the climbing frame to another with spare limbs held away from the body.	17
19. Bs 2	Bimanual suspension with both hands.	32
20. Bs chase	Bimanual suspension chase.	4
21. Qcs	Quadrumanous climbing and scrambling.	9
22. Qcs chase	Quadrumanous climbing and scrambling chase.	1
23. Q stand	Quadrupedal stand.	1
24. Q rock	Quadrupedal rocking backwards and forwards.	18
25. Q bob	Quadrupedal standing repeatedly flexing and extending knee and elbow joints producing a bobbing effect.	5
26. Q stamp	Quadrupedal stamp.	2
27. Q jump	Quadrupedal jump.	19
28. Q walk	Quadrupedal walk.	7
29. Q run	Quadrupedal run.	12
30. Q charge	Quadrupedal charge, generally towards the recipient/s of the display.	57
31. Q chase	Quadrupedal chase after recipient.	9
32. Q swagger	Quadrupedal walk with exaggerated steps swaying from side to side, often accompanied by hair erect, erection and hunched shoulders.	6
33. B stand	Bipedal stand.	37
34. B rock	Bipedal rocking side to side.	6
35. B stamp	Bipedal stamp.	1
36. B jump	Bipedal jump.	18
37. B walk	Bipedal walk.	18
38. B run	Bipedal run.	10
39. B charge	Bipedal charge towards recipient/s.	10
40. B swagger	Bipedal walk with exaggerated steps swaying from side to side, often accompanied by hair erect, erection and hunched shoulders.	49

Outcome classifications are: heavy physical attack; light physical attack; bluff; reassurance; no specific outcome; non-violent assertion of dominance (i.e. mount); victim moves away; victim retaliates; victim submissive; intervention by another individual; grooming session; victim redirects aggression (i.e. victim attacks someone else); attacker moves away. More detailed descriptions of these categories are provide in Goodall (1968).

Vocalisations and behaviours were classified into 40 behaviour patterns, which were easy to distinguish from a distance. Descriptions and observed frequency of behaviours are given in Table 2. χ^2 tests were used to test for associations between the proportion of bipedal and non-bipedal components exhibited in aggressive interactions, and differences in the identity and sex of the protagonist, and the direction, context and outcome of the interactions. The non-bipedal sample is composed of quadrupedalism, tripedalism and quadrumanous climbing and scrambling. All tests were performed on raw data. Significance values are from Sokal & Rohlf (1981).

Results

Behavioural repertoire

Table 3 shows the locomotor profile of the captive chimpanzees in comparison to results for wild animals from Doran (1992b).

Table 3 Locomotor repertoire of captive chimpanzees in comparison to results from a study of free-ranging animals, which used the same method (Doran, 1992b).

Locomotor mode	Free ranging: Travel (%)	Free ranging: Feeding (%)	Captive (%)
Quadrupedalism	92.9	85.2	86.8
Quad. climbing and scrambling	6.4	11.3	11.0
Bimanual suspension	0.5	1.8	1.0
Bipedalism	0.1	1.5	1.1
Leaping & diving	0.2	0.2	0.1

Table 4 demonstrates that the extent of bipedalism exhibited differed substantially between individuals. The context of 361 bouts of bipedalism (189 = postural, 172 = locomotor) were recorded.

Figure 1 shows that there are significant differences between the sexes in use of postural ($\chi^2 = 54.1$, P = < 0.0001) and locomotor bipedalism ($\chi^2 = 85.2$, P = < 0.0001); for the purposes of display, the two are plotted separately as Figures 1a and 1b.

Females primarily use postural bipedalism in more autonomous functional contexts, especially for enhancing vision, whereas in males postural bipedalism is most commonly related to aggression. Male locomotor bipedalism is overwhelmingly used in aggressive situations, whereas the results for females are more evenly distributed across the range of recorded contexts.

Table 4 Study subjects and observations. No. bouts observed refers to the total number of bouts of all modes of locomotion exhibited. Note that rank position for males and females refers to the separate male and female hierarchy. In general all males rank higher than the females. *Results for a mother carrying her infant. She was excluded from the analysis.

Individual	Sex	Age	Rank	No. bouts Observed	% bouts bipedal
Boris	M	27	Alpha male	118	2.4
Friday	M	18	High	112	1
Wilson	M	25	High	102	0
Nicky	M	25	High	109	0.5
Cleo	F	22	Alpha female	123	0.7
Halfpenny	F	18	High	111	1.9
Florin	F	13	High	106	1.8
Kate	F	23	Middle	128	0.3
Heidi	F	21	Middle	100	0.7
Gloria	F	29	Middle	106	0.1
Mandy	F	16	Low	105	13.3*
Rosie	F	21	Low	107	1.7
Farthing	F	18	Low	117	2.1

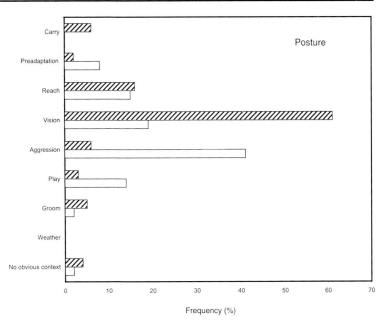

Figure 1a
Frequency of postural bipedalism in different contexts. The hatched bars represent females and the open bars males. Postural: Female $n = 111$, male $n = 78$.

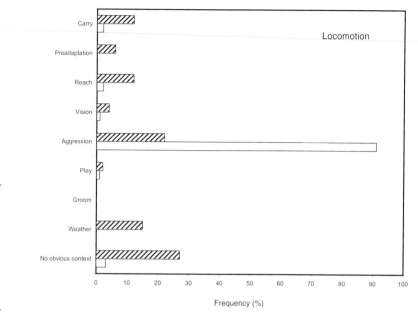

Figure 1b
Frequency of
locomotor bipedalism
in different contexts.
The hatched bars
represent females and
the open bars males.
Locomotion: Female
$n = 67$, male $n = 105$.

Figure 2 shows a substantial difference between the more detailed contexts in which bipedal and non-bipedal locomotion is exhibited ($\chi^2 = 146.5$, P = < 0.0001). Bipedal locomotor bouts are far more characteristically associated with aggression than quadrupedal bouts; quadrupedal bouts on the other hand are characteristically associated with No obvious context and Food gathering.

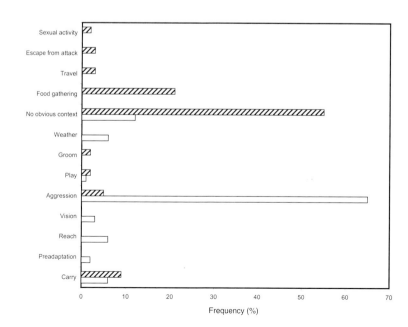

Figure 2
Profiles of bipedal
and non-bipedal
locomotor bouts in
different contexts for
combined male and
female results.
Hatched bars
represent the non-
bipedal sample.

Aggression study

One hundred and fifty two aggressive interactions were recorded, consisting of 667 behavioural components. χ^2 values are provided in Table 5. The most frequently observed form of bipedalism was the bipedal swagger (Table 2) in which the individual walks with exaggerated steps, swaying from side to side, with hair erect, and the arms held out with shoulders hunched. Bipedal standing was also frequently observed in aggressive interactions. The initiator would walk or run quadrupedally to the recipient and then, at close proximity, stand bipedally towering over the recipient. On 20 occasions chimpanzees were observed to run bipedally (Table 2 – B run and B charge). When bipedal running occurred it was generally quite fast and lasted for up to 10 steps. 50% of bipedal running occurred when an individual made a non-violent charging display at an individual or a general display, occasionally using the hands to flail branches or throw twigs etc.

Table 5 Results of χ^2 tests for association between social factors and the proportion of bipedal and non-bipedal bouts in aggressive interactions. ns = not significant.

Variable		χ^2 Value	Level of significance
Individual		18.6	P = < 0.001
Sex of protagonist		3.4	ns
Direction of interaction:			
	Sex	11.3	ns
	Status	3.4	ns
Context		-	-
Outcome		5.9	P = < 0.05

Table 6 shows that there are substantial differences in the frequency, length and bipedal component of aggressive interactions initiated by different individuals. Testing for significant differences in the extent of bipedalism and non-bipedalism in the male sample alone produced a significant χ^2 value (Table 5).

Unfortunately it was not possible to test statistically for differences in the amount of bipedalism exhibited by individual females because the sample was too small (Table 6). Amongst the males, Friday exhibited the highest proportion of bipedalism, which is probably related to his increasing attempts to achieve alpha status. Indeed, Table 9 shows that dominance was the most frequent context of aggressive interactions.

Table 6 Proportion of bipedal and non-bipedal components of aggressive interactions dependent on the protagonist of the interactions.

Individual	Total No. interactions	Total No. components	Average No. components	% bipedal	% non-bipedal
Boris	49	274	5.6	19.0	22.6
Friday	41	202	4.9	31.2	11.4
Wilson	19	70	3.7	18.6	24.3
Nicky	11	45	4.1	13.3	20.0
Cleo	18	41	2.3	12.2	39.0
Halfpenny	2	3	1.5	33.3	33.3
Florin	4	9	2.3	11.1	33.3
Kate	1	2	2.0	0	50.0
Heidi	2	3	1.5	66.7	0
Gloria	3	9	3.0	22.2	33.3
Rosie	1	3	3.0	33.3	33.3
Farthing	1	6	6.0	50.0	0
Male	120	591	4.9	22.7	18.8
Female	32	76	2.3	19.7	32.9

Table 7 Proportion of bipedal and non-bipedal components of aggressive interactions dependent on the direction of the interactions in terms of status. Other = general, humans, unknown and alone.

Direction	Total No. interactions	Total No. components	Average No. components	% bipedal	% non- bipedal
Higher Rank	27	90	3.3	23.3	21.1
Equal Rank	20	85	4.3	24.7	11.8
Lower Rank	53	166	3.1	21.1	22.3
Other	52	324	6.2	22.2	21.3

The difference in extent of bipedal and non-bipedal components exhibited by males and females is not significant, although it is apparent that, in general, males initiate more aggressive interactions than females, and that they are of longer duration (Table 6). Similarly the direction of the interaction in terms of status ranks (Table 7) and sex and age categories (Table 8) does not influence the extent of bipedal behaviour.

Table 8 Proportion of bipedal and non-bipedal components of aggressive interactions dependent on the direction of the interactions in terms of age and sex. Other = male-juveniles, male-unknown, male-alone, female-general.

Initiator	Direction	Total No. interactions	Total No. components	Average No. components	% bipedal	% non-bipedal
Male	Male	40	180	4.5	23.3	14.4
	Female	25	84	3.4	21.4	19.0
	General	28	168	6.0	26.8	19.6
	Human	18	120	6.7	15.8	25
Female	Male	13	31	2.4	12.9	32.3
	Female	12	29	2.4	31.0	27.6
	Juvenile	6	12	2.0	8.3	41.7
Other		10	43	4.3	28.2	20.5

Table 9 Proportion of bipedal and non-bipedal components of aggressive interactions dependent on the context of the interactions.

Context	Total No. interactions	Total No. components	Average No. components	% bipedal	% non-bipedal
Dominance	48	242	5.0	23.6	15.3
Food	15	46	3.1	23.9	28.3
Protection	8	26	3.3	15.4	26.9
Redirected aggression	4	14	3.5	14.3	14.3
Social excitement	30	120	4.0	26.7	21.7
Fear of unknown	3	12	4.0	33.3	16.7
No obvious context	39	190	4.9	17.2	24.2
Retaliation	5	17	3.4	35.3	17.7

Table 9 shows that the chimpanzees exhibited more bipedal than non-bipedal components in Dominance challenges, Social excitement, Fear of unknown noises etc. and Retaliation. It is probable that many of the aggressive acts performed by males during Social excitement and No obvious context are also dominance related (Goodall, 1986). However classifying the context of aggressive behaviour is problematic because knowing the immediate context of an aggressive interaction does not necessarily divulge much about the cause of the aggression. An event that occurred in the recent past, i.e. winning or losing a major fight, can have a temporary or permanent effect on the aggressiveness of an individual (Goodall, 1986) and thus a seemingly trivial situation may result in a violent attack.

Table 10 Proportion of bipedal and non-bipedal components of aggressive interactions dependent on whether the interaction ends in violence.

Outcome	Total No. interactions	Total No. components	Average No. components	% bipedal	% non-bipedal
1. Heavy physical attack	3	14	4.7	14.3	28.6
2. Light physical attack	28	82	2.9	12.2	24.4
3. Bluff	12	53	4.4	28.3	15.1
4. Reassurance	1	8	8	25.0	12.5
5. No specific outcome	57	320	5.6	23.8	20.6
6. Non-violent assertion of dominance	4	17	4.3	35.3	5.9
7. Victim moves away	18	71	3.9	25.4	14.1
8. Victim retaliates	7	18	2.6	22.2	22.2
9. Victim submissive	9	31	3.4	22.6	19.4
10. Intervention by another individual	1	2	2	0	50.0
11. Grooming session	7	23	3.3	26.1	26.1
12. Victim redirects aggression	1	1	1	0	100
13. Initiator moves away	4	27	6.8	11.1	29.7
Violent	40	117	2.93	13.7	25.6
Non-violent	112	550	4.91	24.2	19.3

Also the identity of the other individuals involved, their relative dominance status and the initial level of arousal of all present have direct implications for the behavioural response of an individual to a particular context. Consequently it is inappropriate to statistically test the relationship between bipedalism and context. Table 10 shows the proportion of bipedal and non-bipedal components in relation to the outcome of aggressive interactions. To test these results statistically, the different outcomes were separated into those that were violent (i.e. consisted of some form of physical attack) (1,2,8,10,12) and those that were non-violent (3,4,5,6,7,9, 11,13). Table 5 shows that these results were statistically significant, indicating that bipedalism is exhibited significantly more in interactions which are non-violent, and quadrupedalism is exhibited in violent interactions. Non-violent interactions occur far more frequently than violent ones and last longer.

Discussion

The results suggest that both postural and locomotor bipedalism are context specific behaviours, that are strongly associated with aggressive behaviour in males, but with other, more autonomous functional behaviours in females. These results may be thought to contradict Hunt's (1994) study of free ranging animals, which found that 80% of bipedalism was associated with feeding and only 1% in dominance display. Captivity does provide a false environment for chimpanzees and possibly one in which levels of aggression are increased. Certainly in the present study aggression levels were rather high because the observations were made during a period in which a subordinate male (Friday) was beginning to compete for the alpha position. However Hunt (1994) refers purely to dominance display, and does not report any aggressive behaviour, while studies by Goodall (1968) and Mori (1982) indicate high levels of aggressive behaviour do actually exist in wild chimpanzee populations, although differences in behavioural observation and recording techniques prevent direct comparison.

Equally, the fact that during this study common chimpanzees were observed to run bipedally might appear to contradict the suggestion of Thorpe *et al.* (1999) that they are incapable of exerting the hindlimb muscle stresses required for sustained bipedal running. The opposite view has been presented by, for example, Reynolds (1987) and Taylor & Rowntree (1973). However, chimpanzee running behaviour has neither been properly documented nor kinematically analysed, so that it is impossible to say whether in any reported case the subjects were actually running rather than walking very fast, a distinction which can be made only by calculation of duty factors in 'running' chimpanzees. However, we do know enough to be sure that there are significant differences in the bipedal running of humans and chimpanzees. When chimpanzees were observed to 'run' bipedally in this study they did so for, at most, 10 steps; in addition they did not generally maintain an erect posture for the length of the 'run', but rather increasingly approached a quadrupedal posture as they progressed, so that the transition from bipedalism to quadrupedalism was a gradual, rather than sudden one. One may legitimately conclude that the 'running' of chimpanzees is not directly comparable to that of humans, where erect running can be sustained for hours, and an abrupt transition to walking may be made at any time, either at the commencement or termination of a bout of running.

Conclusion

Our results suggest that, in addition to the more autonomous functional benefits of a bipedal posture (i.e. carrying objects, enhanced vision etc.), bipedalism may play a role as a non-violent threat or display of prowess, designed to elicit submissive behaviour in the recipient, without recourse to physical violence. No single selective factor is likely to have brought about the evolution of bipedalism, but this study has adduced statistical evidence that suggests that amongst other selective influences, aggressive behaviour is likely to have played a role in the evolution of bipedalism.

Acknowledgements

We thank The North of England Zoological Society for permission to carry out observational studies of the chimpanzees in their care.

References

Altmann J. 1974. Observational study of behaviour: sampling methods. *Behaviour.* **49**: 227-267.

Carpenter CR. 1964. A field study in Siam of the behaviour and social relations of the gibbon. In: Carpenter CR. ed. *Naturalistic Behaviour of Non Human Primates.* Philadelphia: Pennsylvania State University Press. 145-271.

Crompton RH, Li Y. 1997. Running before they could walk? Locomotor adaptation and bipedalism in early hominids. In: Slater A, Sinclair A, Gowlett JAJ. eds. *Archaeological Sciences 1995.* Oxford: Oxbow Press. 428-434.

Crompton RH, Li Y, Wang W, Günther M, Savage R. 1998. The mechanical effectiveness of erect and 'bent-knee, bent-hip' bipedal walking in *Australopithecus afarensis. Journal of Human Evolution.* **35**: 55-74.

Doran DM. 1992a. The ontogeny of chimpanzee and pygmy chimpanzee locomotor behaviour: a case study of paedomorphism and its behavioural correlates. *Journal of Human Evolution* **23**: 139-157.

Doran DM. 1992b. Comparison of instantaneous and locomotor bout sampling methods: a case study of adult male chimpanzee locomotor behaviour and substrate use. *American Journal of Physical Anthropology.* **89:** 85-99.

Fleagle JG. 1976. Locomotion and posture of the Malayan siamang and implications for hominoid evolution. *Folia Primatologica.* **26:** 245-269.

Fleagle JG. 1988. *Primate Adaptation and Evolution.* New York: Academic Press.

Fossey D. 1985. *Gorillas in the Mist.* London: Penguin Books.

Goodall J. 1968. Behaviour of free living chimpanzees of the Gombe Stream area. *Animal Behaviour Monographs.* **1:** 163-311.

Goodall J. 1986. *7he Chimpanzees of Gombe: Patterns of Behavior.* London: Harvard University Press.

Hunt KD. 1990. Implications of chimpanzee positional behaviour for the reconstruction of early hominid locomotion and posture. *American Journal of Physical Anthropology.* **81:** 242.

Hunt KD. 1992. Positional behaviour of *Pan troglodytes* in the Mahale Mountains and Gombe Stream National Parks, Tanzania. *American Journal of Physical Anthropology.* **87:** 83-107.

Hunt KD. 1994. The evolution of human bipedality: ecology and functional morphology. *Journal of Human Evolution.* **26:** 183-202.

Ishida H, Kimura T, Okada M. 1974. Patterns of bipedal walking in anthropoid primates. In: Kondo S. ed. *Proceedings of the Symposium of the 5th Congress of the International Primatological Society.* Tokyo: Japan Science Press. 287-301.

Ishida H, Kimura T, Kondo S. 1985. Primate bipedalism and quadrupedalism: comparative electromyography. In: Kondo S. ed. *Primate Morphophysiology, Locomotor Analysis and Human Bipedalism.* Tokyo: University of Tokyo Press. 59-80.

Jablonski NG, Chaplin G. 1993. Origin of habitual terrestrial bipedalism in the ancestor of the Hominidae. *Journal of Human Evolution.* **24:** 259-280.

Jenkins FA. 1972. Chimpanzee bipedalism: cineradiographic analysis and implications for the evolution of gait. *Science.* **178:** 877-879.

Kimura T. 1985. Bipedal and quadrupedal walking of primates: comparative dynamics. In: Kondo S. ed. *Primate Morphophysiology, Locomotor Analysis and Human Bipedalism.* Tokyo: University of Tokyo Press. 81-105.

Kimura T, Okada M, Ishida H. 1977. Dynamics of primate bipedal walking as viewed from the force of the foot. *Primates.* **18:** 137-147.

Li Y, Crompton RH, Günther MM, Alexander RMcN, Wang WJ. 1996 Characteristics of ground reaction forces in normal and chimpanzee-like bipedal walking by humans. *Folia Primatologica.* **66:** 13-159.

Livingstone FB. 1962. Reconstructing man's Pliocene pongid ancestor. *American Anthropologist.* **64:** 301-395.

Martin P, Bateson P. 1986. *Measuring Behaviour: An Introductory Guide.* Cambridge: Cambridge University Press.

Mori A. 1982. An ethological study on chimpanzees at the artificial feeding place in the Mahale Mountains, Tanzania – with special reference to the booming situation. *Primates.* **23**: 45-65.

Mori A. 1984. An ethological study of pygmy chimpanzees in Wamba, Zaire: a comparison with chimpanzees. *Primates.* **25**: 255-278.

Reynolds TR. 1987. Stride length and its determinants in humans, early hominids, primates and mammals. *American Journal of Physical Anthropology.* **72**: 101-115.

Rodman PS, McHenry HM. 1980. Bioenergetics and the origin of hominid bipedalism. *American Journal of Physical Anthropology.* **52**: 103-106.

Rose MD. 1991. The process of bipedalization in hominids. In: Coppens Y, Senut B. eds. *Origine(s) de la Bipedie chez les Hominides.* Paris: Editions du CRNS. 37-48.

Sokal RR, Rohlf FJ. 1981. *Biometry.* New York: W. H. Freeman and Co.

Stern JT, Susman RL. 1981. Electromyography of the gluteal muscles in *Hylobates, Pongo* and *Pan:* implications for the evolution of hominid bipedality. *American Journal of Physical Anthropology.* **55**: 153-166.

Stern JT, Susman RL. 1983. The locomotor anatomy of *Australopithecus afarensis. American Journal of Physical Anthropology.* **60**: 279-317.

Susman RL. 1984. The locomotor behaviour of *Pan paniscus* in the Lomako forest. In: Susman RL. ed. *The Pygmy Chimpanzee: Evolution, Biology and Behaviour.* New York: Plenum Press. 369-393.

Taylor CR, Rowntree VJ. 1973. Running on two or four legs: which consumes more energy? *Science.* **179**: 186-187.

Thorpe SK, Li Y, Crompton RH, Alexander RMcN. 1998. Stresses in human leg muscles in running and jumping determined by force plate analysis and from published magnetic resonance imaging. *Journal of Experimental Biology.* **201(1)**: 63-70.

Thorpe SKS, Crompton RH, Gunther MM, Ker RF, Alexander RMcN, in press. Dimensions and moment arms of the forelimb and hindlimb muscles of common chimpanzees. *American Journal of Physical Anthropology.*

Tuttle RH, Basmajian JV, Ishida H. 1979. Activities of pongid thigh muscles during bipedal behaviour. *American Journal of Physical Anthropology.* **50**: 123-136.

Wescott RW. 1967. The exhibitionistic origin of human bipedalism. *Man* **2**: 630.

CHAPTER TWELVE

Habitat and foraging in great apes

A. E. BEAN

Introduction

Great apes live in a wide variety of habitat types: from lowland to montane areas, and from desert savannah to moist, tropical rainforest. Populations of a number of African apes of different species overlap in habitat, for example: eastern lowland gorillas *Gorilla gorilla graueri* and eastern chimpanzees *Pan troglodytes schweinfurthii* live in the same area, as do eastern lowland gorillas and central chimpanzees *Pan troglodytes troglodytes*; and western lowland gorillas *Gorilla gorilla gorilla* and central chimpanzees.

The great apes exhibit considerable flexibility in their foraging behaviour and this study is a preliminary exploration into the ecological factors affecting this behaviour. A 'habitat index' is constructed in order to summarise the habitat type of 38 great ape study sites. Also, ecological costs for individual ape foragers in each of 28 study sites are assessed using an 'ecological cost index'. The range of great ape foraging strategies in relation to ecology is also explored.

Foraging behaviour

Foraging is defined here as a set of behaviours concerned with the finding and processing of food items that make up an individual's diet. Foraging strategy is defined as foraging behaviour produced in response to biological factors within the individual's habitat (such as food quality and dispersion), energetic requirements (considering body weight and reproductive status), and it also involves the individual's social and reproductive strategies and the behaviour of competitors. In this study, foraging strategy includes the variables: day range; home range; dietary breadth (number of food items in the diet); population density; foraging party size; activity budget (% time spent feeding, travelling and resting); and dietary composition (% fruit, plant parts, bark and invertebrates in the diet) (see Bean, 1998 for definitions).

Dietary Strategy

Although great apes are generally omnivorous, their dietary strategies fall into two main categories: 1) Frugivorous – chimpanzees *Pan troglodytes*, low-altitude gorillas *G.g. graueri* and *G.g. gorilla* (<1000m above sea level) and orang-utans *Pongo pygmaeus* concentrate on fruits (Goodall, 1963; Galdikas, 1988; Williamson, 1988; Williamson, Tutin & Fernandez, 1990 and see Appendix 1); and 2) Folivorous – high-altitude gorillas (> 1000m above sea level –

G. g. beringei) concentrate on leaves (Fossey & Harcourt, 1977; Watts, 1983, 1984; Vedder, 1982 and see Appendix 1). Although bonobos *Pan paniscus* are generally classified as frugivores, they are more folivorous than the above mentioned frugivores (Badrian & Badrian, 1984 and see Appendix 1).

Fruits are generally considered to be a rich source of energy or a high quality food patch. However, the distribution of fruit is patchy in both time and space (Hladik, 1977). In contrast, within rainforest habitats, leaves are abundant and spatially continuous, therefore, folivores do not encounter the same foraging problems as frugivores. However, the distribution advantages of leaves are offset by the fact that cellulose and lignin, which form the cell walls of plants, are indigestible in the natural state (Sullivan, 1966; van Soest, 1977). To overcome this problem, herbivores are either ruminants, must bulk feed or are coprophageous (eat faeces). The most folivorous of the apes are the high-altitude gorillas. They are also large and, therefore, have high nutritional requirements. In order to meet these requirements, they bulk feed (Fossey & Harcourt, 1977; A. Goodall, 1977), processing considerable quantities of plant matter high in structural carbohydrates. To facilitate this dietary strategy, gorillas have a relatively large caecum (Chivers & Hladik, 1980), long gut retention times (Milton, 1984) and have a large hindgut fermentation capacity.

Animal matter is often an important part of an ape's diet. Insects constitute a high-energy food because they are rich in fat. However, individual items are generally small and are not usually found in large concentrations. In the great apes, insect eating varies between the sexes (Bean, 1999). Individuals that forage on insects are usually large (i.e. often males rather than females), so they may have a greater need to supplement their diets in this way (Tutin & Fernandez, 1983; Yamagiwa *et al.,* 1991; Remis, 1994, 1995). In addition, males are often more terrestrial than females, which might facilitate insect foraging (Bean, 1998).

In chimpanzees, however, males are not much larger than females (Johanson, 1974; Cramer, 1977) and, in this species, females are the primary insect forager (McGrew, 1979; Wrangham & Smuts, 1980; Boesch & Boesch, 1981; Conklin & Wrangham, 1991). It has been suggested that the extra energetic costs of reproduction incurred by the female chimpanzees encourage supplementation of their diet with insects (Boesch & Boesch, 1981; Conklin & Wrangham, 1991).

Male chimpanzees, in some populations, hunt vertebrate prey such as reptiles, birds and small mammals (Goodall, 1963, 1965, 1973; Wrangham & Smuts, 1980; Boesch & Boesch, 1981, 1984, 1989), which may be an alternative method of supplementing their diet. However, hunting is energetically expensive, time consuming and very risky (Kaplan & Hill, 1992) and, therefore, the value of this activity as a primary foraging 'strategy' may be marginal.

Male chimpanzees are more social than females (Wrangham, 1977; Wrangham, Clark & Isabirye-Basuta, 1992) and chimpanzee hunting is, mainly, a social occupation that often results in food sharing (de Waal, 1989). The selection of meat-sharing beneficiaries by male chimpanzees is significant. Eighty percent of sharing in chimpanzees involves adults of both sexes getting meat from males (de Waal, 1982), and cycling female chimpanzees are more successful in obtaining meat than are non-cycling females (Teleki, 1973). Thus, chimpanzee hunting of vertebrate meat may also involve the non-subsistence related benefits of status politics and mating opportunities.

Among other primate species, the eating of animal matter may be more frequent in poorer quality habitats, and within habitats it is more common during the dry season when food supplies are more limited (Skinner & Skinner, 1974; Galat & Galat-Luong, 1977; Kavanagh, 1978).

Nutritional requirements

Apes are large-bodied animals, but there is, nevertheless, quite a range of body weights across the species. For instance, male eastern chimpanzees weigh 39.5kg at Gombe (Wrangham & Smuts, 1980), whilst male eastern lowland gorillas can weigh up to 175.2kg at Kahuzi (Leigh & Shea, 1995). Basal metabolic rate (BMR) scales at three-quarters the power of body weight (BMR= 70 $W^{0.75}$ kcal kg^{-1} day^{-1} [Kleiber, 1961]). As a result, the energy requirement, per kilogram of body weight, for maintaining basic metabolic processes is greater for small animals than for large ones, thus large animals need to eat less per unit of body weight than smaller ones. Body weight, therefore, has to be taken into consideration when comparing ecological factors between apes. In this study, the metabolic body weight ($W^{0.75}$) is used as a basis for comparison.

Habitat Type

The habitat type is an important determinant of foraging behaviour, particularly of dietary composition and ranging behaviour. Figure 1 is a vegetation map of Africa and it can be seen from this that the different African ape populations (Figure 2) are generally restricted to the tropical zones; the exceptions are some chimpanzee populations. The habitat characteristics of 38 great ape study sites (Figure 3) are summarised in Appendices 2 and 3.

Characteristics of orang-utan habitats

Orang-utans are limited in distribution to the Indonesian islands of Borneo *P. p. pygmaeus* and Sumatra *P. p. albelii* and, therefore, inhabit only a limited range of habitat types compared to the African apes. Orang-utans inhabit predominantly dipterocarp forests that are relatively poor in terms of fruit production (Caldecott, 1986a, 1986b). It is thought that the costs that would be incurred by a group of frugivorous orang-utans searching for food in these habitats necessitates the solitary foraging of this species (see below).

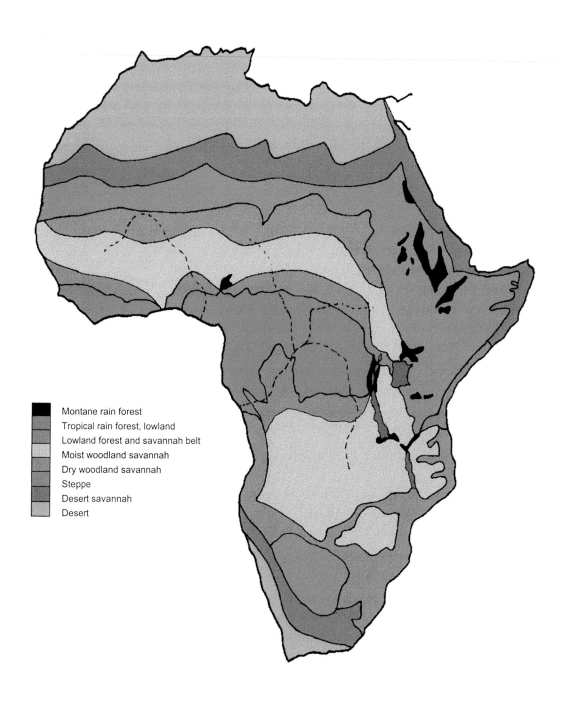

Montane rain forest
Tropical rain forest, lowland
Lowland forest and savannah belt
Moist woodland savannah
Dry woodland savannah
Steppe
Desert savannah
Desert

Figure 1
Vegetation map of
Africa (adapted from
Kano, 1992).

The population densities of orang-utans are variable, ranging from one individual per square kilometre to five individuals per square kilometre (Appendix 1). Overall population density is comparable between the sub-species, which indicates that the habitats of the two islands are quite alike. However, although the different field sites support similar dipterocarp rainforest, they do show specific differences in flora and climate (Appendices 2 and 3). For example, Segama is 250 m higher above sea level than Kutai (Appendix 2) and this causes considerable differences in the tree species that occur in the two areas. The small differences in latitude between the sites (e.g. Kutai is 5° north of Segama) causes climatic differences as well. For example, Kutai shows equatorial uniformity throughout the year, while Segama experiences marked tropical seasonality and monsoons. Most often, orang-utans have been studied in rugged, mountainous areas where the land is full of ridges and valleys. However, the ecotype of Tanjung is markedly different from those of the other study sites (Rodman, 1973, 1979; MacKinnon, 1974); it is a low-altitude site (<30 m above sea level) and is mainly dry ground forest (60%) and peat swamp (27%).

Characteristics of gorilla habitats

Gorillas have both a large vertical (i.e. altitudinal) and horizontal range. They inhabit a variety of lowland tropical rainforests up to the high-altitude montane forests of the Virunga Volcanoes (Democratic Republic of Congo, Rwanda & Uganda). The habitats of gorillas can be broadly divided into two types: high-altitude (>1000 m), and low-altitude (<1000 m) (Appendix 2). The effects of altitude on gorilla populations and behaviour are clearly observable in population density, foraging party behaviour, ranging and dietary composition (Bean, 1998 and Appendix 1).

The population densities of gorillas living above 1000 m are generally higher than those observed at low-altitudes (t=2.78, p=0.027; Appendix 1). This could reflect the greater quantity of fruit in the diet of low-altitude gorillas (Appendix 1). Fruit is a patchy and seasonal resource, which foragers must spread out to search for, thus lowering their population density. High-altitude gorillas eat less fruit and switch to terrestrial herbaceous vegetation (THV) as a major food source (t=5.2, p=0.002; Appendix 1). THV is abundant, widespread and available throughout the year (as opposed to fruit). Therefore, a habitat, such as that occupied by mountain gorillas, that has a lot of THV can support larger numbers of individuals foraging in larger groups (t=3.21, p=0.0024; Appendix 1). In contrast, gorillas living at low-altitude do not forage as 'cohesively' as high-altitude gorillas; instead, the former often disperse into foraging sub-groups, most commonly of two individuals (Tutin & Fernandez, 1984).

Characteristics of bonobo habitats

Bonobos are restricted to the tropical lowland rainforests of Democratic Republic of Congo, a region that is isolated by the Zaire

River. The climate and topography are relatively constant (Kano, 1992) and the monthly variation in temperature (20°-30°C) and rainfall (1600-2000 mm) is low (Appendix 1). Within the bonobos range, altitude varies by just 180 m, reaching 479 m at the highest point and 299 m at the lowest (Appendix 1). The forests are generally primary, consisting of dry and swamp forest. Bonobos have a wide ecological niche, with every stratum of every vegetation type being used in some way (Kano, 1983).

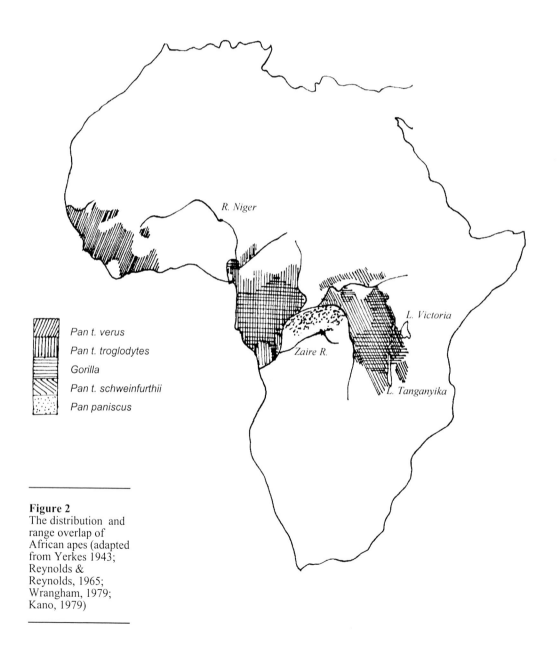

Figure 2
The distribution and range overlap of African apes (adapted from Yerkes 1943; Reynolds & Reynolds, 1965; Wrangham, 1979; Kano, 1979)

Figure 3
Location of major
field sites of African
apes. The key to
these field sites is
given in Appendix 2.

Characteristics of chimpanzee habitats

Chimpanzees, in contrast, have an extensive range from Mali and Senegal on the west African coast, across the northern part of the equatorial rainforest zone of the Zaire River, to both sides of Lake Tanganyika in east Africa and as far south as 8° S (Reynolds & Reynolds, 1965; Goodall, 1968; Hladik, 1977; McGrew *et al.*, 1981, Figures 2 and 3). Their total range is approximately 15 times that of the bonobos and they are the most widely distributed apes (except humans). Whilst the range of habitats in which bonobos are found is limited, it is extreme in chimpanzees (Appendices 2 and 3). The altitudinal range of chimpanzees is from 0-3000 m above sea level (Kortlandt, 1967) (Table 1). Climatic conditions are diverse. For instance, western chimpanzees *P. t. verus* inhabit humid areas in Guinea, where the average annual rainfall is 4350 mm (de Bournville, 1967), across to Senegal, where average annual rainfall is only 954 mm (McGrew, Baldwin & Tutin, 1981). The eastern chimpanzees *P. t. schweinfurthii* of the dry Ugalla hill zone experience only 900 mm or less rainfall per year (Appendix 2).

The wide range of climatic conditions and topographies across chimpanzee habitats means that the floristic characteristics are also diverse. Chimpanzees inhabit the tropical lowland rainforests from west Africa through central Africa, the mountainous forests of Cameroon and east Africa's Western Great Rift Zone and the deciduous woodland-savannah belt in the boundary zone of their distribution. The primary habitat of the chimpanzee is the rainforest. Nevertheless, while bonobos are restricted to a humid habitat, chimpanzees are found not only in the wet, equatorial rainforest belt, but in drier areas to the south and east in mosaic savannah vegetation, woodland, grassland and riverine forest (Appendices 2 and 3), thus inhabiting a much broader range of relative aridity.

Habitat richness

Overall habitat richness, or habitat quality (reliability, abundance and nutritional value of food items) can be estimated using habitat type variables (e.g. rainfall, altitude, latitude, temperature range, seasonality and mean temperature). Fruit is a food source that is rich in calories and easy to process relative to THV; thus, it is assumed that fruit is a favourable food item for apes. As a result, a habitat that supports a lot of fruit is here considered a 'rich habitat', even though a higher density of THV in an habitat can act as a buffer for a lower density of fruit patches.

Habitat richness will influence group size and foraging efficiency. Data from ape species confirm that they may congregate in unusually large numbers at particularly good food sources (orang-utans; MacKinnon, 1974: chimpanzees; Sugiyama & Koman, 1979, Wrangham, 1977: bonobos; Kano & Mulavwa, 1984; Badrian & Badrian, 1984), and Dunbar (1988) presents evidence within species that group size increases when habitat quality improves.

Table 1 Results of partial correlation coefficient matrix for great ape population climatic data.

	Altitude	Rainfall	Degrees from Eq.
NO Control			
Mean temperature	p=0.000, r=-0.62	-	-
Seasonality	p=0.005, r=0.44	p=0.001, r=-0.52	-
Temp. Range	-	p=0.038, r=0.44	p=0.025, r=-0.36
Controlling for ALTITUDE			
Mean temperature	-	-	-
Seasonality	-	p=0.001, r=-0.52	-
Temp. Range	-	p=0.03, r=0.36	p=0.026, r=-0.37
Controlling for SEASONALITY			
Mean temperature	p=0.000, r=-0.57	-	-
Seasonality	-	-	-
Temp. Range	-	p=0.043, r=0.33	p=0.033, r=-0.35
Controlling for RAINFALL			
Mean temperature	p=0.000, r=-0.61	-	-
Seasonality	p=0.006, r=0.45	-	-
Temp. Range	-	-	p=0.01, r=-0.42
Controlling for MEAN TEMPERATURE			
Mean temperature	-	-	-
Seasonality	p=0.028, r=0.36	p=0.002, r=-0.49	-
Temp. Range	-	p=0.042, r=0.34	p=0.023, r-0.37
Controlling for TEMPERATURE RANGE			
Mean temperature	p=0.000, r=-0.62	-	-
Seasonality	p=0.004, r=0.46	p=0.001, r=-0.52	-
Temp. Range	-	-	-
Controlling for ALTITUDE + SEASONALITY			
Mean temperature	-	-	-
Seasonality	-	-	-
Temp. Range	-	p=0.059, r=0.31	p=0.043, r=-0.33
Controlling for RAINFALL + SEASONALITY			
Mean temperature	p=0.000, r=-0.59	-	-
Seasonality	-	-	-
Temp. Range	-	-	p=0.004, r=-0.46

Table 2 Great ape habitat indices.

	Study Site	Habitat Index		Descriptive Statistic	Statistic Value
SO	Ranun	7.37		Orang-utan mean	8.70
SO	Ketambe	7.93	Decreasing	Orang-utan median	8.33
BO	Segama	8.21	Habitat	Bornean Orang-utan mean	9.22
BO	Kutai	8.44	Harshness	Sumatran Orang-utan mean	7.65
BO	Sepilok	9.84		Range	(7.37-10.4) 3.03
BO	Tanjung	10.4		Standard deviation	1.17
				Standard error	0.48
				Variance	**1.37**
ELG (H)	Kahuzi	2.52		Gorilla mean	3.96
MG (H)	Virunga	2.86		Gorilla median	3.60
MG (H)	Karisoke	2.94	Decreasing	Mountain gorilla mean	3.27
ELG (H)	Kahuzi-B	2.98	Habitat	Eastern-L gorilla mean	3.89
MG (H)	Kisoro	3.24	Harshness	Western-L gorilla mean	4.70
MG (H)	Kayonza	3.31		High altitude gorilla mean	3.17
ELG (H)	Tshia'	3.48		Low altitude gorilla mean	4.85
ELG (L)	Itebero	3.60		Range	(2.52-6.87) 4.35
MG (H)	Kabara	4.01		Standard deviation	1.18
WLG (L)	Bai	4.37		Standard error	0.31
WLG (L)	Lopé	4.38		**Variance**	**1.40**
WLG (L)	Likouala	4.44			
WLG (L)	Belinga	4.48			
WLG (L)	Rio Mun	5.84			
ELG (L)	Utu	6.87			
B	Tumba	6.86		Bonobo mean	6.99
B	Yalosidi	6.87	Decreasing	Bonobo median	6.90
B	Lomako	6.90	Habitat	Range	(6.86-7.37) 0.51
B	Wamba	6.95	Harshness	Standard deviation	0.215
B	Lilungu	7.37		Standard error	0.096
				Variance	**0.046**
EC	Ugalla	1		Chimpanzee mean	4.07
EC	Kahuzi	2.52		Chimpanzee median	4.07
WC	Assirik	2.70	Decreasing	Eastern chimpanzee mean	3.08
EC	Gombe	2.82	Habitat	Western chimpanzee mean	5.04
EC	Mahale	3.12	Harshness	Central chimpanzee mean	5.13
EC	Budongo	3.76		Range	(1-6.35) 5.35
CC	Lopé	4.38		Standard deviation	1.64
WC	Bossou	4.92		Standard error	0.47
EC	Kibale	5.25		**Variance**	**2.70**
CC	Rio Muni	5.87			
WC	Sapo	6.20			
WC	Tai	6.35			

BO - Bornean Orang-utan   WLG = Western Lowland Gorilla   EC = Eastern Chimpanzee
SO = Sumatran Orang-utan   H = High Altitude (> 1000m)   WC = Western Chimpanzee
MG = Mountain Gorilla   L = Low Altitude (< 1000m)   CC = Central Chimpanzee
ELG = Eastern Lowland Gorilla   B = Bonobo

Habitat type is summarised into an index using climatic and ecological variables. This habitat index is used to assess habitat richness for great ape study sites. The index provides some measure of habitat richness independent of the animal using the habitat. However, actual resource availability is dependent on the individual forager – its body size and/or taxon, for example.

An assessment of resource availability and hence quality of the habitat to an individual forager is made using an 'ecological cost index' which incorporates foraging party size as an indicator of resource availability.

Foraging party size as an indicator of resource availability and feeding competition

Of particular distinction amongst great ape foraging behaviour is the more or less solitary nature of the orang-utan. Wrangham (1979) has suggested that orang-utans are obliged to forage separately by the severe costs incurred by foraging in groups (termed 'feeding competition' in this study). The most likely costs of grouping for orang-utans derive from the energetic costs of travel for an animal that is both heavy (males reach up to 66.3 kg, Leigh & Shea, 1995) and as arboreally adapted as the orang-utan.

Gorillas, whilst being large, are generally terrestrial. Gorilla foraging party size varies with dietary composition, thus the less frugivorous the population the smaller the foraging party size (Tutin *et al.*, 1991). The same trend is observed in bonobos and chimpanzees; bonobos forage in larger parties than do chimpanzees and are less dependent on fruit as a principal food source (Malenky & Wrangham, 1994). Foraging party size is generally indicative of resource availability (see Bean, 1998 for further review), whether the principal resource is fruit or not; the higher the feeding competition, the lower the foraging party size.

Body size (mass) has to be considered when calculating relative costs to a forager. This is because a suitable habitat for a small frugivore may not necessarily be a suitable habitat for a large frugivore. A multiple of body mass is, therefore, incorporated into the 'ecological cost index'. As noted above, body mass is included as metabolic body weight.

Methods

Habitat index

In order to explore the nature of great ape foraging behaviour in relation to habitat type, the climatic variables are summarised in a single descriptor variable called 'habitat index'. The habitat index provides some measure of variability of habitat type. This index also denotes relative 'richness' of habitat and illustrates divergences and overlaps in the habitat types occupied by great ape populations.

Firstly, interactions between the climatic data were investigated. The bivariate correlation matrix of the climatic variables used to describe habitat type is summarised in Figure 4. Excluding altitude, then rainfall, then degrees from equator, then altitude and seasonality and then seasonality and rainfall by a partial correlation procedure (Table 2), indicates that much of the variation in the climatic data set is accounted for by seasonality, rainfall and altitude.

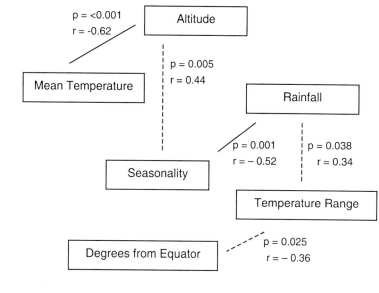

Correlation is significant at the Bonferroni significance level (p = 0.001)
Correlation is not significant at the Bonferroni significance level but still p <0.05

Figure 4
Results of bivariate correlation matrix of the great ape climatic variables.

A less harsh habitat, or 'richer' habitat, was assumed to be characterised by a low altitude, high mean annual rainfall and a low level of seasonality. To account for these patterns altitude and seasonality were multiplied by −1. Altitude, rainfall and seasonality were then saved as z-scores and summed (Equation 1).

[1]   *Raw habitat index value = [Z (altitude[-1])+ Z (rainfall) + Z (seasonality[-1])]*

The resulting variables span both positive and negative values, therefore these values were re-scaled by transforming the most harsh habitat index value to 1. To maintain the degree of difference between habitat indices the remaining values were transformed accordingly: i.e. the most negative value = -4.36, so +5.36 was added to each habitat index value.

[2]
$$'Habitat\ Index' = Raw\ habitat\ index\ value + ([x - (2x)] + 1$$
where x = most negative raw habitat index value

Ecological costs and resource availability

Merely using a 'habitat index' to understand or predict sub-species or population foraging behaviour is probably too simplistic an approach. The 'habitat index' used above codes the habitat into a general habitat type, independent of the animal using the habitat. Further measures are needed to provide an index that is relevant to each individual in each taxon, firstly because resource availability for one taxon is not the same as resource availability for another and, secondly, because, for each individual, the 'suitability' of the habitat or relative 'resource availability' will differ and this will further determine foraging behaviour.

At the population level of comparison, thus sensitive to local resource availability, the great apes are expected to vary in foraging behaviour, particularly in dietary strategy, ranging and foraging party size.

Ecological cost index

Habitat type ('habitat index'), behavioural variables relative to resource availability (foraging party size) and a measure of daily energetic costs incurred by the individual forager (metabolic body mass) are used to calculate an 'ecological cost index' (ECI) (Equation 3).

[3]
$$Ecological\ cost\ index = \frac{Habitat\ Index\ x\ Foraging\ Party\ Size}{Ln\ Metabolic\ Weight}$$

Great ape foraging clusters

Figures 5 to 10 suggest complex interactions between foraging variables. In order to examine whether the original foraging behaviour variables (i.e. excluding climatic variables) cluster into foraging strategies, the foraging data from 44 ape groups were entered into the cluster analysis (Table 3). The foraging data used are shown in Appendix 1. The data were standardised by a rescaling procedure (Norusis, 1994a).

Results

Habitat indices: overall characteristics of great ape habitats

While there are clear differences in the overall habitat types of the great ape study sites (Table 1); there is also considerable overlap between sub-species (Table 1). Some study-sites are inhabited by more than one species, for example Kahuzi-Biega is inhabited by eastern lowland gorillas and eastern chimpanzees, whilst Lopé and Rio Muni are inhabited by both western lowland gorillas and central

Although the gorillas appear to inhabit the 'harshest' habitats overall (Table 1), this may be misleading. The high altitude of mountain gorilla habitats has resulted in the low habitat index for this sub-species, which has affected the gorilla mean. It may be useful to incorporate temperature, rather than altitude, in further estimates of habitat type calculations. Comparisons between the study sites of different sub-species reveal considerable overlap in chimpanzees' and gorillas' habitats (Table 1).

Table 3 Selected outline of clusters produced of great ape foraging strategy as directly transcribed from the SPSS generated icicle plot (see Bean, 1998 for full details of analysis).

Step in Clustering Procedure	Cluster Groups at Step...
7 groups (i.e. Stage 37)	1. Eastern lowland gorillas 2. Mountain gorillas 3. Mountain gorilla outlier (Karisoke) 4. Chimpanzee outliers (Mt. Assirik; Kasakati; Ugalla; Filabanga*) 5. Rest of chimpanzees and bonobos 6. Bonobo outlier (Lake Tumba) and western lowland gorillas 7. Orang-utans
5 groups (i.e. Stage 39)	1. Eastern lowland and mountain gorillas 2. Mountain gorilla outlier (Karisoke) 3. Chimpanzee outliers (Mt. Assirik; Kasakati; Ugalla; Filabanga*) 4. Bonobos, western lowland gorillas and rest of chimpanzees 5. Orang-utans
4 groups (i.e. Stage 40)	1. Eastern lowland and mountain gorillas 2. Mountain gorilla outlier (Karisoke) 3. Chimpanzees, bonobos and western lowland gorillas 4. Orang-utans
3 groups (i.e. Stage 41)	1. Eastern lowland and mountain gorillas 2. Chimpanzees, bonobos and western lowland gorillas　　↓ Leap in clustering Coefficient 3. Orang-utans

Total Stages = 44 (i.e. 44 ape populations)
* dry woodland/savannah chimpanzees

Figure 5
Relation between Ln number of food Items in diet (excluding animal matter) and sqrt of % invertebrates in the diet in great apes (linear trend line presented for illustration).
Food items are particular types of food identified by the researcher as being eaten by great apes. For any one plant species, flowers, nuts, leaves, fruit, etc., all count as separate food items. The number of food items in the diet are used to estimate dietary breadth).

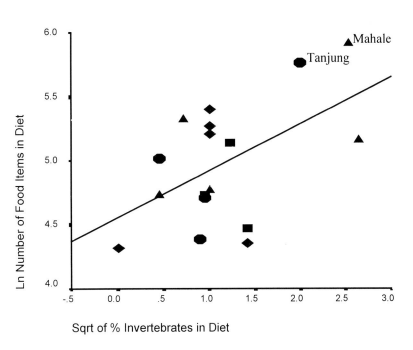

Species

● Orang-utan
◆ Gorilla
▲ Chimpanzee
■ Bonobo

Figure 6
Relation between Ln day range and habitat index in great apes (linear trend line presented for illustration).
(Day range is the measure of distance travelled per day (in kilometres) by a single individual or group, each day).

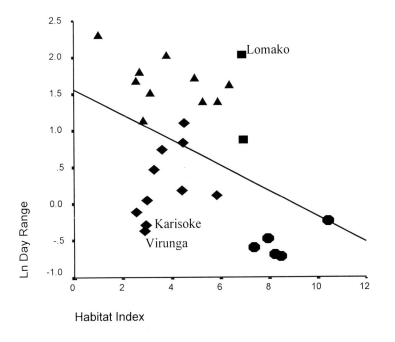

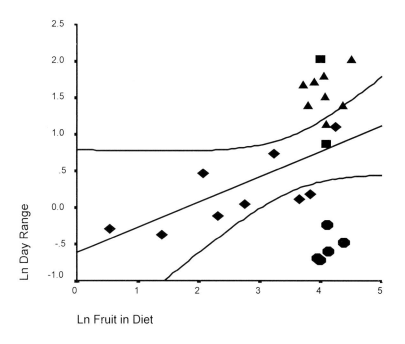

Figure 7
Relation between Ln
day range and Ln of
% fruit in diet in
great apes (trend line
and 95 % confidence
limits shown).

Species

● Orang-utan
◆ Gorilla
▲ Chimpanzee
■ Bonobo

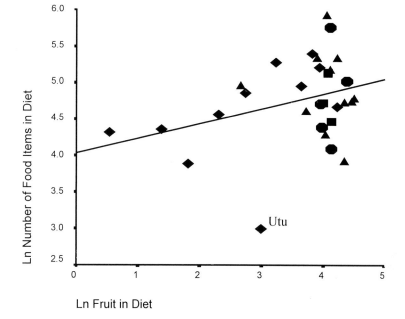

Figure 8
Relation between Ln
of % fruit in diet and
Ln number of food
items in diet (linear
trend line presented
for illustration).

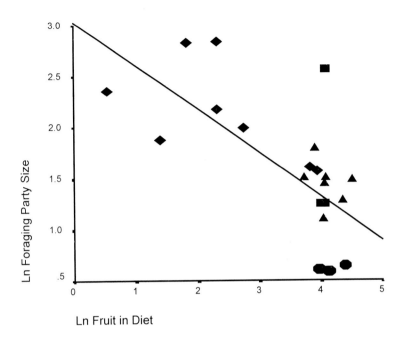

Figure 9
Relation between Ln
of % fruit in diet and
Ln foraging party
size (linear trend line
presented for
illustration).

Species

● Orang-utan
♦ Gorilla
▲ Chimpanzee
■ Bonobo

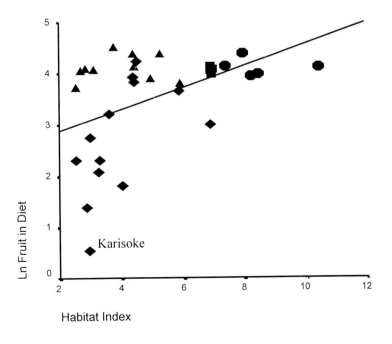

Figure 10
Relation between
habitat index and Ln
of % fruit in diet
(linear trend line
presented for
illustration).

Table 4 Results of Bivariate Correlation Matrix for Great Ape Foraging Behaviour (data from Appendix 1).

	Pop' Dens'	Day Range	Home Range	F' Party Size	Dietary Breadth	Fruit in Diet	Invert's in Diet
Pop' Dens'							
Day Range	p=0.365 r=-0.14						
Home Range	p=0.024 r=-0.34	p=0.010 r=0.386					
F' Party Size	p=0.152 r=-0.220	p=0.700 r=0.060	p=0.520 r=0.995				
Dietary Breadth	p=0.169 r=0.211	p=0.364 r=0.140	p=0.614 r=0.078	p=0.065 r=-0.280			
Fruit in Diet	p=0.200 r=0.197	*p=0.006 r=0.411*	*p=0.038 r=0.313*	*p=0.003 r=-0.441*	p=0.067 r=0.278		
Invert's in Diet	p=0.827 r=-0.034	p=0.065 r=0.280	p=0.111 r=0.244	p=0.068 r=-0.278	*p=0.018 r=0.357*	**p=0.000 r=0.547**	

Pop' Dens' = natural log of population density (n/km2)
Day Range = natural log of mean population day range (km)
Home Range = natural log of mean population home range (km2)
F' Party Size = natural log of mean foraging party size
Dietary Breadth = natural log of mean number of food items in mean annual dietary composition
Fruit in Diet = % fruit in diet
Invert's in Diet = square root of % invertebrates in mean annual dietary composition
Correlations in **bold** = significant at the Bonferroni significance index level (i.e. <0.002)
Correlations in *italic* = <p = 0.05, whilst not significant at the Bonferroni level are still discussed due to the relatively small sample size

Habitat richness and foraging behaviour

A series of bivariate correlations was used to identify patterns in great ape foraging behaviour (Table 4). Variables such as day range can be used as indicators of habitat quality. Day range is longer in poorer habitats than in rich ones (Struhsaker, 1967; Richard, 1978; Anderson, 1981; Figure 6). However, although day range and habitat index have a significant correlation (r=-0.418, p=0.03), Figure 6 shows that there is clearly more going on here than a simple bivariate correlation as the perpendicular distribution of the chimpanzee data points and some gorilla data points suggest. Virunga gorillas have extremely low day ranges (Figure 6) despite the high altitude of this study site. This suggests that the region is actually quite a rich habitat. Whilst altitude may be an indicator of habitat richness for frugivorous apes, it is not for folivorous gorillas.

Figure 7 shows that low altitude gorillas rely more on fruit than do high altitude gorillas (t=5.2, p=0.002) and that great ape day range is dependent on dietary composition.

There is clear species clustering in the regression relationship shown in Figure 7. The orang-utan group has a characteristically shorter day range than expected by the amount of fruit in its diet and falls below the confidence limits. This may be because, compared to the other great apes, orang-utans are more likely to travel arboreally, which is less efficient than terrestrial travel. The chimpanzees have relatively higher day ranges than expected by the amount of fruit in their diet and also fall somewhat below the confidence limits. This may be related to the 'harsher habitat type' in which they are judged to live.

Folivorous apes subsist on fewer plant species than do frugivorous ones and, therefore, have a relatively conservative dietary breadth (see Clutton-Brock & Harvey, 1977; Hladik, 1977; Sussman, 1977; Raemakers, 1979 and Figure 8). Frugivorous apes are more likely to supplement their diet with animal matter, such as invertebrates, during periods of low fruit availability (see Yamagiwa *et al.*, 1991), thereby increasing dietary breadth further (Figure 5). Also related to dietary composition is foraging party size, which decreases as percentage fruit in diet increases (Figure 9).

Habitat index and dietary composition

The type of habitat will determine food items available to any forager. For example, high altitude habitats generally have more THV and are less rich in fruit than low altitude habitats (Schaller, 1963; Fossey & Harcourt, 1977; Watts, 1984). Habitat type will also determine the availability of such foods through the year (i.e. seasonality). However, the forests of Dem. Rep. of Congo, inhabited by bonobos, are low altitude, but are notable for their relatively high level of THV. The availability of food items, both spatially and temporally, will influence dietary composition: as fruit in diet increases so does dietary breadth (Figure 8) although the relationship is weak.

The relationship between habitat index and % fruit in diet (Figure 10), appears to be triangular, or even cubic (and possibly described by a polynomial relationship). This adds further weight to the suspicion that habitat index does not actually express 'resource availability'. There are other factors involved, which are likely to be correlated with habitat index.

As habitat index increases, day range decreases (Figure 6), again, the spread of data points in a triangular formation suggests that habitat index is correlated with other factors influencing these variables.

Ecological cost index

To calculate the ecological cost index one has to assess the resource available to an individual forager, taking its body mass into account. The results of the ECI calculation (Table 5) show that although orang-utans have the highest (mean) habitat index (i.e. rich habitat types) they have low ECIs (low actual resource availability).

Table 5 Great ape ecological cost indices.

Sub-Species	Ecological Cost Index	Study-Site
WC	2.71	Assirik
EC	4.15	Kahuzi
O	4.22	Ranun
EC	4.65	Gombe
O	4.82	Ketambe
O	4.84	Segama
EC	4.86	Mahale
O	4.98	Kutai
MG	5.10	Virunga
O	5.81	Sepilok
WLG	5.84	Bai
ELG	5.98	Kahuzi-B
O	6.04	Tanjung
EC	6.06	Budongo
WLG	6.09	Lopé
EC	6.92	Kibale
MG	7.95	Kayonza
MG	8.48	Karisoke
B	8.73	Tumba
WC	9.88	Bossou
B	9.99	Yalosidi
ELG	11.78	Kahuzi
WC	13.92	Tai
B	16.08	Lilungu
B	17.57	Lomako
MG	18.61	Kabara
CC	23.63	Rio Muni
B	32.86	Wamba

O = Orang-utan   MG = Mountain Gorilla
ELG = Eastern Lowland Gorilla   WLG = Western Lowland Gorilla
B = Bonobo   EC =Eastern Chimpanzee
CC = Central Chimpanzee   WC = Western Chimpanzee

Bonobos, as well as having a relativity high habitat index, have high ECIs. Western chimpanzees have higher HIs and ECIs than eastern chimpanzees. Mountain gorillas and eastern lowland gorillas, whilst having the lowest HIs (apart from eastern chimpanzees), actually have higher ECIs than western lowland gorillas. This confirms the idea that whilst chimpanzees *rely* on fruit, gorillas do not. In habitats that are low in terms of fruit production, gorillas switch to eating THV.

When in sufficient quantity and of sufficient quality (Wrangham *et al.*, 1996), THV can be a better resource than fruit, being more available and of higher nutritional content. Indeed, the bonobos, living in habitats with high ECIs, are observed to rely less on fruit than do chimpanzees (Wrangham, 1987).

Great ape foraging clusters

A leap in clustering coefficient, from a four-stage cluster to a three stage cluster (for details and clustering coefficients see Bean, 1998, illustrated in Table 3), indicates that great ape foraging is best represented by a three-cluster solution.

The interpretation of the cluster analysis (Bean, 1998, summarised in Table 3) indicates that the three most robust clusters are (a) eastern lowland and mountain gorillas, (b) chimpanzees, western lowland gorillas and bonobos, and (c) orang-utans. This suggests a substantial gap between the behavioural ecology of eastern lowland and mountain gorillas with western lowland gorillas, which, in turn, appear to overlap in habitat and foraging strategy with chimpanzees and bonobos.

The steps in the hierarchical clustering solution are shown on the dendrogram in Appendix 4. The dendrogram identifies the clusters being combined. Appendix 4 shows how: bonobos associate with western chimpanzees and central chimpanzees before they cluster with eastern chimpanzees; eastern lowland gorillas and mountain gorillas form a distinct cluster; western lowland gorillas cluster and then associate with eastern chimpanzees and bonobos.

Results were plotted two-dimensionally using a multi-dimensional scaling procedure (Figure 11, for co-ordinates see Bean, 1998). The same data were used as for the cluster analysis, except in multi-dimensional scaling procedures the data are converted to Z scores and are entered into the analysis as a matrix of dissimilarity (Norusis, 1994b). SPSS® (Statistical Package for the Social Sciences) plots the points in space so that the distances between pairs of points have the strongest possible relation to the similarities between pairs of objects.

Cluster analysis, on the other hand, forms clusters by grouping cases into bigger and bigger assemblages until all cases are members of a single cluster (Norusis, 1994a). This is why the dendrogram of the cluster analysis (Appendix 4) and the results of the multi-dimensional scaling procedure (Figure 11) differ.

The results of the multi-dimensional scaling procedure (Figure 11) emphasise the three main clusters of foraging strategies adopted by the great apes.

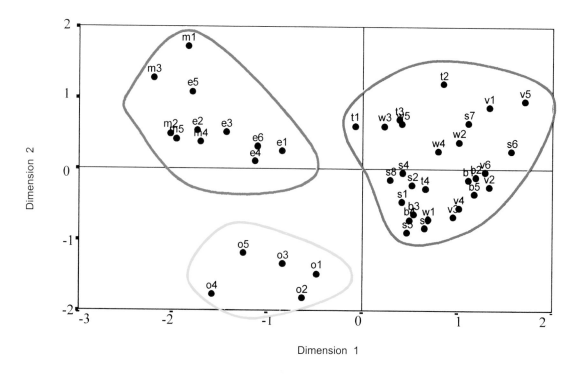

Figure 11
Two-dimensional multi-scaling plot of great ape foraging clusters (Derived Stimulus configuration: Euclidean distance model). For co-ordinates, (Bean, 1998).

m = Mountain Gorilla
e = Eastern Lowland Gorilla
w = Western Lowland Gorilla
o = Orang-utan

s = Eastern Gorillas
v =Western Chimpanzee
t = Central-Western Chimpanzee
b = Bonobo

Discussion

Great ape habitats

The results show that chimpanzees occupy the widest range of habitat types and bonobos the narrowest (Table 3).

This is intuitively sensible when considering the geographical isolation of bonobos in the lowland tropical forests of Dem. Rep. of Congo and the broad range of chimpanzees – from Senegal in west Africa to Tanzania in east Africa (Figure 2). The gorillas occupy the next most variable set of habitat types. However, the gorilla range is not so much a geographical spread (Figure 3) as a vertical spread, ranging from 350 m above sea level (Bai Hokou, Central African Republic, Table 1) to 3150 m above sea level in the Virunga Volcanoes (Dem. Rep. of Congo/Rwanda/Uganda, Appendix 2).

Great ape foraging behaviour

Gorilla foraging behaviour appears to be highly correlated with altitudinal effects and, therefore, with sub-species. However, populations of the eastern lowland gorilla are found at both high altitudes (i.e. above 1000 m) and low altitudes, which reduces the latter correlation as the foraging behaviour in this sub-species varies in different ecological zones. This contrasts with chimpanzee foraging behaviour, which is more variable at the population level.

Great ape habitat indices

Out of the gorilla subset, mountain gorillas have the lowest habitat index and, therefore, the 'harshest' habitat (when defined in terms of fruit production); western lowland gorillas appear to have the richest habitat types. The latter overlap with Central chimpanzees. Eastern chimpanzees have the lowest habitat indices of the sub-species set, while central chimpanzees lie intermediate between eastern lowland and western lowland gorillas. The great ape sub-species habitat indices show considerable overlap (Table 1).

Orang-utans, like bonobos, are geographically isolated. Orang-utans have low variance in habitat index. Orang-utans score highly on the habitat index scale (higher than bonobos), thus they appear to live in relatively rich habitats. However, in this case the habitat index is too simplistic since the forests that orang-utans inhabit are mainly dipterocarp and are relatively poor in terms of fruit production (Caldecott, 1986a, 1986b) for such a large bodied, arboreal frugivore, especially since orang-utans appear to be heavily dependent on fruit (40-65% of their diet).

Resource availability

The type of habitat will largely determine the food items available to the forager (but not in the case of orang-utans). In general, the data indicate that chimpanzees rely more on fruit than do bonobos and that low-altitude gorillas rely more on fruit than high-altitude gorillas (Appendix 2). Ranging behaviour is dependent on dietary composition (Figure 7) as well as habitat type (Figure 6). Also dependent on dietary composition is dietary breadth, which decreases as % fruit in diet decreases (Figure 8), and foraging party size which decreases as % fruit in diet increases (Figure 9). Percentage fruit in diet also increases as habitat index increases (Figure 10). However, the spread of points in these figures suggests that these relationships are far more complex than these simple analyses describe. Dietary composition is therefore a highly flexible behavioural characteristic; being correlated with habitat type and other foraging behaviour variables such as dietary breadth, party size and ranging.

Foraging behavioural ecology

In general, frugivores have larger ranging areas than folivores do (Mace & Harvey, 1983), and this trend was found here for apes (Figure 7). These relationships may be due to fruits being more patchy in distribution than leaves and, once a fruit patch has been exhausted, a group may have to travel a considerable distance to find another (Clutton-Brock & Harvey, 1977).

Bonobos and mountain gorillas occupy habitats rich in terrestrial herbaceous vegetation, which is reflected in their diets (Watts, 1984; Wrangham, 1987). The number of food items in the diet of bonobos is less than in that of chimpanzees (Appendix 1). Bonobos use a smaller proportion of the food resources available (Malenky & Wrangham, 1994). This suggests that the supply of major food is more stable for bonobos and that bonobos do not need to feed on items that are 'hard to process', or difficult to collect, such as bark and insects. It has been suggested that chimpanzee diet is more varied than that of bonobos because the habitat is poorer. High quality THV (Wrangham et al., 1996) is found in far greater quantities in the areas occupied by bonobos than in the habitats of chimpanzees (Wrangham, 1987; White, 1988).

Because of the simplistic nature of the habitat index, this scale was modified to incorporate more specific indicators of resource availability (such as foraging party size) and also included a relative energetic cost to the individual forager (i.e. used metabolic body mass), in the 'ecological cost index'.

Ecological costs

Whilst the habitat index for orang-utans is high, they have the lowest values for ecological cost index. The almost solitary nature of orang-utan foraging indicates that feeding competition is high. Bonobos have the highest ecological cost indices and are, therefore, predicted to experience the highest resource availability amongst great apes. Mountain gorillas and eastern lowland gorillas have higher ecological cost indices than western lowland gorillas. This is due to the greater proportion of THV, which lowers feeding competition as indicated by larger foraging party sizes.

Foraging strategy

The cluster analysis suggests that three main groups best represent great ape foraging strategy: (1) orang-utans (2) eastern lowland and mountain gorillas, and (3) chimpanzees, western lowland gorillas and bonobos. The principal independent variable separating the groups is altitude, which acts through temperature, rainfall and seasonality to determine vegetation.

The variation in foraging strategy suggests that the plasticity in foraging behaviour represents a population response to ecological factors, rather than a fundamental difference between species or sub-species. Differences in great ape foraging behaviour need to be interpreted in the light of variable responses to variable habitats across populations.

Acknowledgements

Many thanks to Phyllis Lee, Mike Linley and Mark Golley for their comments and encouragement. The work on this paper was supported by research awards from the Board of Graduate Studies (University of Cambridge), the Henry Ling Roth Fund (Department of Social Anthropology, Univ. of Cambridge), British Foundation of Graduate Women, Gonville and Caius College (Cambridge), the Anthony Wilkin Fund (Ethnology, Univ. of Cambridge) and the Henry Chadwick Fund (Anglo Saxon, Celtic and Norse, Univ. of Cambridge), to all of which I would like to express my gratitude.

References

Anderson CM. 1981. Subgrouping in chacma baboon *(Papio ursinus)* population. *Primates.* **23:** 445-58.

Attica Won Atlas/WWF. 1996. AirteQ Ltd: Phillip's thematic maps and Phillip's geographical digest (1996-97). Milton Keynes, United Kingdom: Reed International Books Ltd.

Bean AE. 1998. The ecology of sex differences in great ape foraging behaviour and hunter-gatherer subsistence behaviour: The origin of sexual division in human subsistence behaviour. [Unpublished Ph.D thesis], University of Cambridge.

Bean AE. 1999. Ecology of sex differences in great ape foraging behaviour. In: Lee PC. ed. *Comparative Primate Socioecology.* Cambridge: Cambridge University Press.

Badrian A, Badrian N. 1984. Social organization of *Pan paniscus* in the Lomako Forest, Zaire. In: Susman RL. ed. *The Pygmy Chimpanzee: Evolutionary biology and Behaviour.* London: Plenum Press. 325-346.

Boesch C, Boesch H. 1981. Sex differences in the use of natural hammers by wild chimpanzees: a preliminary report. *Journal of Human Evolution.* **10:** 585-93.

Boesch C, Boesch H. 1984. Possible causes of sex differences in the use of natural hammers by wild chimpanzees. *Journal of Human Evolution.* **13:** 415-440.

Boesch C, Boesch H. 1989. Hunting behaviour of wild chimpanzees in the Tai National Park. *American Journal of Physical Anthropology.* **78:** 547-573.

Bournonville D de. 1967. Contribution a l'étude du chimpanzé Guineé. *Bulletin de l'institut francais african noir.* **29:** 1189-1269.

Caldecott JO. 1986a. *An Ecological and Behavioural Study of the Pig-Tailed Macaque.* Basel: Karger.

Caldecott JO. 1986b. Mating patterns, societies, and the ecogeography of macaques. *Animal Behaviour.* **34:** 208-20.

Chivers DJ, Hiadik CM. 1980. Morphology of the gastrointestinal tract in primates: Comparisons with other mammals in relation to diet. *Journal of Morphology.* **166:** 337-386.

Clutton-Brock TH, Harvey PH. 1977. Species differences in feeding and ranging behaviour in primates. In: Clutton-Brock TH. ed. *Primate Ecology.* London: Academic Press. 557-579.

Conklin NL, Wrangham RW. 1991. Dietary strategies and nutrient intakes in Kibale Forest, Uganda. *Philosophical Transactions of the Royal Society of London. Series B,* **334:**11-18.

Cramer DL. 1977. Craniofacial morphology of *Pan paniscus:* a morphometric and evolutionary appraisal. *Contributions to Primatolology.* **10:** 1-64.

Dunbar RIM. 1988. Ecological modelling in an evolutionary context. *Folia Primatologica.* **53:** 234-56.

Fossey D, Harcourt AH. 1977. Feeding Ecology of free-ranging mountain gorilla *(Gorilla gorilla beringei).* In: Clutton-Brock TH. ed. *Primate Ecology.* London: Academic Press. 415-449.

Galat G, Galat-Luong A. 1977. Demographie et regime alimentare d'une troupe de *Cercopithecus aethiops* en habitat marginal du nord Senegal. *Terre Vie.* **31:** 557-77.

Galdikas BMF. 1988. Orangutan diet, range and activity at Tanjung Puting, Central Borneo. *International Journal of Primatology.* **9(1):** 1-35.

Goodall AG. 1977. Feeding and ranging behaviour of a mountain gorilla group *(Gorilla gorilla beringei)* in the Tshibinda-Kahuzi region (Zaire). In: Clutton-Brock TM. ed. *Primate Ecology.* London: Academic Press. 449-479

Goodall J. 1963. Feeding behaviour of wild chimpanzees (A Preliminary Report). *Symposia of the Zoological Society of London.* **10:** 39-48.

Goodall J. 1965. Chimpanzees of the Gombe Stream Reserve. In: de Vore I. ed. *Primate Behaviour.* New York: Molt, Rinehart and Winston. 425-473.

Goodall J. 1968. The behaviour of free-living chimpanzees in the Gombe Stream Reserve. *Animal Behaviour Monographs.* **1:** 161-311.

Goodall J. 1973. The behaviour of chimpanzees in their natural habitat. *American Journal of Psychiatry.* **130:** 1-12.

Hladik CM. 1977. Chimpanzees of Gabon and chimpanzees of Gombe: Some comparative data on the diet. In: Clutton-Brock TM. ed. *Primate Ecology.* London: Academic Press. 481-501.

Johanson DC. 1974. Some metric aspects of the permanent and deciduous dentition of the pygmy chimpanzee *(Pan pansicus). American Journal of Physical Anthropology.* **41:** 39-48.

Kano T. 1972. Distribution and adaptation of the chimpanzee on the eastern shore of Lake Tanganyika. *Kyoto University African Studies.* **7:** 37-129.

Kano T. 1983. An ecological study of the pygmy chimpanzees *(Pan paniscus)* of Yalosidi, Republic of Zaire. *International Journal of Primatology.* **4(1):** 1-31.

Kano T. 1992. *The Last Ape.* Stanford, California: Stanford University Press.

Kano T, Mulavwa M. 1984. Feeding ecology of the pygmy chimpanzees *(Pan paniscus)* of Wamba. In: Susman RL. ed. *The Pygmy Chimpanzee: Evolutionary biology and Behaviour.* London: Plenum Press. 233-274.

Kaplan H, Hill K. 1992. The evolutionary ecology of food acquisition. In: Smith EA, Winterhalder B. eds. *Evolutionary Ecology and Human Behaviour.* New York: Aldine. Chapter 6.

Kavanagh M. 1978. The diet and feeding behaviour of *Cercopithecus aethiops tantalus. Folia Primatologica.* **30:** 30-68.

Kleiber M. 1961. *The Fire of Lift, and Introduction to Animal Energetics.* New York: Wiley and Sons, Inc.

Kortlandt A. 1967. Handgebrauch bei freilebenden Schimpansen. In: Affen, Fruhmenschen. eds. *Hangebrauch und Vertandigung.* 59-102.

Leigh SR, Shea BT. 1995. Ontogeny and the evolution apes. *American Journal of Primatology.* **36:** 37-60.

Mace GM, Harvey PH. 1983. Energetic constraints on home-range size. *The American Naturalist.* **121(1):** 120-132

MacKinnon J. 1974. The behaviour and ecology of wild orang-utans *(Pongo pygmaeus). Animal Behaviour.* **22:** 3-74.

Malenky RK, Wrangham RW. 1994. A quantitative comparison of terrestrial herbaceous food consumption by *Pan paniscus* in the Lomako Forest, Zaire, and *Pan troglodytes* in the Kibale Forest, Uganda. *American Journal of Primatology.* **32:** 1-12

McGrew WC. 1979. Evolutionary implications of sex differences in chimpanzee predation and tool use. In: Hamburg DA, McCown ER. eds. *The Great Apes.* Menlo Park: Benjamin Cummings. 440-463.

McGrew WC, Baldwin PJ, Tutin CEG. 1981. Chimpanzees in a hot, dry and open habitat: Mt. Assirik, Senegal. *Journal of Human Evolution.* **10:** 227-244

Milton K. 1984. Habitat, diet, and activity patterns of free ranging woolly spider monkeys *(Brachyteles arachnoides* E. Geoffroy, 1806). *International Journal of Primatology.* **5:** 491-*514.*

Norusis MJ. 1994a. Cluster analysis. In: *SPSS Professional Statistics 6.1.* Chicago: SPSS Inc. 83-110.

Norusis MJ. 1994b. Multidimensional scaling. In: *SPSS Professional Statistics 6.1.* Chicago:SPSS Inc. 155-222.

Pearce EA, Smith CG. 1994. *World Weather Guide: Third Edition.* Helicon.

Raemakers J. 1979. Causes of variation between months in the distance traveled daily by gibbons. *Folia Primatologica.* **34:** 46-60.

Remis MJ. 1994. Feeding ecology and positional behaviour of lowland gorillas. [Unpublished Ph.D. Thesis], University of Yale.

Remis MJ. 1995. Effects of body size and social context on the arboreal activities of lowland gorillas in the Central African Republic. *American Journal of Physical Anthropology.* **97:** 413-433.

Reynolds V, Reynolds F. 1965. Chimpanzees of the Budongo Forest. In: de Vore I. ed. *Primate Behaviour.* New York: Holt, Rinehart & Winston. 368-424.

Richard A. 1978. *Behavioural Variation: case study of a Malagasy lemur.* Lewsiburg, Philadelphia: Bucknell University Press.

Rodman PS. 1973. Population composition and adaptive organization among orang-utans of the Kutai Reserve. In: Michael RP, Crook JM. eds. *Ecology and Behaviour of Primates.* London: Academic Press. 171-209.

Rodman PS. 1979. Individual activity patterns and the solitary nature of orang-utans. In: Hamburg DA, McCown ER. eds. *Perspectives on Human Evolution. Vol. 5. The Great Apes.* Menlo Park: Benjamin Cummings. 235-255.

Schaller GB. 1963. *The Mountain Gorilla.* University of Chicago Press.

Skinner JD, Skinner CP. 1974. Predation on the cattle egret *(Bulbucus ibis)* and masked weaver *(Ploceus velatus)* by the vervet monkey *(Cercopithecus aethiops). South African Journal of Science.* **70:** 157-158.

Soest van PJ. 1977. Plant fibre and its role in herbivore nutrition. *Cornell Veterinarian.* **67:** 307-326.

Struhsaker TT. 1967. Ecology of vervet monkeys *(Cercopithecus aethiops)* in the Masai-Amboseli game reserve, Kenya. *Ecology.* **48:** 891-904.

Sugiyama Y, Koman J. 1979. Social structure and dynamics of wild chimpanzees at Bossou, Guinea. *Primates.* **20:** 323-339.

Sullivan JT. 1966. Studies of the hemicelluloses of forage plants. *Journal of Animal Science.* **25:** 83-86.

Sussman RW. 1977. Feeding behaviour of *Lemur catta* and *Lemur fulvus.* In: Clutton-Brock TM. ed. *Primate Ecology.* London: Academic Press. 1-36.

Teleki G. 1973. The omnivorous chimpanzee. *Scientific American.* **228(1):** 32-42.

Tutin CEG, Fernandez M. 1983. Gorillas feeding on termites in Gabon, W. Africa. *Journal of Mammology.* **64:** 530-531.

Tutin CEG, Fernandez M. 1984. Nationwide census of gorilla *(Gorilla g. gorilla)* and chimpanzee *(Pan t. troglodytes)* populations in Gabon. *American Journal of Primatology.* **6:** 313-336.

Tutin CEG, Fernandez M, Rogers ME, Williamson LA, McGrew WC. 1991. Foraging profiles of sympatric lowland gorillas and chimpanzees in the Lope Reserve, Gabon. *Philosophical Transactions of the Royal Society of London, Series B.* **334:**179-186.

Vedder A. 1982. Feeding ecology of a group of mountain gorillas. Paper presented at Workshop on Gorilla Ecology. Atlanta, Georgia: IXth Congress of IPS,:

deWaal FBM. 1982. *Chimpanzee Politics.* London: Johnathan Cape.

deWaal FBM. 1989. Food sharing and reciprocal obligations among chimpanzees. *Journal of Human Evolution.* **18:** 433-439.

Watts DP. 1983. Foraging strategy and socioecology of mountain gorillas *(Gorilla beringei).* [Unpublished PhD. thesis], University of Chicago.

Watts DP. 1984. Composition and variability of Mountain Gorilla Diets in the Central Virungas. *American Journal of Primatology.* **7:** 323-356.

White FJ. 1988. Party composition and dynamics in *Pan paniscus. International Journal of Primatology.* **9:** 179-193.

Williamson EA. 1988. Behavioural ecology of western lowland gorillas in Gabon. [Unpublished PhD. Thesis], University of Stirling.

Williamson EA, Tutin CEG, Rogers ME, Fernandez M. 1990. Composition of the diet of lowland gorillas at Lope' in Gabon. *American Journal of Primatology.* **21:** 265-277.

Wrangham RW. 1977. Feeding behaviour of chimpanzees in Gombe National Park, Tanzania. In: Clutton-Brock TM. ed. *Primate Ecology.* London: Academic Press. 503-508.

Wrangham RW. 1979. On the evolution of ape social systems. *Social Science.* **18:** 335-368.

Wrangham RW. 1986. Ecology and social relationships in two species of chimpanzee. In: Rubenstein DL, Wrangham RW. eds. *Ecological Aspects of Social Evolution.* Princeton: Princeton University Press. 352-378.

Wrangham RW. 1987. The significance of African apes for reconstructing human evolution. In: Kinzey WG. ed. *The Evolution of Human Behaviour:Primate Models.* Albany: State University of New York Press. 28-47.

Wrangham RW, Smuts BB. 1980. Sex differences in the behavioural ecology of chimpanzees in the Gombe National Park, Tanzania. *Journal of Reproduction and Fertility Supplement.* **28:** 13-31.

Wrangham RW, Clark AP, Isabirye-Basuta. 1992. Female social relationships and social organization of Kibale Forest chimpanzees. In: Nishida T, McGrew WC, Marler P, Pickford M, de Waal FBM. eds. *Topics in Primatology, Volume 1. Human Origins.* Tokyo: University of Tokyo Press. 81-98.

Wrangham RW, Chapman, CA, Clark-Acardi AP, Isabiyre-Basuta G. 1996. Social ecologyof Kanywara chimpanzees: implications for understanding the costs of great ape groups. In: MeGrew WC, Marchant LF, Nishida T. eds. *Great Ape Societies.* Cambridge: Cambridge University Press.

Yamagiwa J, Mwanza N, Yumoto T, Maruhashi T. 1991. Ant eating by eastern lowland gorillas. *Primates.* **32(2):** 247-253.

Yerkes RM. 1943. *Chimpanzees: A Laboratory Colony* New Haven: Yale University Press.

APPENDIX ONE   Foraging Behaviour Parameters for Great Apes: Dietary

Sub-Species		Study-Site	Population Density (n/km2)	Day Range (km)	Home Range (km2)	Foraging Party Size	No. Food Items	% Fruit in diet
Pongo		Tanjung	2.5	0.79	7.75	1.8	317	61
pygmaeus		Kutai	4	0.49	3.25	1.83	80	53.8
pygmaeus		Segama	1.5	0.5	4.5	1.83	111	52
Pongo		Ketambe	5	0.62	1.5	1.91	151	80.8
pygmaeus albelii		Ranun	1	0.55	3.85	1.8	60	62
Gorilla		Karisoke	1.1	0.75	9.4	10.5	75	1.7
gorilla		Kabara	2.5	0.47	22	16.9	49	6.1
beringei	High Altitude Gorillas	Virunga[3]	1	0.69	4-9.7	6.5	78	4
		Visoke	1	-	-	-	-	4
		Kayonza	0.5	0.5	16	8.75	-	10
		Kisoro	0.96	1.6	10.35	-	-	8
Gorilla		Tshia[r4]	0.55	-	-	-	-	-
gorilla		Kahuzi	0.4	0.9	31	17	95	10
graueri		Kahuzi-B[5]	0.35	1.05	14.75	7.3	129	15.5
		Utu	0.38	-	-	-	20	20
		Itebero	0.29	2.1	-	-	194	25
Gorilla	Low Altitude Gorillas	Rio Muni	0.7	1.13	6.75	-	141	38.3
gorilla		Lopé	0.2	1.172	8.1	5	221	45.5
gorilla		Likoula	2.2	0.94	31	-	-	-
		Bai Hokou	1.14	2.3	22.9	4.8	182	51
Pan		Wamba	2.35	2.4	58	13	170	59
paniscus		Lomako	2	7.6	22	3.5	113	54
		Lilungu	-	-	-	-	-	-
		Tumba	1.7	-	-	3.5	-	58
		Yalosidi	-	-	-	4	87	63
Pan		Gombe	2.6-6	3.1	6	4.5	167	59.4
troglodytes		Mahale	6	4.5	19	4.25	370	57.7
schweinfurthii		Kibale	1	4	18.6	3.6	113	78
		Budongo	3.4	7.5	32	4.4	118	90
		Filabanga	-	-	150	-	206	69
		Kahuzi	4.5	5.3	13.65	4.5	99	41
		Kaskati	-	-	145	-	-	35.7
		Ugalla	0.0075	10	515	-	-	-
Pan		Bossou	4.5	5.5	-	6	205	49
troglodytes		Mt. Assirik	0.09	6	228	3	72	57
verus		Tai Forest	-	5	27	6.55	-	-
		Sapo	0.24	-	9.7	-	-	-
Pan		Rio Muni	0.31	4	15	11.2	-	44.3
troglodytes		Lopé	1	-	-	-	174	61
troglodytes		Bai	-	-	-	-	114	88
		Belinga	-	-	-	-	50	78
		Ivindo	-	-	-	-	141	14.4

1 Plant parts in diet = sum of all plant parts in diet excluding bark and fruit.
2 % Rest = % time per active day (10h) neither feeding or travelling.
3 Virunga = data originally recorded as from non-specified Virunga Volcano sites.

Composition, Ranging, Activity Budget and Foraging Party Size.

% Plant parts in diet[1]	% Bark in diet	% Inverts in diet	% Arboreal	% Feed	% Travel	% Rest[2]	Study-Site	Sub-Species
24	11	4	>85	60	20	19	Tanjung	*Pongo*
31.22	14.2	0.8	>85	45.7	10.8	40.1	Kutai	*pygmaeus*
36	11.1	0.9	>85	32.5	16.7	51	Segama	*pygmaeus*
12.4	6.6	0.2	>90	49.3	12.2	38.5	Ketambe	*Pongo*
23.5	10.5	-	>90	33	15	52	Ranun	*p. albelii*
-	12.5	0.001	20	55.4	6.5	38.1	Karisoke	*Gorilla*
46	18	-	20	41	27.6	31.4	Kabara	*gorilla*
40	20	2	-	-	-	-	Virunga[3]	*beringei*
49	11	-	-	-	-	-	Visoke	
24	35	-	-	-	-	-	Kayonza	
50	13	-	-	-	-	-	Kisoro	
-	-	-	-	-	-	-	Tshia'[4]	*Gorilla*
20	25	-	25	-	-	-	Kahuzi	*gorilla*
18	42.3	-	-	45.5	9.4	45.1	Kahuzi-B[5]	*graueri*
55	5	-	-	-	-	-	Utu	
-	-	1	-	-	-	-	Itebero	
-	-	-	-	45	43		Rio Muni	*Gorilla*
7.5	20.2	1	-	21	39	40	Lopé	*gorilla*
-	-	-	-	-	-	-	Likoula	*gorilla*
10	12	1	58	60.2	13	26.8	Bai Hokou	
15	0	1.5	80	30	13	57	Wamba	*Pan*
12.4	0	0.9	94.6	40.4	16.1	43.5	Lomako	*paniscus*
-	-	-	-	-	-	-	Lilungu	
31	0	4	-	-	-	-	Tumba	
22	0	2	-	-	-	-	Yalosidi	
5	-	Up to 11.9	79.2	55.7	13.8	30.3	Gombe	*Pan*
19.8	-	6.4	-	-	-	-	Mahale	*troglodytes*
1	1.5	0.2	40	57	11	32	Kibale	*schweinfurthii*
2	2	1	-	-	-	-	Budongo	
-	-	-	-	-	-	-	Filabanga	
18	2	-	-	-	-	-	Kahuzi	
-	-	-	-	-	-	-	Kaskati	
-	-	-	-	-	-	-	Ugalla	
15	1	0.5	-	-	-	-	Bossou	*Pan*
15	-	5	7.5	48	35	17	Mt. Assirik	*troglodytes*
-	-	-	-	-	-	-	Tai Forest	*verus*
-	-	-	-	-	-	-	Sapo	
7.66	-	Up to 15.76	65	31	51	18	Rio Muni	*Pan*
14	2	7	-	-	-	-	Lopé	*troglodytes*
5	-	-	-	-	-	-	Bai	*troglodytes*
6	4	8	-	-	-	-	Belinga	
16.2	2.8	Up to 10.8	-	-	-	-	Ivindo	

4 Tshia' = data recorded from Mt. Tshiaberimu study site literature.
5 Kahuzi-B = data recorded from Kahuzi-Biega study site literature.
N.B. All original data sources, study site definitions and parameter definitions are recorded in Bean (1998).

APPENDIX TWO   Climatic Variables for Great Ape Study Sites.

Sub-Species	Study Site	Fig 3 I.D. No	Country	Rainfall (mm/ year)	Mean Alt. (m > sea level)	
Bornean orang-utan	Tanjung	-	Borneo	3000	30	
Pongo pygmaeus	Segama	-	Borneo	3810	870	
pygmaeus	Sepilok	-	Borneo	3962	152	
	Kutai	-	Borneo	2360	(125)	
Sumatran orang-utan	Ketambe	-	Sumatra	3229	675	
Pongo pygmaeus albelii	Ranun	-	Sumatra	3000	(1000)	
Mountain gorilla	Karisoke,	1	Rwanda	1800	3500	
Gorilla gorilla beringei	Virunga (general)	-	Rwanda/ Uganda	1700	3150	High Altitude Gorillas
	Kayonza	5	Uganda	(1750)	2058	
	Kisoro	3	Uganda	1676	2957	
	Kabara	2	Uganda	1750	1413	
Eastern lowland	Tshia'	4	Uganda	(1750)	2621	
gorilla	Kahuzi-B	6	Congo	1700	1954	
Gorilla gorilla	Mt. Kahuzi	-	Congo	1548	2384	
graueri	Iterbero	9	Congo	1700	950	
	Utu	7	Congo	2320	732	Low Altitude Gorillas
	Bwindi	8	Uganda	-	-	
Western lowland	Rio Muni	10	Eq. Guinea	2800	550	
gorilla	Likuoala	-	Congo	(1500)	325	
Gorilla gorilla	Belinga	11	Gabon	2000	850	
gorilla	Bai	14	C.A.R.	1500	350	
	Ndoki	15	Congo	-	-	
	Lopé	13	Gabon	1532	(375)	
Bonobo	Lomako	17	Congo	1960	390	
Pan paniscus	Wamba	16	Congo	2005	400	
	Yalosidi	18	Congo	(1400)	(125)	
	Tumba	20	Congo	1398	(125)	
	Lilungu	19	Congo	1653	(125)	
Eastern chimpanzee	Gombe	21	Tanzania	1600	1138	
Pan troglodytes	Mahale	22	Tanzania	1836	1649	
schweinfurthii	Ugalla	27	Tanzania	1012	1300	
	Kibale	23	Tanzania	1671	1508	
	Kasakati	26	Tanzania	-	-	
	Filabanga	25	Tanzania	-	-	
	Budongo	24	Uganda	1495	1097	
	Kahuzi-B	-	Congo	1700	1954	
Central chimpanzee	Lopé	34	Gabon	1532	(375)	
Pan t. troglodytes	Ivindo	32	Gabon	-	-	
	Rio Muni	33	Eq. Guinea	2800	550	
Western	Sapo	31	Liberia	(1850)	(250)	
chimpanzee	Tai	30	Ivory Coast	1829	203	
Pan t. verus	Bossou	28	R. Guinea	2500	600	
	Assirik	29	Senegal	954	(125)	

No. of months < 50mm rain-fall (approx.)	Temp. Range (°C)	Latitude	Longitude	Study Site	Sub-Species
0	18-37.5	0 3'S	112 E	Tanjung	Bornean orang-utan
0	22-32	5 3'N	117 E	Segama	*Pongo pygmaeus*
0	23-30	5 20'N	117 5'E	Sepilok	*pygmaeus*
0	19-30.5	0 24'N	117 16'E	Kutai	
0	17-34.2	3 40'N	97 40'E	Ketambe	Sumatran orang-utan
0	18-42	(2 49'N)	98 28'E	Ranun	*Pongo pygmaeus albelii*
3	3.8-14.8	1 S	30 E	Karisoke,	Mountain gorilla
3	0-21	0 03'S	29 15'E	Virunga (general)	*Gorilla gorilla beringei*
3	12-26	0 9'S	29 80'E	Kayonza	
2	4.5-17	1 36'S	29 42'E	Kisoro	
2	4-15	1 20'S	29 20'E	Kabara	
2	9-19.5	0 9'S	29 50'E	Tshia'	Eastern lowland
4	9.9-24.6	2 25'N	28 45'E	Kahuzi-B	gorilla
4	10.4-17.9	2 25'N	-	Mt. Kahuzi	*Gorilla gorilla*
4	10.4-17.9	2 25'N	29 80'E	Iterbero	*graueri*
0	20-30	1 12'N	28 45'E	Utu	
-	-	0 9'S		Bwindi	
3	15.5-33.3	1 55'N	10 30'E	Rio Muni	Western lowland
3	(19.4-32)	(0 25'S)	-	Likuoala	gorilla
3	19-31	1 N	13 20'E	Belinga	*Gorilla gorilla*
3	19.4-32.5	2 13'N	16 11'E	Bai	*gorilla*
-	-	2 20'N	16 19'E	Ndoki	
3	20.1-32.8	0 10'S	11 35'E	Lopé	
0	18.5-32	0 5'S	21 5'E	Lomako	Bonobo
0	12.7-31.4	0 2'N	22 50'E	Wamba	*Pan paniscus*
0	17.5-21.5	1 7'S	23 31'E	Yalosidi	
0	22-31	(0 5'S)	18 07'E	Tumba	
0	22.7-32.6	(1 10'S)	(23 16'E)	Lilungu	
6	19-28	4 40'S	29 39'E	Gombe	Eastern chimpanzee
5	18-27	6 7'S	29 44'E	Mahale	*Pan troglodytes*
8	(19-28)	5 43'S	31 10'E	Ugalla	*schweinfurthii*
0	10-31	0 27'N	30 19'E	Kibale	
-	-	5 23'S	29 55'E	Kasakati	
-	-	5 30'S	29 85'E	Filabanga	
2	28-34	1 43'N	31 27'E	Budongo	
3	9.9-24.6	2 25'N	28 45'E	Kahuzi-B	
3	20.1-32.8	0 10'S	11 35'E	Lopé	Central chimpanzee
-	-	0 02'S	12 13'E	Ivindo	*Pan t. troglodytes*
3	15.5-33.3	1 55'N	9 53'E	Rio Muni	
1	22-28	(6 N)	(7 37'W)	Sapo	Western
1	20-28	5 52'N	7 28'W	Tai	chimpanzee
5	(15.5-33)	7 39'N	8 30'W	Bossou	*Pan t. verus*
9	23-35	12 53'N	12 46'W	Assirik	

(x) = estimated from Pearce & Smith (1994) and Attica/WWF World Atlas (1996))

APPENDIX THREE — Summary of Great Ape Study Site Characteristics.

Sub-Species	Study Site	Country	Habitat Summary
Bornean orang-utan	Tanjung	Borneo	Rainforest, dipterocarp forest and peat-swamp forest
Pongo pygmaeus pygmaeus	Segama	Borneo	Primary dipterocarp forest. Almost continuous canopy. Hilly.
	Sepilok	Borneo	Primary forest, mangrove borders, low undulating county and hills.
	Kutai	Borneo	Lowland dipterocarp rainforest
Sumatran orang-utan *Pongo pygmaeus albelii*	Ketambe	Sumatra	Mixed tropical rainforest with high diversity of tree species, abundant ground covering vegetation and closed canopy in lower stratification
	Ranun	Sumatra	Tropical rainforest, hilly and lowland
Mountain gorilla *Gorilla gorilla beringi*	Karisoke, Mt. Visoke (Virunga Volcanoes)	Rwanda	Montane rainforest with open canopy and woodland with dense herb layer. Lush dense undergrowth.
	Other Virunga Volcano Sites	D.R.C./ Rwanda-Uganda	Volcanic mountain range. Montane forest in continuous strip along mountain chain.
	Kayonza	D.R.C.-Uganda	Rugged mountain area covered with forest. Steep and undulating terrain.
	Kisoro	Uganda	Rocky terrain consisting of montane woodland, bamboo, sedge grass meadow with discontinuous canopy and open slopes
	Kabara	Uganda	Meadow land broken by outcrops of rocks and forest. Dry colonising woodland, bamboo and open woodland
Eastern lowland gorilla *Gorilla gorilla graueri*	Tshia'	Uganda	Lower slopes of rift valley are dry, barren covered with bracken, fern, grass and open woodland. Southern hills covered with bamboo. Forest tract and isolated patches
	Kahuzi-B	D.R.C.-	Many hills covered with various sub-types of montane forest. Large swamp areas
	Iterbero	D.R.C.-	Extension of Kahuzi-Biega. Tropical forest, including primary and secondary and abandoned cultivated fields
	Mt. Kahuzi	D.R.C.-	From east to west sclerophyllus plants give way to secondary forest and primary mountain forest and a wide bamboo zone
	Utu	D.R.C.-	Lowland rainforest. Steep terrain. Secondary forest in various stages of regeneration and primary forest
Western lowland gorilla *Gorilla gorilla gorilla*	Rio Muni	Rep. Of Equatorial Guinea	Forests confined to areas of difficult terrain such as river areas and mountainous regions. Forest canopy is uneven and nearly closed. Secondary and regenerating forests in various stages of development and are non-uniform

	Likuoala	D.R.C.-	Permanently saturated swamps with small areas of flooded forest and savannah vegetation. Forests have closed canopy and seasonally saturated soils. Terre firma covered with semi-deciduous forest cover
	Belinga	Gabon	Primary forest covers 95% study area. Small areas of secondary forest
	Bai	C.A.R.	Primary rainforest, Semi-deciduous rainforest and large swamp with swamp vegetation, marshy grassland, sparse undergrowth and mixed species forest
	Lopé	Gabon	Intact lowland rainforest. Mature and secondary forest. 30% savannah

Sub-Species	Study Site	Country	Habitat Summary
Bonobo *Pan paniscus*	Lomako	D.R.C.-	Low elevation forest, predominantly primary, climax, evergreen, polyspecific. Smaller areas of secondary forest and slope, stream, river and swamp
	Wamba	D.R.C.-	Primary forest dominates area, swamp forest is extensive, aged secondary forest, young secondary forest and open land lying in fallow and secondary shrub
	Yalosidi	D.R.C.-	Dryer evergreen forest with tall semi-deciduous trees. Much variation in vegetation due to human activity and tributaries. Swamp forest, primary forest, young secondary forest, oil-palm forest, aged secondary forest and swamp grassland
	Tumba	D.R.C.-	Forest bounded by lake and swamp. Terra firma forests are semi-deciduous, but climax evergreen forests run along edges.
	Lilungu	D.R.C.-	Primary forest, aged secondary forest, young secondary forest and secondary shrub
Eastern chimpanzee *Pan troglodytes schweinfurthii*	Gombe	Tanzania	Evergreen riverine forest, deciduous dry forest, thicket, woodland and grassland moorland. Countyside broken up by thickly forested valleys. Open woodlands cover upper slopes. Vegetation not diverse
	Mahale	Tanzania	Mountainous terrain. Woodland, savannah, bush, colonising forest and climax forest. 80% semi-deciduous. Closed forest with vine tangles and much forest floor cover
	Ugalla	Tanzania	Dry and sparsely wooded. Swamp forms boundary. Area covered in sparse riverine forest

	Kibale	Uganda	Medium altitude tropical rainforest. Undulating terrain, mid altitude mosaic and secondary forest. Tall grassland, swamps and softwood plantations
	Budongo	Uganda	Tropical rainforest. Forest is solid mass. Terrain is undulating. Rattan swamp. Forest is woodland, mixed and Iron wood
	Kahuzi-B	D.R.C. -	Many hills covered with various sub-types of montane forest. Large swamp areas
Central chimpanzee	Lopé	Gabon	Intact lowland rainforest. Mature and secondary forest. 30% savannah
Pan troglodytes troglodytes	Rio Muni	Rep. Of Equatorial Guinea	Forests confined to areas of difficult terrain such as river areas and mountainous regions. Forest canopy is uneven and nearly closed. Secondary and regenerating forests in various stages of development and are non-uniform
Western chimpanzee	Sapo	Liberia	Primary evergreen forest with secondary growth from past areas of agriculture. Areas of swamp
Pan troglodytes verus	Tai	Ivory Coast	Tropical evergreen rainforest
	Bossou	Rep. Of Guinea	Mostly secondary forest of various stages which was abandoned after shifting cultivation. Limited primary forest and grassland
	Assirik	Senegal	Smooth surface plateaus and valleys. Vegetation is hetergenous Sudanian savannah woodland, dominated by grasses, from short-grass plateau to deciduous woodland with grass understory. Small strips of gallery forest is <3%

APPENDIX FOUR Dendrogram Describing the Clustering Procedure of Great Ape Foraging
Strategy   (Using average linking – Between Groups).

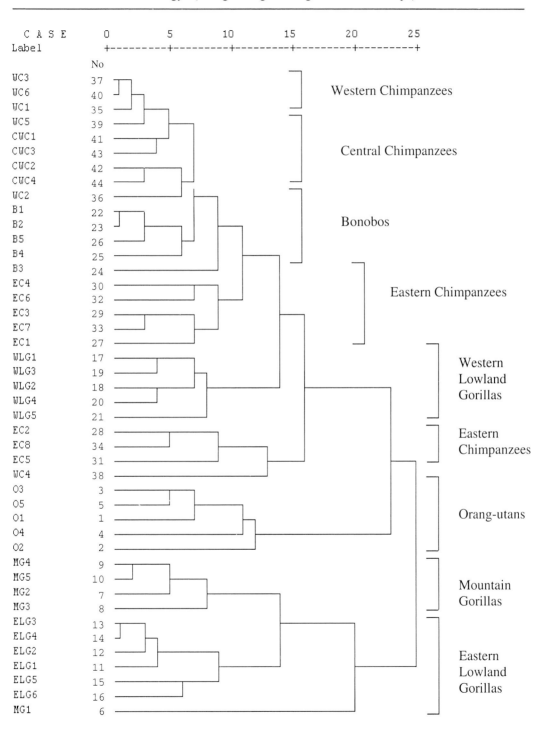

CHAPTER THIRTEEN

Ranging patterns of male chimpanzees in the Budongo Forest, Uganda: range structure and individual differences

N. E. NEWTON-FISHER

Introduction

Despite spending much of their time in small parties of variable composition, individual chimpanzees *Pan troglodytes* Blumenbach, are members of a 'community' who share a common home range (Goodall, 1973, 1986; Wrangham, 1986; Nishida & Hiraiwa-Hasegawa, 1987). Within the community, relationships between males are generally affiliative, whereas relationships between males of neighbouring groups are often intensely hostile (Goodall *et al.*, 1979; Nishida, 1979). The shared community home range is used differently by males and females: female chimpanzees spend the majority of their time within restricted, non-exclusive and extensively overlapping, 'core' areas, while males range more widely (Wrangham, 1977, 1979; Wrangham & Smuts, 1980).

From these observations and theoretical considerations, a model of chimpanzee sociality has emerged in which female 'core' areas, spread through the community range, function as dispersed foraging areas. The size of female 'core' areas prevents a single male from defending access to one or more females (Wrangham, 1979; Mitani & Rodman, 1979; Dunbar, 1988), and so males of one community co-operate to defend access to females against males in neighbouring communities. In doing so, they range fairly evenly across the female 'core' areas within their community range (Wrangham, 1975, 1986). Models of male reproductive strategies (Dunbar, 1988) support the notion that males search for reproductively active, or cycling, females at random throughout their shared range; foraging and defending the community territory in the process.

Further observations suggest, however, that this currently accepted model (Wrangham, 1975, 1979) is an incomplete explanation of male chimpanzee ranging patterns, and thus their reproductive strategies. The idea that males range fairly evenly across the community range rests on the assumption that males form parties for co-operative range defence. This should require relatively *large* parties (Wrangham, 1977). However, it seems that chimpanzee males preferentially form *small* parties with particular individuals (Newton-Fisher, 1997; 1999), in order to pursue the relationships so important to their reproductive success (Wrangham, 1986; Nishida & Hiraiwa-Hasegawa, 1987). The majority of a male's time is, therefore, spent moving about his home range, forming parties with these preferred individuals. Such behaviour is likely to lead to differential use of the home range, so producing observable range 'structure'. As partner preferences vary from one male to another (for example: Halperin, 1979; Goodall, 1986; Newton-Fisher, 1999), preferential associations should also lead to individual differences in range structure.

Such differences have been reported. Males of the Kasakela (Gombe) community were found not to use their community home range evenly, using only 40-60% of the area for 80% of their time (Wrangham & Smuts, 1980). These 'core' areas were similar to those identified for females, evenly distributed over the community range and almost completely overlapping, although larger on average (Wrangham, 1977, 1979; Wrangham & Smuts, 1980). In the Kibale Forest, although males of the Kanyawara community ranged more widely than females, no evidence of a sex difference was found in patterns of range use: both sexes showed a 'clumped' pattern, suggestive of 'core' areas (Chapman & Wrangham, 1993).

Although these observations indicate that male chimpanzees, in both forest and savannah-woodland habitats, have structured home-ranges, the ranging behaviour of males has received less attention than that of females and remains poorly understood. Wrangham's (1975) original model neither predicted nor precluded male 'core' areas, assuming, in the absence of detailed data, no differences between males in their ranging patterns (Wrangham, 1977, 1979). The generality of male 'core' areas has not been assessed, no functional explanation for their existence has yet been made, and no attempt has been made to explain why male ranging patterns might deviate from the expectations of the currently accepted model of chimpanzee sociality. Furthermore, the implications of restricted ranging for male mating strategies have yet to be examined.

This study provides a detailed investigation into the ranging patterns of adult male chimpanzees *(P. t. schweinfurthii)* in the Budongo Forest, Uganda. In particular, the structure of male ranges is examined, and assumptions concerning male ranging behaviour underlying the Wrangham model are tested.

Methods

Study site

The Budongo Forest Reserve is 792 km² of forest and grassland in western Uganda (1° 37′ – 2° 00' N, 31° 22′ – 31° 46' E), of which 428 km² is moist semi-deciduous tropical forest. Much of the forest has been selectively logged since about 1910, and can be divided into four main forest types: *Cynometra* forest, mixed forest, colonising woodland and swamp forest (Eggeling, 1947; Synnott, 1985; Plumptre, 1996). These forest types can be further subdivided to reflect variation in chimpanzee food supply (Newton-Fisher, 1997).

Observations of the study community were made between August 1994 and December 1995 in the Sonso region (1° 44′ N, 31° 33′ E), which lies within the heart of the forest. This study site, including a system of trails allowing rapid access through the forest, was set up and maintained by the Budongo Forest Project (Reynolds, 1992; Plumptre, Reynolds & Bakuneeta, 1997). From October 1994, the chimpanzees were sufficiently habituated to be observed at close quarters on the ground and individually recognisable. Individuals were named and assigned a two-letter identification code. Ranging patterns of all twelve adult males (MG, KK, MA, BY, MU, NJ, TK, DN, VN, JM, BK, CH) are analysed here. For more details of the study site and community, see Newton-Fisher (1997).

Data collection

Individual males were targeted as focal for 30 minute periods, during which behavioural and association data were collected by focal animal and instantaneous scan sampling (Altmann, 1974). The location of the focal male, and that of other party members, was recorded in relation to the mapped trail system at 15 minute intervals as paced distances along east-west and north-south compass bearings. Distances were collapsed to 25 m^2 blocks to avoid spurious levels of accuracy. The co-ordinates of these blocks, taken from a regular grid superimposed on a map of the study area, were the locations used for analysis.

Definitions and analysis techniques

Analyses of ranging behaviour have been hampered by problems with both defining and measuring an animal's range. *Range* is most easily defined as the total area used over a specified time period, while *home range* is that fraction of the *range* 'habitually used'. This is a succinct summary of the generally accepted (Seaman & Powell, 1996) definition: *"...that area traversed by the individual in its normal activities ... Occasional sallies outside the area, should not be considered as part of the home range"* (Burt, 1943). Although no objective method exists to define 'habitual' (Clutton-Brock, 1975), the *home* range can be defined as *"the smallest sub-region which accounts for a specified proportion of its total utilisation"* (Jenrich & Turner, 1969), usually the area enclosing 95% of fixes (Cresswell & Harris, 1988; Harris *et al.*, 1990) to exclude Burt's (1943) *"occasional sallies"*. A range thus defined will be that habitually used.

For many species, measuring the range over any extended period of time is impossible. Instead, the observed sample of locations is used to estimate the total 'utilisation distribution' (*"two dimensional relative frequency distribution for the points of location of an animal over a period of time"*: van Winkle, 1975) which describes the relative amounts of time an animal spends in any place. The result is a range model which specifies the probability of an animal being within a particular area (Seaman & Powell, 1996).

For the model to provide valid estimates, it is important that a sufficiently large sample of locations is used, and that consecutive locations show minimal temporal autocorrelation; location of an animal at time Y is independent of its location at time X (Swihart & Slade, 1985; Harris *et al.*, 1990). The time interval between successive observations must, therefore, be sufficient for an animal to move from any location within the range to any other. When sufficient samples have been taken, a cumulative plot of observed locations against estimated home range area reaches an asymptote such that further sampling does not significantly alter the estimate (Harris *et al.*, 1990).

Three analysis techniques provided by the RANGES V software package (Kenward & Hodder, 1996) were used to examine ranging patterns: minimum convex polygons, cluster analysis and kernel analysis. Each technique uses a different algorithm to estimate range area, and each has particular strengths and weaknesses.

A minimum convex polygon (MCP) is the smallest area polygon to encompass all of an animal's locations. It is the only method directly comparable between studies (Harris *et al.*, 1990), producing an empirical estimate of range size, but is biased by peripheral locations and does not provide information about range 'structure'. Hierarchical cluster analysis (CST) is a non-parametric technique particularly appropriate for identifying range structure (Kenward, 1987). The required percentage of locations are grouped into clusters, around which convex polygons are drawn. Including 100% of locations produces an identical estimate to MCP.

Kernel analysis (Worton, 1989) is the most accurate technique currently available (Seaman & Powell, 1996). This uses the non-parametric kernel density estimator (Silverman, 1986), to model the utilisation distribution. Each observation point is replaced by a kernel with a density corresponding to the amount of time spent at each location. A regular rectangular grid (unrelated to that used to record the observations) is superimposed, and for each grid intersection an estimate of density (time spent) is obtained. Observation points close to a grid intersection contribute more to this estimate than those far away. In essence, the density estimate at an intersection is a weighted average of the densities of all kernels which overlap that intersection (Seaman & Powell, 1996).

The width of the kernel, the 'smoothing parameter', determines the influence that more distant points have on the density estimate at each location. Wide kernels produce a model which emphasises the general shape of the distribution. Narrow kernels produce a model which emphasises structure (Seaman & Powell, 1996; Kenward & Hodder, 1996). During analysis the smoothing parameter is applied in one of three ways: *fixed* (smoothing is the same for all areas), *adaptive* (more smoothing for low density areas, less for high density areas), or *inverse adaptive* (Worton, 1989; Seaman & Powell, 1996; Kenward & Hodder, 1996). The value of the smoothing parameter can be determined objectively by 'least squares cross validation' (LSCV: Silverman, 1986; Worton, 1989).

In the investigation of 'core' areas, cluster analysis tends to emphasise subtle differences and so produce multinuclear 'core' areas, whereas kernel analysis tends to regard these differences as less important, and so produce mononuclear 'cores' (Figure 1).

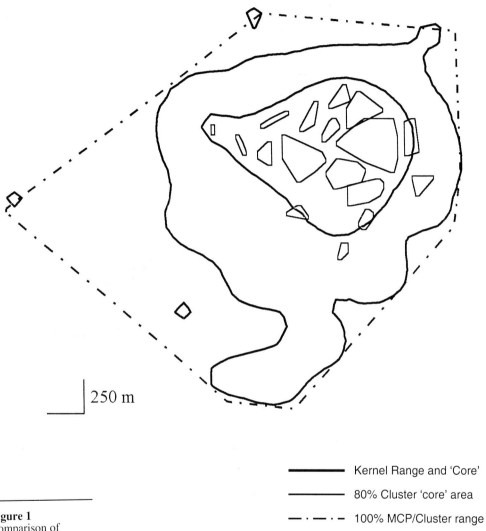

Kernel Range and 'Core'

80% Cluster 'core' area

— · — · — 100% MCP/Cluster range

250 m

Figure 1
Comparison of analysis techniques. Fixed kernel, MCP and cluster analysis estimates of range, and 80% 'core' area, are shown for the same data-set. Data are 250 locations for the adult male chimpanzee DN collected over 15 months.

Analysis conducted

MCPs were constructed to provide initial estimates of range areas, comparable across studies. Kernel analyses, both fixed (KNF) and adaptive (KNA) methods implementing least squares cross validation, were used to provide more accurate estimates of range area and details of range structure. Cluster analysis was conducted particularly to provide details of range structure. Spearman rank correlations were calculated to determine whether estimated range area was independent of the number of locations for each male, and incremental area analysis (Kenward & Hodder, 1996) was used to determine whether range areas reached asymptotes and were thus good estimates of home range.

The time interval necessary to minimise temporal autocorrelation between fixes was calculated by comparing a maximum range area for two wide ranging males with an average travel speed for chimpanzees. Day-range length was not recorded, and therefore travel speed was calculated from data presented by Wrangham (1977) as 2.95 km h^{-1}. This was close to the 3.07 km h^{-1} calculated by K. Hunt (*pers. comm.*). This was not a theoretical straight-line speed of travel, which would have been unlikely to minimise autocorrelation (see: Harris *et al.,* 1990), but took account of the intermittent nature of chimpanzee travel. An interval of between two and four hours between successive locations provided sufficient time for an individual to be capable of travelling from any one location within the range to any other, while pursuing typical foraging, socialising and travel patterns. Purposeful, direct travel, such as shown by chimpanzees travelling to a distant food tree or to reach the scene of a hunt (*pers. obs.*) would have enabled chimpanzees to reach other locations far more rapidly, but such travel was rare, and was only considered to the extent that it influenced average daily travel distances across seasons. For each adult male, a data set of locations separated by at least four hours was extracted from the location records, including only those records when the subject was focal, or first sighted after an interval of over four hours.

For each male, home range area and structure were determined for the period October 1994 to December 1995. To produce estimates of community home range size and structure, individual male's data sets were merged, excluding all same-time, same-location records. A habitat map was constructed using point-sampled forest-type data (Newton-Fisher, 1997) and used to calculate the habitat composition of each male's home range. To determine the degree to which members of each dyad used the same area, 'dynamic interaction analysis' (which compares observed same-time locations with possible distances between dyads [Macdonald, Ball & Hough, 1980; Kenward, Marcstrom & Karlbom, 1993]), was used to determine the tendency of individuals to be in the same part of the forest on the same day. The difference between observed and predicted locations was expressed as indices calculated using median, and geometric mean, distances (Kenward & Hoddar, 1996).

Utilisation plots, the percentage of fixes included in the analysis against the estimate of range area, were used to investigate whether distinct 'core' areas, as indicated by discontinuities in the plots, could be distinguished. Wrangham and Smuts (1980) defined 'core' areas, for both males and females, as the area in which an individual spent 80% of its time (see also, Wrangham, 1979). For probabilistic analysis techniques this corresponds to 80% of the utilisation distribution; the areas where there was an 80% probability of locating the individual at any particular time. The size, location, overlap and habitat composition was determined for these 80% 'core' areas. To test whether males showed individual differences in their use of the community range, and thereby deviated from Wrangham's (1975) model, overlaps between 80% 'core' areas were compared to a set of overlaps generated at random from a uniform 95% to 100% distribution, reflecting the 'almost complete' overlap specified by the model.

A second assumption of the Wrangham model is that males co-operate in the defence of the community range. However, alpha males are expected to benefit disproportionately from group defence of female 'core' areas (Tutin, 1979; Nishida, 1983; Newton-Fisher, 1997), and lower status males may, as a result, withhold their co-operation (Bygott, 1979). Chapman and Wrangham (1993) found dominant males of the Kanyawara (Kibale) community had larger home range areas than subordinate males. If subordinate males participate less frequently in 'border patrols', they should have significantly smaller estimates of range area size, whereas males who assist in range defence should have range area estimates which do not differ significantly in size from that estimated for the community range. To test this, social status for males of the Sonso community was determined using a method which combined directions of dominant and subordinate dyadic interactions (Newton-Fisher, 1997), and analyses were conducted to determine the influence of social status on the size of home ranges, and on the size and overlap of 80% 'core' areas.

If association patterns are at least partly responsible for producing structure in male ranges, then this influence should be detectable. The degree of overlap between 'core' areas should correlate positively with the tendency to associate derived from observed party compositions (dyadic association strength: Newton-Fisher, 1997; 1999). However, while chimpanzees using the same areas have the opportunity to associate and interact, they do not necessarily do so. If association partners were selected simply from those ranging nearby or recently encountered, the dynamic interaction index and the index of association (dyadic association strength) should be positively correlated, whereas if individuals seek out desired association partners there should be no relationship between the two measures. These relationships were investigated using matrix correlation permutation tests, with 5000 permutations (Hemelrijk, 1990; Adams & Anthony, 1996).

Results

Male locations were recorded by 5158 instantaneous samples over 15 months (monthly mean = 343.87 ± 104.05). Of these, subsets averaging 190 locations per male (see Table 1) were used for analysis of ranging patterns. Insufficient data remained after independence criteria were applied to investigate temporal shifts in range patterns, and all analyses were conducted for the entire 15-month data set.

Home range

Estimates of the community home range area varied from 6.78 km^2 to 14.51 km^2 (Table 1; Figure 2), depending on the analysis technique. Observations of patrolling behaviour in the areas indicated as north-east and south-west boundaries, and of unhabituated chimpanzees in the north-east, suggested these boundaries were accurate. However, study animals were occasionally sighted beyond the area in which they were systematically sampled and focal animals were lost when travelling through forest beyond the trail system, particularly in the south-east.

Table 1 Estimates of community (all males considered together) and individual male home ranges, using four analysis techniques: Minimum convex polygons (MCP); Fixed kernels with least squares cross validation (KNF); Adaptive kernels with least squares cross validation (KNA); Cluster analysis (CST). Range estimates based on 100% location inclusion.

Home Range Areas: Size (km²) & Percentage of total (%)									
		MCP		**KNF**		**KNA**		**CST**	
Individual	n	km²	%	km²	%	km²	%	km²	%
All Males	836	6.78	100.0	6.89	100.0	14.51	100.0	6.78	100.0
DN	250	5.89	86.9	4.27	62.0	9.17	63.2	5.89	86.9
VN	242	5.63	83.0	4.52	65.6	12.85	88.6	5.63	83.0
BK	161	5.40	79.6	1.84	26.7	5.69	39.2	5.40	79.6
MG	204	4.57	67.4	4.29	62.2	10.87	74.9	4.57	67.4
MA	238	4.87	71.8	4.36	63.3	8.54	58.9	4.87	71.8
CH	171	5.03	74.2	3.92	56.9	10.69	73.7	5.03	74.2
JM	111	5.16	76.1	4.70	68.2	10.95	75.5	5.16	76.1
BY	182	4.90	72.3	4.89	71.1	13.16	90.7	4.90	72.3
KK	198	4.23	62.4	3.04	44.1	8.76	60.4	4.23	62.4
NJ	173	5.41	79.8	3.45	50.1	7.29	50.2	5.41	79.8
MU	211	3.83	56.5	3.51	51.0	8.27	57.0	3.83	56.5
TK	160	3.17	46.8	1.07	15.5	5.02	34.6	3.17	46.8

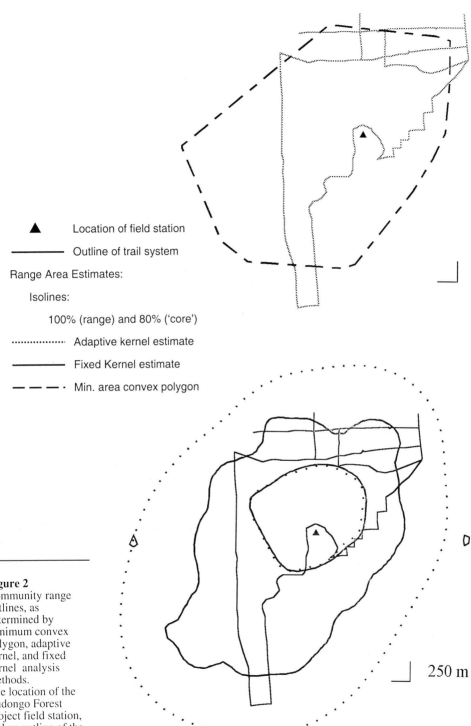

▲   Location of field station

———   Outline of trail system

Range Area Estimates:

    Isolines:

        100% (range) and 80% ('core')

··············   Adaptive kernel estimate

———   Fixed Kernel estimate

— — —   Min. area convex polygon

250 m

Figure 2
Community range
outlines, as
determined by
minimum convex
polygon, adaptive
kernel, and fixed
kernel analysis
methods.
The location of the
Budongo Forest
Project field station,
and an outline of the
trail system are
shown for reference.

This region was separated from the rest by thick swamp forest and the Sonso River, making it difficult to search for, or to follow chimpanzees. As a result, the area enclosing 100% (rather than 95%) of fixes was considered to be the home range. The community range area approached an asymptote after around 350 fixes. MCP/cluster and fixed kernel analyses produced similar estimates, suggesting that 7 km^2 represents community *home* range size. The high estimate produced by the adaptive kernel method may be closer to the size of the *total* range.

The ranges of individual males varied in size (Table 1), although this was not correlated with the number of observations (MCP/CST: $r_s = 0.21$, n = 12, $p > 0.20$; KNF: $r_s = 0.29$, n = 12, $p > 0.50$; KNA: $r_s = 0.24$, n = 12, $p > 0.50$). For nine of the twelve males, range estimates tended to reach asymptotes between 110 and 160 fixes. For one male (CH), the existence of an asymptote was questionable, and range estimates for two males (NJ & JM) did not reach asymptotes. There were no significant differences in habitat composition between male home ranges (100% KNF range: $\chi^2 = 11.25$, $df = 154$, ns; 100% CST range: $\chi^2 = 5.24$, $df = 154$, ns).

Male chimpanzees of the Sonso community were usually found in the same parts of the community range on the same day, regardless of whether they were in association (in the same party), although the extent of this varied between dyads (Table 2). Subjectively, it seemed that at different times, particular parts of the range would be used more heavily with travelling parties consistently heading for the same areas over a period of days or weeks. Two or three parties within a few hundred metres of one another would remain in contact through pant-hoot vocalisation choruses.

Range structure

Male chimpanzees did not range evenly over the community range, but spent the majority of their time within a relatively small area. Slight discontinuities were apparent between 70% and 95% of fixes in utilisation plots constructed for each male, but these were not sufficiently distinct to identify 'core' areas. What was clear, however, was that sub-regions of each male's home range, and thus the community range, were used disproportionately. Male chimpanzees of the Sonso community spent 80% of their time in a restricted area of the community home range, and in *this* sense could be said to have 'core' areas (Table 3).

Kernel analysis produced mononuclear 'cores' which averaged 32% (KNF) of individual home ranges. This compares to the 40-60% reported for Kasakela males and females (Wrangham & Smuts, 1980). Cluster analysis produced smaller, multinuclear, 80% 'core' areas, averaging only 7% of individual home ranges (Figure 3). These 80% 'core' areas did not differ significantly in habitat composition (80% KNF 'cores': $\chi^2 = 10.02$, $df = 154$, ns; 80% CST 'cores': $\chi^2 = 46.02$, $df = 154$, ns).

Table 2 Dynamic interaction indices, assessed by median (above diagonal) and geometric mean (below diagonal) distances. For each dyad *n* observed 'same time' distances are compared to *n* x *n* possible distances (individual 2 at any of its *n* used positions when individual 1 at each of its used locations). Index varies from +1 (observed distances small relative to possible distances) to -1 (observed distances relatively large). The high positive values indicate that individuals tended to be in the same areas on the same days.

Dynamic interaction indices

	DN	VN	BK	MG	MA	CH	JM	BY	KK	NJ	MU	TK
DN	x	0.97	0.95	0.00	0.76	0.84	0.91	0.82	0.11	0.89	0.89	0.88
VN	0.47	x	0.87	0.00	0.99	0.98	0.97	-0.13	0.00	0.96	0.91	0.92
BK	0.96	0.88	x	-	0.00	0.97	0.88	-	-	1.00	-	0.71
MG	0.00	V0.00	-	x	0.96	-	-	0.87	0.88	1.00	0.89	0.34
MA	0.96	0.98	-	0.99	x	-	0.90	0.97	0.95	0.96	0.90	0.96
CH	0.87	0.98	0.89	-	-	x	0.98	-	-	-	-	0.00
JM	0.98	0.93	0.91	-	0.00	0.99	x	-	-	0.81	0.00	0.96
BY	0.88	-0.99	-	0.97	0.53	-	-	x	0.98	0.98	0.89	0.93
KK	0.73	0.00	-	0.64	0.67	-	-	0.68	x	0.79	0.68	0.61
NJ	0.96	0.98	1.00	1.00	0.98	-	0.97	0.99	0.91	x	0.81	0.89
MU	0.95	0.88	-	0.99	0.95	-	0.00	0.66	0.88	0.74	x	0.88
TK	0.62	0.96	0.93	0.05	0.91	0.00	0.96	0.98	0.40	0.91	0.93	x

Table 3 Estimates of 80% 'core' areas; community (all males) and individual males, using four analysis techniques: Minimum convex polygons (MCP); Fixed kernels (KNF) and Adaptive kernels (KNA), both with least squares cross validation; Cluster analysis (CST). Size in km^2, and 'core' as a percentage of both the respective home range (%$_{HR}$), and of the total (community) range (%$_{CR}$).

'Core' Areas: size, % of individual's home range (%$_{HR}$) & of community range (%$_{CR}$)

	MCP			KNF			KNA			CST		
	km^2	%$_{HR}$	%$_{CR}$	km^2	%$_{HR}$	%$_{CR}$	km^2	%$_{HR}$	%$_{CR}$	km^2	%$_{HR}$	%$_{CR}$
All	1.23	18.1	18.1	1.48	21.5	21.5	1.39	9.6	9.6	1.36	20.1	20.1
DN	1.27	21.6	18.7	1.19	27.9	17.3	1.22	13.3	8.4	0.44	7.5	6.5
VN	1.41	25.0	21.0	1.07	23.7	15.5	1.12	8.7	7.7	0.31	5.5	4.6
BK	1.02	18.9	15.0	0.85	46.2	12.3	1.02	17.9	7.0	0.27	5.0	4.0
MG	1.01	22.1	14.9	1.18	27.5	17.1	1.13	10.4	7.8	0.33	7.2	4.9
MA	1.15	23.6	17.0	1.19	27.3	17.3	1.12	13.1	7.7	0.31	6.4	4.6
CH	0.98	19.5	14.5	1.12	28.6	16.3	1.23	11.5	8.5	0.29	5.8	4.3
JM	1.06	20.5	15.6	1.41	30.0	20.5	1.59	14.5	11.0	0.23	4.6	3.4
BY	1.02	20.8	15.0	1.18	24.1	17.1	1.23	9.3	8.5	0.34	6.9	5.0
KK	0.96	22.7	14.2	0.99	32.6	14.4	1.02	11.6	7.0	0.24	5.7	3.5
NJ	1.00	18.5	14.7	1.25	36.2	18.1	1.20	16.5	8.3	0.31	5.7	4.6
MU	1.12	29.2	16.5	1.06	30.2	15.4	1.05	12.7	7.2	0.34	8.8	5.0
TK	0.82	25.9	12.1	0.48	44.9	7.0	0.96	19.1	6.6	0.26	8.2	3.8

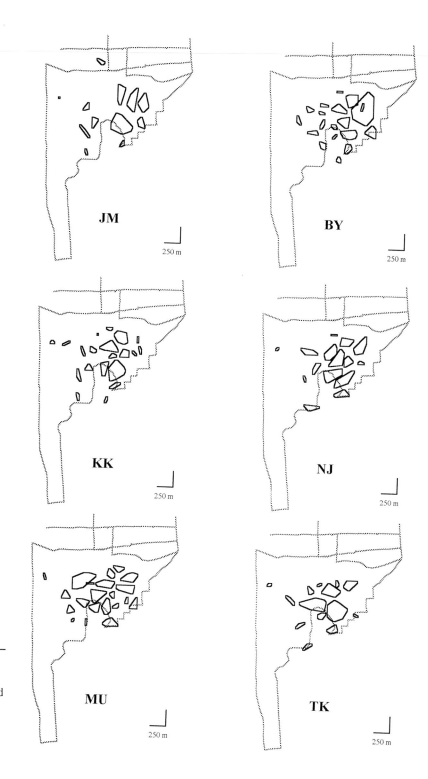

Figure 3
Individual 80% 'core' areas produced by cluster analysis, for all 12 study animals. 80% isopleths plotted against an outline of the trail system (*cf.* Figure 2).

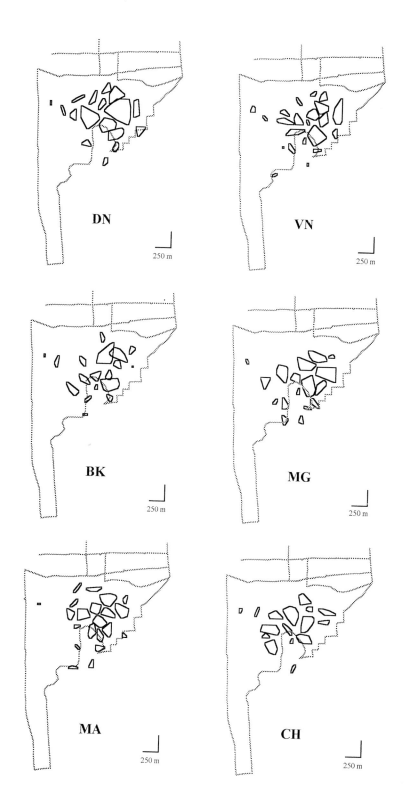

The 80% 'core' areas were geographically distinct, with pairs of 'core' areas only partially overlapping. Percentage overlaps between 'core' areas varied widely between dyads (KNF: range = 32% to 100%, median = 87.5%; CST: range = 31% to 72%, median = 49.8%). This suggested that the ranging behaviour of these males did not appear to fit the assumptions of Wrangham's (1975, 1979) model. The median degree of overlap between male 'core' areas was significantly lower than 95-100%, whether 'cores' were determined by kernel analysis ($U = 1584.5$, $n_1 = 132$, $n_2 = 132$, $p < 0.0001$) or cluster analysis ($U = 0.0$, $n_1 = 132$, $n_2 = 132$, $p < 0.0001$). Cluster analysis produced 'core' areas which overlapped significantly less than those determined by kernel analysis ($U = 1298.5$, $n_1 = 132$, $n_2 = 132$, $p < 0.0001$).

Social status and range structure

Social status appeared to have only minimal effects on the size of male home-ranges and 80% 'core' areas. Home-range size, estimated by either MCP or cluster analysis, was positively correlated with social status ($r_s = 0.74$, n = 12, $p = 0.006$), although estimates produced by kernel analysis were not (KNF: $r_s = 0.38$, $p > 0.50$; KNA: $r_s = 0.61$, $p > 0.50$). MCP estimates are heavily influenced by outlying points, and the significant correlation may indicate that high status males ranged, albeit infrequently, more widely than those of lower status. The size of 80% 'core' areas was not significantly correlated with social status (KNF 'cores': $r_s = 0.22$, n = 12, $p = 0.50$; KNA 'cores': $r_s = 0.24$, n = 12, $p = 0.45$; CST 'cores': $r_s = 0.26$, n = 12, $p = 0.41$). Social status did not significantly influence the overlap of 'core' areas (CST 'cores': $K_r = 165$, $t = 0.25$, n = 12, $p_r = 0.11$; KNF 'cores': $K_r = 53$, $t = 0.08$, n = 12, $p_r = 0.35$).

Association patterns and range structure

The structure of males' ranges appeared to be influenced by association patterns. Overlaps between 80% 'core' areas determined by cluster analysis were significantly and positively correlated with dyadic association strength ($K_r = 315$, $t = 0.49$, n = 12, $p_r = 0.001$) However, overlaps between 80% 'core' areas determined by kernel analysis were not correlated with dyadic association strength ($K_r = 101$, $t = 0.16$, n = 12, $p_r = 0.18$). Differences between male 'core' areas may therefore have been subtle; emphasised by cluster analysis, but potentially masked by the 'smoothing' of kernel analysis. Indices of dynamic interaction were not correlated with dyadic association strength [indices (median distances): $K_r = 37$, $t = 0.06$, n = 12, $p_r = 0.24$; indices (geometric mean distances): $K_r = -8$, $t = -0.01$, n = 12, $p_l = 0.44$]. Although a lack of correlation is only weak support for the hypothesis, this result suggests that males were not simply associating with those whose ranging behaviour happened to make them available as potential social partners, but that they were seeking out desired social partners.

Sonso males have been described as pursuing either *intense* or *gregarious* association strategies (Newton-Fisher, 1999). *Gregarious* strategists divided their association time fairly evenly across the other males in the community, whereas *intense* strategists concentrated on associating with a few, particular, individuals. The strategy pursued did not influence the size of either the individual's home range or 80% 'core' area (CST ranges $U = 14$, ns; CST 'cores'; $U = 8.5$, ns, KNF range $U = 8$, ns; KNF 'cores' $U = 15$, ns; n = 6,5). However, the results of cluster analysis, although not kernel analysis, suggest that the overlap between 80% 'core' areas was related to association strategy. Males identified as *intense* social strategists had 80% 'core' areas which overlapped a larger percentage of other males' 'core' areas than did the 80% 'core' areas of males pursuing a *gregarious* strategy (CST: $U = 853.0$, $n_{intense} = 66$, $n_{gregarious} = 55$, $p < 0.0001$; KNF: $U = 1686.0$, ns; 11 'core' area overlaps per male).

Discussion

Community home range

The Sonso community lives in an area of secondary forest, which is a mosaic of different forest types. The size of the community home range falls at the low end of estimates for other communities (cf. Wrangham, 1986; Table 16.1), with all but the adaptive kernel method estimating a community home range of around 7 km².

However, many of the figures for chimpanzee home ranges may be overestimates. Commonly, range area is estimated using the grid-square technique. For example, the home range of the Kasakela (Gombe) chimpanzees was estimated at 13 km² using 500 x 500 metre grid squares, while that of the Kanyawara chimpanzees was estimated at 8-9 km² using a 200 x 200 metre grid (Wrangham & Smuts, 1980; Chapman & Wrangham, 1993). This technique is sensitive to grid size such that a reduction in grid size leads to a reduction in range area estimates (Clutton-Brock, 1975), and so these communities may have home ranges which are more similar, and absolutely smaller, than the estimates suggest.

Strictly, only the MCP method is comparable between studies (Harris *et al.*, 1990) which suggests that the Sonso community range over an area no more than half that used by the Kanyawara (Kibale) community, particularly in light of recent indications that the Kanyawara community range may in fact be much larger (MCP = 25 km², GPS data: R. Wrangham & M. Wilson, *pers. comm.*).

Community home range size is likely to be indicative of resource availability with low abundance and high dispersal of food resources combining to produce larger ranges (see: Dunbar, 1988). Higher quality habitats may be responsible, bearing in mind the issues of analysis techniques, for smaller community ranges such as reported here for the Sonso community. Comparison of range areas between the Sonso and Kanyawara communities suggests that the resource base differs at the two sites, with resources less dispersed (less patchy) and possibly more abundant at Sonso. Such comparisons will remain speculative until data from a number of sites are collected and analysed with more precision.

Male 'core' areas

Despite ranging widely, males spent the majority of their time within relatively restricted 'core' areas, which, while not exclusive, only partially overlapped the 'core' of each of the other males. Defining these 'core' areas was subjective; any figure greater than 50% of fixes could be used. No precise technique exists to discriminate 'core' areas (Kenward & Hoddar, 1996), although inspection of 'utilisation plots' is a widely used method. This may not, in fact, be appropriate for investigating chimpanzee home range structure, as the conceptual model of a home range with a distinct 'core' does not necessarily reflect the nomadic nature of chimpanzees. There are no permanent, continually reused, nests, lying up sites or dens to which the animals return after each foraging trip. Chimpanzee 'core' areas may therefore represent 'preferred' areas of activity, existing only in a probabilistic sense. Male 'core' areas are now reported from three study sites, each with a different ecology (Gombe: Wrangham & Smuts, 1980; Kibale: Chapman & Wrangham, 1993; Budongo: this study).

Function of male 'cores'

Why males occupy 'core' areas needs further investigation. Males may simply tend to use particular areas, which are most familiar to them, perhaps because these areas were parts of their mothers' 'core' areas. It seems unlikely that male 'core' areas serve an ecological function, as has been proposed for female 'core' areas (Wrangham & Smuts, 1980; Pusey, Williams & Goodall, 1997), as in this study there was no difference between male 'cores' in habitat composition, and no obvious influence of social status. Within any particular dyad, 'cores' were only partially overlapping, and the degree to which each dyad shared 'core' areas was related to the strength of their association relationship. Males appeared to be ranging to associate, rather than associating with those they happened to encounter.

Chimpanzee long distance calls, pant-hoots, are given primarily by males and are thought to summon, or at least notify, the caller's allies of his location (Mitani & Nishida, 1993; Clark, 1993; Clark & Wrangham, 1993, 1994). If males are searching for one another, it may be an advantage for a male's location to be predictable, particularly if it is important for individuals to be found by their allies. While pant-hoots may carry information regarding the caller's identity and approximate direction, they may be less useful for specifying location. In thick forest, attenuation of calls is likely to be fairly rapid and, through a mosaic of vegetation, unpredictable. Where the habitat covers rough terrain, vocalisations may be restricted to a single valley. Highly structured 'core' areas may, therefore, function to increase the probability that males can be located by any individual searching for them. Cycling females, as well as male allies, may make use of this information. Observations suggest that these females do not remain in their 'core' areas, which are important to ensure access to food for females with infants, but that they leave them to associate with males (Tutin, 1979; Nishida, 1979; Goodall 1986; Nishida & Hiraiwa-Hasegawa, 1987). Cycling females may even seek out males (Takahata, Ihobe & Idani, 1996; Gagneux, Woodruff & Boesch, 1997), possibly making use of the predictability conferred by male 'core' areas. Males may therefore monitor the availability of cycling females by having multi-nuclear 'cores' which overlap 'core' areas of a number of females, or by making occasional visits to the female 'cores'.

The multinuclear 'cores' indicated by cluster analysis may be the result of a compromise between the benefits of being locatable, and the possible reduction in foraging efficiency associated with restricted ranging. If location by allies is more crucial to male reproductive success than access to energy rich food, and if females make use of male 'cores' to predict individuals' location, then males may tolerate foraging costs. The degree of tolerance may be related to individuals' social status. However, in this study male social status had little influence on 'core' areas. If multiple food patches are available simultaneously, as is common at Sonso, males may make differential use of these patches, and so be able to occupy subtly distinct 'core' areas. This differential use of feeding trees remains to be investigated, but would serve to overcome potential foraging costs. Superabundant, ephemeral resources could still be exploited: by definition, males spend 20% of their time outside their 'core' areas.

In common with many other species (review in Cheney & Seyfarth, 1990), chimpanzees appear to have mental maps of their home ranges. They are also capable of simple numeracy (Boysen & Berntson, 1990; Perusse & Rumbaugh, 1990), and individual recognition (Bauer & Philip, 1983; Boysen & Berntson, 1987). As a result, chimpanzees should be capable of identifying greater or lesser use of certain areas by particular individuals, and be able to use this information.

Male chimpanzees will travel away from their current location, for example a feeding tree, to meet and groom other individuals, without relying on vocalisations to locate these individuals (*pers. obs.*). This suggests that they have knowledge of the locations of other males. Whether they are identifying certain areas as those where they are most likely to find particular individuals remains to be investigated.

Ranging and territoriality

The 80% 'core' areas occupied by the Sonso males were localised away from community range boundaries. Such boundaries are known to be hazardous for males (Goodall *et al.*, 1979; Nishida, 1979); if caught alone by a group of neighbouring males, the lone male risks serious injury or death. In thick forest, such as Budongo, with low levels of visibility and no strong topographic features to define community range boundaries, these may be ambiguous. If as a result males tend to avoid the boundaries, boundary *zones* would develop. These would function to reduce the chances of males from different communities encountering one another at short range. The conflict between avoidance of boundary zones and possible benefits of individually distinct 'cores' may force males into occupying multinuclear 'core' areas.

However, males cannot defend community boundaries by avoiding them. Boundary patrols are characteristically infrequent, unpredictable and conducted in large, powerful, groups. Range defence is typically by means of loud vocal advertisements of male presence and strength (Goodall, 1986; *pers. obs.*). Such territorial behaviour serves to minimise the risk to each individual. If the risks associated with trespassing into a neighbouring community's range are sufficiently high, and the possibility of encountering resident males unpredictable, range boundaries may be maintained by a system of 'mutual respect' (Frank, 1995). So long as boundaries are defended occasionally, and unpredictably, they should be respected. Males of each community would be expected to test range boundaries, making incursion patrols in strong groups, and the 'mutual respect' system would break down if a strong asymmetry in the strength of these groups, and thus the threat posed, developed between neighbouring communities.

These results can be fitted into a modified version of Wrangham's (1975) model, in which females possess 'core' areas within an area defended by males, if parties are seen as the outcome of social interactions; their primary function is to provide a social milieu, rather than as means of range defence. Large parties specifically concerned with range defence will be formed occasionally, but as community boundaries maintained by a 'mutual respect' system require only a small proportion of each male's time for their defence, males spend most of their time in small parties. These are the outcome of the association patterns of males concerned with intra-community politics rather than defending or searching for reproductively active females.

Male chimpanzees are therefore seen as spending much of their time moving between food resources and social partners in a way, which leads to differential use of the community home range. Males avoid boundaries between community ranges, using occasional, unpredictably timed patrols into boundary zones to maintain range boundaries by a system of 'mutual respect'. It is suggested that boundary zones develop in the absence of obvious geographical markers. Away from community boundaries, males concern themselves with social politics, associating with and avoiding one another. These patterns lead to subtly distinct individual 'core' areas.

It is hypothesised that these 'cores' function to enable males' locations to be predicted by alliance partners and possibly by females.

Acknowledgements

This study was funded by the L.S.B. Leakey Foundation, the Boise Fund, and the L.S.B. Leakey Trust (UK). Fieldwork was conducted with the permission of the Uganda Council for Science and Technology, and the President's Office. P.C. Lee provided support and direction throughout my research and V. Reynolds gave permission to work at the Sonso site. In Uganda, A.J. Plumptre organised the Budongo Forest Project and Geresomu Muhumuza provided invaluable help during fieldwork. The manuscript was improved by comments from R.W. Wrangham and C. Harcourt.

References

Adams DC, Anthony CD. 1996. Using randomisation techniques to analyse behavioural data. *Animal Behaviour.* **51:** 733-738.

Altmann J. 1974. Observational study of behaviour: Sampling methods. *Behaviour.* **49:** 227-265.

Bauer HR, Philip M. 1983. Facial and vocal recognition in the common chimpanzee. *Psychological Record.* **33:** 161-170.

Boysen S, Berntson G. 1987. Conspecific recognition in the chimpanzee: Heart-rate indexes of significant others. *American Journal of Primatology.* **12:** 332-333.

Boysen ST, Berntson GG. 1990. The development of numerical skills in the chimpanzee (*Pan troglodytes*). In: Parker ST, Gibson KR. ed. *'Language' and Intelligence in Monkeys and Apes: Comparative developmental perspectives.* Cambridge: Cambridge University Press. 435-450.

Burt WH. 1943. Territoriality and home range concepts as applied to mammals. *Journal of Mammalogy.* **24:** 346-352.

Bygott JD. 1979. Agnostic behaviour, dominance, and social structure in wild chimpanzees of the Gombe National Park. In: Hamburg DA, McCown ER. eds. *The Great Apes.* Menlo Park, California: Benjamin/Cummings Publishing. 405-428.

Chapman CA, Wrangham RW. 1993. Range use of the forest chimpanzees of Kibale: Implications for the understanding of chimpanzee social organisation. *American Journal of Primatology.* **31:** 263-273.

Cheney DL, Seyfarth RM. 1990. *How Monkeys See the World: Inside the mind of another species.* Chicago: University of Chicago Press.

Clark AP. 1993. Rank differences in the production of vocalisations by wild chimpanzees as a function of social context. *American Journal of Primatology.* **31:** 159-179.

Clark AP, Wrangham RW. 1993. Acoustic analysis of wild chimpanzee pant hoots: Do Kibale Forest chimpanzees have an acoustically distinct food arrival pant hoot. *American Journal of Primatology.* **31:** 99-109.

Clark AP, Wrangham RW. 1994. Chimpanzee arrival pant-hoots: Do they signify food or status? *International Journal of Primatology.* **15:** 185-205.

Clutton-Brock TH. 1975. Ranging behaviour of red colobus (*Colobus badius tephrosceles*) in the Gombe National Park. *Animal Behaviour.* **23:** 706-722.

Cresswell WJ, Harris S. 1988. Foraging behaviour and home-range utilisation in a suburban badger (*Meles meles*) population. *Mammal Revue.* **18:** 37-49.

Dunbar RIM. 1988. *Primate Social Systems.* London: Croom Helm.

Eggeling WJ. 1947. Observations on the ecology of the Budongo Rain Forest, Uganda. *Journal of Ecology.* **34:** 20-87.

Frank SA. 1995. Mutual policing and the repression of competition in the evolution of cooperation groups. *Nature.* **377:** 520-522.

Gagneux P, Woodruff DS, Boesch C. 1997. Furtive mating in female chimpanzees. *Nature.* **387:** 358-359.

Goodall J. 1973. Cultural elements in a chimpanzee community. In: Menzel EW. ed. *Precultural Primate Behaviour: Fourth International Congress of Primatology, Symposia Proceedings.* Basil: Karger Press.

Goodall J. 1986. *The Chimpanzees of Gombe: Patterns of behaviour.* Cambridge, Massachusetts: Belknap Press.

Goodall J, Bandora A, Bergmann E, Busse C, Matama H, Mpongo E, Pierce A, Riss D. 1979. Intercommunity interactions in the chimpanzee population of the Gombe National Park. In: Hamburg DA, McCown ER. eds. *The Great Apes.* Menlo Park, California: Benjamin/Cummings Publishing. 13-53.

Halperin SD. 1979. Temporary association patterns in free ranging chimpanzees: An assessment of individual grouping preferences. In: Hamburg DA, McCown ER. eds. *The Great Apes.* Menlo Park, CA: Benjamin/Cummings Publishing. 491-500.

Harris S, Cresswell WJ, Forde PG, Trewhella WJ, Woollard T, Wray S. 1990. Home range analysis using radio-tracking data: A review of problems and techniques particularly as applied to the study of mammals. *Mammal Revue.* **20:** 97-123.

Hemelrijk CK. 1990. Models of, and tests for, reciprocity, unidirectionality and other social-interaction patterns at a group level. *Animal Behaviour.* **39:** 1013-1029.

Jenrich RJ, Turner FB. 1969. Measurement of non-circular home range. *Journal of Theoretical Biology.* **22:** 227-237.

Kenward RE. 1987. *Wildlife Radio Tagging: Equipment, field techniques and data analysis.* London: Academic Press.

Kenward RE, Hoddar KH. 1996. *Ranges V: An analysis system for biological location data.* United Kingdom: Natural Environment Research Council.

Kenward RE, Marcstrom V, Karlbom M. 1993. Post-nestling behaviour in goshawks *Accipiter gentilis*. II. Sex differences in sociality and nest switching. *Animal Behaviour.* **46**: 371-378.

Macdonald DW, Ball FG, Hough NG. 1980. The evaluation of home range size and configuration using radio tracking data. In: Amlaner CJ, Macdonald DW. eds. *A Handbook on Biotelemetry and Radio Tracking.* Oxford: Pergamon Press. 405-424.

Mitani JC, Nishida T. 1993. Contexts and social correlates of long-distance calling by male chimpanzees. *Animal Behaviour.* **45**: 735-746.

Mitani JC, Rodman PS. 1979. Territoriality: The relation of ranging patterns and home range size to defensibility, with an analysis of territoriality among primate species. *Behavioral Ecology and Sociobiology.* **5**: 241-251.

Newton-Fisher NE. 1997. Tactical behaviour and decision making in wild chimpanzees. [Unpublished PhD thesis], University of Cambridge.

Newton-Fisher NE. 1999. Association by male chimpanzees: a social tactic? *Behaviour.* **136**: 705-730.

Nishida T. 1979. The social structure of chimpanzees of the Mahale Mountains. In: Hamburg DA, McCown ER. eds. *The Great Apes.* Menlo Park, California: Benjamin/Cummings Publishing. 73-122.

Nishida T. 1983. Alpha status and agnostic alliance in wild chimpanzees. *Primates.* **24**: 318-336.

Nishida T, Hiraiwa-Hasegawa M. 1987. Chimpanzees and bonobos: Cooperative relationships between males. In: Smuts BB, Cheney DL, Seyfarth RM, Wrangham RW, Struhsaker TT. eds. *Primate Societies.* Chicago: University of Chicago Press. 165-177.

Perusse R, Rumbaugh DM. 1990. Summation in chimpanzees (*Pan troglodytes*): Effects of amounts, number of wells, and finer ratios. *International Journal of Primatology.* **11**: 425-437.

Plumptre AJ. 1996. Changes following 60 years of selective timber harvesting in the Budongo Forest Reserve, Uganda. *Forest Ecology and Management.* **89**: 101-113.

Plumptre AJ, Reynolds V, Bakuneeta C. 1997. The effects of selective logging in monodominant tropical forests on biodiversity. *Overseas Development Agency, Project Report, R6057.*

Pusey A, Williams J, Goodall J. 1997. The influence of dominance rank on the reproductive success of female chimpanzees. *Science.* **277**: 828-831.

Reynolds V. 1992. Chimpanzees in the Budongo Forest, 1962-1992. *Journal of Zoology.* **228**: 695-699.

Seaman DE, Powell RA. 1996. An evaluation of the accuracy of kernel density estimators for home range analysis. *Ecology.* **77**: 2075-2085.

Silverman BW. 1986. *Density Estimation for Statistics and Data Analysis.* London: Chapman and Hall.

Swihart RK, Slade NA. 1985. Testing for independence of observations in animal movement. *Ecology.* **66**: 1176-1184.

Synnott TJ. 1985. *A Checklist of the Flora of the Budongo Forest Reserve, Uganda, with Notes on Ecology and Phenology.* Commonwealth Forestry Institute, Occasional Paper. Oxford: Oxford Forestry Institute.

Takahata Y, Ihobe H, Idani G. 1996. Comparing copulations of chimpanzees and bonobos: Do females exhibit proceptivity or receptivity? In: McGrew WC, Marchant LF, Nishida T. eds. *Great Ape Societies.* Cambridge: Cambridge University Press. 146-155.

Tutin CEG. 1979. Mating patterns and reproductive strategies in a community of wild chimpanzees (*Pan troglodytes schweinfurthii*). *Behavioral Ecology and Sociobiology.* **6:** 29-38.

van Winkle W. 1975. Comparison of several probabilistic home-range models. *Journal of Wildlife Management.* **39:** 118-123.

Worton BJ. 1989. Kernel methods for estimating the utilisation distribution in home range studies. *Ecology.* **70:** 164-168.

Wrangham RW. 1975. The behavioural ecology of chimpanzees in the Gombe National Park, Tanzania. [Unpublished PhD thesis], University of Cambridge.

Wrangham RW. 1977. Feeding behaviour of chimpanzees in Gombe National Park, Tanzania. In: Clutton-Brock TH. ed. *Primate Ecology.* London: Academic Press. 504-538.

Wrangham RW. 1979. Sex differences in chimpanzee dispersion. In: Hamburg DA, McCown ER. eds. *The Great Apes.* Menlo Park, California: Benjamin/Cummings Publishing. 481-490.

Wrangham RW. 1986. Ecology and social relationships in two species of chimpanzee. In: Rubenstein DI, Wrangham RW. eds. *Ecology and Social Evolution: Birds and mammals.* Princeton, New Jersey: Princeton University Press. 352-378.

Wrangham RW, Smuts BB. 1980. Sex differences in the behavioural ecology of chimpanzees in the Gombe National Park, Tanzania. *Journal of Reproduction and Fertility, Supplement.* **28:** 13-31.

CHAPTER FOURTEEN

A biology of primate extinction, at two temporal and spatial scales

A. H. HARCOURT

Introduction

To investigate the biology of primate extinction (and, therefore, the process of evolution), I attempt to distinguish the biological traits of taxa at risk of extinction from the traits of less susceptible taxa. The suggestion is that understanding of the biology of extant susceptible taxa by contrast to the biology of less susceptible ones should improve both our understanding of the process of evolution and also our ability to predict the future (Diamond, 1984a; Jablonski, 1986; Foley, 1987; Johns & Skorupa, 1987; Brown, 1995; Harcourt, 1998). While small-scale extinction of populations probably precedes large-scale extinction of species, nevertheless, debate occurs about whether there exist qualitative differences between the effects of short-term, local environmental perturbations and long-term, regional environmental perturbations, and, consequently, the biological traits associated with them (Brown, 1995, Ch 9). Generally, is macroevolution indeed a different process from microevolution?

I use 'natural experiments' that have occurred at two spatial and temporal scales to investigate both the biology of extinction and the possibility of scale effects. Taxa go extinct when their habitat changes or it shrinks. Change probably precedes the shrinkage and disappearance and, at least initially, mere change should have less impact than fragmentation and disappearance. Thus, I investigate susceptibility to local extinction in the short-term by analysing the effects of habitat alteration. Susceptibility to regional extinction in the long-term, I investigate by analysing the effects of habitat removal.

The habitat alteration experiment involves selective logging, or other partial habitat alteration, and subsequent comparison of densities of primate taxa in the 'experimentally altered' plots with their density in the 'control' plots of unaltered primary forest (see Skorupa, 1986; Johns & Skorupa, 1987; Grieser Johns & Grieser Johns, 1995; Struhsaker, 1997; Harcourt, 1998). Taxa at risk are those whose density is far lower in the 'experimental' plots than in the 'control' plots. The habitat removal experiment involves flooding with sea-water a continental shelf, the Sunda Shelf of south-east Asia, and 10,000 years later investigating presence of primate taxa in relation to size of the islands left by the raised sea-level (Wilcox, 1980; Heaney, 1984; Harcourt, 1999). Susceptible taxa are classified as those that survive only on large islands by comparison to their co-taxa that also survive on smaller islands, on the assumption that all taxa were formerly more widespread.

At both scales, the traits of taxa at risk are compared with those of the less susceptible taxa. The traits chosen for analysis were those that several other studies of primates, or of other taxa, had shown to be correlated with risk of extinction. Nine traits were examined. Population density is a measure of rarity, and rare taxa are at risk because of various problems of small population size; large-bodied taxa are at risk because of low population size, greater requirements for resources and slow reproductive rate; minimum inter-birth interval is an index of potential population recovery rate; year range and group mass are measures of resource requirements and should therefore correlate with risk; diet is a measure of specialisation, and requirement for rare resources; altitudinal range and maximum latitude are measures of the variety of zones inhabited and, therefore, potentially of plasticity; and taxa with small geographic ranges are more likely to have their whole area of distribution affected by the adverse change (Diamond, 1984b; Skorupa, 1986; Johns & Skorupa, 1987; Jablonski, 1991; Lande, 1993; Caughley & Gunn, 1996; Cowlishaw & Hacker, 1997; Harcourt, 1998; Harcourt, submitted).

Methods

The precise measures used are as follows, with medians being used where more than one study was available per species (genus is median of species): population density; body mass – of females; minimum inter-birth interval; year range – the average minimum convex polygon per year per social group; group mass – female body mass x number individuals per group; diet – % fruit, flowers or seeds; altitudinal range; maximum latitude; and the taxon's geographic range. Age at first birth, arboreality, and territoriality were also investigated, but the first correlated almost perfectly with birth interval and produced fewer data, and the second two had too few terrestrial and territorial taxa, respectively, for useful results.

In the case of short-term, local alteration of habitat, taxa categorised as at risk are those, that suffered at least a 50% drop in density in the secondary forest (resulting from regrowth after logging) by comparison to density in the adjacent unaltered primary forest. In order to increase the reliability of assessment of susceptibility, I counted only taxa for which data from more than one site existed, and counted as susceptible or not only those taxa in which all contrasts in density were in the same direction. In order to minimise confounding factors, I counted only those studies in which densities were measured in altered and *adjacent* unaltered forest. While the measure of vulnerability is copied from Skorupa and from Johns (see above), these criteria are specific to this study (Harcourt, 1998).

For the analysis of responses to long-term, regional loss of habitat, the size of the smallest island on which the taxa were recorded was the base datum. The crucial assumption is that taxa found only on large islands have gone extinct on the smaller islands isolated several thousand years ago as a result of the end-Pleistocene global rise in sea level (Rohling *et al.*, 1998). Of the nine genera or sub-genera statistically compared (below), six are still widespread across many islands in the Sunda region and beyond; and one, *Pongo*, is known to have been formerly far more widespread across Asia (Jablonski, 1998). Evidence for extinction on small islands comes from analysis of number of species in relation to size of islands and distances between them: the data show fewer species on smaller islands, and no relation of number of species per island to distance between island and nearest 'mainland' source, as would be expected if differences in number of species resulted from extinction alone (Heaney, 1984; Harcourt, 1999). Also, sub-fossil evidence exists of mammal species, including *Pongo*, on some of the smaller islands on which the taxa are no longer found (Hooijer, 1975).

In the analysis of short-term response to local alteration of habitat, the 28 species compared are:

Africa – At Risk – *Cercopithecus diana, Procolobus badius, Pan troglodytes;* Other – *Cercopithecus mitis, Cercopithecus ascanius, Colobus guereza, Cercocebus torquatus, Gorilla gorilla*;

Asia – At Risk – *Presbytis comata, Nasalis larvatus, Hylobates syndactylus, Pongo pygmaeus*; Other – *Macaca nemestrina, Macaca fascicularis, Presbytis melalophos, Presbytis obscura, Hylobates lar, Hylobates muelleri*;

South America – At Risk – *Cebus albifrons, Callicebus torquatus, Lagothrix lagotricha, Alouatta seniculus, Ateles paniscus*; Other – *Callithrix argentata, Saguinus fuscicollis, Saguinus midas, Cebus apella, Callicebus moloch, Saimiri sciureus*.

This sample allowed up to 10 comparisons (see below for method of comparative analysis).

In the analysis of long-term response to regional loss of habitat, the 19 species considered are: *Hylobates agilis, lar, moloch, muelleri; Hylobates syndactylus; Macaca fascicularis, nemestrina; Nasalis larvatus; Nycticebus coucang; Pongo pygmaeus; Presbytis comata, frontata, hosei, melalophos, rubicunda; Tarsius bancanus; Trachypithecus auratus, cristatus, obscurus.*

This sample allowed up to nine comparisons (see below for method of comparative analysis). In order of largest island on which the taxa are extant (i.e. decreasing risk of extinction), the genera are: *Nasalis, Pongo, Hylobates (Symphalangus) syndactylus, Hylobates, Presbytis, Trachypithecus, Macaca, Tarsius* and *Nycticebus*.

The taxonomy used was that of Purveys (1995), with alterations and additions of Asian colobines following Oates, Davies & Delson, (1994).

Analysis was designed to take account of taxonomic dependence in the data, i.e. the fact that intrageneric species are likely to have similar values and, therefore, not to be strictly independent data points for statistical analysis. The method used was comparative analysis by independent contrasts (CAIC) (Purvis & Rambaut, 1995). The method, in effect, sets as positive the difference between related taxa in size of minimum island and then asks the degree and direction of differences between those same taxa in the correlated measures of interest. Thus two colobines would be compared, and two cercopithecines, and then the average value for the colobines compared to the average value for the cercopithecines, and then the average for the Old World monkeys compared to the average for apes, and so on. If there is a significant association between island size and a measure, the majority of differences between the taxa in the measure should be either positive or negative. That being the case, correlation between the independent and dependent variables can be tested with a Binomial or a Wilcoxon matched pairs signed ranks test (Siegel, 1956).

Obviously the traits are not necessarily independent of one another: taxa of large body size generally live at low density, for instance. Thus the analysis here of the separate traits is not to argue that they are independent influences; of course they are not. It is an attempt to elucidate the mechanism by which the traits have their effect. Independence of effects was investigated by correlating the contrasts from the CAIC. Where confounding effects exist, I discuss them.

Wilcoxon tests were performed with Statview (Abacus Concepts, 1990-91), and regressions and correlations with JMP (SAS Institute Inc., 1995). Wilcoxon matched-pairs, signed-ranks tests assessed the likelihood that the CAIC results were significant: were there more and larger contrasts than expected in the predicted direction? Probability is one-tailed, because predictions of the direction of difference were made beforehand on the basis of other studies or general biology.

Details of the methods, tables of data, and sources of data are in Harcourt (1998; submitted), for which Rowe (1996) was a valuable source of references. In brief, each species' value is the median value from all studies of that species that reliably provide the measure. Minimum inter-birth interval has been added here as a trait in the habitat alteration analysis since Harcourt's (1998) study; Harvey & Clutton-Brock (1985), chapters in Smuts *et al.* (1987) and Ross (1988, 1991) were main sources of data.

Results

In the Habitat Alteration analysis, of ability to survive in the short-term in locally altered forest, two of the nine factors were significantly (one-tailed) associated with risk, i.e. with decreased density in the altered forest by comparison to the primary forest (Table 1, Figure 1). Two of nine is a proportion more than would be expected by chance alone. Taxa with large year range by comparison to their partner taxon were at risk, and perhaps so also were taxa with low maximum latitude. In Harcourt's (1998) analysis, local density in the adjacent unaltered primary forest (as opposed to the species' average density, as here) was also analysed as a potential correlate of vulnerability. Unexpectedly, no relation existed: species in dense (large) populations in primary forest did not do better in the adjacent secondary forest than did species that lived at low density in the primary forest. The lack of association is exemplified by the highly susceptible red colobus monkey *Procolobus badius*, which in primary forest lives at densities twice those of the unsusceptible black and white colobus *Colobus angolensis*.

Table 1 Statistics of associations between biology and susceptibility to extinction. The environmental changes are, Table A, short-term, local habitat alteration (conversion of primary to secondary forest), and, Table B, long-term, regional loss of habitat on the Sunda Shelf of south-east Asia (due to end-Pleistocene sea level rise).

Table A: Row 1 : *T* value and probability value (one-tailed) for Wilcoxon matched pairs, signed rank test of CAIC results (N=10); Row 2 : Measures whose contrasts correlated with contrasts in listed measure (see below for key).

Table B: Rows as for Table A, but only for contrasts at deeper than specific level (N = 8). * – P value for geographic range is from binomial test on total range for genus (7/8 contrasts showed susceptible taxon to have smaller geographic range); *T* value is insignificant.

In correlated contrasts, Alt.R = altitudinal range; B.M = body mass; Frug% = % fruit, flowers, seeds in diet; G.R. = geographic range; PD = population density; YR = year range; ML – maximum latitude.

A. Habitat Alteration: decades, local.

Statistics	Body Mass	Pop.Density	Year Range	Max. Latitude	Geog. Range
CAIC Wilcoxon T	-	-	1 ; 0.01	11 ; 0.04	-
Correlated contrast	-Frug %; +Alt.R	-	+G.R	+G.R	+Frug %; +YR; +ML

B. Loss Habitat: millennia, regional.

Statistics	Body Mass	Pop.Density	Year Range	Max. Latitude	Geog. Range
CAIC Wilcoxon T	1 ; 0.01	3 ; 0.02	8; 0.02	1 ; 0.01	7; 0.035 *
Correlated contrast	-	-YR; -GR	+Frug%; -PD	-	-PD

Potential confounds exposed by the correlation of contrasts are (Table 1a): body mass and frugivory might have cancelled one another as correlates of susceptibility, because while large-bodied taxa should be at risk, so should be frugivorous taxa. Similarly with body mass and altitudinal range; geographic range and frugivory might have cancelled one another out, because taxa of small geographic range should be at risk, but not taxa with low percent frugivory.

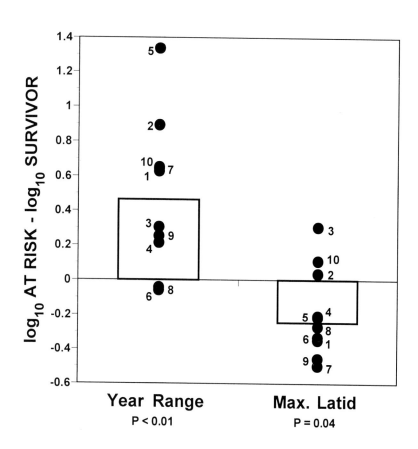

Figure 1
Direction of differences in measures between independent pairs of 'At Risk' and 'Survivor' taxa that showed a significant correlation with vulnerability to short term, local Habitat Alteration. Taxa at risk are those that experienced a drop in density of 50% or more in secondary compared to primary forest.

Filled circles = taxonomically independent contrasts; histogram = median contrast. (Values were logged before subtraction to ensure equal 'distance' either side of zero in the Figure; and columns with original values of less than 1, were multiplied by 10 to ensure positive log values). Measures are year range (km^2) and maximum latitude. (See Table 1 for statistics). (Wilcoxon Signed Ranks (one-tailed)).

The ten pairs of independent taxa, with the more susceptible listed first are: 1. *Cercopithecus diana* and the mean of *C. ascanius* and *C. mitis;* 2. *Procolobus badius* and *Colobus guereza;* 3. *Pan* and *Gorilla;* 4. *Presbytis comata* and *P. melalophos;* 5. *Nasalis larvatus* and *Trachypithecus obscurus;* 6. *Hylobates syndactylus* and *H. lar;* 7. *Pongo* and mean remaining *Cercopithecines;* 8. *Cebus albifrons* and *C. apella;* 9. *Callicebus torquatus* and *C. moloch;* and 10. mean Ateline and mean remaining New World taxa.

Year range was a correlate of risk despite the opposing correlation of its contrasts with geographic range (taxa of small geographic range should be at more risk); and maximum latitude was associated with risk, despite positive correlation of its contrasts with geographic range, which was not associated with risk. Thus it seems that associations of measures with risk might have been hidden by correlation with other measures, but it does not seem that false positive associations with risk have been produced by correlation of contrasts.

In the analysis of ability to survive in the long-term on small islands of remaining habitat in the Sunda Shelf, analysis starting at the level of species showed no effects. However, if analysis is done

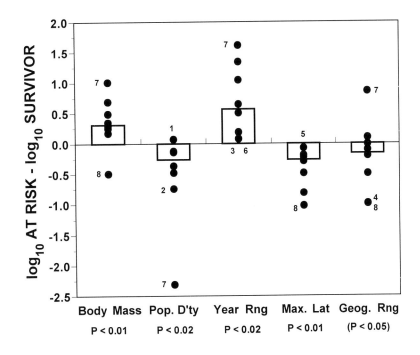

Figure 2
Direction of differences in measures between independent pairs of 'At Risk' and 'Survivor' taxa (genera and deeper) that showed a significant correlation with long term, regional Habitat Loss. Taxa at risk are those that did not survive on islands as small as did their sister taxa.

Filled circles = taxonomically independent contrasts; histogram = median contrast. Pop. D'ty = Population density; Year. Rng = year range; Max. Lat = Maximum latitude; Geog. Rng = Geographical range (for which P value is for Binomial Test using total range for each genus (not mean specific value per genus, which are data shown)). *(See Table 1 for statistics)*
(Wilcoxon Signed Ranks (one-tailed)). Logged values were used to ensure equal 'distance' either side of zero in the Figure; the result is equivalent to the ratio of the absolute values. The eight pairs of independent taxa (at deeper than specific level), with the more susceptible listed first, are: 1. *Presbytis* x *Trachypithecus*; 2. *Nasalis* x Colobines; 3.*H. syndactylus* x other *Hylobates*; 4. Colobines x *Macaca*; 5. *Pongo* x Hylobatids; 6. Apes x Monkeys; 7. *Tarsius* x Anthropoids; and 8. *Nycticebus* x All.
Only the extreme pairs are labelled.

at deeper than the species level, i.e. sub-genera and deeper, primate taxa of large body mass, living at low density, in large year range, with low maximum latitude were significantly at risk, as perhaps also were taxa with small geographic range (Table 1, Figure 2). This number of significant associations is far too many to be accounted for by chance alone. Some of the contrasts correlated with one another (Table 1b). The negative correlation of contrasts in population density with contrasts in year range prevents separation of their effects (low density, large year range at risk); while year range contrasts correlated positively with frugivory contrasts, nevertheless frugivory did not appear as an effect; and the negative correlation of contrasts of population density with geographic range could have masked an effect of geographic range.

Discussion

To repeat, the analysis here of the separate traits is not to argue that they are independent influences; of course they are not. It is an attempt to elucidate the mechanism by which the traits might have their effect. We know, for instance, that population density, year range, group mass, diet, and inter-birth interval all correlate with body size (Clutton-Brock & Harvey, 1977; Harvey & Clutton-Brock, 1985). However, body mass itself is only an index of the risk factor. It is not an explanation in itself, as it sometimes appears to be treated. Thus I argue that the fact that in this analysis of long-term habitat loss, only population density and year range, in addition to body mass, correlate with risk of extinction, tells us something about how extinction might be occurring. Furthermore, obvious exceptions exist to the generalisation that large-bodied and rare taxa are at risk: for instance, the gorilla survives forest alteration better than does the chimpanzee (Harcourt, 1998. See also Vermeij, 1986; Pimm, Jones & Diamond, 1988; Brown, 1995, Ch 12).

Primate taxa susceptible to extinction seem not to be a random, accidental selection of the total fauna. Biological traits that distinguish them from surviving taxa can be identified, as is true of other taxa (Brown, 1971; Terborgh, 1974; Diamond, 1984b; Laurance, 1991; Kattan, Alvarez-López & Giraldo, 1994; Brown, 1995; Jablonski & Raup, 1995; Jernvall, Hunter & Fortelius, 1996; Leach & Givnish, 1996). Among primates, the traits associated with risk differ according to whether risk is measured in the short-term, local scale, or long-term, regional scale. On the short-term, local scale of habitat alteration, taxa at risk are those with large year range and, perhaps, low maximum latitude; on the long-term, regional scale of habitat loss and fragmentation, taxa at risk are those with a large body mass, living at low density, in large year range, with low maximum latitude, and, perhaps, in a small geographic range.

Together, the traits appear to indicate that requirements for a large resource base, lack of plasticity, and in the long-term, a small population size, might predispose primate taxa to extinction.

Frugivores, especially large frugivores, require a large resource base (Clutton-Brock & Harvey, 1977). The fact that diet appears not to correlate with risk in these analyses is therefore anomalous. However, the measure of diet is crude and, in the case of habitat alteration, the exact nature of the secondary forest by comparison to the primary forest will strongly determine whether in fact frugivores are at risk (Fimbel, 1994; Plumptre & Reynolds, 1994).

If different traits are important at different scales, the question is whether different phenomena are at work at the different scales, or whether the short-term, local extinctions are simply a prelude to large-scale ones. Brown (1995, Ch 9) argues that we do not yet know the answer. It could be the case, he suggested, that species that go extinct during periods of stability are different from those that are at risk in unstable environments. For instance in the short-term, in a stable environment, small-bodied species could be more at risk (instead of the usual large-bodied), because their populations fluctuate more (Pimm *et al.*, 1988). By contrast, in a severe environmental change, ability to recover from low population size might be crucial (Brown, 1995). Certainly, the traits in marine taxa associated with risk differ between periods of mass extinction and background extinction (Jablonski, 1991). In the case of primates under the two scales of time and space examined here, most of the traits that correlate with short-term, local risk seem to be a subset of those that correlate with long-term, regional risk. Such is to be expected if a taxon that went extinct in the short-term cannot survive in the long-term, and if more severe change over longer time simply places more severe stress on taxa, and thus involve more traits more intensely. Nevertheless, the appearance of overall population density (rarity) as a risk factor in the long-term regional scale might be a qualitatively different risk factor from those apparent in the short-term, local scale of habitat alteration. The database is small, however, and in the analysis of habitat alteration, removal of the two opposing extreme values produced a significant effect of population density (Harcourt, 1998).

None of the traits was a surprise as a correlate of risk. They were chosen for analysis precisely because other studies of primates, or studies of other taxa, had shown them to be such. Nevertheless, a correlation is not an explanation, and explanations for some of the associations need more investigation. Why is year range a correlate of risk? It has, to my knowledge, been shown to be a factor for only one other taxon, African carnivores (Woodroffe & Ginsberg, 1998). Woodroffe & Ginsberg argued that species with large ranges were killed when they went outside protected areas. I have not addressed hunting as a cause in this analysis and, indeed, have assumed that it is not an issue. In the analysis of habitat alteration, I specifically analysed only sites where the primary and altered forest were adjacent to one another in order to minimise contrasts in human influence. Also, Skorupa's (1986) results for one site without hunting (Struhsaker, 1997) not only showed year range as a significant correlate of risk, but are also not obviously different from other individual sites where there might have been hunting, nor from the results of analysis across several sites (Johns & Skorupa, 1987; Harcourt, 1998). In the case of the Sunda Shelf islands, year ranges of the primate species are very small by comparison to the size of the islands, or remaining forest on them, indicating that the Woodroffe-Ginsberg effect was not operating. The other explanation for year range as a correlate of risk is that it indicates a requirement for a large resource base. Nevertheless, year range is at the same time highly labile, correlating strongly with group mass, and habitat (Clutton-Brock & Harvey, 1977). Why is it not the case that individuals in difficulty reduce the size of the group of which they are a member, and hence their range requirements? Is it possible that predation risk (Janson & Goldsmith, 1995) or competition with other groups prevents them from doing so (Wrangham, 1980; van Schaik, 1989; Isbell, 1991; Wrangham, Gittleman & Chapman, 1993)?

The finding that risk correlates with maximum latitude, with the most tropically confined taxa being at higher risk, might be a novel finding for primates. It has, however, been found to be a factor for some taxa in some past eras, for example brachiopods (Jablonski, 1986). The explanation offered here for maximum latitude being a risk trait is that it is an index of plasticity (accepting that the concept of plasticity of a taxon is by no means a simple one (West-Eberhard, 1989)). The finding matches the general perception that specialists are at risk (Brown, 1971), although we still need reliable measures to distinguish specialists from generalists. In the case of primates, Temerin & Cant (1983), Jablonski (1998), and Harcourt (submitted) have suggested that apes are more at risk than are monkeys. They did so with respect to changes in, respectively, the end of the Miocene in the Old World, end of the Pleistocene in mainland Asia, and recently in the south-east Asian Sunda Shelf region. Temerin & Cant (1983) and Jablonski (1998) related the greater susceptibility of apes to a smaller diet breadth. While the results here do not support the idea of diet as important (though only one crude measure was used), they do support the concept of breadth of response to environmental change as a factor in susceptibility to extinction. Again, specialists (apes) are at risk.

It remains to be seen how applicable these results are to extinct primates and how useful they are, in general, to the understanding of the process of evolution, because, of course, different taxa respond differently to environmental change and the same taxa respond differently in different eras (Diamond, 1984a; Jablonski, 1995). Foley (1994) argued that environmental change in the Pliocene and Pleistocene was correlated with extinction of hominid species, but not their appearance, i.e. not with speciation. Nevertheless, the hints from the results for primate extinctions about the importance of plasticity and of efficient use of resources seem relevant to the evolution of an organism, *Homo*, with a large brain, given that important benefits from a large brain are surely increased plasticity (in effect stabilising the environment) and increased efficiency (in effect allowing more gain from a smaller resource base).

Finally, if we are to study the process of extinction in primates, we need to study primates in adverse environments. However, most studies of all organisms are done in prime environments, for obvious reasons. Consequently, we have extremely few available data so far on the response of primate species to environmental adversity. Thus, from a total of over 200 primate species (Groves, 1993), only ten pairs of taxonomically independent comparisons (only eight pairs of intrageneric comparisons) were considered reliable enough for analysis of response to habitat alteration (Harcourt, 1998). This paucity occurs despite the massive environmental adversity that humans are inflicting on most of the world, especially the habitat of most primates, tropical forest. The tragedy is that the very changes that might allow study are daily diminishing the chances of there being primates left to study.

Acknowledgements

I thank Caroline Harcourt and Bryan Sherwood for the invitation to write this chapter, and Guy Cowlishaw, Robin Dunbar, Robert Foley, Phyllis Lee, John Oates, Carel van Schaik, and Kelly Stewart for valuable discussion and criticism.

References

Abacus Concepts Inc. 1990-91. *Statview SE+.* Berkeley, California: Abacus Concepts, Inc.

Brown JH. 1971. Mammals on mountaintops: nonequilibrium insular biogeography. *American Naturalist.* **105:** 467-478.

Brown JH. 1995. *Macroecology.* Chicago: University of Chicago Press.

Caughley G, Gunn A. 1996. *Conservation Biology in Theory and Practice.* Cambridge, Massachusetts: Blackwell Science.

Clutton-Brock TH, Harvey PH. 1977. Primate ecology and social organization. *Journal of Zoology.* **183:** 1-39.

Cowlishaw G, Hacker JE. 1997. Distribution, diversity, and latitude in African primates. *American Naturalist.* **150:** 505-512.

Diamond JM. 1984a. Historic extinctions: a Rosetta Stone for understanding prehistoric extinctions. In: Martin PS, Klein RG. ed. *Quaternary Extinctions. A Prehistoric Revolution.* Tucson, Arizona: The University of Arizona Press. 824-862.

Diamond JM. 1984b. 'Normal' extinctions of isolated populations. In: Nitecki MH. ed. *Extinctions.* Chicago: University of Chicago Press. 191-246.

Fimbel C. 1994. Ecological correlates of species success in modified habitats may be disturbance- and site-specific: the primates of Tiwai Island. *Conservation Biology*. **8**: 106-113.

Foley R. 1987. *Another Unique Species.* Harlow, United Kingdom: Longman Scientific and Technical.

Foley RA. 1994. Speciation, extinction and climatic change in hominid evolution. *Journal of Human Evolution*. **26**: 275-289.

Grieser Johns A, Grieser Johns B. 1995. Tropical forest primates and logging: long-term coexistence? *Oryx*. **29**: 205-211.

Groves C P. 1993. Order Primates. In: Wilson DE, Reeder DM. ed. *Mammal Species of the World: A Taxonomic and Geographic Reference*. Washington: Smithsonian Institution Press. 243-277.

Harcourt AH. 1998. Ecological indicators of risk for primates, as judged by susceptibility to logging. In: Caro TM. ed. *Behavioral Ecology and Conservation Biology*. New York: Oxford University Press. 56-79.

Harcourt AH. 1999. Biogeographic relationships of primates on south-east Asian islands. *Global Ecology and Biogeography*. **8**: 55-61

Harvey PH, Clutton-Brock TH. 1985. Life history variation in primates. *Evolution*. **39**: 559-581.

Heaney LR. 1984. Mammalian species richness on islands on the Sunda Shelf, southeast Asia. *Oecologia*. **61**: 11-17.

Hooijer DA. 1975. Quaternary mammals west and east of Wallace's Line. In: Bartsra G-J, Casparie WA. eds. *Modern Quaternary Research in Southeast Asia, 2*. Rotterdam: A.A. Balkema. 37-51.

Isbell LA. 1991. Contest and scramble competition: patterns of female aggression and ranging behavior among primates. *Behavioral Ecology*. **2**: 143-155.

Jablonski D. 1986. Causes and consequences of mass extinctions: a comparative approach. In: Elliott DK. ed. *Dynamics of Extinction*. New York: John Wiley & Sons. 183-229.

Jablonski D. 1991. Extinctions: a paleontological perspective. *Science*. **253**: 754-757.

Jablonski D. 1995. Extinctions in the fossil record. In: Lawton JH, May RM. ed. *Extinction Rates*. Oxford: Oxford University Press. 45-54.

Jablonski D, Raup DM. 1995. Selectivity of end-Cretaceous marine bivalve extinctions. *Science*. **268**: 389-391.

Jablonski NG. 1998. The response of catarrhine primates to Pleistocene environmental fluctuations in east Asia. *Primates*. **39**, 29-37.

Janson CH, Goldsmith ML. 1995. Predicting group size in primates: foraging costs and predation risks. *Behavioral Ecology*. **6**: 326-336.

Jernvall J, Hunter JP, Fortelius M. 1996. Molar tooth diversity, disparity, and ecology in Cenozoic ungulate radiations. *Science*. **274**: 1489-1492.

Johns AD, Skorupa JP. 1987. Responses of rain-forest primates to habitat disturbance: a review. *International Journal of Primatology*. **8**: 157-191.

Kattan GH, Alvarez-López H, Giraldo M. 1994. Forest fragmentation and bird extinctions: San Antonio eighty years later. *Conservation Biology.* **8:** 138-146.

Lande R. 1993. Risks of population extinction from demographic and environmental stochasticity and random catastrophes. *American Naturalist.* **141:** 911-927.

Laurance WF. 1991. Ecological correlates of extinction proneness in Australian tropical rain forest mammals. *Conservation Biology.* **5:** 79-89.

Leach MK, Givnish TJ. 1996. Ecological determinants of species loss in remnant prairies. *Science.* **273:** 1555-1558.

Oates JF, Davies AG, Delson E. 1994. The diversity of living colobines. In: Davies AG, Oates JF. eds. *Colobine Monkeys: Their Ecology, Behaviour and Evolution.* Cambridge: Cambridge University Press. 45-73.

Pimm SL, Jones HL, Diamond J. 1988. On the risk of extinction. *American Naturalist.* **132:** 757-785.

Plumptre AJ, Reynolds V. 1994. The effect of selective logging on the primate populations in the Budongo Forest Reserve, Uganda. *Journal of Applied Ecology.* **31:** 631-641.

Purvis A. 1995. A composite estimate of primate phylogeny. *Philosophical Transactions of the Royal Society of London.* **B 348:** 405-421.

Purvis A, Rambaut A. 1995. Comparative analysis by independent contrasts (CAIC): an Apple Macintosh application for analysing comparative data. *Computer Applications in the Biosciences.* **11:** 247-251.

Rohling EJ, Fenton M, Jorissen FJ, Bertrand P, Ganssen G, Caulet JP. 1998. Magnitudes of sea-level lowstands of the past 500,000 years. *Nature.* **394:** 162-165.

Ross C. 1988. The intrinsic rate of natural increase and reproductive effort in primates. *Journal of Zoology.* **214:** 199-219.

Ross C. 1991. Life history patterns of New World monkeys. *International Journal of Primatology.* **12:** 481-502.

Rowe N. 1996. *The Pictorial Guide to the Living Primates.* East Hampton, New York: Pogonias Press.

SAS Institute Inc. 1995. JMP, 3.2.2. Cary, NC, USA.: SAS Institute Inc.

van Schaik C P. 1989. The ecology of social relationships amongst female primates. In: Standen V, Foley RA. eds. *Comparative Socioecology.* Oxford: Blackwell Scientific Publications. 195-218.

Siegel S. 1956. *Nonparametric Statistics for the Behavioral Sciences.* Tokyo: McGraw-Hill Kogakusha Ltd.

Skorupa JP. 1986. Responses of rainforest primates to selective logging in Kibale Forest, Uganda: a summary report. In: Benirschke K. ed. *Primates. The Road to Self-Sustaining Populations.* New York: Springer-Verlag. 57-70.

Smuts BB, Cheney DL, Seyfarth RM, Wrangham RW, Struhsaker TT. eds. 1987. *Primate Societies.* Chicago: University of Chicago Press.

Struhsaker TT. 1997. *Ecology of an African Rain Forest.* Gainseville: University Press of Florida.

Temerin LA, Cant JGH. 1983. The evolutionary divergence of Old World monkeys and apes. *American Naturalist.* **122:** 335-351.

Terborgh J. 1974. Preservation of natural diversity: the problem of extinction prone species. *Bioscience.* **24:** 715-722.

Vermeij GJ. 1986. The biology of human-caused extinction. In: Norton BG. ed. *The Value of Biological Diversity.* Princeton: Princeton University Press. 28-49.

West-Eberhard MJ. 1989. Phenotypic plasticity and the origins of diversity. *Annual Review of Ecology and Systematics.* **20:** 249-278.

Wilcox BA. 1980. Insular ecology and conservation. In: Soulé ME, Wilcox BA. eds. *Conservation Biology. An Evolutionary-Ecological Perspective.* Sunderland, Mass.: Sinauer Associates. 95-117.

Woodroffe R, Ginsberg JR. 1998. Edge effects and the extinction of populations inside protected areas. *Science.* **280:** 2126-2128.

Wrangham RW. 1980. An ecological model of female-bonded primate groups. *Behaviour.* **75:** 262-300.

Wrangham RW, Gittleman JL, Chapman CA. 1993. Constraints on group size in primates and carnivores: population density and day range as assays of exploitation competition. *Behavioral Ecology and Sociobiology.* **32:** 199-209.